WARNING

THIS BOOK IS ALREADY OUT OF DATE!

This is the thirteenth edition of my guide. And even with tight deadlines, not one of the previous editions ever made it to the shelf without at least one restaurant closing. I'm sure the curse has afflicted this edition, as well.

There's nothing I can do to keep the volatile world of restaurants from changing. But I can see to it that you know about the changes. And so, every six months, I will publish an update bulletin for purchasers of The New Orleans Eat Book. It will list all the closings, openings of note, and major changes.

Your first update is free. All you need to do to get it is cut out this page (no photocopies accepted), fill in your mailing address at the bottom, and mail it in. If you would like to receive all future updates until the next publication of this book, send $15 along with this page.

FREE UPDATE

Mail to: **MENU, P.O. Box 51831, New Orleans, LA 70151**

☐ Please send me a free update of The New Orleans Eat Book, when published.

☐ I enclose $15. Please send all updates until the publication of the next edition of the Eat Book, as well as all past updates which may have come out previous to my request. I understand that this also entitles me to a year's subscription to the New Orleans MENU magazine.

Name _____

Address _____

City, State, Zip _____

THE NEW ORLEANS EAT BOOK

By TOM FITZMORRIS
Editor, Menu Magazine

Thirteenth Edition

New Orleans, Big Bend & Pacific Company, Publisher
P.O. Box 51831
New Orleans, Louisiana 70151-1831

Copyright ©1991 Thomas G. Fitzmorris. All rights reserved, including the right of reproduction in whole or part by any means.

A condensed version of this book is available in bulk quantities for conventions, corporations, and other groups. Call (504)524-0348 for more information.

ISBN 1-878593-25-0

To Mary Ann,
who still hates bearnaise sauce.

"It is not the critic who counts—not the man who points out how the strong man stumbled, or where the doer of deeds could have done them better. The credit belongs to the man who is actually in the arena; whose face is marred by dust and sweat and blood, who strives valiantly; who errs and comes short again and again; who knows the great enthusiasms, the great devotions; who spends himself in a worthy cause; who, at best, knows in the end the triumph of high achievement and who, if he fails, at least fails while daring greatly."—Ovid

"A dinner chosen according to one's needs, tastes, and moods, well-prepared and well-served. is a joy to all senses and an impelling incentive to sound sleep, good health, and long life."—Count Arnaud

"Faire de la bonne cuisine demande un certain temps. Si on vous fait attendre, c'est pour mieux vous servir, et vous plaire."—Antoine's menu

A as in andouille

ABOUT THIS BOOK. Use it like an encyclopedia. Everything except the indexes in the back is in alphabetical order. Some 300 individual restaurants are listed. But you can also look up a style, a dish, or some other aspect of dining out and find an explanation and cross-references. For example, if you look up **Buffet, Chinese, Romantic Atmosphere, Oysters Rockefeller,** or **Wine Lists,** you will find the names of the restaurants we recommend for all of those things; then you can check the listings on those restaurants for more details.

The New Orleans Eat Book is an expanded version of a restaurant guide I have written annually since 1977. As in previous editions, all the information was gathered by first-hand experience. With the exception of a few restaurants from which I have been banned (this fact is noted where appropriate), I gathered the material by dining in the restaurants myself. Five visits is the typical research on major restaurants; I've dined in some of them over a hundred times.

I dine exactly as you would. I order a normal meal, pay for it, and then ask myself: "Well, did I enjoy that? How come?" The cartoon of a critic who takes a bite, chews thoughtfully with cocked eyebrow, then jots a note is not my style. I enjoy dining out for its own sake before I think of the critical aspect of a meal.

Cooking is an art, and its merits can only be determined by the person who does the eating. Since I can't speak for the tastes of others, the comments herein spring from my own likes and biases. While I think my tastes are well within the normal range, I have my quirks. For example, I like antique restaurants more than most people do. In the reviews, I try to own up to the eccentricities in my taste that have been pointed out to me consistently.

My critical qualifications are that I eat out with great enthusiasm at least ten times a week and have been writing about it on at least a weekly basis since 1971. By now I have dined in every major restaurant in the area and most of the minor ones. I have also eaten my way through most of America and Europe. The main thing that keeps me honest is the fear that I'll lose this delightful occupation if I put out inaccurate, useless data. The 50 to 100 phone calls and letters I get from readers every week is constant pressure to keep high standards.

I think every responsible critic should state his opinions unambiguously, and that's why I rate restaurants on a scale of zero to five stars. Here are my nebulous translations of the constellations:

★ ★ ★ ★ ★ —*One of the top few restaurants in New Orleans.*
★ ★ to ★ ★ ★ ★ —*Recommended, with varying degrees of enthusiasm*
★ —*Acceptable.*
NO STARS—*Unacceptable.*

The ratings are arrived at by no exact method; this is an art, not a science. I'd say I'm impressed about 75 percent by quality of food, and about 25 percent by service, atmosphere, wine list, and other amenities. Value is considered something like this: a three-star meal for $25 would probably be a two-star meal if it cost $35. Price structure inspires certain expectations; fulfillment of expectations is what makes a meal a success.

The *Eat Book*—in the fine old New Orleans tradition of provincialism—sees the universe as ending fifty miles from New Orleans in all directions. So by giving a restaurant five stars I'm not comparing it with anything in New York or France—although I do think New Orleans has world-class restaurants. Since there are something like 2,500 restaurants in the area, the two-star and better places represent the top ten percent of the dining options here. So don't look down on those two-star places—they're good.

The listings include address, telephone number, hours, and credit card acceptance as they stood at the time of publication. However, all of that info and even the very existence of a restaurant has a way of changing. I advise you to call ahead to unfamiliar restaurants.

I have also included an estimate of how much you're going to spend for a typical meal at each restaurant, not including drinks or tips. The shorthand here is a dollar sign for each ten dollars or part thereof the meal costs, up to "$$$$$". So the notation "$" would denote meals for $10 or less, "$$$" would indicate an expenditure of between $21 and $30 per person, and "$$$$$" means $41 or over.

The last revision of this edition was in March 1991. I guarantee that there will be some changes in the restaurant scene by the time you read it. But this book, unlike all other restaurant guides in the world, updates itself. I publish updates at regular intervals; the first one is free, and can be had by sending in the coupon at the back of the book. In the meantime, I welcome any comments you have about the book or reports on discrepancies between what you read here and reality. Send them to me at Menu, P.O. Box 51831, New Orleans, LA 70151.

I hope you have a great New Orleans meal today.

★ ★ Acme Oyster House

724 Iberville, French Quarter. 522-5973. 11 a.m.-10 p.m. Mon.-Sat.; Noon-7 p.m. Sun. AE, MC, V. $.

The Acme was once the acme of New Orleans oyster bars; now it's just one of the better ones. Behind a heavy marble counter stand shuckers who usually keep the dirt, broken shell, and other detritus out of the oyster. The Acme's source of product and handling thereof is also pretty good, since the oysters are almost always big, cold, and salty.

The Acme also makes poor boys of acceptable but not genius quality, and there is a terrific juke box. The place could be a lot cleaner than it is.

In case you're new to raw-oyster-eating, see **Oysters**.

★ ★ ★ Alberto's

611 Frenchmen, Faubourg Marigny. 949-5952. 6- 11 p.m. Mon.-Sat. No credit cards. $$

A tiny, ramshackle little second-story dining room with a quaint decor (the tables are mounted atop old sewing machines), Alberto's is a very good neighborhood Italian cafe. The chef and co-owner, Alberto Rodriguez (Spanish name, but he grew up in Genoa) learned most of his moves by working for Jimmy Moran. And so we get some curious tastes—tomato sauces with cream added, for example.

The abbreviated menu starts off with terrific mussels and clams in their shells, awash in a lusty marinara sauce. There's always a good soup on the stove; the lentil is particularly memorable. Cannelloni here are made with crepes rather than pasta; both the seafood-stuffed and the spinach-and-cheese versions are quite delicious either as a starter or light main course. Linguine pasta—a touch overcooked, a preference of the chef—comes with tasty, tiny meatballs, chicken cutlets with eggplant and tasso (one of several Creole tastes here), or veal.

Bread pudding (light, cinnamony) is the best of the few desserts. Service is friendly but perfunctory. The main element of atmosphere is that most of the customers come from the neighborhood, and frequently.

★ ★ ★ Alex Patout's

221 Royal St. 525-7788. 11 a.m.-2:30 p.m. Mon.-Fri.; 6-10:30 p.m. seven nights. AE, DC, MC, V. $$$.

Alex Patout made a big splash during the heat of the Cajun cooking craze that swept the country a few years ago, getting big-time publicity in *Esquire* and *Food & Wine*, among other places. After building an empire of restaurants with his family (and eventually closing much of it), he split off on his own and opened this place in 1988. It's a handsome room that previously hosted rather formal restaurants; for it, Patout polished his New Iberia-Cajun cooking somewhat. The style has never done much for me. I find it uniformly overcooked and usually oversauced. Patout buys fine fresh fish and other quality raw materials. Why he feels that they must be overwhelmed with a rich, creamy, spicy, salty sauce—usually one studded with crawfish, shrimp, crabmeat, or a combination—is beyond me.

But some of the food here is good. The starters of boudin, chicken-andouille gumbo, and shrimp remoulade are beyond reproach. The crawfish tails sauteed in butter and their own fat, with a minimum of other additions, is pleasantly spicy and good. The cochon du lait—roasted baby pig, well trimmed, sliced, and abetted with a well-made pork-stock sauce—is an edible version of a dish one usually finds only at church festivals. Plain grilled fish, sans sauce, is well-seasoned and delicious. But beware stuffed anything—fish, eggplant, and even the seductively-described duck, all of which taste confused at best.

They make a great side dish here: sweet potatoes, mashed up and sweetened further with caramelized sugar, and studded with pecans. Much better than the totally overcooked green beans or whatever that is next to the yams. Desserts are not especially good.

Service here is quite hospitable and prompt. Upstairs, there's a jazz club where, for $35 a person, you get a five-course meal from a limited (but decent) menu while a good combo plays a set or two.

ALFRESCO DINING. A local restaurateur whose establishment was famous for its outdoor tables was once presented by his ad agent with a radio commercial that invited one and all to come to the place for alfresco dining. The restaurateur took the cigarette out of his mouth and said, "Who the — — is Al Fresco?" Well, I know Al Fresco, and I just plain hate Al Fresco. See **Patio Dining.**

★★Alonso & Son

587 Central Ave. (between Jefferson and Airline Hwys.), Jefferson. 733-2796. 10 a.m.-10 p.m. Mon.-Sat. No credit cards. $

Alonso's is one of the great old-time neighborhood "Bar & Rest." joints that used to dominate the everyday eating scene before the advent of fast food. It's crowded, noisy, smoky, and refreshingly shabby. The television is on all the time, and the walls are covered with artifacts of mysterious origin.

The best eating at Alonso's is seafood. The fried oysters in particular are outstanding, coming out sizzling, crisp, and greaseless. They're equally good as a platter or as an oyster loaf. The boiled seafood is also delectable and the matching beer is agreeably cold. The plate specials are uniformly satisfying, and the poor boys are classic. I have always felt that places like this make the best roast beef poor boys, and Alonso's is a good proof of that theory.

ALLIGATOR. Even old native Orleanians are tickled a bit by the idea of eating alligator. The ferocious, rather stupid biting machine teems in the marshes (it's hardly endangered, and occasionally turns up in populated areas). It has surprisingly tender, delectable meat—mostly in its tail. Its flavor has a certain seafoodiness to it, but other aspects suggest fowl or veal. The closest thing I can think of to alligator in taste is turtle meat—for which alligator is frequently substituted. (A great example of this is the alligator soup at **Antoine's**, made in the style of turtle soup.)

Creole and Cajun cooks serve alligator in almost every imaginable way. The three most popular ways are in soup, in a stew called alligator sauce piquant (the sauce is light in color, but packs a peppery wallop), and deep-fried. It is also sometimes made into a light sausage. All of these are great, but unfortunately few have found permanent places on local menus. Look for alligator dishes on daily special lists and at festivals

★ ★ Altamira

701 Convention Center Blvd., CBD. 581-6870. 11:30 a.m.-3 p.m. and 6-10 p.m. Mon.-Sat. AE. $$

Altamira is the only restaurant in the city serving the food of Spain. Spanish cooking is very different from the much more familiar Latin American food; the biggest difference is that there are not many spicy Spanish dishes. Altamira's proprietor came from Seville and tries to stay authentic; his food may be a little too authentic for local tastes, and runs to blandness at times.

You start with tapas, the complimentary snacks served with drinks in Spain. At Altamira, the tapas have been things like marinated mussels on the half shell or small potato omelettes. Soup is a reasonable next course; they make a gazpacho here that, despite its creamy appearance, tastes right on the money. The garlic soup is also nice, if very light. Other appetizers include large orders of the mussels and a big baking dish full of broiled veal kidneys.

The best entrees are the various grilled fish, served with a cold vinaigrette, peppers and onions—light, refreshing. The roast pork, chicken, and beef all come out in very large portions, abetted with a hint of garlic and a broad hint of olive oil.

You could not have a Spanish restaurant without rice dishes; that endeavor here is represented by paella, the ancestor of jambalaya, made here with chicken, shrimp, scallops, and fish, scented with saffron. It's enough to feed several. Oddly, they don't cook things like rice with squid—a disappointment.

There's a decent flan for dessert and homemade sangria for washing things down. The dining room is much more inviting than the rather stark exterior of the reclaimed warehouse the restaurant occupies; service is also better than one would expect. Altamira is especially popular on Fridays and Saturdays, when there is live flamenco. They have live music most other nights, too.

AMBERJACK. A tasty, tender, very white Gulf fish with large flakes, amberjack began appearing on grills when redfish became rare, and it surprised everyone with its goodness. It is now a common catch of the day, and tastes particularly good grilled. **Christian's** occasionally smokes amberjack to fine effect. See **Fish**.

ANDOUILLE. A dense, thick-skinned, moderately spicy, smoked sausage of pork and garlic. It is identified as a Cajun item and its name is French, but I have always detected a German aspect to the andouille. That's logical, since the best andouille comes from Laplace, just upriver of New Orleans in an area historically called "The German Coast." Andouille is most often seen cut into thick coins about an inch in diameter. Its customary hangouts are with chicken in a gumbo or flanking a plate of red beans. It is also very good grilled. Restaurants serving especially good andouille are **Mr. B's**, **Emeril's**, and **Commander's Palace**.

★ ★ ★ ★ ★ Andrea's

3100 19th Street, Metairie. Reservations 834-8583. 11:30 a.m.- 10:30 p.m. seven days. Brunch 11 a.m.-3 p.m. Sun. AE, CB, DC, MC, V. $$$
NOTE: I collaborated on Andrea's cookbook. I have a financial interest in the book, though not in the restaurant. Andrea's had a five-star rating long before I began work on the book, for what that's worth. But I would be remiss in not pointing out the connection.

Andrea's is easily the city's most polished, ambitious, and delectable Italian restaurant. In 1984, after eight years as chef at the Royal Orleans Hotel, Andrea Apuzzo and his cousin Roberto De Angelis—both from Capri— created the kind of restaurant they both always wanted. The dining rooms, despite their low ceilings, are handsome and comfortable. The waiters are knowledgeable, attentive, and stylish. And Roberto has assembled the finest stock of Italian wines in the city.

Andrea's menu covers many styles of Italian cooking, but the emphasis is the top of the boot. Northern Italy is the wellspring of classical European cuisine, and its cooking techniques, raw materials, and sauces are among the most elegant and complex in the world. If you didn't know any better, you might identify some of this food as French. Northern Italy is not red-sauce-and-garlic country—although Andrea's kitchen uses quite a lot of tomatoes in its cooking.

Scrupulous standards of freshness give Andrea's food a tremendous head start. All the fish come in fresh and whole. All pastas are made on the premises. The herbs are fresh and vivid-tasting.

Some fine cold appetizers. Vitello tonnato is pretty sliced veal with a tuna mayonnaise sauce, a classic Italian dish almost never seen in New Orleans. Similarly tasty is the carpaccio—raw beef pounded thin, served with mustard sauce. The table adjacent to the front door is laden with appetizing caponata, marinated escarole, tomatoes with provolone, and other tempting antipasti. The chef makes his own caciotta cheese and serves soft, white disks of it over arugula and other nice greens.

The steamed clams or mussels—with a white-wine-and-herb sauce or a lusty red marinara sauce—are spectacular. The broiled oysters en brochette have too much bacon wrapped around them, but the leeks and creamy lemon butter sauce set them off well.

The best soups here are the country-style varieties like pasta fagioli—an incredibly aromatic broth of beans, pesto, and pasta. In cold weather, I can think of almost nothing I'd rather eat. Vegetable cream soups, on the other hand, tend to be very light and something less than satisfying.

In a traditional Italian meal, pasta would be the next course. But pasta is also a great way to start. The angel hair with smoked salmon and caviar, fettuccine with cream pesto sauce, ravioli stuffed with cheese (or, occasionally, with the rich, earthy porcini mushrooms), and linguine forestiere (with morel mushrooms) are delicious individually or as parts of a pasta assortment.

The chef's range is so broad that it's tough to pick out a best section of entrees—let alone specific dishes. But the dovetailing of beautiful fresh Gulf fish with Northern Italian cooking methods results in spectacular eating. Several species of fish are available daily. My favorite is the pompano with the pale-green, basil-fragrant pesto cream sauce; the fish is enormous and oozing goodness from deft sauteeing. Similarly wonderful is the buttery, herbal basilico sauce. In season, the chef sends out great soft-shell crabs with the entire range of fish sauces, and shrimp of enormous size are awash in a spicy, chunky, tomatoey fra diavolo sauce.

The veal is so intrinsically good here that I prefer the simplest renditions of it. The simplest of all is the paillard—a veritable sheet of veal, grilled for just seconds and brought forth with a great lemony, herbal sauce. For veal Tanet—another superb choice—the same large slice of veal is panneed, then deposited atop a stack of romaine leaves with Italian dressing. The restaurant is famous for its veal chop Valdostana, stuffed with cheese and prosciutto and covered with a heady light brown sauce, but I prefer the lovely chop unadorned.

The beef is prime, cut off the loin in too-big slabs to order, and frequently served with overcomplicated sauces. I get lost while eating the filet Andre—somewhere between the shrimp and the mushrooms. But the chef whips up as fine a version of steak au poivre as I've eaten, and he also makes a textbook bearnaise. A crusty rack of American lamb is always available; some wonderful venison steaks sometimes are.

Duck is crisp on the outside and tender on the inside, and comes with a number of different sauces; my preference is for the green peppercorn cream sauce. At lunch (when the place is a real bargain) they feature a tremendous roast chicken, pizzas, osso buco, and other hearty eating.

The pastry department here is one of the best in town. Its best work is an unusually elegant manifestation of the ethereal cake called tirami su ("pick-me-up"). It's a sponge cake moistened with espresso and layered with sweetened mascarpone cream cheese and cocoa, and you don't eat it as much as you inhale it. A dry cake called torta di mandorle, tasting more of chocolate than almonds, is great by itself, or with ice cream or zabaglione. The chocolate mousse is intense (the dark version is considerably better than the white, no matter what the chef or the waiter says). Fine cappuccino and espresso and a bar stocked with many unusual Italian liqueurs round out the best Italian meals ever served in this city.

Andrea's is not perfectly consistent; I think the chef stretches himself and his staff far too thin with special events. But I've never had a bad meal here, and the place performs at or near peak most of the time.

★ Andy Messina's

2717 Williams Blvd., Kenner. 469-7373. 11 a.m.-3 p.m. Mon.-Fri.; 3 p.m.-Midnight Mon.-Sat.; Noon-10 p.m. Sun. AE, CB, DC, MC, V. $

One of the oldest restaurants in Kenner, Messina's is a neighborhood restaurant specializing in a very old-fashioned style of Italian cooking. The red sauces have clearly been cooked a very long time, and come out sweet and thick. The pastas, veal dishes, and seafood are all edible, if not brilliant. You can also get a good poor boy sandwich here.

★★★ Angelo Brocato

214 N. Carrollton Ave., Mid-City. 486-1465. 9:30 a.m.-10 p.m. Mon.-Thurs.; till 10:30 p.m. Fri. & Sat.; 9:30 a.m.-10 p.m. Sun. • 537 St. Ann (in the Lower Pontalba), French Quarter. 525-9676. 10 a.m.-6 p.m. Mon.- Thurs.; till 10 p.m. Fri., 11 p.m. Sat. 9 a.m.-9 p.m. Sun. No credit cards. $

The third generation of Brocatos continues the traditions of this seminal Sicilian-style ice cream parlor. All of Brocato's ice creams are made at the Mid-City location, and include the last words in spumone (four layered flavors), torroncino (a wonderful flavor of cinnamon and nuts), cassata (like spumone, but with a layer of cake), bisquit tortoni (a nutty-tasting frozen souffle), and the entire array of other flavors. But the crowning glory is Brocato's lemon ice. It's served not only here but in restaurants all over town. Nothing could be more refreshing on a summer day. The other ices are also delectable. And then there is the cannoli—a sort of giant corn flake stuffed with a mixture of ricotta cheese, fruits, nuts, sugar, and chocolate. The glass cases further reveal cheesecakes, candies and cookies; espresso and cappuccino are available to go with it all. In short, a delightful place to go after a Chinese meal or any other time you need a dessert.

★★ Annadele Plantation

Covington; turn west from US 190, seven miles north of the north end of the Causeway, at Popeyes. Signs direct you through a series of small roads for a few blocks. Reservations 1-893-4895. 11:30 a.m.-2:30 p.m.

Tues.-Fri. 5:30-10:30 p.m. Tues.-Sat. Sun. brunch 11 a.m.-3 p.m. AE, CB, DC, MC, V. $$

After you wind your way through the piney woods path, you feel nicely deep in rural territory—even though you're just off the main highway through Covington. The restaurant is a well-renovated old house on a large parcel of land, complete with lagoon. It has several small dining parlors; the best room, a bricked-in porch at the rear, has a lot of windows for observation of the trees.

The food here is basic Creole with interesting twists. Start with the combination of oysters Rockefeller, Bienville (best) and a third kind with eggplant and apples (worst). The shrimp remoulade has an extra-spicy, refreshing sauce. The gumbo is just okay.

Seafood: trout Swisscourt is inlaid with a duxelles of mushrooms, moistened with a bit of butter, mellowed with pecans. The very simple and tasty trout meuniere is sauteed nicely and served with brown butter. The fried soft-shell crab is very good; the zippy cream sauce with shrimp, mushrooms and peppers looks like a bit much, but clicks with the crab.

Meat: a filet mignon is deposited atop a slice of bone with easily-accessible marrow, and the whole thing is covered with a good bearnaise and an okay marchand de vin. This is quite a dish. The rack of lamb for one is roasted till crusty and brought forth with a honey mustard sauce—a good, original taste. Many polite veal and chicken dishes.

Good bread pudding and marginal other things are the desserts. The wine list, with eight selections served by the glass, is better than average. Service is a little spotty but not too bad. The setting is great for Sunday brunch.

ANTIQUE RESTAURANTS. In most American cities, a restaurant is thought of as old if it's been open ten years. In New Orleans, the yardstick is much longer, given the presence of places like Antoine's (founded 1840), Tujague's (1856), Commander's Palace (1880), Delmonico (1898), Galatoire's (1905), Arnaud's (1918), and Broussard's (1920). There's a still longer list of restaurants which have passed their 50th anniversaries.

I admit to a special love of antique restaurants, and I tend to rate them higher than the average person might. For example, **Antoine's** unswerving adherence to century-old styles of cooking and service is maddening in a modern context. But since I go there specifically to *remove* myself from the modern context, the quirks become set-pieces of an enjoyable fantasy. If you have no taste for such historical mind games, you should probably deduct at least one star from all my ratings of the older restaurants in this book.

Or, go to an old restaurant which has kept its antique looks while forging ahead on the operational front. **Commander's Palace**, for instance, can be avant-garde in its cooking. **Arnaud's** and **Broussard's** also cook up to date. **Delmonico** is up to about 1965.

The best of New Orleans' antique restaurants is **Galatoire's**. In every way it is unmistakeably the product of its age, but its food has a timeless appeal that relegates the historical landmark status of the place to a footnote.

★ ★ ★ ★ Antoine's

713 St. Louis, French Quarter. Reservations 581-4422. Noon-2 p.m. and 5:30-9:30 p.m. Mon.-Sat. AE, CB, DC, MC, V. $$$$$

Antoine's is the grandfather of New Orleans restaurants, with all the endearing and exasperating qualities that implies. In 1990, it celebrated its 150th anniversary with Antoine Alciatore's descendents still at the helm (Bernard Guste, fifth generation, is the titular proprietor). In the latter part of the 1800s, Antoine's defined Creole restaurant cuisine. The original recipes of many Creole commonplaces are still served; in some cases, they are the best versions of those dishes to be had.

Antoine's traditions are so many and so strong that the restaurant autopilots on them. Many of these lend a museum-like fascination to the dining experience. Other traditions, their origins and meanings long forgotten, are more like ruts. In any case, it takes years of regular patronage to figure out the place. Even the menu is inaccessible: 138 dishes are listed in French with no explanations of any kind.

If you're a first-timer, your enjoyment of Antoine's hangs by the threads of luck and your taste for antiquity. On the other hand, I greatly enjoy my regular meals at Antoine's, despite all the inconsistencies and pecadillos. The good dishes are approximated by no other restaurant, and the ambience is inimitable.

To have a peak Antoine's experience, it helps to be well-known by a waiter, or to be with someone who is. Failing that, if you can follow exactly what I'm about to tell you, ignoring contrary pushes from the waiter, you have a decent shot at enjoying yourself.

Make a reservation, preferably for a weeknight. Or go for lunch, when the dining room population will probably be sparse (the menu and, unfortunately, the prices are the same as at dinner, and the food may actually be better). When you arrive, insist on a table in the Annex—the big, dark, Germanic red room in the back where all the regulars sit.

Begin with loaves of the hot, toasty French bread—the best in town— and a basket of pommes de terre soufflees. The latter item is the ultimate in French fries—very thin, fried twice to result in irresistable hot, hollow potato balloons.

Next, order an abundance of appetizers—the restaurant's best course—and pass them around the table, Chinese-style. Certain of these are essentials. The oysters Rockefeller are the originals, with their unique topping of fennel-flavored greens, rich and slightly peppery. Oysters Foch are fried, placed atop toast slathered with foie gras, and covered with a thick, dark brown, slightly sweet, aromatic Colbert sauce. (I think this is the best dish in the house, and the sauce also goes well with any other seafood.) Escargots come with either garlic-and-herb butter or (better) the unique brown sauce with chunks of garlic, sherry, and a little cheese. Shrimp remoulade and crabmeat ravigote are great cold starters. The soups tend toward heaviness, but some are good anyway. The shrimp and crawfish bisques are so similar that the waiters never seem to know which is which; either is tasty, as is the highly unusual potage alligator. That one tastes just like a traditional New Orleans turtle soup, but it's made with alligator tail meat in whitish, tender morsels. The gumbo, the darkest in town, contains a lot of seafood. The vichyssoise is a bit too rich for me. The salads are barely adequate these days, although you might get a kick out of the cubist-looking salad Bayard, a rather salty affair with minced greens and anchovies atop an artichoke bottom.

Antoine's beef is the equal of any in the world—no kidding. The entrecote (strip sirloin), filet mignon and similar but smaller tournedos are prime, well-trimmed, and intensely beefy. The steaks may or may not be enhanced by the various sauces which, in the old style of doing things, are sold separately. The good ones are the beef-stock-and-red-wine marchand de vin sauce or the sharper, mildly-peppery brown Medicis sauce. The lamb chops and the noisettes d'agneau (the latter with an inexplicably delectable fine brown pineapple sauce) are also tasty stuff.

Most Antoine's diners have a seafood entree—usually a confused one. The waiters love to ruin a perfectly good fillet of fish with some kind of gloppy sauce. The two worst travesties are the fried trout covered with crawfish etouffee and (the waiters' favorite) pompano en papillote, an anonymous fish stew baked in a parchment bag. Both of these are made of very fine elements whose tastes cancel each other.

Far better—in fact, extremely delicious—is the plain grilled pompano. It's expensive, but the portion is enormous and there is no better local fish. The crusty fried trout or soft shell crabs (they always give you two, no matter how huge they may be) with Colbert sauce are also reasonably irresistable, if rich.

The most underrated dishes here are made with chicken. Poulet Rochambeau is a baked and boned half-bird with two sauces: a slightly-sweet, translucent brown sauce and the restaurant's weird, bright yellow, lemony bearnaise. Extremely rich, but good. Poulet bonne femme is rib-sticking and hearty, the chicken surrounded with a smoky sauce of bacon, potatoes, and onions. Poulet au champignons is simply that: a broiled chicken half with mushrooms and way too much butter. Get them to pour some of it off and a fine bird emerges.

Vegetables are generally not worth the added expense; they murder fresh asparagus. Potatoes, however, are better, including the best brabants—buttery fried dice—I've ever eaten. The creamed spinach is the local benchmark.

One of the world's greatest desserts is here, and must be ordered at the beginning of the meal. It's baked Alaska, a handsome mound of decorated meringue in the shape and size of a football, baked to a light brown with a plug of ice cream at its center. Some eat this with chocolate sauce; they should be taken out and shot. On Friday lunches, they have a superb bread pudding. There are a few sundae-like ice cream desserts, the best of which is the peche Melba. The coffee is rich, strong, and habit-forming.

The waiters play a more important role here than at other restaurants. If you're a regular, the waiter gets you in through the back door for dinner, gives you an appraisal of what's up that night, and fixes special combinations. By modern standards, Antoine's waiters are casual, to say the least; they dispense with ceremony and get the food and wine onto the table.

After, before, or during dinner, you should take a tour of the expansive premises, which could be turned into a museum tomorrow with few changes. The most impressive stop is at the entrance to the wine cellar, a temperature-controlled alley that looks four blocks long. There are some 35,000 bottles in there, and in recent times the selection and pricing of them has raised Antoine's wine list to the top rank locally.

★ ★ ★ ★ Arnaud's

813 Bienville St., French Quarter. Reservations 523-5433. 11:30 a.m.-2:30 p.m. Mon.-Fri. 6-10 p.m. Sun.-Thurs.; till 10:30 on Fri. & Sat. Jazz brunch 10 a.m.-2:30 p.m. Sun. AE, CD, DC. MC, V. $$$$

Arnaud's is an example of the right way to restore a restaurant. When proprietor Archie Casbarian took over a few years ago Arnaud's—the greatest of New Orleans restaurants in the Thirties and Forties—was a smelly, barely-operating shambles. The new proprietor restored the sparkle to the distinctive tile floors, beveled glass, old ceiling fans, and tin ceilings. The classic Arnaud's dishes remained, too, with polish and updating applied as appropriate.

The famous appetizer is shrimp Arnaud, the best shrimp remoulade in town, with its tart, pleasantly oily, smooth orange sauce. If you like baked oysters, you can find three different great ones (plus a couple of mediocrities) on one plate under the name "oysters Arnaud." There are Rockefellers and Bienvilles, of course, but also oysters Suzette, with a highly original sauce of peppers and bacon. The soups, led by superb essays with shrimp and oysters, are rich, intense, and creamy.

Arnaud's old-style menu extends far beyond the list of the restaurant's specialties. The good and not-so-good dishes are well-mixed. Fortunately, the waiters are pretty candid, so it's a good idea to ask probing questions, especially about such things as the freshness of fish.

Arnaud's most famous seafood entree is trout meuniere, with its brown lemon-butter sauce. However, it has been too variable for me to recommend it. So get the pompano en croute, a delectable treat wrapped in a fish-shaped pastry, moistened with a creamy, light peppercorn sauce.

Pompano Pontchartrain has a good brown butter and crabmeat on top.
The beef is probably the most reliable thing on the menu, owing to the excellent quality of the meat and some well-made classic sauces. I like the quail and Cornish hen, each stuffed with pate and covered with, respectively, a white-wine sauce and a heady red-wine-and-pepper sauce. Duck Ellen is a pretty array of duck breast slices with blueberries. There are some nice veal dishes: veal Lafitte, with a light artichoke sauce and sauteed lettuce, and veal Wohl, with an overcomplication of crawfish and crabmeat in two sauces. The sweetbreads are unusual, with a sauce of mustard and bearnaise: tasty, rich stuff.

Vegetables and salads are taken seriously here and are generally excellent. The bread is a trademark, being the old-style "cap" bread, a thick, squat French loaf, warm and good.

Dessert is led by a terrific bread pudding, custardy and cinnamony, with a good, hot whiskey sauce. Bananas Foster and creme brulee (a rich, semi-liquid custard) are also very fine, as is the aromatic, mouth-filling coffee.

Arnaud's wine cellar has become one of the best, with a startling variety and a great many curiosities. The prices are a little on the steep side, though, and the waiters are not uniformly well-educated in oenology. But that's about all the bad news I have about the wait staff, which shows considerably more polish than the norm for these old places.

Not all is perfect. The raw materials are not always of the top quality, and the success of the cooking is somewhat variable. I think much of this has to do with the extensiveness of the menu and the size of the restaurant, which does a heavy private-party business. But most nights, Arnaud's provides an unforgettable evening in the old style.

Lunchtime is a spectacular bargain here, with four-course repasts for $8 to $12 and a house full of local people.

★ ★ Asia Garden

224 Poydras, CBD. 525-2742. 11 a.m.-10 p.m. Mon.-Sat.; till 11 p.m. Fri. & Sat. AE, MC, V, CB. $$

Here, in one of the last remaining old buildings on canyon-like Poydras Street, the office-building crowd finds Chinese lunches far better than the dismal chopsticks fodder generally available downtown. Cold noodles Szechuan style, a great first course, are mixed with chicken and spice and sesame oil for a highly unusual flavor. The fried dumplings are fat with a meaty, herbal stuffing. The hot-and-sour soup is very.

The entrees show a lot of polish in both flavor and appearance. The best choices are the spicy Szechuan dishes, the most complex of which has been General Cho's chicken—fried to a near-perfect tenderness and coated with a ruddy, slightly-sweet, spicy sauce. The deep fried whole fish in hot sauce is also handsome and toothsome. The shrimp in garlic sauce one night was powerful both in levels of pepper and garlic. The long list goes on to include a great many Cantonese items; even so prosaic a thing as pork in black bean sauce achieves a decent level of excitement. Avoid dishes with sweet sauces, which go a bit overboard in the sticky-gooey department. They do good apple or banana fritters for dessert. Service is helpful.

★ ★ ★ Assunta's

2631 Covington Hwy. (US 190), Slidell. 1-649-9768. 5:30-10 p.m. Tues.-Sun. MC, V. $$.
This is a quaint cottage way out on the highway between Slidell and Mandeville. Most of the seating is on enclosed porches surrounding a big room with a unique bar. The front and back parts of the bar are a matched set of intricately-carved wooden altars, bought from a church somewhere. It's a good thing the bar is nice to look at, because chances are you'll look at it for quite a spell while waiting for a table. Assunta's is extremely popular, and it takes no reservations.

Assunta is a smiling, middle-aged lady from Naples, and her cooking is easily accessible to even the most unadventuresome eater of Italian food. The menu is deceptively basic: fried eggplant, calamari, fettuccine with cream and cheese, spaghetti and meatballs, Italian sausage, veal Parmigiana, oysters with spaghetti aglio olio. All of this is exceptionally well prepared, featuring an intense, smooth tomato sauce of unaccustomed elegance.

There are a few surprises on the menu. The croquettes are balls of mashed potatoes enclosing slices of cheese and prosciutto: very good. The gnocchi, served in that fine red sauce, are also made with potatoes and are just about perfect in both taste and texture. The portions are very large and the prices quite low.

They have a few interesting wines at very attractive prices. The cheesecake is the only dessert, rich and made on the premises. Service is by very friendly young servers, and Assunta herself makes the rounds of the tables.

ATMOSPHERE. A good car stereo is pointless if the car doesn't run. That is my analogy to the place of atmosphere in a restaurant: it's a nice accessory to the food. But atmosphere is one of the few things over which a restaurateur has total control. Once the restaurant design is created, it stays created. Chefs and waiters, on the other hand, change unpredictably from hour to hour. So the temptation is great for a restaurateur to put too much emphasis on physical premises. While this is not as true in New Orleans as it is elsewhere, we certainly have our share of places that deliver little beyond good looks.

Nevertheless, it's a welcome trend that more attention than previously is being paid to chairs, lighting, silverware, china, noise level, flowers, art, music and interior design. Here is a list, grouped by architectural style, of the most atmospheric restaurants in the area.

CLASSIC NEW ORLEANS
Antoine's
Arnaud's
Brennan's
Broussard's
Commander's Palace
Court of Two Sisters
Galatoire's

MODERN OPULENCE
Caribbean Room
Henri
Isadora
Le Jardin
Louis XVI
Windsor Court Grill Room

INTERESTING ARCHITECTURE
Emeril's (converted factory)
Christian's (converted church)
Palace Cafe (coverted music store)
Emeril's (ultramodern)
La Provence (French country inn)
Sazerac (European classicism)
Trey Yuen (Oriental palace)

SWELL FUNKY
Cafe du Monde
Casamento's
K-Paul's Louisiana Kitchen
Ralph & Kacoo's (French Quarter)
Napoleon House
Uglesich's

DARK & SECRETIVE
Antoine's
Beef Room
Flagons (wine bar part)
Versailles

See also **Music, Plantations, Romantic Atmosphere** and **View.**

AU GRATIN. Properly, this adjective means that the dish involved has had its upper surface encrusted. But in New Orleans au gratin usually means cheese: in, under, and especially on top. The most popular entree au gratin is crabmeat au gratin, prepared well at the **Bon Ton, Galatoire's, La Cuisine** and the **Steak Knife.** Au gratin vegetables are epitomized by the potatoes, broccoli, cauliflower, spinach and peas (!) au gratin at **Ruth's Chris Steak House;** they're more popular than good. Au gratin potatoes reach apotheosis at **Crozier's,** where the gratin dauphinois is not only elegantly creamy but also touched with garlic. They also do this dish well at **Louis XVI** and **Henri—** which, incidentally, also has a gratin of strawberries and ice cream (sabayon sauce is what gets the glaze).

Augie's Glass Garden

3300 South I-10 Service Rd., Metairie. 835-3300. 11 a.m.-11 p.m. seven days. AE, MC, V. $$$.

A greenhouse of mirror glass, with waterfalls and streams coursing through the interior jungle, contains a high-profile but consistently mediocre suburban restaurant. The menu offers seafood, Italian food, steaks, lobster, and just about anything else you might be hungry for. They especially love to combine two or even three entrees on the same plate, and to top dishes with crabmeat. The steaks—prime grade, accurately broiled—are the best food I've had here. Almost everything else has shown some degree of careless preparation. Nor has my pointing this out had any effect on the mechanical service staff.

★★Avenue Sandwich Shop

520 City Park Ave., Mid-City. 482-7335. 10 a.m.-2:30 Mon.-Fri. No credit cards. $

For years this little corner poor-boy emporium was a quiet place where a long line of people waited while the elderly proprietress made sandwiches one by one. Now a younger generation has taken over, cleaned the place up, installed a few tables, speeded up the assembly line, and . . gadzooks! *kept the flavor intact!* The Avenue puts forth a mammoth roast beef poor boy which hits squarely in the center what lifelong Orleanians would identify as the classic roast beef poor boy taste. The beef is not impressive to look at (so don't look at it), but that's authentic (after all, it is called a "poor boy"). The gravy, on the other hand, is delectable, and there's plenty of it. The bread and the dressings are fresh and good.

Distinction extends to the rest of the poor boy selection, which covers most of the bases. The grilled ham is a good alternative; shrimp and oyster loaves are eminently edible. All are easily big enough to share.

B as in bread pudding

★ ★ ★ Back to the Garden

936 St. Charles Ave., Uptown. 522-8792. 7 a.m.-7:30 p.m. Mon.-Fri., 9 a.m.-5 p.m. Sat. • 207 Dauphine, French Quarter. 524-6915. 11 a.m.-4 p.m. Mon.-Sat. No credit cards. $.

These vegetarian lunchettes prove that natural foods can be served with some flavor and without the irritating smugness for which health-foodies are infamous. All the dishes are meatless and prepared more or less according to dietary fads current among the overly health-conscious. As you might expect, the menu board offers a number of salads in which sprouts and sunflower seeds are unavoidable, but the other ingredients are very fresh (ripe avocados!) and the dressings are good. Sandwiches are made with superb whole-grain breads; the best of them are a tuna club and an avocado and cheese.

The plate specials here are the most interesting eating. They have a few tasty Mexican items — a meatless chili, cheese enchiladas with a zippy red-brown sauce, and firm beans. The meatless meat loaf, made with nuts and cheese, is shockingly delicious. Soups are wonderful — particularly those made with legumes. Smoothies and various fruit items make up the sweet part of the menu. The restaurants are self-service; orders are prepared quickly.

★ ★ Bailey's

Fairmont Hotel, 123 Baronne, CBD. 529-7111. Open 24 hours, seven days. AE, CB, DC, MC, V. $$.

The coffee shop of the Fairmont Hotel is one of the very few decent restaurants open 24 hours. Unfortunately, lately it's been just barely decent. The menu (except for the higher prices here) is that of a New Orleans neighborhood cafe — sandwiches, seafood (including oysters on the half shell), red beans, gumbo, and the like. Most of these things are reasonably edible, and occasionally very good. The sandwiches employ very classy fillings, including wonderful pastrami. Lox is silky and tasty; with a bagel and cream cheese, it makes a fine late-night snack. At any hour Bailey's prepares a good breakfast. Omelettes are especially well-made. Service is iffy; some of these boys and girls seem never to have worked in a restaurant before, and they break down when the place is busy—as it usually seems to be in the wee hours.

BAKED ALASKA. The best fancy dessert in town is either this one or bananas Foster. Baked Alaska is a plug of ice cream surrounded and insulated by a dome of sweet meringue, then baked to a golden brown. The final item is the size of a football, at least. It's a specialty of **Antoine's**, which shames all competitors in both the taste and the decoration of this old-style extravaganza. I can't imagine anything better matched to a bottle of Sauternes.

BAKED POTATOES. The problem restaurants have with baked spuds is that they take over an hour to bake, and then can't be held for very long. So they can't really be prepared to order. The best restaurants for baked potatoes are those that serve a lot of them—**Port of Call**, **Ruth's Chris Steak House**, and **Snug Harbor** have consistently good ones. Insist that baked potatoes be served (and baked, if possible) without the absurd aluminum-foil jacket. It makes the skin soggy, you have to fool around with it at the table (and maybe splash butter all over yourself), and worry about whether a tiny piece of it will hit a filling. Connoisseurs of baked potatoes always eat the skin, and the skin doesn't get crispy and nutty when it's wrapped with foil.

BANANAS FOSTER. The only flaming dessert worth the trouble, bananas Foster was created at **Brennan's**, which still does them well—although not *quite* as well as **Arnaud's** and **Commander's Palace**. The bananas are sauteed in butter, caramelized sugar, cinnamon and brandy, and are served atop ice cream. The blend of flavors is remarkable—even the most stuck-up French chefs of my acquaintance like it.

★ ★ ★ Bangkok Cuisine

4137 S. Carrollton Ave., Mid-City. 482-3606. 11 a.m.-3 p.m. Mon.-Fri.; 5-10 p.m. Sun.-Thurs.; 5-11 p.m. Fri. & Sat. AE, MC, V. $$.

The second location of the city's first Thai restaurant looks much better inside (a wide open expanse of dimly-lit dining room, with Thai fabrics and furnishings) than outside (an old shopping center). The food is less than perfectly consistent, but you'll have a good meal of Thai classics, prepared with reasonable authenticity.

The best starter is the Thai tray, which contains six different appetizers, each with its own sauce for dipping. The spring rolls are firm and full of shrimp, pork, mushrooms, and glass noodles; the fascinating carrot sauce lifts them out of the ordinary (it's also good with the shrimp toast). Bangkok chicken is incredible: the middle part of a chicken wing is stuffed with minced pork and served with a spicy peanut sauce. Beef Rama (a cold, spicy sliced-beef salad) and todd munn (a fried fish cake with curry) complete the starter list.

Soups are delicious. I particularly like the chicken soup with lemon grass and coconut milk, velvety and aromatic, and the shrimp Siam soup—a hot-and-sour affair.

Paht Thai is to Thai cooking what jambalaya is to Creole. Noodles are pan-fried and tossed with morsels of chicken, shrimp, bean sprouts, and scallions to form an amorphous, moist, light-tan pile. At the Bangkok, the dish is a little stickier and much hotter in taste than I like, but it's still satisfying. When I feel like eating something this hot, I usually order one of the four curries. Thai curry neither looks nor tastes much like its Indian cousin. For example, the green curry—my favorite—is light and creamy with coconut milk, eggplant and chicken bits. It is very hot, but the coconut milk adds a soothing effect.

The remainder of the menu holds a wide range of surprises. Best bets: Siam whole fish, fried and slathered with a gingery sauce. Enormous Rama squid, stuffed with shrimp and pork. Peppermint chicken, which tastes better than it sounds. Also there are a few deep-fried and stir-fried dishes for those who want something familiar.

The best drinks are the Thai beer—which is delicious—and a creamy, rich concoction called Thai iced tea. Service is good and helpful.

BANQUETS. Few conclusions about the quality of a restaurant's banquets can be drawn from its a la carte service, or vice-versa. Many restaurants and hotels that specialize in large private parties even have separate kitchens and staffs for the purpose. Furthermore, the success of a banquet depends as much or more upon the taste and the budget of the host than the abilities of the restaurant. So, if you're at a dinner that seems a little cheesy, it may be that the host is a cheapskate.

Here are the ten restaurants which, in my opinion, acquit themselves especially well in the serving of large parties.
 1. Antoine's
 2. Andrea's
 3. Windsor Court Hotel
 4. Arnaud's
 5. Royal Orleans Hotel
 6. Fairmont Hotel
 7. Le Meridien Hotel
 8. Commander's Palace
 9. Versailles
 10. Brennan's

BARBECUE. New Orleans is not a barbecue town. There are few barbecue restaurants of any kind, let alone good ones. That is either the cause or the result of a serious lack of barbecue education on the part of the population. Although each part of the country has a different style of barbecue, all the good barbecue I've eaten (and I'm something of a barbecue buff) had two attributes in common. First, good barbecue is uniformly well-smoked, but never to the point of bitterness. Second, it has a satisfying, slightly chewy, tight texture. Notice I said nothing about sauce. Sauce is secondary; it's a lot easier to make a decent sauce than to smoke a slab of ribs or brisket nicely.

Only two barbecue restaurants here could even hope to survive in Memphis, Austin, Kansas City, or North Carolina. The first and easily the best is **Tipton County Tennessee Pit Barbecue**, which does the Memphis "dry" style of pulled pork and spectacular small, smoky spare ribs. **Harold's Texas Barbecue** puts out a first-class, smoky beef brisket with a superior sauce and excellent side dishes. **Creech's** across the lake puts out nice brisket and pulled pork, although the ribs and side dishes leave me cold. **Copeland's** is not a barbecue restaurant, but they do make the city's best barbecue baby back ribs. (They should bring back their stellar lamb ribs, which were unforgettable.) **Luther's** is fast-foody and just okay.

If there is such a thing as New Orleans-style barbecue, it is epitomized at **Podner's** and **BBQ King**, two rough-and-ready take-out places. The chicken and beef are edible, but the ribs appear to be boiled, which causes the meat to be far too tender. This effect, which results in the meat remaining on the plate when you pick up the bone, is totally wrong and terrible in my book. You find a similar thing playing to big crowds at **Houston's**.

BARBECUE SHRIMP. A misnomer, but still one of the most exciting — and messiest — dishes in the local cuisine. Barbecue shrimp was introduced in the 1950s at Pascal's Manale, where a customer from Chicago supplied a recipe and asked to have them made. The dish became so popular that Manale's nearly became a one-dish restaurant as a result. This dish is relatively simple: huge whole shrimp in a tremendous amount of butter and black pepper. Every restaurant that serves barbecue shrimp seems to have its own approach, but anything far afield of the Manale's style is less good. Other restaurants that prepare great barbecue shrimp are **Mr. B's** (a spectacular, herbal version), **Kolb's, Briar Rose** and **Stephen & Martin**.

As far as the eating is concerned, barbecue shrimp is two dishes in one. The first is the shrimp themselves, drenched with the sauce and eaten with the fingers. I pull the head, legs and tail off, but I eat all the rest of the shell. I have never had a problem with this, although I hesitate to recommend shell-eating to you. The other dish is bread dunked in the sauce, which some maintain tastes better than the shrimp.

Although Manale's maintains an aura of secrecy about the recipe, the preparation is no big deal. Since I think the dish is one of the ten best dishes in the local cuisine, here is a recipe. It makes barbecue shrimp that I find indistinguishable from the classic original. The most essential element in this recipe is the requirement for head-on shrimp. It's the fat in the heads that makes the sauce.

BARBECUE SHRIMP
6 lbs. fresh Gulf shrimp with heads on, 21-25 count to the pound
1½ lbs. salted butter
½ lb. margarine
1 newly-purchased 6-8 oz. can black pepper
1 tsp. granulated garlic
2 tsp. hot paprika

Preheat the oven to 400 degrees.
1. Wash the shrimp and more or less dry them. Place the shrimp on their sides, crowded together and slightly overlapping, two layers deep, in aluminum baking pans.
2. Melt the butter and margarine together without getting them hot. Stir in the pepper, granulated garlic and paprika until well blended. Pour the butter mixture over the shrimp, making sure that all the shrimp get sauced.
3. Bake the shrimp in a preheated 400-degree oven for 10 minutes. Turn the shrimp and return to the oven for another five minutes. They will probably not be fully cooked yet, but you must gauge how much longer to leave them in the oven. You want the finished product to be just starting to soften, with shells the texture of thick cellophane. You do *not* want soft, wrinkled shells.
4. Serve the shrimp in soup plates with lots of the sauce and toasted crescents of French bread. Also plenty of napkins and perhaps bibs.
Serves six to eight.

BARD-O-TERIA. See Parky's Ungulate's Bard-O-Teria.

★ ★ ★ Barreca's

3100 Metairie Road, Old Metairie. 831-4546. 11 a.m.-3 p.m. Mon.-Fri.; 4-10 p.m. Mon.-Sat. AE, MC, V. $$

Barreca's occupies a building that has hosted a succession of cheap neighborhood cafes. Indeed, that's what Barreca's itself was at first. But after a year it evolved into a very good, creative restaurant. The ambience, prices, and service are those of a corner eatery, but the food is considerably more ambitious and delightful.

Start off with the shrimp or crawfish remoulade, served cold and in ample portion, with a mellow, orange sauce. The baby soft shell crabs are fried with ideal lightness and abetted, if you like, with a crawfish sauce that allows you to still taste the crab. (A pair of these is also good as an entree.) Soups are just okay; they have a way of being overloaded with seasoning vegetables.

A blackboard listing the day's half-dozen or so specials is the best place to look for your entree. Various species of fish are grilled with a nice seasoning balance, although if it's tuna you'd better tell them to ease off on the cooking time. The trout with pecans is one of the best around, comparing favorably with the original at Commander's Palace. The best part of this—one which shows up on a few other seafood entrees as well—is the old-style meuniere sauce. It is an exceptionally well-made version of the thick, translucent, light brown flow that has otherwise all but departed local kitchens.

The specials usually include a roast duck, usually with a spicy peach sauce, a crisp skin, and a very moist, pleasantly overcooked interior. It is a wonderful duck, resting atop a pile of dirty rice. The grilled chicken with mustard sauce is a fine lighter dish. Both of these come with fine baked yams.

Without a doubt the least interesting food here is from the Italian dishes. The chicken Parmigiana, veal Sorrentino, and lasagna are all edible, but not much more than that.

Service here is unusually friendly and helpful. The restaurant tends to be very crowded in the early evening hours, but the staff handles the stress with great diplomacy and cordiality.

★ ★ ★ Barrow's Shady Inn

2714 Mistletoe (just off Earhart Blvd. near Orleans Parish line), Uptown. 482-9427. 5-10 p.m. Tues. & Wed.; 11:30 a.m.-10 p.m. Thurs.; 11:30 a.m.-Midnight Fri.; Noon-Midnight Sat. No credit cards. $.

Catfish Central! This restaurant opened in the Forties, but only its adherents knew about it until the new Earhart Expressway made it easy to find. I have always liked Barrow's for its one-dish dinner menu: catfish, delivered fresh and whole from Des Allemands, filleted on the premises, coated with cornmeal and fried to an incomparable light golden brown. This is such good catfish that you practically inhale it. The plate currently costs $8.50 (the signs on the walls show current market price), and comes with a great potato salad made from freshly-boiled new potatoes. On the three days they serve lunch, the offerings expand to include some pot cooking, and that's good too.

★ ★ Bart's Lighthouse Inn

8000 Lakeshore Dr., Lakefront. 282-0271. 11:30 a.m.-10 p.m. seven days; till 11:30 p.m. Fri. & Sat. AE, MC, V. $$.

Bart's is an old name in the annals of lakefront seafood dining, but the restaurant currently bearing it is a recent creation, built on the site where the original Bart's burned down in the early Seventies. The setting is promising: the second-floor dining room and its balcony overlook Lake Pontchartrain. The lounge is almost as large as the dining room, and on most nights a lively young singles scene swings well into the night.

Bart's menu is more ambitious than those of most of its competitors on the lakefront, but attempts to stray from the basics of local seafood dining have proven to be bum steers. The place is close to the front rank in the Worst Hollandaise Competition, for example. The best food here is the grilled fish, which comes out in reasonably good shape, tasting fresh. The second-best food is soup: they put out an especially good crawfish bisque, spicy and full of crawfish flavor. The shrimp Clemenceau is an original treatment; the shrimp are sauteed with artichokes, mushrooms, peas, onions, and garlic, and this is quite delicious. The fried seafood platters are well fleshed out with food, but have never been as hot, crisp, or well enough seasoned for me.

Nothing exciting for dessert. Service is a bit disorganized, especially at lunch.

★ ★ ★ ★ Bayona

430 Dauphine, French Quarter. Reservations 525-4455. 11:30 a.m.-2:30 p.m. Mon.-Fri.; 6-10 p.m. Mon.-Sat.; till 11 p.m. Fri. & Sat. AE, MC, V. $$$.

This is the latest edition of a restaurant known to avid diners as "Susan Spicer's Place." Spicer is a youngish chef who first attracted attention in the early Eighties at Savoir-Faire. She accumulated an enthusiastic, room-packing following—not to mention glowing notices in the national food press—at the Bistro at the Maison de Ville. Bayona is the first restaurant in which she is a proprietor as well as chef. (The name, by the way, is what the Spanish used to call Dauphine Street.)

Spicer's fans, weary of the battle for tables at the tiny Bistro, are ecstatic to find that Bayona is roomy. The space was occupied for years by the stuffy old Maison Pierre. Spicer's designers freshened it up and took advantage of the many windows and the patio to create a very comfortable dining room.

Susan Spicer's celebrity is not without cause. I have met few chefs who combine such a sense of adventure with such unerring taste. She always has a dish or two you never heard of before, but never do these go crashing into the pitfalls of silliness or pretentiousness. And, just in case, the menu includes a few exercises in elegant familiarity.

Bayona just opened as this book went to press, but a couple of early meals assure me that Chef Spicer has lost no momentum. Her specialties tend to be foods and dishes that few other restaurants have much luck with. Veal sweetbreads, for instance. They show up at Bayona sauteed with mushrooms and a sauce of sherry, mustard, and butter as a somewhat filling appetizer, and in the classic, simple, crusty meuniere style with capers as an entree. Grilled duck breast, sharpened with a glaze of pepepr jelly, was the big hit for the chef at the Bistro, and here it is again, good as ever. Here too is the soup that was Susan Spicer's first signature dish: cream of caramelized garlic, nutty and slightly sweet.

If none of that catches your fancy, you can still start off most deliciously with the roasted eggplant salad, served with tapenade (a semi-puree of olives, anchovies and olive oil) and feta cheese—a bunch of intense Mediterranean flavors that jolts your palate from its slumber. They have a boudin noir—blood sausage—served with apples and onions. At lunch, there's a wonderful croustade of crunchy, slightly peppery arugula and prosciutto with a pair of fried quail eggs on top. The underlayer is toasted, buttered brown bread that seems relatively impervious to the mustard-laced sauce all around. The proscuitto adds a satisfying note of richness.

The most obvious evolution in the chef's style with the opening of Bayona is a greater number of Italian-inspired dishes than before. Paella risotto (why not just add "jambalaya" to the name and cover all the bases?) includes shellfish, sausage, and chicken in a matrix of saffron-scented Arborio rice. There's a vegetable lasagna with three cheeses, and the quail is sent out with an Abruzzese herb sauce and sage polenta. But we still get French tastes, like pan-roasted salmon with choucroute and Gewurztraminer. And Creole: rabbit fricassee with artichokes (a chicken potpie version of this same idea appears at lunch).

Desserts change daily. The best of them by a million miles is a sort of sandwich of thin, hazelnut-encrusted, hard-baked meringue cookies with intense chocolate mousse in the center: irresistible. That this could steal me from Spicer's lemon tart, especially since I'm no chocoholic, is a recommendation of considerable weight.

Finish the meal with the excellent espresso, and lubricate it with wines from a list that at this writing is rather quirky and too expensive. But food prices here are a good deal lower than those of comparable restaurants—certainly within the French Quarter. Four courses with wine might be brought in under $30 per person.

★ ★ ★ ★ Bayou Ridge Cafe

5080 Pontchartrain Blvd. (I-10 at Metairie Road), Mid-City. 486-0788. 11:30 a.m.-2:30 p.m. Mon.-Sat.; 5:30-10 p.m. Mon.-Thurs.; 5:30-11 p.m. Fri. & Sat. AE, MC, V. $$.

The best new restaurant of 1988, this convivial cafe opened with a trendy gimmick: a wood-fired stone oven for baking pizzas. It took them awhile, but they seem to have mastered the art of making a good pizza crust: crisp at the edges, bready-aromatic, not spongy. The pizzas make a great shared appetizer or a light entree for one. The toppings are offbeat: smoked salmon, goat cheese, sun-dried tomatoes, and Italian sausage. Most unusual is the muffuletta pizza, topped with the meats, cheeses, and olive salad of that sandwich: a great idea.

The kitchen is run by Kevin Vizard, one of the best younger chefs in town. We previously enjoyed Mr. Vizard's work at various Uptown cafes; he has the rare ability to innovate without losing sight of the ABC's. For example, he's not at all ashamed to feature a basic, no-frills, crisp-skinned, juicy, elemental roast chicken half.

The best of the non-pizza appetizers are small orders of pasta. Some of these fill the mouth explosively: oysters saltimbocca, with ham, cheese, and a zippy brown sauce, for example. Two soups daily: a thick, dark gumbo, and something else good. Salads are exceptionally well made. A small one would be something like spinach, belgian endive, melted Gorgonzola, pecans and apples. A big salad—and a great lunch—is the salade Nicoise with fresh tuna.

The roast chicken would be my first entree pick, but there is much else toothsome. Rabbit tenderloin grilled to a spicy, light crustiness, moistened with a veal-stock reduction that runs into a pile of angel hair pasta: tremendous food. The beef tenderloin is sliced thin to reveal a marvelous contrast between crusty exterior and rare inside. Sauces change with every new menu (they re-invent the wheel here every few months).

The Bayou Ridge is definitely a fish house. Two fresh fish species appear daily, grilled and otherwise prepared. I've enjoyed the likes of mustard-glazed salmon with arugula and grilled fish with artichoke confit. Mussels marinara are a big pile of gaping black shells with great fresh mussels in a spicy red sauce.

Several original desserts, the most outrageous of which is the fruit pizza. The sauce is a blend of cream cheese with honey; the toppings are raspberries, strawberries, kiwi, or whatever else is around, finished with fresh mint. This is really great. I also like the rich, crusty creme brulee, and the "chocolatines"—little piles of stiff chocolate mousse atop cookies in raspberry sauce. Coffee, espresso, and cappuccino are all rich and strong.

The wine list is interesting; right up with the times. Service is casual and decent. The premises consist of two simple rooms with exposed ceiling beams and columns of finished wood; large mirrors add further dimension. Prices at all meals are well below those prevailing in the Uptown bistros with similar menus; dinner entrees are between $10 and $15.

★★Bean Pot

8117 Maple, Uptown. 866-2904. 11 a.m.-2 p.m. Mon.-Sat.; 5:30-10:30 p.m. seven nights. MC, V. $$.

The look is authentic: a couple of small rooms claimed from a former residence. But what the Bean Pot lacks in looks it makes up for in its food, which is offbeat and better than you think it's going to be. The Mexican chef/owner is a creative soul who likes to develop sauces. For example, his avocado sauce, bright green and mildly peppery, is a great match for his crabmeat enchiladas. So is a fascinating tart sauce made from the tomatillo, a small green tomato. Salsa Azteca, made from pumpkin seeds, is herbal and unique. These and other, more familiar sauces— like a rich, dark, peppery, bitter-chocolate mole poblano—are slathered over chicken, pork, beef, fajitas, or seafood.

The usual combination platters of various manifestations of the tortilla are prepared and assembled well. The refried beans, appropriately enough, are far above average—spicy, flavorful, and not a gloopy mass. Good rice, too. It's bothersome that the place looks and acts barely open, but it in fact has been there for years. The prices are a poco higher than they ought to be.

BEARNAISE. Probably the world's richest and most delicious sauce, this is a thick, pale yellow blending of butter and egg yolks, flavored with tarragon and other aromatic herbs. It seems to have possibilities with virtually every food, but the classics are steak (especially chateaubriand, with which it is de rigeur), lamb, and chicken. Particularly good bearnaise is made in the kitchens of **Louis XVI**, **Galatoire's**, the **Versailles**, **Arnaud's**, and **Andrea's**. Antoine's makes a very peculiar fluffy, lemony bearnaise which works better on fish than on meat.

Beef Baron

541 Oaklawn (at Veterans), Metairie. 837-5949. 11 a.m.-3 p.m. Sun.-Fri., 5-10 p.m. seven nights (till Midnight Fri. & Sat.). AE, CB, DC, MC, V. $$$.

The Beef Baron moved to Metairie a few years ago after a long run on Canal Street. The premises are pleasant, suburban, and feature an interesting bit of Sixties kitsch: curtained booths, with a light on the outside to signal the waitress. This would be more fun if they hadn't made the booths a little too small, but at least they have plenty of them.

The Beef Baron has always served prime beef. But of all the prime steaks I've eaten, I like these least for texture, flavor, and especially temperature. Is the grill not hot enough? That dullness extends through all the other food in the house: oily onion rings, pale onion soup, indifferent salads, and overcooked vegetables. The sharp edges that turn me on and make me want to come back are missing.

They have very inexpensive lunch specials (which are countered by plastic covering over the tablecloths and paper napkins, even when you pop for top dollar menu items). And the menu includes as many seafood items as steak.

★ ★ ★ Beef Room

2750 N.Causeway Blvd. (between I-10 and Veterans), Metairie. 837-0431. 4 p.m.-Midnight seven nights. AE, CB, DC, DS, MC, V. $$$.

If you want to have a decent meal with someone you shouldn't be seen with, come here. The Beef Room is dark, a little hard to get to (despite the seemingly prime location), and it's strictly regulars at the other tables. The dining room is out of the late Sixties: patterned velvet wallpaper with

dark wood Olde English embellishments.
This is a very good steak house. The beef is USDA prime and broiled to a sizzle. They don't trim the steaks very well, but they are of such size that there can be no argument about portion. The prices are below market average for prime beef. The salads and spuds, both well turned out, come with the steak. If you want an appetizer, go for the fettuccine. Service is efficient and that's all. In recent times, they've started grilling fish here like everywhere else, but for me this is still a. . . well, beef room.

BEEF WELLINGTON. A cut of beef tenderloin covered with duxelles (a semi-sauce of chipped mushrooms), wrapped with pastry, and baked. It is almost always served with sauce Perigourdine, a translucent beef reduction studded with truffles. It sounds like a much better dish than it actually is. The beef never cooks just right and has a peculiar texture. This is especially true if the Wellington is cooked for one. Restaurants which do a good job with the dish are **Louis XVI** (which introduced it to the area), the **Versailles** and **Crozier's** (it's not on the menu at either place, but they'll prepare it with a day's advance notice), and the **Mystery Street Cafe**. The **Blue Room** puts out an excellent cold beef Wellington on its Sunday brunch buffet.

★★Begue's

Royal Sonesta Hotel, 300 Bourbon, French Quarter. 586-0300. Noon-2:30 p.m. Mon.-Sat.;6-11 p.m. seven days; Sun. Brunch 10:30 a.m.-2:30 p.m. AE, CB, DC, MC, CB, V. $$$.

The flagship restaurant of the Royal Sonesta Hotel borrows one of the most famous names in the annals of New Orleans dining. Madame Begue's restaurant, which was where Tujague's is now, was the Commander's Palace of the late 1800s. But Madame Begue would probably be shocked to see her name associated with the Sonesta's restaurant. In its recently-built new room, fronting on the hotel's beautiful courtyard, Begue's is an overpackaged hodgepodge of Creole-Cajun cliches gilded with European slickness.

It's not a total disaster, however. They give good soup—particularly the creamy seafood bisques and the turtle soup. The Begue's salad is very fine, with an interesting assortment of greens, feta cheese, and pecans. The pastas with seafoods and the simply broiled or sauteed fish are more than edible. The thick prime sirloin strip is broiled nicely and served with a fine sauce with wild mushrooms. At lunch there is a satisfying roasted half chicken.

Where they get into trouble here is with awful parodies of local cooking like blackened fish, fish fillets covered with thick, creamy sauces studded with crawfish or some such, and overuses of assertive ingredients like tasso and andouille. Whenever I've eaten this fare, I always wish I'd asked them to hold the glop, because the fish or veal or whatever tastes good enough all by itself. Begue's is famous for a hot spinach salad made tableside; its preparation makes the whole dining room smell like bacon.

They do an okay Sunday brunch, when desserts are at their peak of the week. Service is not rigorous; the wine list is decent but overpriced.

BEIGNETS. These are the square, sugar-dusted doughnuts served at the **Cafe du Monde, Cafe Beignet,** the **Morning Call,** and a few other places. You must keep two things in mind when eating beignets. They are heavier than they look. And never laugh while biting into one, or else you'll create a cumulo-nimbus of powdered sugar dust around your head.

Here is the recipe my mother used to produce beignets that tasted exactly like those in the Market. Buy a can of regular Ballard biscuits (not buttermilk or flaky), and stretch out each biscuit three times its original size. Then cut the dough into squares (or any other shape you want), and fry them in 350-degree vegetable oil, turning once, until golden brown. Dust with powdered sugar, and accompany with cafe au lait.

★ ★ ★ Berdou's

300 Monroe St., Gretna. Reservations 366-2401. 11:30 a.m.-1:30 p.m. and 5-8:30 p.m. Tues.-Sat. No credit cards. $$.

Berdou's continues to serve its Creole specialties as if there were no tomorrows, only yesterdays. Many yesterdays ago, restaurant food was cooked, served, and priced like this. But nowadays, how many restaurants are left which still feature among their appetizers hearts of celery, sardines, tomato juice, or olives? How many restaurants close for dinner at 8:30? And how many offer a five-course meal for under $10?

There are two dining rooms, each with a certain charming antique plainness. Attached to the menu is a list of the table d'hote specials of the day. These are even more of a bargain than the regular menu, which has few prices over $10. Once past the good shrimp remoulade and the homemade soups of turtle, vegetables, or oysters, your best option is to have a seafood entree. Pompano en papillote, not what it once was, is still reasonably good: a light sauce is baked with the fish inside a paper bag. Trout Marguery is pleasantly rich and shrimpy. If you like garlic, the crabmeat Berdou casserole has quite a bit of it. Fried seafood comes out hot and crisp.

Aside from the seafood, Berdou's does a nice job with lamb chops (they even put those little paper things on the bones!). They cook up eminently edible versions of chicken Clemenceau and bonne femme.

Desserts, wines, and service, like the surroundings, are simple and just good enough.

BISQUE. It depends on where you are. If you're reading "lobster bisque" from a menu in a fancy French place, it'll be a creamy, rich soup—maybe with chunks of lobster meat. The best of these are at the **Sazerac** and **Le Jardin**. If you're in a Creole or Cajun place, chances are it's crawfish bisque. Then you'll have a reddish-brown concoction with a lot of pepper and slivers of crawfish. Usually floating in there are crawfish heads stuffed with a mixture of crawfish meat and seasonings. I wish that this tradition would die out and be replaced by crawfish boulettes, which are fried balls of the same stuffing without the troublesome shell. Outside of crawfish season, similarly good soups are made with crab or shrimp. Some restaurants serve a creamy, ivory-hued shellfish bisque; these are, to my taste, far less interesting than the brick-red varieties. Good Creole-Cajun bisques are found at **La Cuisine**, **Bon Ton**, **Christian's**, **Antoine's**, the **Gumbo Shop**, **Ralph & Kacoo's**, the **Peppermill**, **Kabby's**, the **Rib Room**, and **Mike Anderson's**.

★ ★ ★ Bistro at Maison de Ville

Hotel Maison de Ville, 733 Toulouse. Reservations 528-9206. 11:30 a.m.-2:30 p.m. Mon.-Sat. 6-10 p.m. seven days; till 11 p.m. Fri. & Sat. AE, CB, DC, DS, MC, V. $$$.

A 40-seat cafe attached to a small, first-class hotel, the Bistro was—until she left in early 1990—better known as "Susan Spicer's Place." The appropriately-named Ms. Spicer was the chef and creative force behind the room from the day it opened in 1986, and her stamp remains. The style of cooking here is basically that of a French bistro, but with lots of fascinating amendments.

Start with a plate of grilled shrimp, awash in a light butter sauce flavored with the pungent coriander. The best part of the dish is a thick disc of well-cooked black beans, nicely seasoned and abetted with a dollop of sour cream. Even more unusual as a first course is the plate combining tapenade (a spread made of anchovies and olives) with "eggplant caviar" (the center part of the vegetable). The snails with prosciutto, tomato, and fresh thyme sounds complicated, but it has a fine rich, herbal flavor.

The soups, which vary daily, have perfect texture, temperature, and flavor. Especially good is the sweet garlic soup. There's a fascinating salad of well-roasted, smoky quail on spinach; another good one is the feta cheese with tomatoes and marinated vegetables.

The entree everybody talks about is the sweetbreads. They are prepared simply and classically: flour-dusted, sauteed, and served with lemon butter and capers. At lunch, there are interesting variations on the sauce. My second choice is the filet mignon with a French-style brown bordelaise sauce, redolent of garlic; the steak has a stratum of herbal boursin cheese stuffed into its center. Grilled duck breast with pepper jelly is edgy and brilliant. Tender rabbit tenderloins are sauteed with the interesting combo of tomato, artichokes, and olives.

Each day's menu at the Bistro includes a pair (at least) of lovely fresh fish, cooked different ways but always with great delicacy. The list of meat possibilities goes on to include peppered pork loin, lamb chops, and cutlets of venison—all eminently edible. Desserts are very straightforward; my favorite of them is the custardy, puckery lemon tart—thicker and richer than most such things. The espresso and cappuccino are among the best in the city. The wine list is short but very well chosen, both for quality of the vintages and for matching with the food. Service is efficient and knowledgeable; most of the staff has been here since the place opened.

My only complaint about the Bistro is the small size of its tables for two, which are cramped for six-foot, 200-pound guys.

BLACKENED. Everywhere except Louisiana, blackening is the best known of Cajun cooking techniques. It involves coating the redfish, chicken, prime rib, or whatever with a liberal dusting of a salty, very peppery seasoning blend and then cooking it rapidly in a superheated black iron skillet. The style was named and popularized by Paul Prudhomme at **K-Paul's Louisiana Kitchen**, the prototype for many of the Cajun restaurants which flourished for a few years around America. Chef Paul liked the hickory-grilled redfish he helped develop at Mr. B's; the story is that he couldn't install a grill at K-Paul's, so he developed the blackening method as a substitute.

A good blackened dish can be delicious. The best are blackened fish (especially tuna or pompano) at K-Paul's, **Gambrill's** or **Copeland's**. Blackened prime rib at **Brigtsen's** or **Flagons** show the way to prepare meats in this style; the success rate elsewhere is even worse than for the fish.

But any kind of blackened dish runs the risk of being overseasoned and overcooked. For blackened fish to come out right, the fillet has to be about eight to ten ounces—a much bigger portion of fish than most restaurants will give you.

These days, blackened dishes are most likely to be found in tourist-oriented or pop restaurants. The patrons, not familiar with the cuisine, order the one dish they have inevitably heard of. It's like a request for "New York, New York" in a piano bar. We would all be better off eating the grilled dishes that the blackened concept sought to imitate. See **Grilled.**

★★Blue Room

Fairmont Hotel, University Place, CBD. Reservations 529-4744. Brunch Sun. only, 10:30 a.m.-2:30 p.m. AE, CB, DC, MC, V. $$$$.

The Blue Room was New Orleans' glamorous supper club, with big-name entertainment and a house orchestra, but all that came to an end in 1989. Now it's only open on Sunday for a very popular and—as buffets go—very good brunch. Unlike most buffets, in which the availability of unlimited quantity obviates the need for quality, the Blue Room's artful displays are replete with edible food. The cold buffet and desserts are particularly impressive. The former has, interspersed with dozens of salads, such savories as boiled shrimp, raw oysters, pates and sausages, cold beef Wellington, smoked salmon, crab claws, marinated squid, and lots more. You can put together a very substantial and appetizing meal of just starters. The entrees show more variability. But the half-dozen or so selections will constitute the mediocre part of your meal. Better to get the omelettes and pastas, which are prepared to order.

The dessert table holds 25 or so different desserts, as well as fresh fruit and cheese. At the table, glasses and cups are kept filled and the detritus of previous courses is removed by effective waitresses; don't forget to tip 15 percent. The $20 tab is a little higher than for most buffets, but the Blue Room's is a lot better.

BOILED SEAFOOD. Crabs, shrimp, and crawfish boiled with a lot of salt, pepper, and herbs are ubiquitous casual foods in New Orleans. The ethos reaches a crescendo in the springtime, when crawfish—which lend themselves to boiling better than anything else—reach their peak. Then you'll see dainty women convert small mountains of brick-red boiled mudbugs into scatterings of parched shells with astounding speed. They can do this because they know how to "squeeze the tips and suck the heads."

It takes practice. What you do is break the crawfish where the thorax ("head") meets the abdomen ("tail"). Next, peel off the two biggest shell sections from the tail. Then squeeze the tip of the tail with thumb and forefinger. If you did it right, the tail meat should pop right out. If not, peel off another section or two of shell. Now the head-sucking part. There is a dollop of rich, delicious crawfish fat in there which can be extracted by a deft tonguing-sucking action which seems decidedly lewd. This is optional, but serious crawfish-eaters would rather slit their wrists than give up head-sucking.

Boiled shrimp are easy: just peel off the inedible-looking parts and eat the rest. Boiled crabs, in contrast, are the most complicated, despite the presence of a natural pull-tab. Opening crabs requires a bit of strength in the hands and perhaps some banging with the handle of a knife. In fact, I wonder whether the energy expended in opening a crab is replaced by the eating. The best course is to get an experienced eater to show you the ropes, but here's the basic technique. The best parts of the crab are the "lumps" found sort of in the armpits of the claws. To get at them you pull the tab on the underside, break the crab in half front to back, and start peeling away shell. There are two noxious grey organs called "dead-man's fingers" which must be removed; the lumps are just beyond. You also have some tasty meat in the claws, which open in an obvious way.

Boiled seafood is unquestionably better eaten at someone's home than in a restaurant, mainly because most restaurants serve the stuff refrigerated. It is much better hot. The only consistent sources of hot boiled seafood I know about are **Jaeger's** on Elysian Fields and **West End Cafe**. West End Park is a traditional setting for boiled seafood; good purveyors out there are **Bruning's, Maggie & Smitty's, Sportsman's Paradise,** and **The Bounty**. Other good restaurants for boiled seafood are Bozo's, Cafe Atchafalaya, Alonso's, and Sid-Mar's.

★★Bombay Club

1019 Dumaine, French Quarter. 586-0972. 6-10 p.m. (bar open much later), Tues.-Sun. MC, V. $$.

A smallish motel lounge was converted a few years ago by the tasteful Marc Turk into a stylish late-evening rendezvous. A pianist fills those parts of the air that aren't already crammed with clever conversation, and the whole place has a certain English spin. There is food, consisting mainly of inconsistent nightly specials and a very good hamburger. But the place is so small that I find eating here uncomfortable. There may be no better place to which to repair after dining somewhere else.

★★★Bon Ton Cafe

401 Magazine, CBD. Reservations 524-3386. 11 a.m.-2:00 p.m. and 5-9:30 p.m. Mon.-Fri. Closed Sat. & Sun. AE, MC, V. $$$.

The Bon Ton is a popular restaurant with a long-term national reputation for Cajun cooking. But this is the most lightly-seasoned Cajun food you're likely to find. It is not, however, inauthentic. Cajun food has regional variations, and the Bon-Ton's is the Bayou Lafourche style — the other end of the spectrum from K-Paul's Opelousas style. Start with the catfish fingers, served with a tasty, cold, orange sauce like a mild remoulade. The mock turtle soup is light in color and tasty, with a shot of sherry.

Without a doubt the best dish here is redfish Bon Ton, a big flank of well-trimmed fish (probably not really red) with a buttery orange sauce and a drift of crabmeat on top. In season, the crawfish dishes are satisfying as long as you're not expecting blow-your-brains-out pepper levels. The best crawfish repast is the crawfish dinner; it takes the delicious tails through a half-dozen or so different dishes. It includes etouffee, bisque, fried croquettes, and—best of all—a crawfish omelette. Out of crawfish season, things get even milder. The shrimp etouffee is a mellow stew over rice—shrimpy and elegant. Oyster pan roast with shallots is a deftly-wrought version of an old, seldom-seen item. The newer oysters Alvin are fried and sauced with another zingy, butter-like sauce.

If you like crabmeat, this is the place for you. The crabmeat salad is replete with white lump meat under a mellow dressing. Crab Imperial has the same lumps with green and red peppers and a good bit of margarine. The only way you could not like this is if you didn't like crabmeat. Crab au gratin has a bit too much cheesy, creamy sauce, but it's a good example of the dish.

The bread pudding is a hot cube with a very alcoholic whiskey sauce. It is not my style, but it's clearly well-made and its adherents swear it's the best there is. Service is by wonderful old-line New Orleans waitresses with lots of personality.

Those on low-cholesterol diets will be happy to know that all the cooking at the Bon-Ton is done with margarine. This is not a gimmick; the place has never used butter.

BORDELAISE. This term, applied to a wide range of dishes in New Orleans, causes much confusion among those familiar with the classic bordelaise sauce (a robust brown sauce made with demi-glace, tomato, and red wine). In these parts, bordelaise almost always refers to some variation on garlic butter—like the kind you get on snails. The most familiar manifestation is spaghetti bordelaise, at its apex at **Mosca's**; it's spaghetti with butter, olive oil, and garlic—period. Many of the local steak houses offer this same bordelaise sauce to abet your beef. Avoid this old-fashioned practice. An especially wonderful classic French bordelaise sauce is served with a boursin-cheese-stuffed filet mignon at the **Bistro at the Maison de Ville**. La Provence occasionally does a great version of the same sauce for its steaks.

BOUDIN. Pronounced "BOO-danh." Boudin is one of the tastiest of Cajun snacks; you'll find that you can eat a much bigger piece of it than you might imagine. By far the most common variety is a sausage casing stuffed with very spicy rice mixed with pork. This boudin is sold widely in stores, particularly in the Cajun country, where it's often kept hot and ready to eat. It is almost unavoidable at festivals. It is, unfortunately, very rarely encountered at sit-down restaurants.

Boudin noir is an entirely different animal—a Cajun blood sausage with a puddinglike interior. It's better than it sounds, but you needn't worry about it in any case. It is available only very rarely, in small meat markets in the Cajun country, and only if they know you.

BOUILLABAISSE. When a New Orleans waiter describes bouillabaisse as a thick, slightly spicy soup with redfish, shrimp, oysters, crab, and lobster, the usual response from the uninitiated is "Oh! Something like gumbo!" Well, no, nothing like gumbo. Nor is it much like a real Marseilles bouillabaisse. Regardless, it is good stuff and more than enough for an entree, since the pieces of fish are usually rather large. The best bouillabaisse in New Orleans is made at the **Versailles**, where the fish is present in beautiful form, the stock is delicious, and the fragrance and taste of saffron (the world's most expensive foodstuff) is obvious. Other good bouillabaisses are those at **Christian's** (a bit light, with a spicy garlic mayonnaise for thickening and spicing) and **Galatoire's** (order a day in advance). At **Andrea's**, they make the Italian version of the dish, called cioppino—and this too is in the front rank.

★★The Bounty

1926 West End Park. 282-9333. 11:00 a.m.-10:30 p.m. Tues.-Sun.; till 11:30 p.m. Fri. & Sat. AE, CB, DC, MC, V. $$.

The Bounty looks nicer inside than the other restaurants on stilts at West End. You get to it by walking down a covered ramp over a section of lakefront unusually prone to floating trash. The dining room is distinguished from its competitors' in having tablecloths. The large windows offer an unobstructed view of the lake, the shore, and the moving lights on the Causeway.

The Bounty uses West End Menu A: shrimp and crab cocktails, gumbo, fried and broiled seafood platters, and a few stuffed items. The only prominent concession to changing times is the presence of blackened fish. Don't start with gumbo, as you ordinarily would in a place like this; it's overthick and stale-tasting. The traditional fried seafood platter here is well above average; everything seems fresh, comes out light and crisp, and is blessed with fine seasoning balance, crinkle-cut fries (haven't seen those in awhile), and a trio of hushpuppies. Smaller quantity but equally good taste is found in the delicious broiled stuffed trout. Dessert is a good if very sweet bread pudding. Service is by youngish waitresses who don't seem to have all the answers to your questions.

★★★★Bozo's

3117 21st Street (half-block east of Causeway Blvd., near Lakeside Shopping Center), Metairie. 831-8666. 11 a.m.-3 p.m. and 5-10 p.m. Tues.-Sat.; till 11 p.m. Fri. & Sat. MC, V. $.

Bozo's is my favorite casual seafood restaurant. It has been in its completely public Metairie location for the last ten of its 55 years, and although the restaurant has no easily visible sign, it's full at most normal dining hours. The second-generation owner, Chris "Little Bozo" Vodonovich, is always on hand, supervising the meticulous kitchen operation. Through large windows you can see each strictly fresh seafood prepared to order in its own pot of oil, constantly skimmed and renewed. The result: perfect, crackling-hot cornmeal-coated catfish, oysters, and shrimp.

The best starting point is the oyster bar, where some of the best bivalves you will ever eat are shucked by masters. At the table—if your party is big enough to handle all this food—get some boiled shrimp or (in season) boiled crawfish. Alternately, there are sublime marinated crabs or crawfish, drenched with a thick cold concoction of lemon, artichokes, fat of the animals being marinated, and who knows what else: unbelieveable. The gumbo is a unique, light one of chicken, andouille, and seafood. It starts slowly on the palate but gets better by the spoonful.

The best entree in the house is broiled shrimp, peeled and butterflied tails sprinkled liberally with salt and pepper and broiled in margarine. This is unforgettable, and so light that it qualifies as diet food. Broiled catfish is also good. The stuffed crab is small, inexpensive, and makes a good side order; it's mostly crabmeat.

If you're used to the run-of-the-mill seafood place, be advised that French fries, hush puppies, and other plate fillers have to be ordered separately. The focus is on the perfect fish. Also, since the stuff is not sitting under heat lamps already cooked, it takes a few minutes to appear. Worth the wait.

Bozo's has a few other items. The hamburger steak with onions is not bad. Nor is the killer hot sausage poor boy, delicious but almost sure to make its presence felt later. There's a fruity bread pudding for dessert.

BRABANT POTATOES. Cube-shaped French fries—sort of. Great brabants are first fried, then drizzled with garlic butter and baked until crispy. Nobody does all of that, but **Antoine's** still has great ones. Okay brabants are at **Galatoire's, Crescent City Steak House, Bayou Ridge Cafe,** and the **Peppermill** (when they're made to order). To be avoided are the brabants covered with bread crumbs (such as at Arnaud's.)

BREAD. Orleanians have always favored French bread over sliced white. Several large commercial bakers of French bread—each in business for decades—bake the light New Orleans-style loaf in many different shapes. The two best are **Leidenheimer's** and **Angelo Gendusa.** Recently, some new bakeries with the heavier, more traditional French bread have been well-received—most notably **La Madeleine.**

The French bread typically served in restaurants is the gigot or pistolette—a loaf about a foot long and two inches in diameter, toasted to a slightly burned top right before being brought out. It should smell as good as it tastes. A great variation is the thicker, shorter "cap" bread. The bread available commercially is so good that few restaurants bake their own.

Here are the restaurants serving the best bread of any kind.
1. Antoine's (French bread)
2. K-Paul's (home-baked rolls; great jalapeno cheese bread)
3. La Louisiane (heavy Italian seeded bread)
4. Arnaud's (cap bread)
5. Pelican Club (heavy, herbal focaccia bread)
6. Commander's Palace (French bread and herb-garlic bread)
7. Moran's Riverside (French bread)

8. Andrea's (home-baked whole-wheat rolls)
9. Hummingbird Grill (cornbread)
10. Galatoire's (French bread)
11. Louis XVI (French bread, served with garlic butter)

BREAD PUDDING. Creole bread pudding is my favorite dessert. It's a glorious, rich goodness, a far cry from the poor man's dessert that goes under the same name in other parts of the country. Like gumbo, bread pudding has endless variations of shape, texture, and flavor, despite the fact that the ingredients are more or less the same. The sauces, most of which contain whiskey, rum, or brandy, also differ from cook to cook. Despite that (or perhaps because of it), there are many more good bread puddings than bad.

The finest products of bread pudding evolution are the totally different versions at **Arnaud's** and **Commander's Palace**. The former is a rather firm square with discrete layers separated by strata of custard and cinnamon, served hot with a great brandy sauce. Commander's regular light bread pudding is good to start with, but they blend it with meringue to make a fluffy, hot souffle. The light whiskey sauce goes down the middle, and the effect is wonderful. Other great bread puddings are served at the **Bon Ton, Mr. B's, Pascal's Manale, Ruth's Chris Steak House, La Cuisine,** and **Crozier's**.

Here is a recipe for a bread pudding that combines ideas from Commander's Palace and my mother:

BREAD PUDDING
 ½ stick butter or margarine
 ¾ cup sugar
 1 quart half-and-half cream
 5 large eggs
 3 Tbs. vanilla (Mexican, if available)☆
 2 Tbs. cinnamon
 Stale French bread
 ½ cup golden raisins

Preheat oven to 300 degrees. This pudding contains an almost obscene custard component, and to keep it from burning you should bake it as you would a custard. I use a Pyrex baking dish 9x5x3 inches, and set it inside a slightly larger pan of water once it's in the oven.

1. Melt the butter in a mixing bowl. Stir in the sugar until well creamed. Blend in half-and-half, vanilla, cinnamon and egg yolks. Reserve three of the whites, and add the other two to the mixture—a liquid custard.

2. Lightly butter the inside of the baking dish. Slice the French bread into ¼-inch-thick slices. Place a layer of bread at the bottom of the baking dish, squinching the sides of the slices to cover most of the bottom. Sprinkle with cinnamon and raisins. Pour in enough of the custard mixture to soak the bread. Lay down another layer of bread slices, this time

overlapping each slice slightly. Sprinkle with cinnamon and raisins. Soak with custard. Continue adding layers of bread with cinnamon, raisins, and custard until dish is ⅔ full, then pour on the remainder of the custard. (There should be more than enough custard to completely soak all the bread. It may slightly float the entire bread mass.)

3. Bake for one and one-half hours at 300 degrees. Remove from oven and allow to cool. Meanwhile, make a meringue with these ingredients:

3 egg whites (reserved from first step)
Pinch cream of tartar
¼ cup sugar
1 Tbs. vanilla

4. In a completely clean, grease-free bowl (copper is best), beat egg whites with cream of tartar at high speed until peaks begin to form. Add sugar a little at a time, followed by vanilla, until completely blended. After bread pudding has cooled for 30 minutes, top pudding with a thick layer of meringue and put back in 350-degree oven until meringue is lightly browned on top. No sauce is needed.

BREAKFAST. I am told by those who should know that there is no way for a restaurant to make money with breakfast. On the other hand, **Brennan's** has made a fortune by serving the most spectacular breakfast imaginable. (See **Eggs.**) But most places that serve breakfast only do it because they have to—hotels, for example. As a result, some of the best places to take the morning meal are hotel coffee shops.

The most impressive is the **Windsor Court Grill Room**, with its lovely setting, fresh pastries, and classy service of both standard and more elegant egg dishes. The most traditional is the **Cafe Pontchartrain**, where a round-robin of local businessmen crowd in at a table in the corner every morning promptly at seven to scan the newspapers and scam some freshly-baked blueberry muffins, made-to-order eggs and bacon, hot grits, and dense, great chicory coffee. Other good hotel coffee shops are **La Gauloise**, the gleaming brasserie in Le Meridien; **Cafe Royale** in the Royal Orleans, which before 10 a.m. serves some superb pastries and croissants in a glorious room of marble, mirrors, and skylight; and **Bailey's**, the 24-hour place in the Fairmont, which has the city's best Danish and coffeecake. The coffee shops at the Hyatt, Hilton, and Westin Canal Place I find substandard.

Of the independent restaurants that serve breakfast, the best are the **Coffee Pot, Riverbend, Rick's Pancake Cottage,** and **Tiffin Inn**.

★ ★ ★ ★ Brennan's

417 Royal, French Quarter. Reservations 525-9711. 8 a.m.-2:30 p.m. and 6-10 p.m. seven days. AE, CB, DC, MC, V. $$$$$.

Breakfast at Brennan's is rightly one of New Orleans' most famous meals. Cheery dining rooms with big windows surround a classically lovely French Quarter courtyard. The atmosphere is celebratory and the food terrific. But brace yourself for the highest prices in town—at around $35, here is the most expensive morning meal you'll ever eat. (Although it must be said that after breakfast at Brennan's, you won't have room for lunch.)

The classic Brennan's breakfast begins with either oyster soup or a baked apple in cream, then proceeds into the poached-egg department. I like eggs Sardou (creamed spinach, artichoke bottom), eggs Owen (corned beef hash), eggs St. Charles (fried trout), eggs Nouvelle Orleans (crabmeat), and Hussarde (Canadian bacon, grilled tomato, marchand de vin sauce). All of the above involve eggs poached with unerring perfection, wiggly snow-white spheres with viscous liquid centers; all except eggs Owen are crowned with the best hollandaise in town.

The ideal table d'hote breakfast at Brennan's starts with a single egg Sardou, followed by grillades and grits. This is the best version I've ever had of that old Creole breakfast specialty. The grillades are slices of baby white veal, awash in a spectacular red Creole sauce redolent with peppers and herbs. The grits have the perfect lava-like texture, hot and buttery.

The hot French bread and the dense coffee are fine companions to the eggs. Bananas Foster, invented here, are better elsewhere but still a treat. Crepes Fitzgerald—cream cheese inside, strawberries outside—are good if you get them to put the crepes in the pan with the berries. The chocolate suicide cake is rich enough to make your head spin.

The best time to have breakfast at Brennan's is late morning on a weekday. Earlier, and all day Saturday and Sunday, the place is so jammed that even with a reservation you may have to wait for a table, and service may take on a mass-feeding aspect. Dress nicely; although jeans and t-shirts are allowed, that policy subtracts much from the gloriousness of the ambience.

Brennan's is much less frantic at dinner—romantic, even. In the past few years the menu and the cooking have improved tremendously. Unfortunately, at the same time the prices rose to a point that Brennan's is now probably the most expensive restaurant in town. There is a consolation: the best wine list in the city, full of Bordeaux and Burgundies from vintages now at their peaks, at prices below what you'd pay in a store—if, indeed, you could find these wines for sale.

For the most part, Brennan's sticks with old-style Creole tastes. Appealing places to begin: oysters Rockefeller and oysters casino (with a warm cocktail sauce and bacon), fine little buster crabs (small soft-shells, sans appendages) with pecans or bearnaise, the only escargots in New Orleans still served in their shells, a fine thick turtle soup, the Jackson salad of greens, Roquefort, bacon, and hearts of palm.

Because I will have one of those old red wines, my entree thoughts turn to steak. Luckily, Brennan's buys excellent prime beef, and its menu offers more steak dishes here than at any other New Orleans restaurant. My favorite is strip sirloin Stanley, a delicious if unlikely combination: a red-wine beef-reduction sauce topped with a horseradish cream sauce, with a sauteed banana on the side. Second choice would be either steak Diane or steak au poivre, both manufactured tableside to the accompaniment of much mouth-watering aroma and obscene richness.

The veal is of superb quality and needs little help from sauces. Veal Kottwitz, sharpened with artichokes and mellowed with mushrooms, is second only to the aforementioned grillades and grits. The veal Alana Michelle, topped with crabmeat and bearnaise, is good for high camp. Seafood is less a specialty; the kitchen tends to grossly oversauce. Trout with pecans, trout Nancy (capers, crabmeat, and lemon butter), and fish (used to be redfish, but redfish is now banned) Jaime, with a unique spicy brown sauce, are the best shots.

Desserts are the same as at breakfast, and service is a little more formal. Culinary consistency is not as reliable as it is at breakfast—an old story here. A card of specials lets you out of the place for about $40.

★ ★ ★ ★ Brigtsen's

723 Dante (three blocks from Carrollton at St. Charles), Riverbend area, Uptown. Reservations 861-7610. 5:30-10 p.m. Tues.-Sat. AE, MC, V. $$$$.

It's a small house, only slightly reconfigured since its residential days despite the fact that three previous restaurants have occupied it. All of the small rooms are kept full by the clamoring fans of Frank Brigtsen who, in 1986, left K-Paul's to open his own place. From that moment this has been one of the best bistro-style restaurants in the city, with one of the strongest creative flows anywhere in America.

Brigtsen (pronounced "bright-sen") is scrupulous about purchasing fresh, good-looking, and sometimes unusual foodstuffs; his recipes release intensities of uncomplicated flavor. The menu changes daily, but certain dishes have emerged as regular specialties. The better part of a whole rabbit loin is grilled quickly and hotly, then sent out with greens: a great way to begin. So is shrimp remoulade, with its zippy, mustardy sauce over big, plump shrimp. A pair of sausages—one of rabbit, the other a refined but properly peppery boudin, each with its own sauce—is filling for a first course but you gobble it down anyway.

The entree selection employs all the latest foodstuffs. Panneed tenderloin of bunny comes out as tender, oozy, and pure-tasting as baby white veal. And the rabbit livers, sauteed and abetted with caramelized onions, are as delicious as they are unusual. (A similar thing is done with duck livers to no less admirable end.)

Brigtsen's work with fresh seafood is impressive. They have a master touch with grilling fish here; a hunk of tuna comes out looking like a strip sirloin steak, with all the juiciness and robustness that implies. I like the sauteed trout with pecans and crabmeat. In season soft shell and buster crabs, sauteed with lemon butter, have a marvelous toasty crust and a rich interior ooziness of fat lumps. They like to serve soft-shell crawfish here, but this is no favorite of mine anywhere.

Blackening is pretty much limited to one superb specialty: prime rib. I am not one for blackened meats, but this version is exceptional, completely avoiding the burned-grease taste that such things often have. The interior is juicy and the seasoning satisfying—sort of a Cajun steak au poivre, if you will. Venison appears occasionally in a variety of forms, all robust and satisfying.

Good birds. The marinated, grilled chicken with sweet and hot peppers is a regular menu item, and hits you from several different directions. I've also had wonderful simply roasted chicken and duck here.

All the desserts, including the ice creams, are made on the premises and tend to the very rich. A two-layer chocolate cake with a thick, dense chocolate icing, for example, rested atop a plate painted with a couple of sauces—as if they were needed. They also serve good fresh fruit here, both in and out of pastries. The wine list is much more extensive and interesting than one would expect from a place this size. Service is on the very casual side; do not expect that everyone will get his or her entree at the same time.

BRISKET. Brisket—a flavorful, rather fibrous cut of beef—is used to make stocks for soup, but then the meat itself is served in big chunks as a main course, usually at lunch. It is a triumph of Creole cooking that this stuff can actually be delicious after being boiled for four hours. The definitive brisket is at **Tujague's**, where it is served between the soup and the entree as a curious but delectable extra course. **Clancy's, La Cuisine**, and the **Regency Room** are lunchtime sources of tasty brisket. **Galatoire's** works some enormous chunks of it into its vegetable soup. **Harold's Texas Barbecue** does the best thin-sliced barbecue version in these parts.

★ ★ ★ ★ Broussard's

819 Conti, French Quarter. Reservations 581-3866. 5:30-11 p.m. seven days. AE, CB, DC, MC, V. $$$$.

Broussard's was founded in 1920, extensively renovated in 1976, and brought to its present excellence in 1987. Then it was taken over by two restaurateurs of some repute: Evelyn Preuss (co-owner of the Versailles) and George Huber (previously of Louis XVI). They have kept the basically Creole cooking style, but they've added a few Continental touches—pretentiousness and higher prices among them.

The premises are beautiful. Three rooms, none of which looks like the others, keep a cool darkness and reserve. Outside is one of the Quarter's nicest courtyards, on which you can have a pre-or post-prandial drink.

If it's summer, start with the delice Broussard's—a combination of cold crabmeat ravigote and shrimp remoulade. In cooler times the baked oysters Rockefeller and Bienville are far above average, and the crabmeat Imperial—with a complex white sauce—is the best in the city. An appetizer portion of shrimp and crabmeat Lafitte has an herbal, light sauce of white wine with a little garlic. I have had pretty bad luck with the soups. The house salad is a beautiful combination of greens with a creamy vinaigrette.

Meats are the most interesting entrees. The veal sirloin is a thick, vivid pink mini-steak with three sauces napped in a web: the meat is better than the sauces. There's a good roasted rack of lamb with a well-made brown mint sauce, and the steak au poivre is covered with a salty but otherwise well-made cream sauce with peppercorns. The sauce for wonderful roasted, stuffed quails also includes peppercorns, and the dish is accompanied by wild rice.

I've not been too pleased by the seafood entrees. The redfish Conti, topped with hollandaise and either crawfish or crabmeat, is the best of them, but I find it a complicated over-richness. The better trout meuniere is distinguished by two sauces, alternating tan and brown: very unusual, but it doesn't help the flaccid fish.

They have some good fancy desserts—bananas Foster, cherries jubilee, a couple of crepes—flamed not before you but out in the vestibule. You can watch if you want (I don't). The wine list is above average only in price.

BRUNCH. What *is* brunch, anyway? In most places, it's just lunch with a few egg dishes added. Most brunches occur on Sunday (a day when, as a result, it's almost impossible to find lunch), and they fall into two categories. The more popular are the buffets; I find these distinctly less appetizing than brunches ordered from a menu and delivered by a waiter.

Here are the best brunches in town right now:
1. Commander's Palace
2. Arnaud's
3. Windsor Court Grill Room
4. Mr. B's
5. Le Jardin (buffet)
6. Brennan's
7. Kabby's (buffet)
8. Andrea's
9. Blue Room (buffet)
10. Marriott Riverview (buffet)
11. Inter-Continental Veranda (buffet)

See also **Buffets** and **Eggs**.

★ ★ ★ Bruning's

West End Park, Lakefront. 282-9395. 11 a.m.-9:30 p.m. seven days; till 10:30 p.m. Fri. & Sat. AE, MC, V. $$.

West End Park's best restaurant is its oldest. Everything Bruning's serves seems to be fresh and prepared to order—albeit with less consistent care than one might desire. Bruning's seafood generally comes to the table lightly-fried and grease-free, and the portions are large for the prices charged. The seafood platter is a classic of the genre, with fried shrimp, oysters, soft-shell crab, mystery fish (trout, usually) and a delicious ball of spicy crab stuffing. The whole flounder—served either fried or broiled, stuffed or not—is the best example around of that old but hard-to-find treat. Boiled crabs, shrimp, and crawfish are served in big platters for hands-on, messy enjoyment. After indulging, you can wash your hands at a sink right there in the middle of the dining room—a bit of Orleaniana that's fast disappearing around town. The big dining room has windows on all sides and a great view of the lake.

BUCKTOWN. The oldest part of Bucktown looks like any of a hundred little fishing communities on the waterways of South Louisiana. The fact that it's right in the middle of a busy suburb makes it striking and unique. The Bucktown area—like nearby West End—has a number of restaurants, most of them specializing in seafood. The most atmospherically distinctive—a shack with a lake view—is **Sid-Mar's**. The most popular (but not with me) is **Deanie's**. The best food is at **R&O's**, a poor boy specialist. **Carmine's** provides decent Italian food.

★ ★ Bud's Broiler

500 City Park Ave., 2338 Banks, 6325 Elysian Fields, 3151 Calhoun, 801 Carondelet (lunch only), 9820 Lake Forest Blvd., 2800 Veterans Blvd. (Kenner), 112 Sauve Rd. (River Ridge), 3521 18th (Metairie), 605 Lapalco Blvd. (Gretna). Hours in most cases are 11 a.m.-9 p.m., later on weekends. No credit cards. $.

Bud's distinction is that it grills its burgers over live charcoal, which lends a great smoky taste. The buns are toasted, the cheese is grated Cheddar, and the dressings are fresh. I like the Number One sauce, a blend of mayonnaise, hickory smoke sauce and relish. When you get a good one here, it's a peak hamburger experience; unfortunately, Bud's is anything but consistent. They also have weenies with chili and rich fried pies.

Bud's has been on an expansion kick lately, but most of its restaurants have the traditional worn-out, somewhat dirty look. Wooden tables and benches get carved-in messages shortly after they're installed.

BUFFETS. A beautiful display of food from which one can help oneself in unlimited quantities has enormous appeal to the greed department of our appetites. But from a fine dining perspective buffets have a lot of problems. The most obvious is the troublesome walk to the buffet. With plate in hand, we stand in line until it's our turn to figure out just what the hell the pink-and-green stuff is. Clumsy. Second problem: buffets must limit themselves to dishes that can be kept in a steam table or served cold. It's no wonder that the best buffet dishes are salads, chilled seafoods, and desserts, and that the worst things are the entrees. To get around this, the better buffets have stations where omelettes or pastas are cooked to order. Finally, there is so much waste in a buffet — the spread has to look as good at one as it did at eleven — that unless the buffet is a loss leader (as it is in the bigger hotels), the restaurant has to cut back greatly on the quality to make a buck.

As of this writing buffets (the good ones, anyway) are largely limited to Sunday brunch. The best are at the **Blue Room** in the Fairmont Hotel, **Le Jardin** in the Westin Canal Place, **Kabby's** at the Hilton (especially strong in cold seafood), and **La Gauloise** at the Meridien. (La Gauloise also has buffets daily for breakfast and lunch, and a very unusual seafood buffet on Fridays and Saturdays.) **Veranda** at the Inter-Continental, the Hyatt **Top of the Dome** and the **RiverView** at the Marriott are acceptable. Much less interesting to me are the buffets at **Begue's** in the Royal Sonesta and **Le Chasseur** in the Monteleone.

The tip for the service at a buffet is the standard 15 percent minimum. Some tightwads object to this. "Hey! I have to carry my own plate!" Yes, but the waitress does everything else she usually does: picks up the used plates (probably more of them for the price than you would have used if you were ordering from a menu), brings fresh silverware, water, and coffee, and pours the wine. If you don't tip the buffet server at least 15 percent, you're an unsophisticated pig.

BUSTER CRAB. Soft-shell crab with a couple of differences: it's small (no more than three inches across), and its old hard shell was removed by human hand. That results in a more concentrated crabmeat, since the first thing a crab does when it sloughs off its shell on its own is to pump up with water. A real buster crab has no legs or claws, since these are too delicate to survive the shell-removing procedure. **Brennan's** always has buster crabs (which means that sometimes they're frozen, but this doesn't seem to hurt 'em much); a tasty fried trio of them is napped with bearnaise or topped with pecans as a first course. **Antoine's** usually has them, too, but reserves them for use in topping a pompano Pontchartrain. Elsewhere, the item is hit or miss.

BUSY DAYS AND TIMES. A few years ago Jim Quinn, my counterpart in Philadelphia, wrote a book entitled *But Never Eat Out On Saturday Night.* His reasoning was that because it is the busiest night of the week for restaurants, food and service are below peak on Saturday or other busy days. The worst part of Saturday night is getting a table—either with a reservation or by waiting at the bar. It also seems to me that fine points of service go into abeyance. But in any well-organized kitchen, the food may actually get better when the kitchen is busy. This is certainly true at **Commander's** and **Arnaud's**, for example. And since the restaurant stocks up for its busy period, the food is at its freshest.

But if you are persuaded to avoid busy times, here is when they are. (This is the average; it varies from place to place.) From busiest to least busy:

1. Saturday
2. Friday
3. Sunday brunch
4. Wednesday
5. Thursday
6. Tuesday
7. Monday
8. Sunday dinner

The busiest lunch of the week by far is Friday. Holidays to be avoided if you dislike crowds are Mother's Day, New Year's Eve, Valentine's Day, Easter brunch, Halloween (in restaurants with a younger crowd), and the weekend before Mardi Gras. Hotel restaurants are frequently very crowded on Thanksgiving and Christmas.

C as in crawfish bisque

★★ Cafe Atchafalaya

901 Louisiana, Uptown. 891-5271. 11 a.m.-10 p.m. Wed.-Sat.; 5-10 p.m. Sun. AE, CB, DC. $

An old neighborhood seafood joint, Joe Petrossi's, was cleaned up and got a name change a few years ago. The result is this pleasant little cafe. Much of the menu and kitchen staff remains from the old days. The fish and shellfish are all fresh, fried to a light, grease-free exterior, and served in ample portions at neighborhood restaurant prices. Can't ask for much more than that—and you wouldn't get it here, anyway.

★★ Cafe Beignet

620 Decatur, Jackson Brewery, French Quarter. 566-1225. Open 24 hours, seven days. No credit cards. $

There have been many attempts over the years to open up a third French Market coffee-and-beignet stand, but this is the first one that feels right. Cafe Beignet's design is reminiscent of the old Morning Call: stools along mirrored walls, with one central marble counter with a light-bulb-studded arch overhead. The product tastes right, too. The cafe au lait involves powerful coffee and chicory and frothy hot milk. The beignets are relatively grease-free, hot, and lightly crisp at the skin. The waiters act slightly goofy. The only odd note here is that they serve an onion mum—a fancy alternative to onion rings.

CAFE AU LAIT. Dark-roast coffee and chicory, poured into the cup with hot milk, this is the staple of the French Market coffeehouses and some of the older restaurants. The classic places to drink cafe au lait are the **Cafe du Monde** and the **Morning Call**. They also pour a good sample at **Crescent City Steak House**.

★ Cafe Degas

3127 Esplanade. 945-5635. 11:30 a.m.-3 p.m. Mon.-Fri.; 10:30 a.m.- till Sat. and Sun; 5-10:30 p.m. seven days; till 11:30 p.m. Fri. & Sat. AE, MC, V. $$

It functions as a neighborhood cafe for the Esplanade area, but it's a lot different from the usual such place. Most of the tables are in a pleasant open-air, well-fanned wooden porch surrounded by greenery and a view of the avenue. And the food is French. Frenchness, we find here, does not always equate with good. The kitchen seems careless, and cuts a lot of corners. The vichyssoise, for example, tastes like it was made without stock. And I have seen better raw materials.

The best entree I've had here was a pepper steak, whose crust of pepper and sauce provided a reasonably decent flavor. Also okay is the bavette of beef — slices of flank steak with an oniony butter sauce. I have not had a successful fish entree here. Omelettes and crepes are prepared reasonably well. Side orders of vegetables are both ample and well-prepared. The small salads are good, but the popular salade Nicoise is little more than a can of tuna opened onto some lettuce.

Prices are low; service is friendly and very casual.

★ ★ ★ Cafe du Monde

French Market, 800 Decatur, French Quarter. 525-4544. Open 24 hours every day except Christmas. No credit cards. $

An essential element of the New Orleans culinary culture, the Cafe du Monde is the classic French Market coffee stand. It's busy around the clock, dispensing an admirable version of cafe au lait. The coffee and chicory is so blue-black and potent that, even if you always drink coffee black, you'd better cut this with hot milk. The coffee's partner is a plate of three beignets — square doughnuts dusted with powdered sugar. These pose a twofold hazard: that you will eat too many before realizing how they can expand in your stomach, and that you will laugh while biting into one, thereby creating a cumulo-nimbus of powdered sugar. There is a small dining room, but the place to get your coffee and beignets is the large covered patio overlooking Jackson Square. Afterwards, you can go for a walk along the river or through the touristy shops which have been mushrooming in the neighborhood lately. The Cafe du Monde is the classic rendezvous point for Orleanians finishing an evening's entertainment.

★ ★ ★ Cafe Florida

1228 Jefferson Hwy., Old Jefferson. 838-9574. 11 a.m.-11 p.m. Mon.-Sat. MC, V. $$

A quaint cafe in the neighborhood of Ochsner Hospital serves a menu of convincing Cuban food. There are two dining areas; the first room is a sort of lunch counter, the second a more formal room used for dinner. They cook up the entire range of Cuban-style sandwiches — rich, filled with roast pork and ham, sharpened with mustard and pickles, flattened and toasted at the same time in a sandwich press. But you can eat a very filling meal of plate specials, too. Start with the delicious Cuban tamale or the fried chorizo, spicy and aromatic. They make a terrific black bean soup. The daily specials are things like roast chicken with rice and black beans, ropa vieja ("old clothes"—shredded beef in a mellow sauce), Cuban steak (with or without peppers or onions), picadillo (sort of like the inside of taco without the lettuce, but much better), and sauteed pork with congri and yuca. All of this is eminently satisfying, particularly given the prices. (At lunch, it's tough to spend a fiver here.) During the dinner hours, they shove big casseroles of rice with squid or chicken and paella into the oven with good effect. The Cuban steak stuffed with shrimp is better than I would have guessed.

The cooler behind the counter is full of Latin American beers, juices, and soft drinks. And they make *batidos*—shakes involving not only vanilla and chocolate but also guananbana, tamarind, and mango. These are great either as a snack or as a dessert. The owners are nice folks who are very pleased to have non-Cubans try their tasty food.

★ ★ ★ Cafe Maspero

601 Decatur, French Quarter. 523-6250. 11 a.m.-11 p.m. seven days; till Midnight Fri. & Sat. No credit cards. $

How is it that almost every tourist who comes to town hears about Maspero's and gets in its often-lengthy line? It's a mystery, because the place doesn't advertise, and it looks like any of a hundred other tourist feederies in the Quarter. Never mind. Maspero's serves sandwiches of uncommonly large size and fine quality at very low prices. The bread is an interesting French-style roll in the shape of a giant hamburger bun; inside it is fine pastrami, baked ham, corned beef, or roast beef, with whatever dressings you want. A hamburger can also be had, but this is much less good. In recent times, Maspero's has added a few decent seafood platters to its menu, but to my palate it remains a sandwich specialist. Don't come in a hurry; thirsty is better.

★ ★ Cafe Pontchartrain

2031 St. Charles Ave., Uptown. 524-0581. 7 a.m.-4 p.m. seven days; till 3:30 p.m. Sat. & Sun 4:30 p.m.-8:30 p.m. seven days. AE, DC, MC, V. $$

The coffee shop of the Pontchartrain Hotel is one of the few halfway decent breakfast places in town. The basic breakfast standards are first-class. Eggs are accurately cooked, and they don't scorch the omelettes unless you have the bad taste to ask them to do so. Bacon and sausage appear to be grilled to order—a seldom-seen practice around town. Even the toast is good. Pancakes and waffles are passable, and the famous blueberry muffins have returned to edibility. The biggest improvement here is that the fancy egg dishes—particularly the Sardou version with spinach, artichoke bottoms, and hollandaise—are now consistently excellent. The juices are freshly-squeezed, and the coffee, while a little weak by New Orleans standards, is always fresh.

The lunch menu is designed strictly for the diehard daily customer (of which there are many) and the convenience of hotel guests. The weakness of the Cafe Pontchartrain is service, which can be slow and incompetent—although not always. This is especially true on weekends.

★★ Cafe Savanna

8324 Oak, Uptown. 866-3223. 11 a.m.-2:30 p.m. and 5-10 p.m. Mon.-Sat.; till 11 p.m. Fri. & Sat. 10:30 a.m.-3 p.m. Sunday brunch. MC, V. $$

There's a tiny front dining room, a smaller rear dining room that you have to go outside to get into, and a substantial and popular patio with a fan big enough to make the heat tolerable. The feeling is casual, with plants and posters and minimal service and prices to match. At lunch, the sandwiches are quite good—particularly the thick, hand-made hamburger, which is beautifully grilled and served (if you want) on French bread.

At night, the emphasis changes to plate food, including some delicious grilled fish, crunchy fried catfish, a couple of pasta dishes, and a surprisingly good chicken fried steak. The French fries are cut from fresh potatoes and dusted after frying with a delectable garlic salt. The assortment of fried vegetables makes a tasty first course or side dish. Dessert is decent pie. The consistency of the kitchen is less than perfect. A fun hangout, with a slight Sixties feel; next door, the Maple Leaf Bar is a good place to listen to live jazz and folk music.

CAJUN. The Cajuns are descendents of the French-speaking Acadians who were banished from Nova Scotia in the early 1700s. They settled in Southwest Louisiana and lived in isolation until modern times. Until the oil boom came, they had to fight to survive; the Cajun farmers, fishermen, and hunters sold the best of their gatherings and subsisted on the worst. This condition produced the genius of Cajun cooking, which can make a great meal out of practically nothing.

Acadiana is a big enough place to show regional differences in its food. The most robust and interesting cooking comes from Opelousas, Henderson and Ville Platte. Milder but no less good forms of Cajun are found in Avoyelles Parish and along Bayou Teche and Bayou Lafourche.

Unalloyed Cajun food is almost never found in restaurants, not even in Cajun country. I suspect the reason for this is that Cajun cooking, for all its glorious flavor, looks ugly (unless, of course, you grew up with it). Much of it is pot food from very big pots. Getting the polished look restaurant patrons require screws up the flavor. Restaurants also tend to eschew authentic trashy ingredients in favor of things like baby white veal, and this too throws things off.

The kind of Cajun food served in chic restaurants outside Louisiana during the past few years was created by Paul Prudhomme in the late Seventies. Prudhomme is a real Cajun from the Opelousas area, but his very personal cuisine has moved far beyond the limits of traditional Cajun cookery. And that's what you get at **K-Paul's Louisiana Kitchen,** easily the world's most famous Cajun restaurant. A K-Paul's imitator, **Copeland's,** is also near the mark on a number of dishes. **Bon-Ton Cafe** is a very mild form of Cajun. **Alex Patout's** and just-plain **Patout's** grew from a New Iberia restaurant; they cook in a distinctly Cajun style, but not one I would number among my favorites.

Around Lafayette, all the restaurants are Cajun-influenced to one degree or another. I like **Angelle's, Chez Pastor, Pat's, Las's,** and **Don's. Mulate's** is a special treat; not only does it serve pretty good food, it is an enormous hall of Cajun music and dancing—worth a trip.

The best dining in Cajun country is during crawfish season—Thanksgiving through June (see **Crawfish**). Crawfish is the king of Cajun cookery, and dishes made with it have more currency than any other Cajun concoction. Especially around Henderson and Breaux Bridge, great little cafes pop up serving unbelievable crawfish. But these tend to be as transitory as the mudbug himself, and when I return to them they're invariably gone.

CAJUN POPCORN. An appetizing name thought up by Paul Prudhomme for a fairly common dish: fried crawfish tails. The term has been expanded to cover fried shrimp or crab fingers when crawfish are out of season.

CALAMARI. Italian for squid—which see.

★ ★ ★ Camelia Beach House

2025 Lakeshore Drive, Mandeville. 1-626-8500. 11:30 a.m.-10:30 p.m. Wed.-Sun.; till 9 p.m. Sun. $$

Pat Gallagher, the owner and chef, started a wildly popular place called the Winner's Circle about 10 years ago next to a race track in Folsom. After moving into too-fancy quarters for a couple of years, he closed the Winner's Circle in late 1989 and started over. He bought Bechac's—one of the oldest restaurants in the state, with a history that goes back beyond the Civil War—and renamed it after a steamboat that used to take passengers across Lake Pontchartrain. (The boat's name had only one "L," hence the odd spelling.)

The Beach House is indeed right across from the lakeshore. The premises are charming, particularly the upstairs dining rooms. The menu, however, picks up where the Winner's Circle left off. Gallagher's long suit always is basic food, very deftly cooked (usually grilled) in large portions, served with few sauces or other frills.

The charcoal grill is the principal focus of the entree side of the menu. Fish, quail (raised on a nearby farm), lamb chops, gigantic shrimp and steaks get stripes of char and a pleasant, slightly smoky flavor tinge. All of it comes out juicy and well-seasoned—very, very satisfying eating.

They have barbecued pork ribs, the small, tender ones; these are messy and wonderful, pleasantly chewy and meaty. Barbecue shrimp are, as usual around here, not really barbecued; the butter-pepper sauce has more garlic than I remember ever running into before, and either that or the slight sweetness of the sauce throws the dish off for me.

Ample piles of crisp, light fried seafood round out the regular menu. A specials card reveals some more ambitious food. Here are things like veal chops with peppercorn sauce, crab cakes with orange buerre blanc, grilled tuna with ginger, and—surprise!—it's all as good as the regular fare. (Actually, to grill and fry food as accurately as they do requires more than enough talent to handle sauces and such.)

Service is efficient. There's enough well-chosen wine on the list to fill all the glasses at your table agreeably.

★ ★ ★ Camellia Grill

626 S. Carrollton Ave., Uptown. 866-9573. 8 a.m.-1:00 a.m. seven days.; till 2 a.m. Thurs; till 3 Fri.-Sat. No credit cards. $

"A glorified hamburger joint." That's how the late Jimmy Shwartz described his 29-stool diner, now over a half-century old. Although the Camellia Grill's menu is limited to sandwiches, omelettes, and a few platters, everything about the place is classy. A maitre d' seats you; the napkins are linen. The waiters and the grill cooks are snappy performers. And the food is great. What separates it from the more formulaic restaurants serving the same menu is that everything is prepared to order—usually in your sight.

The hamburger is still the star. It's made from fresh, hand-formed beef, grilled to order and served on a toasted bun. It's good enough that you don't need to put any kind of dressings on it —a state of affairs rarely seen in the world of burgers.

The other sandwiches are deli-style. The Camellia Special of ham, Swiss, and cole slaw is almost too thick with the meats; that pattern is repeated in many other sandwiches. The turkey on the club sandwich is roasted on the premises. A delicious recent addition to the venerable menu is Harry's Yankee Special. It's sort of like a Philly cheese steak: roast beef topped with grilled onions and melted Swiss cheese on a hoagie bun, served with a brown mushroom gravy for dipping.

The omelettes are more famous than good: two eggs are whipped into a light froth and scorched to dryness. Other breakfast items are good sometimes, iffy others — with one exception. The waffles are the best in town — either the plain or the pecan version. I often have a waffle as a dessert. Other good desserts are pecan pie — the high-water mark of that dish locally — and the heavy, small slice of cheesecake. The coffee may be the worst in New Orleans, but nobody's perfect.

★ ★ Cannon's

Terry Parkway side of Oakwood Mall, 197 Westbank Expressway, Gretna. 364-1047. 11 a.m.-10 p.m. Mon.-Sat.; till 11 p.m. Fri.& Sat. 11 a.m.-10 p.m. Sun. AE, MC, V. $$

Although it's locally owned, Cannon's looks and acts like a franchise concept restaurant. It's a casual, open dining space with lots of greenery, an emphasis on the brass-railed bar, soft rock music, neon signs, glassbrick walls, and the like. The menu has thick burgers of better than average quality, smoky ribs cooked a little too soft for me, a very good grilled chicken, a wide selection of large, well-made salads, some fried and grilled seafood platters, soups of the broccoli-and-cheese school, a couple of steaks, and a scattering of semi-fancy veal and chicken dishes. Desserts are sweet and goopy (I can see the chocolate sauce flowing now). All of this is strictly mainstream eating for young adults who are more interested in hanging out at a sorta fun place than they are in eating great food. But they could do much worse: the ingredients are fresh and the cooking is usually decent.

CAP BREAD. An old-fashioned form of French bread made by a few local bakers. It's a somewhat oblong loaf, about eight inches long, four inches wide, and two inches thick, with a curious long, thin appendage extending from the end over the top. It reminds me of a chrysalis or (for topology buffs) a Klein bottle. Anyway, it's delicious and uniquely New Orleans (I think), and is the house bread at **Arnaud's, Peppermill, Tujague's,** and **Cafe Sbisa.**

CAPPUCCINO. Despite the response one usually gets to a request for it, cappuccino does not mean "out of order" in Italian. It's a great afterdinner (or, more properly, after-breakfast) beverage of hot espresso with steamed milk dusted with cocoa and cinnamon. The measures of a good cappuccino are the robustness of the coffee and the stiffness of the head of steamed milk (which, by the way, should never be faked with whipped cream). Good cappuccino has become much easier to find in New Orleans lately. The places that do it consistently well are **Andrea's, Angelo Brocato's, Bistro at the Maison de Ville, Flagons, Louis XVI, P.J.'s,** and the **Windsor Court Grill Room.**

CARAMEL CUSTARD. Second only to bread pudding as the most available dessert in New Orleans restaurants, this eggy dessert also goes by the names creme caramel, creme renversee, flan, and egg custard. It is usually baked in a cup and sometimes served in it; most commonly, it is removed from the cup and sits upside down in a pool of the caramel sauce in which it was baked. Without a second thought I nominate the flan at **El Patio** as the city's best; it has a spectacular silky texture and the incomparable flavor of Mexican vanilla. Bunched up in the second tier are the works of **Mandina's, Louis XVI, Sazerac,** and **Galatoire's.**

Creme brulee is a variation on caramel custard in which the custard part is much richer, yet semi-liquid in texture. The caramel part is baked into a hard shell over the top. The best version by far is at **Bayou Ridge Cafe;** they also have a good one at **Arnaud's.** At the **Windsor Court Grill Room,** creme, brulee is served in a pastry, which is not classic but delicious nevertheless.

★ ★ ★ Caribbean Room

Pontchartrain Hotel, 2031 St. Charles Ave. Reservations 524-3178. 11:30 a.m.-2 p.m. Sun.-Fri; 6-10 p.m. seven days. AE, CB, DC, MC, V. $$$$

The Pontchartrain Hotel's flagship dining room is one of the handsomest, most comfortable, and most romantic restaurants in town. The several big rooms are bright and plush pink with profusions of plants; my favorite tables are the two deuces by the fountain.

Since the Aschaffenburg family sold the hotel in 1987, the C-Room has undergone too many changes of personnel and culinary style. An interesting concept called Creole-Provencale was occasionally good, but it was unfamiliar to the regulars, who rejected it. Then another new management team came in and re-installed many of the Caribbean Room specialties from the old days—along with Douglas Leman, maitre d'hotel for over 35 years here and one of the best-liked people in the entire local industry. At this writing there are still wobbles, but things are better.

Crabmeat remains a specialty of the Caribbean Room. My favorite way is crabmeat Remick—a small casserole of jumbo lumps in an understated sauce of chili, mustard, and bacon. Crabmeat Monte Carlo is a light, cold crab salad that's mostly crab lumps. Oysters Lafayette, baked on the shells, have a fluffy bechamel rendered lavish by yet more crabmeat.

The most popular dish in the house, trout Eugene, is better than it's ever been. The substantial shrimp and crabmeat garnishes remain autonomous, so that you get three wonderful tastes instead of a conflicting mishmash. Trout Veronique has also been repaired: the hollandaise is lightly glazed over the poached fish, which is studded with halves of white grapes. Shrimp Saki is simple and delightful: big sauteed shrimp abetted with a deftly-flavored herb butter.

Those are all old dishes. Some of the Creole-Provencale ideas are worthwhile, too. The soft-shell crab is big and crusty, moistened with an inspired, extra-herby red Creole sauce and lemon butter. Through the same clever use of herbs, the kitchen has made a great improvement in a local cliche, shrimp Creole. Tournedos Belle Louisiane, a split filet with two sauces: one light and spicy, the other brown and spicy in a different way. Crabmeat Provencale is a slightly-dry puff pastry filled with a delicious blend of crabmeat, mushrooms, and herbs. Less good is poached pompano aioli; I don't think that pompano poaches well, and the sauce is too subtle for me.

The big-deal dessert (in more ways than one) is the mile-high ice cream pie, the best part of which is visual. They make a great chocolate sauce here, and anything—ice cream, profiteroles, or whatever—dressed with it is a winner. The lemon ice box pie remains definitive.

The wine list is well-selected, with a superb selection of California Cabernets and Chardonnays; the prices are on the high side. You can choose from among eight wines by the glass.

★ ★ Casa Garcia

8814 Veterans Blvd., Metairie. 464-0354. 11 a.m.-10 p.m. Sun.-Thurs., till 11 p.m. Fri. & Sat. AE, DC, MC, V. $$

The casa is a large, handsome corner of a Veterans Blvd. strip shopping center, and the menu is lightly-Americanized Mexican. Its most distinctive dish is an appetizer, queso fundido: melted cheese with peppers and beef bubbling in a casserole. You scoop it up with hot flour tortillas. Messy but good. The tortilla soup would be a good onion soup were it not for the flaccid tortillas in it.

They make a specialty of Latin American-style steaks. I like steak picada, a huge dish made with tasty, tender slices of filet mignon and an interesting sauce of peppers, onions, mushrooms and herbs. Also well-prepared is fajitas, available with beef, chicken or shrimp. The many combination plates of tacos, enchiladas, and the like are reasonably tasty. These are filled out with fine Mexican rice and excellent charro beans in a light, almost soupy sauce. Desserts are marginal; the interesting-sounding Mexican bread pudding is terrible. Service is very friendly and the place has a festive feel.

★ ★ ★ Casamento's

4330 Magazine, Uptown. 895-9761. 11:30 a.m.-1:30 p.m. and 5:30-9:00 p.m. Tues.-Sun. Closed June through August. No credit cards. $

The premises are a relic of a wonderful earlier age: tiles everywhere, from the exterior facade straight back into the kitchen. Some of them are embossed with pastel designs, but all of them are spotlessly clean.

With the glossy enamel ceiling and the curved corners, it looks and sounds like a gigantic bathroom.

Casamento's is Uptown's oyster specialist. So reliant is its menu upon the bivalve that the restaurant closes during the months in which the oyster is traditionally (but not really) inedible. The rest of the time, they shuck good, cold, salty ones at the bar. At the tables, you get perfectly-fried mollusks, coated in cornmeal and brought to a crisp, crackling exterior, well-seasoned and utterly free from grease, fried to order (so don't come in a hurry). The oysters can be had as is or in Casamento's distinctive oyster loaf, made with buttered "pan bread"—regular white, sliced thicker. Other seafoods—particularly soft-shell crabs—are as good as the oysters when they're available, which is not always. The French fries are made from fresh-cut potatoes—incomparably better than frozen. There is also some Italian food, but it's just passable.

★ ★ ★ Castillo's

620 Conti, French Quarter. 525-7467. 11:30 a.m.-2:00 p.m. Mon.-Fri.; 5-10:30 p.m. seven days; till Midnight Fri. and Sat. AE, MC, V. $$

Castillo's, the city's oldest Mexican restaurant, occupies a yellowed, brick-walled French Quarter space that doesn't look like it's had a really thorough cleaning or painting in decades. Despite that, an enthusiastic regular clientele enjoys distinctive Mexican food here. Castillo's menu is more Mex-Mex than Tex-Mex; it apologizes for serving chili, "a Texas stew that's not Mexican."

Caldo xochil is a chicken broth with rice made with cilantro, the pungent parsley; it makes a good starter. The guacamole is mild but not bad; tortilla chips stick up from the green avocado concoction like sails on the lake. The great entree is mole poblano, a wonderful broiled chicken half slathered with a dense, dark sauce of pepper and bitter chocolate; it's one of the best versions of that sauce around. Enchiladas de res, another terrific item, are filled with a peppery beef. Chilmole de puerco is a pork tenderloin grilled in an oily, gritty sauce with burned peppers—better than it sounds. The huevos rancheros are also nice. Lots of other interesting food.

Good flan (caramel custard) and Mexican hot chocolate appear for dessert. Service is usually more than a little slow, particularly at night.

CATFISH. See Fish.

★ ★ Central Grocery

923 Decatur, French Quarter. 523-1620. 8 a.m.-5:30 p.m. seven days; from 9 a.m. Sun. No credit cards. $

The muffuletta was created at the turn of the century by a Sicilian grocer in the French Quarter. The Central Grocery claims to have been the originator, but so do others. The question is worth arguing about. The muffuletta is a singular sandwich: a large, round Italian loaf filled with ham, salami, mortadella, provolone, and mozzarella. The distinctive flavor comes from the garlicky dressing of whole olives and other marinated vegetables. The Central Grocery still makes a good muffuletta, although it's not what it once was (the quality of the meats, it seems to me, have slipped). The sandwich is served at room temperature the way God intended. There are now a few stools and a counter for eating on the premises, but I prefer to repair to the great outdoors and to make a picnic of it.

The Central Grocery and its neighbor the Progress Grocery (which also makes a good muffuletta) are wonderful, fragrant emporiums of imported foods. They carry pastas, cheeses, herbs, and other Italian foodstuffs that are impossible to find elsewhere.

CEVICHE. A cold collection of marinated seafood, this dish is found throughout Latin America and in a surprising number of restaurants in New Orleans. Shrimp, redfish, lobster, crabmeat, and scallops are common components; raw morsels of them are covered with lime juice, cilantro (a pungent parsley), green peppers, onions, and other herbs and allowed to marinate for a day or so. Afterwards, the seafood has the appearance of poached, but it's definitely uncooked. Ceviche has a nice bite and makes a great appetizer. There is not as much of it around as there once was, however. I like the versions at **El Patio, Casa Garcia,** and (occasionally) **Upperline.**

★ ★ ★ Charlie's Steak House

4510 Dryades, Uptown. 895-9705. 11 a.m.-3 p.m. Tues.-Fri. 5-11 p.m. Tues.-Sat. AE, CB, DC, MC, V. $$

Charlie's demonstrates how important the proverbial sizzle on the steak can be. Sizzle makes the choice steaks here taste better than the prime served in some other places. No menu; the offerings include a filet, strip, or T-bone, large or small. For most eaters, small is big enough (too big in the case of the T-bone). The steaks come out erupting in butter sauce: you have to hold your napkin in front of you until the sizzling dies down. Most of the time, the steak is better than you think it's going to be, given the prices. On the other hand, there is the occasional meal that might make you swear never to come back. In any case, you practically have to be rolled out, because this is heavy, heavy eating.

Many Charlie's regulars are attracted as much by the side dishes as for the steaks. The thinly-sliced, lightly-fried onion rings are the best around. Fried potatoes are cut extra-large from fresh. The salad is a sixth of a head of lettuce, still retaining its shape, draped with raw onions and covered with good freshly-made dressings. The Roquefort is the most powerful (and, to my tastes, the best) you'll ever eat. Not much in the way of appetizers, wines, dessert, service, or atmosphere. The two scruffy rooms are served by an assortment of Italian waiters and by the charming Dottye Bennett, one of the owners.

★★Chart House

801 Chartres, French Quarter. 523-2015. 6-11 p.m. Mon.-Fri.; till Midnight Fri. 5 p.m.-Midnight Sat. & 5-11 p.m. Sun. AE, DC, MC, V. $$

What started out as a pop concept restaurant run by the world's biggest franchisee of Burger King evolved into a relaxing, reliably decent neighborhood steakhouse in a singularly distinctive neighborhood: Jackson Square. The restaurant is upstairs, and from the balcony you get a good view of the square. The menu is very basic: several kinds of steak, prime rib, some grilled fish, and that's about it. They have an interesting variation on the salad bar idea: they bring a bucket of salad fixings and dressings to the table. Desserts are gloopy, fudgy things like mud pie. The wine list is minimal but reasonable. Service is uniformly excellent. All in all, a surprisingly good place. If you're visiting New Orleans from the Midwest, save this for when you get homesick.

CHATEAUBRIAND. Properly, this is the blunt end of a tenderloin beef roast, but in most restaurants it is a double filet mignon, typically roasted whole and usually served with bearnaise sauce and a whole bunch of vegetables which, because of their proximity to the Chateaubriand, become "bouquetiere." The dish depends on the quality of the beef and the exactitude of the roasting—it should be a crusty char around the outside, tight and juicy inside. The chateaubriands I have enjoyed most are those at **Louis XVI**, **Antoine's** (with the Robespierre sauce—you have to specify this in advance), the **Sazerac**, and **Arnaud's**.

CHEESECAKE. It's not really a New Orleans specialty, but that doesn't stop any number of restaurants from taking a shot at it. Most of them attempt to make up for the oversweet uncheesiness of the cake by covering their mistakes with gloopy strawberry, blueberry, or (worst of all) praline sauce. The definitive cheesecake here is the tiny oblong slice they serve at the **Camellia Grill**: it's heavy, it's slightly sour, it tastes like cheesecake. In the second tier are **Andrea's, Flagons, Martin Wine Cellar Deli** (which gets them from elsewhere and has several varieties), and **Tavern on the Park**.

★ ★ ★ Chehardy's

3528 18th St., Metairie. Reservations 455-2433. 11 a.m.-3:30 p.m. Mon.-Fri. 5-11 p.m. Mon.-Sat. AE, CB, DC, MC, V. $$$

   This flashy restaurant was the hottest thing going when it opened in 1988, and the vogue lasted until the namesake proprietor had a falling out with his partners and left. Since then, there have been too many changes to keep up with. Some refugees from the closed five-star LeRuth's turned up here just as we went to press, but I'm not placing any bets on Chehardy's renaissance yet.

★ ★ Chelsey's

2400 Lapalco Blvd., Harvey. 368-2121. 10:30 a.m.-11 p.m. seven days; till Midnight Fri. & Sat. No credit cards. $

   The building has the neat stainless-steel look of a Forties hamburger grill, and serves a treat just as old-fashioned: frozen custard. This is ice cream with a richness born not so much of cream as of egg yolks. Unlike the frozen custard of the Midwest, this is not a soft-serve product, but a hard-frozen, hand-dipped ice cream. It is the work of Warren Leruth, and it is a singular treat. The available flavors change daily and include some ideas that are as long on whimsy as they are on flavor. Besides straight cones, the stuff is made into all the classic sundaes and something called a St. Louis Concrete—a shake so thick you can turn the cup upside down.

   Chelsey's also grills up okay hamburgers, hot dogs, and a few other savory foods. But the main focus is on the frozen custard, which is in a class by itself locally.

CHERRIES JUBILEE. Cherries—almost always canned bing cherries—get flamed in liqueur (usually Kirsch) and dumped over ice cream. Usually more trouble than it's worth. **Antoine's** does them traditionally, including the part where the waiter pours the flaming sauce all over the tablecloth.

★ ★ ★ Chez Daniel

2037 Metairie Road, Old Metairie. 837-6900. 5-9:30 p.m. Tues.-Sat. AE, MC, V. $$$.

   Chef Daniel Bonnot is a dominant figure in the last 20 years of New Orleans dining. He was the man who conceived Louis XVI, the city's first successful French restaurant. He oversaw the creation of a few other good places, most notably L'Escale and Savoir-Faire. His reputation was tarnished somewhat by the splashy, bold Tour Eiffel—the reconstruction here in town of the original Eiffel Tower restaurant. It took a long time for Bonnot to recover from that disaster, whose problems were more related to scope and marketing than to food.

Chez Daniel is his comeback effort. It's a tiny bistro in Old Metairie, serving a limited menu of simple French food. There is a certain amount of eclecticism here. A giant mural in the French Impressionist style dominates one of the two dining rooms, whose floors are concrete painted to look like stone. The food is also offbeat, but just a little bit. For example, they serve mussels not with the usual wine-and-herb sauce but with a light cream sauce. You are likely to run into the likes of coq au vin, choucroute, and cassoulet here—all indicator dishes for the French bistro.

This restaurant opened just as this book was going to press—too soon to make much of a judgment. However, early indications are good, and the prices are so moderate for cooking of this caliber that I feel the place is a safe bet. (See **Update**.)

★★Chez Helene

1540 N. Robertson (near intersection of N. Claiborne and St. Bernard Ave.), Downtown. 947-1206. 11 a.m.-1 a.m. seven days. AE, CB, DC, MC, V. $$

Chez Helene has a widespread reputation as the city's premiere soul food restaurant—although I find no real distinction between soul food and good Creole eats. The dining room looks to be unchanged for decades; there's a bar in an adjacent room. The neighborhood is black, but the clientele is mixed, and quite a few tourists find their way here—especially since the television show "Frank's Place," which was pattered against Chez Helene.

The specialty is fried chicken. I find it a bit on the oily side, but it is fried to order with a tasty coating. The classic platter is three pieces of chicken with a stuffed bell pepper and potato salad; I also like the chicken with the zippy red beans and rice as the side dish.

Chez Helene also whips up unassailable fried seafood in all the usual platter configurations: it's crackly and seasoned right. I would avoid the fancier dishes like trout Marguery and the green-food-colored oysters Rockefeller. They'll bring you a complimentary cup of the great seafood gumbo, but if you want more of it it'll set you back $9. For dessert, there's tasty bread pudding with a sugary sauce. Service is friendly and good—at least at lunch, which is the best time to go.

★ ★ ★ Chez Pierre's

2505 Whitney Ave., Gretna. Reservations 362-6703. 11:30-2 p.m. Tues.-Fri.; 6-10 p.m. Tues.-Sat.; 10:30 a.m.-3 p.m. Sun. AE, CB, DC, MC, V. $$

The building is the former home of Willy Coln's, and Pierre is Perry Fusilier, who for many years was the maitre d' at LeRuth's. As chef-owner here, he has taken quite a bit of his culinary inspiration from that laudable source, although his Cajun background is also clearly visible on the menu. More apparent, however, are the very attractive prices at which Chez Pierre's sells what looks like—and then turns out to be—ambitious, delicious food. This is especially true at lunch and in the early evening, at which times one wonders whether the restaurant's food costs are being covered.

The best first courses are small casseroles of seafood. Crabmeat St. Pierre is served in a shell with a light-colored, herbal sauce echoing with pepper. The oysters casino are an original: the oysters are broiled with bacon and jalapeno chips, mellowed with mozzarella. The shrimp or crawfish pie is an understatement; a delicious little casserole of the crustaceans is topped with a cap of flaky pastry.

They put out a superb, cold, tart shrimp remoulade and a fine Godchaux salad—crabmeat and shrimp in a light mayonnaise, tossed with greens. Soups are somewhat overpowering, particularly the dense, dark, smoky chicken-andouille gumbo. The artichoke-oyster soup is choked with oysters in not enough of a beguiling, herbal, light broth.

Many entrees at Chez Pierre's are so rich that I find them difficult to eat more than a little of. I would stay away from dishes topped with seafood in some sort of rich sauce, for example. But the sirloin steak au poivre, with its creamy green peppercorn sauce, is a solid dish. So is the duckling St. Gabriel, stuffed with oyster dressing and moistened with another peppercorn sauce. It's a close copy of the duck at LeRuth's.

A bit more elemental are combinations like the soft-shell crabs topped with crabmeat—a toasty, wonderful plateful that's at its best in the spring and early summer. The trout Cecilia, abetted with shrimp and crabmeat in a light brown butter sauce, also stops satisfyingly short of Too Much. Also here are a handful of out-of-vogue but great Creole classics. I will always have a taste for a well-prepared, non-greasy chicken Clemenceau like the one here.

Desserts include homemade ice cream with just about the highest butterfat content I've ever encountered, as well as a great sweet potato and pecan pie. The wine list is minimal. The premises are a collection of white stucco rooms—a bit on the stark side, but not unpleasant. Service is not what you could call polished but is competent.

CHICKEN. Among the most versatile and wholesome of foodstuffs, chicken gets short shrift in restaurants, where diners eschew it as too commonplace. This is a shame, because some local chicken dishes are spectacularly delicious. To wit:

Chicken bonne femme, in all its many variations, is one of the best dishes in the Creole cuisine. (And, like all the other dishes about which I say that, I've included a recipe. It's at the end of this section.) At **Antoine's** chicken bonne femme is baked with potato chunks, ham, bacon, and mushrooms—very hearty. At **Tujague's**, however, the chicken is fried and covered with fried potato discs and a butter sauce with a staggering amount of garlic and parsley. Chicken Clemenceau is very similar to Antoine's bonne femme; peas are present, but the taste is essentially the same. **Galatoire's** and **Berdou's** do a good Clemenceau.

Chicken Rochambeau is baked and abetted with ham, a red-wine brown sauce, and bearnaise—very, very rich. It is terrible everywhere except at Antoine's, which created it.

Chicken Grandee is Mosca's dish, but it has spread elsewhere, notably to **La Louisiane**. The pieces are broiled with potatoes and mushrooms in an incredible amount of olive oil and garlic. It's terrific, of course.

Simple **roast chicken**, for which I have a soft spot, is hard to find prepared well in any restaurant. The good ones are at **Andrea's, Delmonico, La Louisiane, Bayou Ridge Cafe,** and **Galatoire's**.

Grilled chicken has become a welcome commonplace. I like the pairings with grilled andouille and mustard sauce at **Commander's**, and **Mr. B's**. The latter also grills a spectacular chicken with sweet garlic. Simpler but also tasty is the grilled breast with three sauces at **Stephen & Martin's**.

Fried chicken: Popeyes dominates this arena, and their very spicy chicken is usually pretty good. But this is fast food, and therefore inconsistent; the oil and pepper levels are sometimes out of control. The best fried chickens come from **Miss Ruby's, Chez Helene, Dooky Chase,** and—believe it or not—**Galatoire's**.

Chinese restaurants prepare a bewildering array of chicken dishes. Two of them stand out in my mind. One is the rice-smoked chicken at **Fortune Gardens**. It's just a plate of chicken chunks—no sauce or vegetables—with an incomparable mild smoky flavor. The other great Chinese chicken dish is the lemon chicken at **Trey Yuen**, deftly stir-fried and covered with an elegant, translucent lemon sauce.

This recipe for chicken bonne femme is similar to the one used at Antoine's, but (I think) a little better.

CHICKEN BONNE FEMME
4 slices bacon, cut into 1-inch squares
2 medium frying chickens, quartered
Flour
Salt

White pepper
1 cup ham, cut into 1/2-in. dice
1½ Tbs. chopped garlic
2 cups coarsely-chopped green onion tops
1 cup coarsely-chopped yellow onion
2 dashes Tabasco
1 cup dry white wine
3 large white potatoes, diced
Vegetable oil for frying
2 cups sliced fresh mushrooms
1 stick butter, melted
Salt and pepper to taste

1. Fry the bacon in a broiling pan or large skillet until crisp, then remove. Drain excess fat.
2. Dust (don't coat) chicken pieces lightly with flour, salt, and pepper. Raise the heat to high and brown the chicken pieces lightly on all sides in the same skillet you cooked the bacon in. Remove the chicken pieces and keep warm.
3. Lower the heat to medium. In the same pan saute the ham, garlic, green onions, and yellow onions until the latter turn translucent. Add wine and Tabasco and reduce the liquid by about half.
4. In a separate skillet fry the diced potatoes in 375-degree oil until very lightly browned. Drain them well and add to the sauce, along with mushrooms and bacon. Continue simmering sauce until all of the liquid is absorbed; agitate the pan (don't stir!) to distribute ingredients. Remove from heat.
5. Salt and pepper the chicken pieces and brush them with melted butter. Arrange the pieces in the sauce skillet and spoon the sauce over and around them. Put the skillet into a preheated 450-degree oven and cook for 25 minutes. Pierce a thigh with a skewer; if the juices run out clear, the chicken is done. Serve with lots of the sauce, including the juices.
Serves four.

CHICKEN-ANDOUILLE GUMBO. Another from my list of the ten best New Orleans dishes. Description and recipe under **Gumbo**.

★ ★ ★ China Doll

830 Manhattan Blvd. (in the shopping center at West Bank Expy.), Harvey. Reservations 366-1111. 11 a.m.-10 p.m. Mon.-Fri.; till 11 p.m. Fri.; Noon-11 p.m. Sat. and 5-10 p.m. Sun. AE, MC, V. $$

Like other Chinese restaurants in shopping centers, the China Doll doesn't look like much from the outside. Inside, however, the several dark, heavily-decorated rooms look like a scene from a Fifties movie set in Hong Kong, and comfort is far above average. They serve a little of everything, but what makes the place adventuresome is that more than half the menu is seafood. Here is one of a handful of Oriental restaurants willing to play with Maine lobster, for instance. They bring it forth with a mouth-filling, aromatic ginger and garlic sauce that pairs well with the lobster meat. The scallops, sauteed with pineapples and straw mushrooms, are also an unaccustomed delicacy. Crawfish, shrimp, soft-shell crabs, oysters, and fresh Gulf fish get interesting treatments. And the satay squid, stir-fried with a fiery Indonesian-style sauce, is delicious and original.

My favorite non-seafood here is sesame chicken—a loaf of white meat covered with seeds, toasty and unique. They also do a reasonably good moo-shu pork, ma-po bean curd (a soupy, spicy dish of soft tofu with pork morsels) and Cantonese-style barbecue duck. About the only endeavors these folks perform roughly are appetizers and soups (average at best).

Service is generally excellent. Prices are just a touch over those of the neighborhood places, but the food is a lot better. The place is rather crowded at lunchtime, which extends into the late afternoon.

★★China Orchid

704 S. Carrollton Ave., Riverbend. 865-1428. 11:00 a.m.-10 p.m. Mon.-Fri.; till 10:30 Fri.; 4:30-10:30 p.m. Sat.; 4:30-9:30 p.m. Sun. MC, V. $

The menu of this neighborhood Chinese cafe is riddled with dishes made popular at other local Chinese restaurants. We can forgive that, because the China Orchid cooks them well. Begin with a satisfying hot and sour soup, brought forth with thick, lean slices of roast pork. The pot stickers have fillings that look less savory than I'm used to, but the flavor is right on the money—as is the consistency of the noodle wrapper. There is also the funny Cantonese specialty called umbrella chicken, which involves pushing the meat on the fore portion of the wing up to one end and frying it; this is greaseless and tasty with sweet-and-sour.

Lots of seafood: live Maine lobster, lomi-lomi (giant shrimp wrapped with pineapple and bacon), soft-shell crab, crawfish in black bean sauce with roast pork (which they seem to throw into a lot of different dishes here). The moo-shu pork was once brilliant, but now lacks delicacy. The pancakes that come with it have more of the texture of a flour tortilla than a proper moo-shu pancake. And, of course, chicken, pork, shrimp, and sometimes even lobster and beef come together in single dishes. These are popular but taste nondescript.

Service is straightforward and pleasant; prices are about average.

★ Chinese Kitchen

3327 S. Carrolton Ave. 482-1122. 11:30 a.m.-10 p.m. Mon.-Fri.; till 10:30 p.m. Fri.; Noon-10:30 p.m. Sat. MC, V. $

A tiny room in which stridently mediocre Cantonese standards are served to an enthusiastic crowd which often forms a line. Reason: prices are low, portions are huge, nothing is outright terrible. Very popular among college students, who have an excuse.

CHINESE FOOD. New Orleans' 100-plus Chinese restaurants compete quietly but furiously with one another, with the result that they are among the cheapest places to eat in town. However, a new battleground is emerging: Chinese restaurateurs, having found a demand for new dishes—particularly those involving seafood—are quick to innovate. In a way. See, as soon as one Chinese place starts doing well with a new dish, suddenly lots of other Chinese places serve it and claim they originated the dish. So, while New Orleans is still not a great Chinese restaurant town, it's a lot better than it was five years ago, and there are now a few very serious, good-looking Chinese places with adventuresome menus.

Tastes in Chinese food are more individual than I have noticed for any other kind of eating. One becomes accustomed to the way one's favorite little neighborhood Chinese cafe cooks, and measures all others by that yardstick. (My own favorite is the **Peking**.) So take the ratings with an extra grain of salt (or MSG, if you prefer).

Here is a list of Chinese restaurants recommended in this book. listed
FRENCH QUARTER/CBD
  ★★ Asia Garden
  ★★ Mandarin Cafe
UPTOWN
  ★★ China Orchid
  ★★ Five Happiness
  ★★★ Kung's Dynasty
METAIRIE
  ★★★ Dragon's Garden
  ★★★ Fortune Gardens (Kenner)
  ★★★ Golden Dragon
  ★★★ Great Wall
WEST BANK
  ★★ China Doll
  ★★★ Christina's Empress of China
NEW ORLEANS EAST
  ★★★ East China
  ★★ Jade East
  ★★★★ Peking
NORTH OF THE LAKE
  ★★★★ Trey Yuen

CHOCOLATE MOUSSE. Chocolate pudding with class: chocolate held together in an whipped cream matrix. Without a doubt the best chocolate mousse in New Orleans is that made at the Royal Orleans and served in the **Rib Room**. The texture is extremely dense, almost crumbly; the chocolate is bittersweet. It comes out in a ramekin with chocolate shavings on top. A close second is the mousse at **Andrea's**—because Andrea used to work at the Royal Orleans and borrowed the recipe. Other good chocolate mousses are those at **Antoine's**, **Christian's**, and **La Gauloise**. **Commander's Palace** makes an incomparable chocolate mousse ice cream that kills at 40 paces.

★ ★ ★ ★ Christian's

3835 Iberville, Mid-City. Reservations 482-4924. 5:30-10 p.m. Mon.-Sat. AE, DC, MC, V. $$$

Obviously, the building was once a church. Inside, pews are used as banquettes, a pulpit is a waiter's station, and more ecclesiastical accoutrements are adapted for other uses. But it's not a theme restaurant; Christian is the Christian name of the proprietor, Chris Ansel. Ansel is a member of the family that owns Galatoire's, and his restaurant's style is reminiscent of the old place: fairly basic, very good food made from great ingredients, served unfussily at prices a bit below average.

Oysters are the best starting point. Oysters Roland bubble beneath a crusty, green-brown sauce of parsley and mushrooms. Oysters en brochette are identical to Galatoire's and just as toasty. The shrimp remoulade is one of the best, with big, spicy, firm, pink shrimp and a ruddy sauce that jumps up the back of your nose after you swallow. Christian's smokes its own salmon to good effect. The fish bisque has a rough-edged charm; the changing daily vegetable-cream soups are up and down. There's a fine salad with a terrific, mustardy French dressing.

Seafood comprises over half of the entree list. The most distinctive dish here is the smoked soft-shell crab. It's fried and brown-buttered, and the delicacy of the smoke makes the thing irresistable. Christian's other innovation was its use, long before anybody would touch the stuff, of species of fish other than trout and redfish. Now that the trout and redfish are banned, everybody is serving Norwegian salmon, sheepshead, mackerel, amberjack, lemonfish, etc.—and Christian's still handles all of them deftly. The poisson au poivre vert, for example, treats firm fish fillets to a tan, opaque sauce with green peppercorns. Sauteed fish with artichokes and mushrooms are herbal and satisfying.

More seafood: the bouillabaisse is a bit light, made with local fish, and enriched with a spicy, garlicky rouille (garlic mayonnaise) that you can add as you like. Crawfish etouffee in season varies from pretty good to scrape-up-every-rice-grain great. The rich shrimp Madeleine puts large, tender crustaceans in a matching pink-orange cream sauce; lately this has been a bit bland.

The meat entrees are led by a couple of spectacular steaks. The filet or strip au poivre employs a dense demi-glace sauce with black peppercorns to create a mind-focusing intensity. A milder brown sauce moistens the filet mignon "Bayou La Loutre," which is stuffed with oysters: tremendous. Lighter but also powerfully flavorful are the baby white veal medallions with a nutty sauce of morel mushrooms. Sweetbreads are moist and light, with a sherry-laced brown sauce and mushrooms. Great lamb chops—doubles, simply broiled.

There's a modest but good selection of wine at very attractive prices. The dessert list is dominated by ice creams and ices, which the restaurant makes itself. Caramel custard and chocolate mousse round out the list. Good coffee. Service at all times is pleasant and knowledgeable, and absent any kind of silly ceremony.

★ ★ ★ Christina's Empress of China

429 Wall Blvd., Gretna. 392-9393. 11 a.m.-3 p.m. Mon.-Fri.; Noon-4 p.m. Sat.; 5-10 p.m. seven nights, till 11 p.m. Fri. and Sat. AE, MC, V. $$

Christina Tsang made a lot of friends at the China Doll, then spun off into her own flashy restaurant. The dining rooms, fenced off by various kinds of dividers, are handsome and vaguely mysterious. I think there is no experiment which Christina will refrain from asking her cooks to try; over the years I have eaten dishes that smack as much of Japanese, Korean, and even Creole and Italian cooking as Chinese. It would all work better with a step up in the quality of the raw materials.

Start off with the creamy crab Rangoon—a won-ton filled with Philadelphia cream cheese and crabmeat. The lomi-lomi—fried, bacon-wrapped shrimp with pineapple—make a good first course, too. Soups are up and down.

Well over half the entree selection is seafood. Some of this is rather exotic by local standards; the satay-style giant squid with vegetables is peppery and interesting, for example, and Maine lobster is cooked up with a sauce sharpened with ginger. I like the fried oysters, either with vegetables or sweet-and-sour, for a cheap thrill. Soft-shell crabs, shrimp, and crawfish emerge from the kitchen in numerous guises; shrimp and eggplant and the crab claws with garlic and black bean sauce are especially good. The kung-bo scallops, in their spicy sauce with peanuts, make an interesting taste.

I have had less good luck with the chicken, beef, and pork dishes, most of which duplicate ideas found among the seafood entrees. The crispy Mandarin duck, an old local favorite, is done well here; the sauce has the right sweet tanginess.

The dessert to get is the odd banana ice cream with bananas.

★★ Ciro's

7918 Maple, Uptown. 866-9551. 4 p.m.-1 a.m. seven nights. No credit cards. $

Tables and art line two long walls of a quiet room that looks as if it has been serving pizza and spaghetti, undiscovered, for a long, long time. Although Ciro's has run through a few sets of owners, the service style remains the same. The staff seems to be as much at home behind the counter as they would be in their living rooms. Between glances at the TV, they'll assemble a pizza from scratch for you. The crust is one of the best in town, retaining a semi-crisp texture regardless of what sorts of greasy things you've ordered for the topping. The sauce I find a bit lacking in finesse and flavor, but the end product is satisfying enough. While you wait for it, have one of the excellent Italian salads.

★★★★ Clancy's

6100 Annunciation, Uptown. Reservations 895-1111. 11:30 a.m.-2:30 p.m. Wed.-Fri.; 5:30-11 p.m. Mon.-Sat. AE, CB, DC, MC, V. $$$

Clancy's was a neighborhood barroom located on the kind of obscure corner where such places are found. It was gentrified during the Uptown Restaurant Boom of 1983. From that time to this, it has been a most interesting, personable, and consistent little cafe. The 20-table dining room has big windows and mirrors; the main element of atmosphere, however, is that everybody in the room seems to know everybody else. The bar, a post-yuppie hangout whose TV is tuned to either sports or the stock market ticker, offers lubrication by Jimmy Collins, one of the two or three best mixologists in the city.

Clancy's menu, which changes seasonally, is a good mix of traditional Creole dishes and some new ideas. The signature appetizer is rabbit sausage en croute, served with a creamy peppercorn sauce: terrific. A small portion of sweetbreads, cooked different ways different days, is served as a first course; a recent such essay with a reduction of sherry vinegar and sweet peppers was astounding. Very good oysters Rockefeller come in trios. Snails are some of the best, abubble with garlic butter and topped with pastry. Good soups sometimes.

The entree specialty is mesquite-smoked this or that. Absolutely the best of it is the smoked soft-shell crab. It is fried to a beautiful lightness, and the background smokiness—comparable to that of good smoked salmon—makes for glorious deliciousness. The smoked shrimp with honey mustard sauce and smoked leg of lamb are also satisfying.

What I like about restaurants like this is that some very unlikely but welcome dishes emerge as signature items. At Clancy's, a substantial number of customers come for the liver, which is without question the tastiest in New Orleans. It's startlingly tender, completely free of even small sinews. They prepare it with a sauce of Madeira and onions and send it out sizzling and pink on the inside.

Filets mignon are abetted with highly-refined, flavorful sauces—one with Madeira and mushrooms and another with green peppercorns have been especially good. The veal and lamb chops have been more variable; the latter are cut too thin for my liking, although they do give you enough of them. Grilled chicken with herb butter is a reliable, simple, lighter dish. Nice fish: the specied du jour Nantua, for example, is beautifully broiled and napped with a zingy orange cream sauce redolent of crawfish. Grilled fish has always been delicious.

The wine list here is far better than what one would expect of such a small place. The choices include obscure delights. The dessert course is very weak; the coffee is a great blue-black New Orleans dark roast with chicory. Waiters are efficient and knowledgeable.

COFFEE. That New Orleans has the best food in America is a strong case, but debatable. Much less at issue is that Orleanians drink the best coffee in the country. When I go out of town, I find the coffee so tasteless that I stop drinking the stuff completely.

Coffee gourmets are very picky about the varieties of coffee beans they grind. They insist on arabica beans. But what sets New Orleans coffee apart is not the beans—some of which are rather cheap—but the roast. It is darker than all but one Ethiopian roast, and causes the oils in the beans to break into beads on the side of the bean.

The richness that derives from these oils is what makes our coffee great. Richness differs from strength, which comes from bean tannins and aldehydes. I've tasted many strong coffees which lacked richness. You feel the flavor elements of bitterness and nuttiness in your mouth more than you taste them. Most espressos here (but not in Italy) are like that. So also is all the cafe filtre (that's the coffee that waiters "squeeze" for you in glass pitchers) I've sampled.

The classic New Orleans coffee is blended with chicory by the roaster. Chicory, the roasted root of a lettuce, was originally used as a cheap filler. But Orleanians are so accustomed to its taste that most prefer coffee with chicory to pure. I find the flavor of chicory inherently interesting. And it's a wonderful way to cut down on caffeine. Chicory contains no caffeine at all, and since chicory-blended coffee brews much stronger than pure, it contains less than half the caffeine. Dark-roast beans also have less caffeine than light roasts. So the blue-black brew that colors the side of your coffee mug here has far less caffeine than the taste-free, see-through swill served in the rest of America. This may explain the popularity of the French Market coffeehouses late at night. The sleep-inducing effects of the hot milk blended into the incredibly strong coffee and chicory served at the Cafe Du Monde may more than counteract the caffeine.

The best coffees served in restaurants in New Orleans—and, therefore,

in America—are at these restaurants and coffeehouses:
1. Antoine's
2. Morning Call
3. Cafe Du Monde
4. Commander's Palace
5. Mr. B's
6. Cafe Beignet
7. Clancy's
8. Galatoire's
9. PJ's Coffee & Tea Co.
10. Crescent City Steak House

The majority of these get their coffee from Merchants Coffee Company, whose supermarket brands are French Market and Union. Union Coffee and Chicory is my own favorite; after you brew it, you find a palpable layer of oil on the side of the pot.

★ ★ ★ Coffee Pot

714 St. Peter, French Quarter. 524-3500. 8 a.m.-Midnight or later seven days. AE, MC, V. $$

This cafe occupies the parlor and carriageway of an 1829-vintage townhouse. It has been one of the best neighborhood restaurants for Quarterites since the Forties. A recent major renovation brought the Coffee Pot to its highest point in decades: the place sparkles, but retains the raffish charm that befits its station.

The Coffee Pot cooks the basic Creole canon: gumbo, red beans and rice, poor boys, fried chicken, shrimp Creole, and fried seafood are prepared consistently well daily. A blackboard lists a few lunch and dinner specials—hearty, homely things like meatloaf with brown gravy and rice. The salad Jayne, a entree-size affair with shrimp, egg, cheese, and buttermilk dressing, is one of the best large salads in the city.

The Coffee Pot is best known among locals for its breakfasts, served at all open hours. Omelettes and buttermilk biscuits are especially good, but they also turn out fine pancakes, grillades and grits, and the only surviving manifestation of an old Creole street food called calas. These are spherical rice cakes, full of cinnamon and sugar, eaten with syrup—delightful. The only thing missing from the Coffee Pot's breakfast is, ironically, decent coffee. Service is carried on by personable waiters and waitresses like Pearl, who has been waiting on me since the Sixties.

★ ★ ★ ★ ★ Commander's Palace

1403 Washington Ave., Garden District. Reservations 899-8221. 11:30 a.m.-2 p.m. Mon.-Fri. Jazz Brunch 9:30 a.m.-12:30 p.m. Sat. & Sun. Dinner 6 p.m.-10 p.m. seven days. AE, CB, DC, MC, V. $$$$

When I have somebody in from out of town, Commander's is where I bring them. I don't think there's another restaurant that shows off our local cuisine better. As old as it is (it opened in 1880), Commander's remains on the cutting edge. And its standards for raw materials and preparations are front rank.

There's no more beautiful New Orleans setting. Upstairs, the view through the treetops is of the lovely, romantic courtyard below. You can dine down there when the weather's nice, or have a cocktail other times. The newly-renovated downstairs dining room has mural paintings of Southeastern Louisiana scenes and long, dark, flowery tablecloths.

Polished but traditional Creole flavors live side-by-side with culinary adventures at Commander's. The chefs (whose activities you are invited to observe in the kitchen, through which you have to pass to get to the bar) are encouraged to experiment. Raw materials are fresh and selected with unusual care. There's no better crabmeat, veal, or fish. New Orleans' best food is seasonal, and among the specials at Commander's you'll find foodstuffs that make fleet passages through the marketplace—rarities like Louisiana caviar, reef oysters, squab, and veal kidneys. They'll try anything here.

The best first course—once you're past the French bread crescents oozing garlic, butter, cheese, and dill (don't eat too many)—is soup. Here is the apotheosis of Creole turtle soup, spicy and chunky with turtle meat, well-seasoned and hearty. Corn and crab soup, artichoke bisque, and gumbo ya-ya are also memorable. You can sample all the day's soups through the agency of "soups 1-1-1." They also do fine starters of shellfish: oysters Commander (a delicious collection of fat bivalves with artichokes) and shrimp remoulade (tart, mustardy sauce over big, firm, spicy shrimp). The smoked mushrooms with angel hair pasta sounds a little odd for an appetizer, but it's seriously delicious.

A wood-stoked open grill turns out some great meat and fish dishes. My favorite of these—and, in fact, the best dish in the house—is veal chop Tchoupitoulas, a beautiful thick cut of pink veal on its nibblable bone, grilled to a char with Creole seasonings and served with a lightly sweet veal essence. This is almost too delicious. Rivaling the veal chop is the grilled rack of lamb, served for one and given the same exciting exterior treatment and a fine sauce of natural juices. The grilled fish is crusty and lightly smoky, served atop a pile of vegetable strips for a low-cal but delectable dish. The grilled chicken with andouille is a terrific lunch special, as is the trio of grilled lean lamb patties.

Trout with pecans was invented here and is definitive. The sauce on this, as well as on the fish Grieg's crabmeat topping, is a great beef-stock version of meuniere sauce, spicy and lemony. Commander's puts out spectacular soft shell crabs. During crawfish season, the saute of crawfish in a rich, spicy orange sauce is wonderful either with pasta or rice. Crabmeat Imperial, an old classic, is a very mild-tasting casserole with a glazed mayonnaise.

The veal comes in more polite forms than the chop: Veal Kottwitz (artichokes and mushrooms), veal Marcelle (crabmeat and hollandaise), and veal with wild mushrooms. At lunchtime, there's a near-perfect panneed veal with a crumby, herbal coating and fettuccine. The steaks are prime and beautiful; if you can get the sirloin Stanley, do so. (Two sauces: a red-wine beef-stock affair, and a horseradish sauce, abetted with a sauteed banana.) Avoid steak Diane, which is inexplicably terrible.

Brunch is served on Saturdays and Sundays to the accompaniment of great old-line Dixieland blowers and strummers. The menu is replete with the fancy poached egg dishes for which the Brennans are celebrated. I like eggs Sardou (fresh artichoke bottoms and creamed spinach), eggs de la Salle (atop crab cakes, covered with wild mushrooms), and eggs Creole (with an underpinning of fried grits and a spicy sauce with big chunks of andouille, the spicy Cajun ham-and-garlic sausage). There are specials at brunch, too, and the lighter food from the regular menu.

The great dessert is the irresistably aromatic, fluffy souffle of bread pudding — a great example of what Commander's can do with everyday Creole dishes. Bananas Foster, lemon crepes, and classic crepes Suzette are prepared tableside — well, too. If you like chocolate, there are several richnesses: the chocolate Sheba (a hemi-disc of solid, rich, gooey chocolate "cake"), the chocolate mousse ice cream, and the Celebration (a hill of chocolate and raspberry ice cream with a raspberry sauce). The coffee is some of the best in town — classic New Orleans-style dark roast with chicory.

The wine list is very strong in California Chardonnays and Cabernets, and offers a lot of French choices. Its weakness is that there are few older bottles.

The only consistent problem at Commander's is that the restaurant does such volume that service can become mechanical. The captains and waiters are generally good and friendly, however. Special requests or problems are handled very graciously, and regular customers receive treatment that equals that offered by any other restaurant in the city.

★★ Compagno's

7839 St. Charles Ave., Uptown. 866-9313. 11 a.m.-2 p.m. and 5-10 p.m. Tues.-Thurs.; 11 a.m.-10:30 p.m. Fri.-Sun. MC, V. $$

At one time there must have been fifty neighborhood cafes that looked like this. Compagno's is one of the few survivors. A short brick wall running through the place separates the bar from the red-checked-cloth tables. The menu is also divided equally, between Italian food and seafood.

Both are good. There is a decent lasagne with a thick, satisfying red sauce; cannelloni, spaghetti, Italian sausage, and all the rest of it are also edible. The ravioli is a specialty, made from scratch on the premises. It's meaty and cheesy, served with a robust, smooth red sauce. Seafood is lightly fried, free of excess grease, and crisp. Everything's fried to order, which right there puts the platters well above average. The soft-shell crabs are especially meaty and nutty. Service is leisurely, so don't come in a hurry. Prices are a touch higher than it seems they should be.

CONCEPT RESTAURANTS. "After they outgrow fast-food hamburgers," asked the mass-marketing geniuses in the restaurant industry, "what then?" The answer: give them bigger, more expensive hamburgers, and serve them in a place that is perceived as a real restaurant. Thus was born the concept restaurant, where there's a bar (usually as a brass-railed island in the middle of the place), a lot of pop-culture antiques (sometimes an incredible clutter of them), and a menu full of semi-gourmet-sounding dishes with kicky descriptions. Potato skins and a scattering of Mexican dishes are common. The kitchens and dining rooms, however, dispense with the fine points and generally get as close to fast-food operation as they can without tipping off the diner.

The better concept restaurants go a step further than one would expect, and serve fresh product of reasonably high quality. But the kitchens still operate according to strict procedures written at headquarters. You don't need a very skillful cook—let alone a creative one—to do that. Oddly enough, inconsistency is the main problem in these places.

Concept restaurants tend to be fast, inexpensive, reasonably wholesome, and fun if you're in your late teens or early twenties. Four of them locally even serve good food. **Copeland's** is the best of the lot; it captures a real New Orleans flavor and uses great raw materials. **Houston's** groceries are also above average, particularly its fresh fish and burgers; some of its recipes, however, lack interest. **Cannon's**, a local outfit, gives good grill and remembers the salt and pepper. **Cu-Co's**, another place with a strong accent on freshness, is the best of the Mexican concept places.

Acceptable (but not recommended) concept restaurants are **T.G.I. Friday's**, **Monroe's**, **Houlihan's Old Place**, and **Seaport Cafe**. Unacceptable: **Bennigan's**, **Colours**, **Wellington's**, and **Birraporetti's** (a pseudo-Italian concept).

CONSISTENCY. The pitfall of dining out and the worst enemy of a guide like this one is inconsistency. There is not a restaurant in town that is totally consistent—but who could expect such a thing? After all, the cook's art relies totally on human effort, a notoriously inconsistent resource. Operations which have tried to circumvent humanity wind up working in the straitjacket of formula or, worse yet, get all their food prepared in a factory and shipped in nearly finished.

Some restaurants have a remarkable consistency record, however. Here is my top ten for reliability:
1. Bozo's
2. Crozier's
3. Mr. B's
4. Galatoire's
5. Camellia Grill
6. Christian's
7. Commander's Palace
8. Versailles
9. Delmonico
10. Mosca's

★ ★ ★ Constantin's

8402 Oak, Carrollton. Reservations 861-2111. 11:30 a.m.-2:00 p.m. Mon.-Fri.; 6-10 p.m. Tues.-Sat. MC, V. $$$

Patti and Paul Constantin, young veterans of several restaurants and the catering biz, opened this cafe in 1987 in Lee Barnes' former cooking school. The style is robust, full-flavored, and distinctly Creole; they're meticulous about raw materials, and even grow fresh herbs in the large garden you wind through on your way to the entrance.

The menu is on the short side, abetted by a handful of daily specials. There are especially few first courses; the brie wrapped in spinach and fried is the good regular item. The crawfish croquettes with basil and the smoked quail, both good niblets, appear as specials. Soups are well-conceived twists on standards. Onion soup, for instance, is made with three different kinds of onions, and has an interesting sweetness.

The entree that illustrates the chef's style is the hearty baked pork chop, stuffed with andouille and zucchini, moistened with a savory brown sauce. Other chops—veal and lamb—have been eminently edible, too, although the sauces verge on the overpowering. Chicken breast meat is rolled up with spinach and feta cheese, then sliced to form tasty, light pinwheels. Also interesting is chicken turkonion, a breast with smoked sausage and fried eggplant all covered with a peculiar turkey gravy abetted with caramelized onions.

In compliance with the Ordinance on Uptown Cuisine, Constantin's grills fish. They also bread a trout with crushed almonds, sautee it, then slather it with a hollandaise made with orange instead of lemon juice: amusing and good.

The wine list is abbreviated but good enough; I would advise drinking white wines even with meats here, because the seasoning levels beg for something cold and wet. Desserts lean a little too heavily toward the chocolate end of the spectrum. They make their own ice creams, including one flavored with fresh peppermint.

Service is casually good. The dining rooms are spacious, comfortable, and colorful. The bar is a beautiful oaken affair, and is probably the best-looking room in the house.

★★★ Copeland's

1001 S. Clearview Parkway, Elmwood Village. 733-7843. ● *701 Veterans Blvd., Metairie. 831-3437.* ●*4338 St. Charles Ave., Uptown. 897-2325.* ●*1700 Lapalco Blvd., Gretna. 364-1575.* ●*1337 Gause Blvd., Slidell. 643-0001. All: 11 a.m.-Midnight, seven days.; till 1 a.m. Fri.& Sat., and 11 p.m. on Sun.; Sat. & Sun. Brunch 11-3. AE, MC, V. $$*

Copeland's plays the greatest hits of the recent K-Paul's-inspired Cajun era of local cuisine, in fern restaurant surroundings. An extensive menu is made possible by techniques borrowed from the fast-food industry (Al Copeland also owns Popeyes). The ingredients are fresher and of better quality than one usually finds in a place like this, and the recipes were developed by an all-star group of local chefs.

The levels of pepper, salt, oil, and general richness are all rather high, which gives rise to the biggest flaw of Copeland's food: a lot of it tastes the same. The basic taste is summed up in the fettuccine Lamborghini, with cream, butter, and tasso. You get two good bites before the richness overwhelms you. If you're not careful, you'll get this same taste several times in the meal.

The menu is very large, however, and there are more than a few dishes that break away from the rest. I like to start with an order of the great creamy red beans, the shrimp Carribe, or the onion mum. The latter is a whole fried onion, sliced before frying to resemble a chrysanthemum. A spicy orange dipping sauce is where the stamens would be.

Blackening, logically enough, is a popular cooking method at Copeland's. I am no fan of the technique, but they do it well here. The blackened fish is remarkably consistent: an enormous fresh fillet, heavily peppered and charred on a hot grill. Grilled fish is even better: it's a similar flavor, but since it's not encrusted it's tenderer. An odd number called ricochet catfish is covered with crushed pecans and a great, spicy sauce.

Other good stuff: Pleasantly chewy, smoky barbecued baby back pork ribs. White veal in rich sauces. Decent prime steaks. A chicken-and-spinach salad in the style of Buffalo wings, with a spicy sauce and blue cheese. Baked chicken. To be avoided: any entree with tasso, anything Mexican, the rabbit dishes, and anything with hollandaise.

In lieu of bread are great, oozy buttermilk biscuits. Good, rich Mexican vanilla ice cream, bread pudding, and a funny but acceptable bananas Foster are the desserts to get. The coffee is pretty weak. There is a tolerable wine list; everything is served by the glass. Service is very friendly and good.

★ ★ ★ Court of Two Sisters

613 Royal, French Quarter. Reservations 522-7261. Brunch-lunch buffet 9 a.m.-3 p.m. seven days. Dinner 5:30-11 p.m. seven days. AE, CB, DC, MC, V. $$$

Although the diners are overwhelmingly from other cities, and although the waiters automatically assume you are too, this is not a bad place to have dinner. The courtyard is pure New Orleans, with lots of trees and vines and fountains and crumbling buildings all around, complete with enough fans to make the air tolerable except on the hottest summer nights.

The daily brunch buffet is only decent. Dinner is by far the better meal, with a menu strictly limited to the safest old-style Creole cuisine. Start off with oysters Rockefeller or casino, both of which are superbly rendered. Escargots are also good, served with the inevitable butter sauce inside upended mushroom caps. The seafood gumbo is one of the best, with lots of seafood, spice, and firm long-grain rice. They also put out a very good turtle soup.

I've enjoyed the soft-shell crabs with crabmeat and bearnaise; the smooth crabmeat au gratin; and the delicious stuffed, roasted Cornish hen they call coq d'or. But the best dish in the house is a combination of two specialties: shrimp Toulouse and crabmeat Rector. Both are loose, mildly-spicy, buttery casseroles which are dominated by the flavors of the seafoods, served over rice. Also served over rice is a Court specialty I've never liked, shrimp Creole. Most of my experiences with the fish, duck, and lobster dishes have been less impressive.

For dessert there is some edible bread pudding, pecan pie, and the usual flamed things. Coffee is wimpy by local standards. The wine list is minimal. The waiters are very friendly, and seem to be particularly solicitous if you let on that you're local.

CRAB. The blue crab is abundant in the lakes surrounding New Orleans, as well as on local menus. In their most natural form, crabs are served whole—usually a few at a time—after being boiled in water zapped with spicy crab boil. You also clearly see what animal you're eating when you order a soft-shell crab. Soft-shells have just molted and were plucked from the water before the new shell had a chance to harden. After the noxious gills are removed, the crab is cooked (usually deep-fried) and served whole. It is completely edible—or should be.

Crabmeat removed from the shell is far more common. Crabmeat is made into salads, soups, au gratins, and stuffings. It is also extremely popular as a topping for everything from flanks of fish to slices of veal. In most such cases, the flavor of either the crabmeat or the underlayer, or both, is lost.

Crabmeat comes in two basic forms: lumps from the body of the crab, and strings from the claws. The lump crabmeat looks a lot better and is the usual medium for salads, toppings, and casseroles. The claw meat, despite its darker and less appealing appearance, actually has a more pronounced flavor; it's the stuff of stuffings and the base for crab soups and gumbos.

The classic cold crabmeat dish is crabmeat ravigote. "Ravigote" means "revived," a reference to the dish's origins as a way to make over-the-hill crabmeat taste good again. The sauce of mayonnaise, peppers, onions, and sometimes mustard (there are many variations) does nice things for perfect fresh crabmeat, too. The best ravigote in town is at **Commander's Palace**, which gets beautiful fat lumps. The **Windsor Court Grill Room**, **Galatoire's** (where it's called "crabmeat maison"), **Antoine's**, and **Broussard's** also have fine versions. Some restaurants—notably **Galatoire's** and **Christian's**—serve a *hot* crabmeat ravigote. Other tasty cold crabmeat dishes are Christian's crabmeat Iberville, with green peppercorns; the **Caribbean Room's** crabmeat Monte Carlo, the richest cold crabmeat dish imaginable; and the marinated crabmeat and crab salad at **Mosca's**.

The variety of hot crabmeat dishes is endless. Sometimes a single restaurant will have two or three of them. The most common is crabmeat au gratin, with a sauce of cream and cheese, served exceptionally well by the **Bon Ton**, the **Steak Knife**, and the Caribbean Room. Crabmeat imperial is baked with a good deal of white sauce (sometimes it's a mayonnaise, sometimes it's more like a bechamel) sharpened with peppers, onions, and pimientos. The best imperial is at Broussard's; the Bon Ton, Commander's, and **Gambrill's** also cook good ones.

More great hot crabmeat dishes: Crabmeat Remick, with a chili sauce and bacon, **Caribbean Room**. Crabmeat Yvonne, sauteed with artichokes, mushrooms, and pimientos to oily goodness at **Galatoire's**. Crabmeat Rector, the best dish at the **Court of Two Sisters**, a light, buttery, elemental crab stew over rice.

In the casual seafood restaurants, there is inevitably some form of stuffed crab. (Crab balls, croquettes, or chops are stuffed crabs without a shell.) Far and away the best is at **Bozo's**, where the crabmeat-to-bread ratio is easily the highest in town; it has a great crabby, buttery flavor, and makes a good side dish. Other good stuffed crabs are at the **Coffee Pot** (Fridays), **Bruning's**, **Ralph & Kacoo's**, **Visko's**, and the **Bounty**.

See **Boiled Seafood**, **Buster Crab**, and **Soft Shell Crab** for the best of those dishes.

CRAWFISH. Without a doubt crawfish—called "crayfish" by those who don't eat them—are the greatest delicacy from the wetlands around New Orleans. They look like small lobsters and are in season from about Thanksgiving till Independence Day—the opposite, oddly, of the animal's season almost everywhere else. The culinary possibilities of crawfish are almost without limit, but staggering numbers of them are devoured in their boiled form. This is shirt-sleeves eating, involving a technique known as "squeezing the tip" (of the tail, which pushes the meat out once you've broken the crawfish in two) and "sucking the head" (which is just what it sounds like, for the purpose of extracting the delicious fat lodged in the animal's thorax). The best restaurant for boiled crawfish is **Jaeger's** (only the one on Elysian Fields), where they are served hot out of the pot. Boiled crawfish are also good at **Mike Anderson's**, **West End Cafe**, and **Bozo's**.

Among the many dishes made from crawfish, the two most common are bisque and etouffee. The first is a thick soup, usually involving a thick roux and some stuffed crawfish heads. I like **Antoine's**, the **Peppermill**, and **Ralph & Kacoo's** for this. Crawfish etouffee—literally, smothered crawfish—is a stew of tail meat served over rice. It is not often enough done well in restaurants; **Bart's**, **Christian's**, **Bon-Ton**, **La Cuisine**, and **Galatoire's** make my favorite etouffees. **K-Paul's** makes an incredibly fiery version.

A commonplace in crawfish season is the crawfish dinner, in which several courses of different crawfish dishes constitute the entire repast. Especially good crawfish dinners are served at Ralph & Kacoo's, Mike Anderson's, La Cuisine, and Bon-Ton Cafe.

I think that crawfish bisque is one of the ten greatest dishes in the local cuisine. And so, as for the other nine, here is the recipe I use to make it. This recipe starts with live crawfish, but you can shorten it considerably by using boiled or picked crawfish.

CRAWFISH BISQUE
  20 pounds of live crawfish
  8 large lemons, quartered
  6 yellow onions, quartered
  1 bunch celery, with leaves, cut into eighths
  1 bunch Italian parsley
  4-6 bay leaves
  1 bunch green onions, cut up
  1 bulb of garlic, cut in half
  4 bags crab boil
  1 1/2 cups salt
  1 Tbs. cayenne
  3 lbs. whole new potatoes

1. Fill a bucket or your kitchen sink with two or three gallons of cold water with about a half-cup of salt dissolved in it. Dump the crawfish in; the salted water will purge them. Repeat this process with new water two or three times until the water is only slightly dirty.

2. Bring a large stockpot with five gallons of water to a boil. Add all the other ingredients except the potatoes and return to a boil. Let it cook for ten minutes. Add the crawfish and the new potatoes. Return to a boil and continue boiling for 15 minutes. Make sure there's enough water to completely cover the crawfish.

3. Remove one crawfish after 15 minutes and see if it's cooked through. If so, turn off the heat and let the crawfish steep until the potatoes are tender.

4. At this point, we commence the peeling and eating process which, if you haven't learned it, you're better off picking up from a friend than reading about. The potatoes are a side dish. After you and the rest of the people in the house have eaten their fill of crawfish, there should be about five pounds of them left for the actual bisque.

> 5 lbs. boiled crawfish from above recipe
> 1 Tbs. olive oil
> 2 Tbs. onion, chopped
> 1 tsp. garlic, chopped
> ½ rib celery, chopped
> ½ red bell pepper, chopped
> ½ cup dry white wine
> ¼ cup brandy
> 1 small lemon, sliced
> ⅔ cup flour
> 1 stick butter
> 5 sprigs Italian parsley leaves, chopped
> 2 sprigs fresh oregano leaves (optional; don't use dried)
> 1 pint whipping cream

5. Rinse the boiled crawfish with lukewarm water. This will remove some of the salt, which will otherwise get concentrated later. Peel all of the crawfish and reserve both the tail meat and the shells. Get some kid to pull off all the claws from the shells. Put all the claws onto a dishcloth and fold the cloth into a bag. Using a meat mallet, bash the claws enough to break most of them open.

6. In an eight-quart (or larger) saucepan, heat the olive oil over medium heat. Add the onions, garlic, celery, and bell pepper. Saute until the onions are clear. Add the crawfish claws and shells and wine, and bring to a boil. When most of the liquid has evaporated, carefully pour the brandy over the shells and touch a flame to it. Let the flames die out, then add the lemon. Fill the pot the rest of the way with water. Bring it to a boil, then lower to a simmer for an hour and a half, spooning out the scum from the top of the pot as you go.

7. Strain the stock into another saucepan and discard the solids. Simmer until reduced to one gallon. Strain through cheesecloth or a fine sieve. (At this point, the stock can be refrigerated for up to three days or frozen for later use.)

8. In a large saucepan over medium-low heat, make a dark roux with the flour and butter, stirring constantly to avoid burning. When the roux is the color of chocolate, stir it into the crawfish stock with a wire whisk until completely blended in.

9. Add parsley and oregano. Reserve three large crawfish tails per per-

son, and chop the rest of the tail meat. Add this to the soup and return to a boil for five minutes. Taste the bisque and add salt and hot sauce if necessary. Stir in the cream.

10. Place the whole crawfish tails in soup plates, and ladle the bisque over them.

Serves six to eight.

CREME BRULEE. See Caramel Custard.

CREOLE. Properly, a Creole is one born in this land of parents who immigrated from Europe—most particularly France, Spain, and Portugal. In New Orleans, the distinction became important once the Americans took over. In time, the French Quarter became the Creole sector of town, with the Americans on the other side of Canal Street. (From that division grew the expression "neutral ground," which referred to the median in the center of Canal Street, where the Americans and Creoles could meet without infiltrating one another's area. To this day, the many street medians in New Orleans are all called neutral grounds.) Creole also has the widespread, if inaccurate, connotation of a racially-mixed person.

The observation that there was a distinctive Creole cuisine was first made in 1880 by the writer George Washington Cable. His book *Old Creole Days* created such a sensation that it crystallized the culture and its cuisine. A few years later, around the time of the Cotton Centennial Exposition (New Orleans' first World's Fair), Cable and Lafcadio Hearn collaborated to write the first guidebook to New Orleans, including in it some good (and, from our perspective, highly recognizable) descriptions of the food. Orleanians have been bragging about Creole cooking ever since.

Yet nobody has ever succeeded in defining it—at least not in a few words. Its roots are pretty clear: Creole cuisine evolved from French and Spanish styles of cooking through the interpretations of black cooks. Many blacks in the New Orleans area can trace their lineage to a migration from Haiti in the late 1700s. The Caribbean influence in New Orleans cooking is obvious. Certain Creole dishes—red beans and rice, for example—have identical counterparts in the Caribbean. There is also a German input, from the many German communities immediately upriver of New Orleans. Andouille looks and feels like a German sausage, despite its French name and Creole taste.

My favorite definition of Creole cuisine is one word: more. More salt, more peppers, and more oils, among more other things. It adds up to more intense flavors. When you eat Creole food, you know you've eaten something. Beyond that broad statement, it's hard to say anything definite. Many Creole dishes begin with a roux—a browned (different shades, depending on the dish) mixture of flour and oil or butter. But there are many Creole ways to skin a catfish, and you don't find roux or even pepper hotness in all Creole dishes.

One practice seems to me to be distinctly Creole: brown sauce on fish.

You rarely see this in other cuisines, but it's so pervasive in Creole cooking that there are many different brown sauces used on seafood, from the nutty browned butter at **Galatoire's** to the thick, mahogany Colbert sauce at **Antoine's**.

You need no help finding Creole cuisine in New Orleans. It's hard to avoid. It infiltrates even ethnic cuisines here—most notably Italian, with which it has hybridized to form a distinctive Creole-Italian style. There are few French restaurants here that have avoided Creolization.

Nor is Creole cuisine static. Every ten years or so, a new wave sweeps through and revitalizes things. Justin Galatoire in the early 1900s, Count Arnaud in the Twenties, Pascal Radosta of Manale's in the Thirties, Owen Brennan in the Forties, Warren LeRuth in the Sixties, and Dick and Ella Brennan at Commander's in the Seventies—all have added new dimensions to the cuisine with their restaurants.

The Eighties wave has been the biggest of all, involving for the first time a lot of chefs from other places. Europeans like Andrea Apuzzo and Daniel Bonnot inspired many kitchens other than their own. And New Orleans has had its share of the New Young Genius phenomenon. Many of these chefs, like Emeril Lagasse at Emeril's and Gerard Maras at Mr. B's, are products of the culinary schools of the Northeast. These guys are adventuresome and stringent in their selection of ingredients and cooking methods. The resulting trend has been a great lightening of the eats, with no loss of flavor. In fact, there may be more intensity than ever. The principal exponents of Eighties Creole are Bayou Ridge Cafe, Brigtsen's, Clancy's, Commander's Palace, Emeril's, Flagons, Gambrill's, Gautreau's, Mr. B's, and Upperline.

I am not ignoring Paul Prudhomme. The success of his restaurant and his knack for drawing publicity have made people around the country take Cajun food seriously. Another effect of the K-Paul's-inspired Cajun craze was that Creole and Cajun styles of cooking—always related—have now more or less merged. The current Creole cuisine incorporates lots of elements of its country cousin. Spice levels are higher than they were ten years ago, for example, and crawfish are much more commonly used. (Let's hope that puts an end to the heretofore endless and unresolvable argument about the difference between Cajun and Creole.)

CREOLE SAUCE. Elsewhere around the country this thickish, tomatoey concoction, chunky with peppers and onions, is thought to be a part of any Creole dish. In fact, it is not widely used here. Nor is it one of the better Creole ideas. The most frequent apparition of Creole sauce is as a matrix for shrimp Creole, a stew which I have sampled from the hand of innumerable cooks, but which I've never particularly enjoyed. (I keep trying, because I suspect that a forgotten secret—flecks of shrimp fat in the sauce, or something—will one day surface and explain why the dish is so famous.) Probably the best use of Creole sauce is in the old breakfast dish grillades and grits, particularly the way they do it at **Brennan's**. A recipe for this dish appears under **Grillades and Grits**.

CREOLE TOMATO. This is Louisiana's finest vegetable and the greatest tomato you'll ever eat. They are in season late spring through early summer (although some hothouse growers are trying to make them a year-round treat). They are extremely large, somewhat misshapen, always picked completely ripe, and more than a little sweet. The ultimate way to eat a Creole tomato is out of your hand while leaning over the sink, but these juicies are wonderful in any kind of salad, omelette, sandwich, or wherever else they appear in unaltered form.

★★Crescent City Steak House

1001 N. Broad, Mid-City. 821-3271. 11:30 a.m.-11 p.m. Tues.-Sun. AE, CB, DC, MC, V. $$$

This 55-year-old restaurant, still operated by its founder (nothing much else has changed, either) is the originator of the New Orleans-style prime steak in butter sauce. It still serves a great steak. The cut to get is the strip. It's trimmed just right, is very well aged (indeed, it has a pronounced agey flavor which not everyone likes), and comes out in a modest pool of politely-bubbling butter. For two or more, the porterhouse—combining a strip and a filet in an enormous cut something like a T-bone—is equally magnificent. The filet mignon alone is less good because it's wrapped in bacon, which interferes with the beef's own flavors. The T-bone, while certainly not skimpy, is cut too thin to get a good broiling. The rib-eye is to me never a good cut for prime beef (too much fat).

The salads are dressed with peculiar sauces of the restaurant's devising. The potatoes are all fresh; the best of them is the Lyonnaise version, cut up and cooked with onions and butter. The onion rings are terrible. For dessert, there's a good warm bread pudding and some wonderful strong coffee with hot milk.

The interior is unusual: tile floor, chandeliers, stainless-steel columns, curtained booths along one wall, an uninteresting bottle of wine on each table. The funny thing is that those tables are usually empty: most of the few customers are die-hard regulars of many years' patronage.

★★★Croissant d'Or

617 Ursulines, French Quarter. 524-4663. 7 a.m.-5 p.m. seven days. No credit cards. $

In the former digs of Angelo Brocato's, this is the larger and more spacious sister pastry shop of La Marquise, owned by the same French master baker Maurice Delechelle. It is one of the best-liked hangouts of French Quarter residents, who fill most of the tables and keep a line going at the counter. In the glass cases you'll find an assortment of terrific, flaky croissants; rich, fruity flans and tarts; eggy brioches, and the rest of the French pastry pantheon. The carrot-laced bran muffins are the apotheosis of the genre. Croissant d'Or's regular coffee is weak and terrible, but the chicory blend, espresso, and cappuccino are better.

★ ★ ★ ★ ★ Crozier's

3216 W. Esplanade, Metairie. Reservations 833-8108. 11:30 a.m.-2 p.m. Mon.-Fri.; 6-10 p.m. Mon.-Sat. AE, DC, MC, V. $$$

There's nothing pretentious or ambitious about Crozier's, the city's first and best real French bistro. But what it promises it delivers, and then some—consistently. There are very few restaurants about which that can be said. It's modest but comfortable, small but spacious. The owner is in the kitchen, and his wife is in the dining room; both are from the area of Lyon. The menu of familiar French dishes is completely free of Creole influences.

Most of the action is in the entree section, but there are some good starters: porky homemade pate de campagne, escargots in an aromatic garlic butter, light soups of this or that, and a fine salad of crisp, cold romaine with a textbook French dressing.

A great example of Crozier's food is coq au vin, a cliche French dish if ever there was one. Here the capon is baked with an inspired rich sauce of red wine, salt pork, and pearl onions: hearty and intensely flavorful. The beef dishes have great sauces. The steak au poivre has a richnessof cream, peppercorns and demi-glace. Tournedos Gerard employs the unlikely but wonderful combination of shrimp, foie gras, and a cream sauce. The steak Perigourdine has a glistening, powerful, translucent sauce of beef essence and foie gras.

The chef has been playing around with veal lately, coming up with a lightly-tomatoey sauce on Thursdays, a polished cream-and-butter affair on Saturdays, and some others. Veal sweetbreads, sauteed and served with burned butter, are always available and delicious.

Fish has been occupying a larger and larger part of the menu at Crozier's, particularly as nightly specials. Trout with fennel or capers is nice enough, and the new poached salmon with a finely-wrought bearnaise is a good lighter dish. Sides often include rice, which the chef does better than anybody else in town: it's nutty-tasting. The gratin Dauphinois is a little casserole of beguilingly garlicky and buttery potato scallops.

At lunchtime, they make what are without doubt the best omelettes in town: perfect yellow at the outside, moist on the inside. Crawfish in hollandaise makes a nice filling.

The wine list is entirely French and attractively priced. Desserts are various little pastries, a creme caramel, and a pie-slice of bread pudding, all made well on the premises. Service is performed easily by young waitresses, most of whom have been here for many years.

★ ★ Cuco's

1340 S. Carrollton, Uptown. 861-3322. 11 a.m.-11 p.m. seven days; till Midnight Fri. & Sat. ●Lapalco Belle Chasse Plaza, Gretna. 393-7766. 11 a.m.-10 p.m. seven days; till 11 p.m. Fri. & Sat. ● 5048 Veterans Blvd., Metairie. 454-5005. 11 a.m.-10 p.m. seven days; till Midnight Fri. & Sat. and till 11 p.m. Sun. All locations: AE, MC, V. $$

Cu-Co's isn't really Mexican or anything close, but whatever it is, it's reasonably edible. A locally-based regional chain of kicky concept Mexican restaurants, it's better than most such squeaky-clean places. The ingredients are fresh and of obviously good quality. It is only slightly maddening that they twist around classic Tex-Mex for the apparent purpose of writing clever menu prose, but the results could be a lot worse. The "fresh-itas," for example, are like fajitas except that the garlicky pico de gallo is missing, and that they bring the sizzling platter of meat, onions, and peppers with a plate of miscellaneous salads and sauces for wrapping in the crepe-like flour tortillas. They make "fresh-itas" with beef or chicken; the latter makes a tasty light supper. Most of the menu is composed of different combinations of the tortilla dishes: tacos, chimichangas, enchiladas, and like that, covered with loads of melted cheese, guacamole, sour cream, lettuce, tomatoes, or innocuous red sauce. Strictly pop-Mex cuisine for the unadventuresome; no mole poblano or anything else really interesting. Cinnamon-sugar-coated fried ice cream is the only decent dessert; the flan is the worst I've ever encountered. Service is excellent; prices are low.

CUSTARD. See Caramel Custard.

D as in dirty rice dressing

★ ★ ★ Dante's Pizza Cafe

Plaza in Lake Forest, Lakeside Mall, and Esplanade Mall. Open mall hours in each location. Also Bourbon at Conti and 700 block of St. Peter, French Quarter. 11 a.m.-till. No credit cards. $

As unlikely as this may sound, Dante's little shopping-mall kiosks and French Quarter-strip cafes serve the best pizza in New Orleans. Not consistently, mind you—but even at its worst Dante's is hard to beat. When it's at peak, the crust is perfect: thin, with a firm, crusty bottom and a just-thick-enough bready layer. It's as close to the superb pizza of the Northeast as you'll find hereabouts—including the by-the-slice aspect, which is how they sell most of their pie. The varieties are usually just cheese (my pick), pepperoni, sausage, or a pepper-and-olive combo; the topping ingredients could be better, but with a crust like this it almost doesn't matter.

Deanie's Seafood

1713 Lake Ave., Metairie. 831-4141. 11 a.m.-10 p.m. seven days; till 11 p.m. Fri. & Sat. AE, MC, V. $$

Deanie's appeal is simple: they serve a staggering amount of seafood for a very low price. Like a dozen and a half or more each of oysters and shrimp, seven catfish fillets, a couple of crabs, and titanic piles of fries for around $10. However, I have never had what I thought was an acceptable meal here, and I fail to see the logic in the idea that a lot of bad food is better than a little bad food. (I'd say it's worse.) Deanie's mounds of fried seafood have been, in my experience, tepid and lacking in crispness. The gumbo comes not in a bowl, but in a small kettle; it has never held my interest past the third or fourth spoonful. And so on. If quantity is your main concern, this is the place for you.

★ ★ ★ Delerno's

619 Pink (at Focis, one block lake side of Metairie Road), Old Metairie. 832-3087. 11:30 a.m.-2:30 p.m. Tues.-Fri. 4:30-9:30 p.m. Tues.-Thurs.; till 10:30 Fri. & Sat. 11 a.m.-9 p.m. Sun. AE, CB, DC, MC, V. $$.

For decades, Delerno's was the best place to eat in Old Metairie. When J.B. Delerno died, the place went into limbo until 1989. Then Larry Lindelow—who had a good culinary track record at La Coquille—reopened Delerno's. He installed many of the old specialties of the restaurant, along with an assortment of Galatoire's-style dishes. The neighborhood-cafe style of the place was also kept.

One of the best of the old dishes is a great appetizer for the whole table: crawfish tapas. It's a flat fried flour tortilla, spread with melted cheese and topped with spicy crawfish etouffee—gooey and good. They send out an excellent shrimp remoulade, served beautifully with both the red and white remoulade sauces. This makes a good summertime lunch. Soups are savory and spicy.

Absolutely the entree to get here is "the combo": a luscious, delicate smoked-then-fried soft shell crab, a half eggplant stuffed with shrimp and crabmeat, and a toasty, buttery trout meuniere. All three elements are wonderful, and the variety of flavors keeps the palate interested. Delerno's invented the crawfish dinner: bisque, fried tails, remoulade, etouffee, and crawfish pie, all wonderful in the old style of such things.

Most of the entree list is more seafood. The trout with pecans or with the artichoke and mushroom sauce are both fine eating. They grill fish here, too—but only moderately well. There is some Italian food: the cannelloni, stuffed with veal, cheese, and spinach is very rich and good, and the pesto-enhanced lasagna is a nice twist on the standard.

The best of the few meat dishes is the carpetbag steak, an old, neglected classic: an oyster stuffed inside a filet mignon. Here spinach is added to the oyster and, as unlikely a combination as it all sounds, the taste is magnificent.

Delerno's is not the most consistent restaurant around. More unexpectedly clumsy food than I can ignore has appeared before me. And I have yet to have a decent dessert here. But these are problems typical of inexpensive neighborhood places, and they're not enough to keep me from recommending this rebirth of a venerable Metairie institution.

DELI. New Orleans has never been a deli city. At times, reasonably authentic kosher-style delis have opened here. These died a quick death, because even the Jewish population here mostly eats Creole. (I once saw "gefilte fish remoulade" on a menu, and I'm still puzzling over it.) The closest approximation to New York deli here is **Martin Wine Cellar Deli**. (Just before this book went to press, a place called **Cajun Kosher Deli** opened in Metairie. It's *real* kosher—glatt meats and all.)

In a completely different vein, several supermarkets have good American delis. Easily the best is at the **Whole Foods Market**, a natural-foods supermarket with a superb cheese, smoked fish, and meat selection. The larger stores of the **Canal Villere** chain and **The Real Superstore** also have impressive selections of cold cuts, cheeses, and sandwiches. The smaller, more specialized **Magazine Cuisine** and **Chez Nous** have a more gourmet-oriented line of take-outs.
All are good bets for stuffing picnic baskets.

★ ★ ★ Delmonico

1300 St. Charles Ave., near Lee Circle. Reservations 525-4937. 11:30 a.m.-9:30 p.m. Mon.-Sat.; till 9 on Sun. AE, CB, DC, MC, V. $$

Delmonico hasn't changed very much in the past few decades. Its premises and menu allow one to eat as one did in the Fifties and Sixties. This is all honest; the restaurant has been around since before the turn of the century. Rose Dietrich and Angie Brown, daughters of the founder, run the place with a welcome more genuine than most.

The gleaming facade of Delmonico is deceptive. There is nothing fancy about the dining room, the food or the service—all of which are comfortable in a neighborhood-cafe way. At dinner, four substantial courses runs you between $12.50 and $19.

Start with soup. Seafood gumbo is light in texture, well seasoned, replete with crab and shrimp. The turtle soup is also light and has a great taste, and the old-style vegetable soup is good too. Firm shrimp with a nose-filling, smooth remoulade sauce and the well-made oysters Rockefeller are more solid options. The house salad is a collection of marinated vegetables in a hand of lettuce with a tangy house vinaigrette.

The menu is dominated by seafood. The best of it is catfish meuniere, served with a trio of spicy stuffed shrimp. They also do a great job with trout amandine, broiling the fish and moistening the almonds in a good lemon butter. When soft-shell crabs are in season, Delmonico's cooks up several different good versions of them. Those who like light food will enjoy the seafood kebab, with redfish, scallops, oysters, and shrimp all grilled together.

Delmonico's has the city's best basic broiled chicken. The bird can also be had with a variety of more-than-edible stuffings and sauces. Good steaks, and decent broiled calves' liver with onions and bacon, and a veal selection or two.

By 1990 standards Delmonico overcooks a lot of its food, particularly the vegetables. Some dishes are oversauced or overstuffed. Amenities which have only recently become de rigeur—a great wine list, for example—are absent. But there will always be a place for this kind of restaurant. And my reaction to the check is always that I have been undercharged.

DESSERT. I feel funny if I don't have dessert after a meal. While that hunger is going out of style, it is one which I share with many other diners. Tastes for dessert tend to fall into three rough categories: for chocolate, for custards, or for fruit. I am a custard person. Specifically, my favorite dessert is Creole bread pudding, about which I have a lengthy dissertation elsewhere.

Here are the dozen best desserts served in New Orleans restaurants:
1. Baked Alaska, Antoine's.
2. Bread pudding souffle, Commander's Palace.
3. Bananas Foster, Commander's Palace or Arnaud's.
4. Chocolate cake, Mr. B's.
5. Tiramisu, Andrea's.
6. Creole cream cheesecake, Emeril's.
7. Hot souffles, Morton's.
8. Chocolate mousse, Rib Room.
9. Tres leches, Tula's Kitchen.
10. Flan, El Patio.

Some restaurants—notably Oriental ones—don't have much in the way of dessert. After dining at such places, one looks for a dessert specialist. The best of these are **Angelo Brocato**, **Haagen Dazs**, **La Madeleine**, **La Marquise**, **Croissant D'Or**, and **P.J.'s**. Also popular for dessert are the French Market coffeehouses, **Cafe Beignet**, **Cafe du Monde** and **Morning Call**.

DIM SUM. Chinese tidbits, designed to be taken with tea early in the day. They range from little pieces of meat to steamed dumplings to meat-stuffed buns, and are classically sold by the piece from a cart. As of this writing, real dim sum has not hit New Orleans yet, although two restaurants—**China Rose** and **Five Happiness**—take a stab at it on weekends. Both are just okay, and will be disappointing if you've sampled dim sum in New York or San Francisco.

★ ★ ★ DiPiazza's

337 Dauphine, French Quarter. 525-3335. 11:30 a.m.-10 p.m. Tues.-Fri.; till 11 p.m. Fri. 5-11 p.m. Sat. AE, MC, V. $$

This cafe serves the best food per unit floor space in New Orleans. A miniscule room (for many years "Eva's Spot") is nicely decorated and furnished with 30 or so seats. The pair of pews out on the sidewalk are frequently occupied, especially in the evening, with people waiting patiently for their turn at some highly imaginative Italian cooking.

The best way to order here is to speak two magic words: "Feed me." Then, for a tab ranging between $15 and $25 per person (depending on how hungry you are), a procession of the day's specials will come to the table, along with plates for splitting each. Six to eight courses is typical. All of it except the desserts (which I suspect come from outside) will be delicious. Most of it will be unusual.

For example, a recent meal started with marinated calimari with bell peppers. Then came an oval baking dish with baked oysters Giovati (garlic, bread crumbs, and a bit of bacon) on one end, and spicy roasted red and yellow peppers with mozzarella on the other. Next, grilled "squid steak" — something the chef was experimenting with that day. (It had the texture and color of lobster and the shape of a hamburger pattie — very good.) Next was a quail atop fresh spinach and mushrooms in a very buttery sauce. Then broad noodles with a sauce of white beans and lentils with herbs. Finally, veal sirloin with mushrooms, peppers, and onions.

There is also an a la carte menu that includes the standard Italian appetizers, a dozen ways to have pasta, and four ways each to have veal, beef, chicken, pork, shrimp, or fish.

Service is very friendly, as are the fellow diners who, because of the cramped quarters, will inevitably join the conversation. Despite the closet effect, the restaurant is completely comfortable.

DOE'S EAT PLACE. This restaurant is 300 miles from New Orleans in Greenville, Mississippi, the major river town between Memphis and Vicksburg. Since the title of this book was inspired by Doe's, I think it's only right that I should tell you about the place. It's ramshackle, to say the least; stoves and other cooking gear share rooms with tables. No alcohol is served, so everyone brings his own hooch in polished flasks in handsome satchels. The menu at Doe's Eat Place is peculiar: gumbo, hot tamales, steaks (they display several of them for you to choose from), spaghetti and meatballs — that's about it. All of it is tasty stuff, especially those tamales, of which you should order at least a dozen regardless of what else you're eating. Anyone in Greenville can tell you how to find Doe's Eat Place, which despite its looks is the city's great meet-and-eat institution. The address is 502 Nelson in Greenville, MS; the phone is (601) 334-3315.

★ ★ ★ Dooky Chase

2301 Orleans Ave., Mid-City. 821-0600. 11:30 a.m.-Midnight seven days; till 2:30 a.m. Fri. & Sat. AE, DC, MC, V. $$

Ever since the major renovation to Dooky Chase's, this first-line restaurant of the black community has been one of the most comfortable places to take a meal — particularly late at night. I don't find Dooky's food as consistently good as it once was. But it would take a long fall before Dooky's became bad. It's still an interesting place to eat what is widely thought of as "soul" food (actually, the menu and the style of cooking is identical to that of any other Creole family restaurant). The dining room staff is unusually friendly.

The biggest loss here has been the gumbo, which used to be one of the great ones. Lately, it has not tasted fresh, and the ingredients are out of balance. A better starter is shrimp Dooky, with its extra-spicy remoulade sauce.

The entree specialty is stuffed shrimp. Don't break your brain try to figure out how you put crabmeat inside a shrimp—the stuff is wrapped around the outside, and the whole thing is fried. It's a great recipe, full of crabmeat, pepper, and herbs. All the rest of the seafood is made with equal skill: the fried things are crisp, flavorful, and free of grease. Chicken is available fried or broiled, and both of those are as good as any. And you can even order a more-than-decent steak with marchand de vin sauce. At lunchtime they turn out classics like baked chicken, red beans and rice, and jambalaya, all more than edible.

Dooky's is open extremely late—in fact, it's busier in the wee hours than it is at more ordinary dinnertimes. There is a good children's menu.

★ ★ ★ Doug's

348 Robert Road, Slidell. 1-649-1805. 11 a.m.-2 p.m. Tues.-Fri. 5-10 p.m. Tues.-Sat. AE, CB, DC, MC, V. $$

One of the surprisingly few decent restaurants in Slidell, Doug's is owned by Floyd Bealer. For many years Floyd did most of the cooking at Commander's Palace. While a substantial part of Doug's menu is reminiscent of Commander's, the place does have a casual style of its own—"good food with a Creole taste," to quote the menu. The two dining rooms are pleasant if far from fancy; heavy gardening outside the big windows provides the main element of atmosphere.

Start with the fried oysters with artichokes and lemon butter, a fine pairing. The shrimp remoulade is satisfyingly zingy. They make several good soups nightly, including a great old-style gumbo.

Trout with pecans is the most memorable of the entrees, followed closely by the spicy grilled chicken and andouille. I've had better andouille in my life, but the flavor of the whole dish makes the grade. They grill several different species of fish; I would ask them to ease off a touch on the charring, which has a way of getting out of control. Panneed veal with fettuccine Alfredo, fried seafood, and steaks—all more than decent—round out the menu.

Desserts include a rich chocolate mousse pie and a somewhat heavy bread pudding. They have a better selection of wine than one would expect. One thing they could do for New Orleans diners is provide bottled water; the Slidell tap water is heavy with sulphur, which the locals are used to but which puts hair on my teeth.

★★★ Dragon's Garden

3100 17th St., Metairie. 834-9065. 11 a.m.-2 p.m., Mon.-Fri.; 5 p.m.-10 p.m. Mon.-Sat. AE, CB, DC, MC, V. $

Two locations and I don't know how many owners ago, the Dragon's Garden led the movement of New Orleans' Chinese restaurants out of the dreary sameness of Cantonese cooking into the fascinations of Szechuan, Mandarin, and Hunan cuisines. Spinoffs of the Dragon's Garden became some of the best Chinese restaurants in town. After a few recent years of inconsistency, the Garden itself has returned to goodness. The room is acceptable but hardly atmospheric; the food, however, shows polish, particularly in the consistency and flavors of the sauces.

Start off with the fine hot and sour soup, the well-made Mandarin egg rolls (smooth skin, dense interior), the superb shrimp toast, or the rich roast pork. They do a great Peking duck here with a day's notice. Equally grand and good is moo-shu pork, the fine Mandarin crepe-wrapped classic. That dish balances off the spicy Szechuan dishes, of which my favorites are the stir-fried pork string and the kung-pao chicken with peanuts. There's a tasty version of chicken with walnuts, beef with a variety of different vegetables, and a vegetarian dish or two. Fried candied bananas make a better dessert than is usually found in a Chinese restaurant.

★★★ Drago's

3232 N. Arnoult Rd., Metairie. 888-9254. 11 a.m.-9:30 p.m. Mon.-Sat.; till 10 p.m. Fri. & Sat. AE, CB, DC, MC, V. $$

Two good restaurants in one. The more accessible menu is of New Orleans-style seafood. The oyster bar, presided over by the very friendly proprietor Drago Cvitanovich, is one of the best. At the table, you can order from an enormous selection of seafood platters. The fried stuff comes out agreeably crisp and light. They also prepare very fine broiled seafood as well. An especially enjoyable new dish is char-broiled oysters—a dozen, served on their shells, basted liberally with garlic butter and licked with flames.

Drago's other aspect is its Yugoslavian menu. The selection is broad and it's entirely authentic (there's a large Yugoslavian community in Southeast Louisiana). If you like squid, this is the place for it; they're great either as a starter or entree. I also like the bright green, creamy, spicy spinach soup (with or without oysters) and the lentil soup. The best of the Yugoslavian platters are the muckalicka (grilled pork with green peppers and onions), sarma (stuffed cabbage rolls), and musaka (something like the layered meat-and-potatoes Greek dish moussaka, but denser and more powerfully flavored).

The dining room is pleasant. Waitresses are very helpful with the less familiar parts of the menu.

DRINKS. It has been said that when one dies of cirrhosis of the liver in New Orleans, the death certificate reads, "natural causes." Bars are open 24 hours a day, 365 days a year—even on Election Day. Despite that, New Orleans has a shocking paucity of good mixologists. It's not at all easy to find a place that does consistently good mixed drinks.

Which is a shame, since there are a number of fairly complicated cocktails which are New Orleans originals. When made properly, these are wonderful drinks.

Sazerac is the trademark of a bottled concoction produced by the Sazerac Company, a large liquor producer here—but when you order a Sazerac in a bar, it will almost certainly be made to order from Herb-Saint (an absinthe substitute), Peychaud bitters, and rye whiskey. It's the Peychaud connection that supports a claim that the Sazerac is the original cocktail. Antoine Peychaud, a New Orleans druggist in the mid-1700s, served his friends an elixir made of brandy (from the Limoges, France firm of Sazerac-de-Forge) and his bitters. He served it in an egg cup. (The word "cocktail" is supposed to be a corruption of "coquetier," the French word for egg cup.) But another story has it that it was made up by a bartender at the Imperial Cabinet on Baronne Street.

At any rate, a Sazerac is properly made by putting a few drops of Herbsaint in an Old Fashioned glass (the Old Fashioned, by the way, was also created in New Orleans), twirling it to coat the sides of the glass, and then adding the other chilled ingredients. The only place I ever see this technique anymore is at the **Sazerac Bar** in the Fairmont Hotel, although I have also had good Sazeracs at **Commander's Palace** and **Clancy's**.

The **Ramos Gin Fizz** is a terrific, unique drink made with egg whites, gin, soda, a little sugar, and orange flower water. Unfortunately, not a single bar in town prepares it consistently well, although I have gotten good versions now and then at **Brennan's**, **Commander's Palace**, and the **Esplanade Lounge** in the Royal Orleans Hotel. The versions at the Sazerac Bar in the Fairmont (which owns the trademark) and the Pontchartrain's **Bayou Bar**, despite their fame, are marginal.

Absinthe Suisesse and **brandy milk punch** are among the better "eye-openers" made popular by the breakfast at Brennan's; both have spread to other Sunday brunches. They're both made with half-and-half, sugar, and liquor. The absinthe Suisesse is the better of the two drinks; the anise taste of the Herbsaint goes well both with the milk and the almond-flavored orgeat syrup.

The **Hurricane** is the creature of **Pat O'Brien's**, and although the drink is sold everywhere on Bourbon Street, Pat O's is the only place you should get one. It's a fruit-juice drink with four or five ounces of Myer's rum, and comes in a distinctive glass you get to keep. My limit is three-fourths of a Hurricane.

The **Cajun Martini** is the only cocktail served at **K-Paul's Louisiana Kitchen**. The idea, Paul Prudhomme told me shortly after his restaurant opened, was to repel the old drunks who used to hang out in the bar he'd taken over for K-Paul's. But the drink caught on—inexplicably, if you ask me. It's a pint or a quart Mason jar filled with vodka with marinated hot peppers. One sip was enough to last me a lifetime. A few other restaurants serve Cajun martinis; you can also buy it bottled.

Mint juleps are widely pooh-poohed as a corny, touristy drink. What a pity—a good one can be wonderful. The best mint julep is made at the bar in the kitchen at Commander's Palace, where they muddle fresh mint leaves and serve the thing incredibly cold.

DRUM. See Fish.

DUCK. There's a lot of duck hunting in the swamps around New Orleans, but state laws prevent wild duck from appearing in restaurants. So we get the Long Island ducklings (none of which, incidentally, come from Long Island anymore) just like everybody else. More duck is being served in restaurants now than at any time in recent memory, and there are plenty of good ones. My favorite is available by special order at the **Sazerac**; Canard Bernard is a big slab of duck meat that's first roasted and then sauteed to an incomparable melt-in-the-mouth crispness at the skin, brought forth with some great sauteed spinach. But the current thinking about duck is that you grill it, and they do so very well at **Mr. B's** and **Upperline** (some wonderful seasonal sauces here). The more traditional roast ducklings—you know, a l'orange and all that—are prepared best at **La Provence** (orange sauce), **Andrea's** (orange, cherry, plum, or au poivre), **Versailles** (port wine sauce), **Cafe Sbisa** (orange or green peppercorn), and **Feelings Cafe** (orange).

But the real duck fanatics are the Chinese. Peking duck, the most festive Chinese duck dish, is rubbed with herbs for a day and slowly roasted so the fat drips off and the skin turns crisp. The ceremony goes like this: The waiter brings the whole roasted duck to the table—just for show. Then it's returned to the kitchen and sliced up. You put a couple of pieces of meat and a couple of pieces of skin onto a thin pancake slathered with the slightly sweet, thick, red-brown hoisin sauce and some strips of scallions. You roll up the pancake to make something like a burrito, pick it up and eat it. Peking duck makes a great first course for four to six people. The best Peking duck in town is at the **Great Wall**; other good ones are at the **East China, Peking, Fortune Garden, Trey Yuen,** the **Dragon's Garden,** and **Kung's Dynasty**. (Peking duck must be ordered a day in advance at all these restaurants.) Trey Yuen probably has the best array of other duck dishes, including a spectacular tea-smoked duck and wor shu op (mandarin duck to you—strips of fried duck meat with vegetables and a great spicy sauce called tong-cho).

E as in eggs sardou

★ ★ ★ East China

9830 Lake Forest Blvd., New Orleans East. 241-6600. 11 a.m.-3 p.m. and 4:30-10 p.m., seven days; till 11 p.m. Fri. & Sat. AE, MC, V. $$

This small cafe is somewhat hidden in a strip shopping center in New Orleans East, but it's worth seeking out. The food is prepared in a modern style: raw materials are fresh and the cooks are not given to overcooking them. The sauces are refined, free of excess oil, and made without MSG. And while the cooking is done with an eye to lightness, there is no loss of flavor.

Start with the very good hot and sour soup. The crawfish roll and the fried dumplings are also nice. The East China's Peking duck is one of the city's best; the contrast between the crisp skin and moist meat is ideal, and the bird is almost fat-free. This makes a great first course divided several ways.

The entree specialty here is seafood. My favorite item is the scallops Szechuan style; the big white scallops are cooked to precisely the point where they're bulging and juicy. The sauce is mildly peppery and more than mildly garlicky; it abets the scallops deliciously. The shrimp are big and fresh-tasting, and figure in about a dozen different concoctions; all I've tried were delectable.

The sesame chicken consists of large nuggets rolled in sesame seeds and moistened with a dark, slightly sweet brown sauce and vegetables: excellent contrast of flavors and textures. Beef with orange peel, the spicy River Shang pork, and kung-pao anything (peppery, with peanuts), and the old-fashioned lo mein dishes are other winners here. The dining room, which is cursed with those sheets of glass atop the tablecloths, is not grand but is comfortable enough, and the restaurant has so many regulars that the atmosphere is friendlier than that of the average Chinese place.

★ ★ ★ Eddie's

2119 Law (about midway between N. Broad—the easiest point of access—and Elysian Fields), Gentilly. 945-2207. 11 a.m.-10 p.m. Mon.-Sat.; till 11:30 p.m. Fri. & Sat. AE, MC, V. $

This is the best "underground" restaurant in New Orleans. The first time you go looking for it, you may give up after not being able to find the street (Law Street runs underneath the Elysian Fields, Franklin, and Almonaster overpasses; the best way to get to it is from N. Broad and A.P. Tureaud). Things used to be worse. The restaurant once had no sign. However, there's nothing wrong with the neighborhood, the dining room, and certainly not the food, which is ideal everyday Creole cooking. The robust red beans and rice come with a potent hot sausage if you want. The fried chicken is crisp and has a delicious coating. Fried seafood is also hot, well-seasoned, and crackly, prepared to order. Chicken filé gumbo is one of the best. And poor boy sandwiches are flawlessly executed with hot French bread and good, fresh fillings. That's about the extent of the menu, save for the bread pudding they sometimes serve for dessert. On Thursday nights, there is a popular and very inexpensive buffet dinner. Bill Cosby talked hilariously about Eddie's one night on Johnny Carson, and recommended it highly—with good reason.

EGGS. Imitations of breakfast at Brennan's, particularly at Sunday brunch, possibly has made New Orleans the Fancy Egg Dish Capital of the World. Most of the dozens of creations involve poached eggs slathered with hollandaise. That's eggs on eggs, folks, but it works if they remembered the cayenne.

Here is a list of the best egg dishes in New Orleans.

Eggs Sardou. This is a pair of poached eggs atop creamed spinach, in turn atop artichoke bottoms, all covered with hollandaise. **Brennan's** poaches eggs and makes hollandaise exceedingly well, which goes a long way in explaining the merits of their vaunted (and expensive) breakfast, of which this dish is the apotheosis. Other great eggs Sardou are at **Commander's, Galatoire's, Arnaud's,** and **Antoine's** (where the dish was actually created, and where they omit the spinach).

Eggs Hussarde. Poached eggs atop a thick slice of Canadian bacon, slices of grilled tomato, and Holland rusk (an almost inedible item used for its resistance to sogginess). The whole thing is drenched with marchand de vin sauce and topped with hollandaise. This was dreamed up at Brennan's, which still does it well, as does Commander's.

Eggs Creole. This lends itself to interpretation, but always includes red, chunky-with-peppers Creole sauce. At Commander's and **Mr. B's** brunches, they fry grits cakes as an understratum for the eggs, and serve the whole thing with lengths of spicy andouille.

Eggs St. Charles. I don't see this many places other than Brennan's, but the idea is sound: poached eggs on fried trout with hollandaise. Crunchy.

Eggs Windsor Court. This is only served at the eponymous hotel's **Grill Room.** It's a pair of poached eggs with smoked salmon and caviar and hollandaise.

The everyday egg dishes such as scrambled and sunny-side up are almost as hard to find prepared well as the fancy dishes. Nothing could be worse than scrambled eggs made by the tub and spooned out from a steam table, but that's what a lot of places do. For good simple eggs to order, I like the **Camellia Grill**, the **Cafe Pontchartrain**, the **Hummingbird Grill**, and the **Windsor Court Grill Room**.

Omelettes are another story. Literally. (See Omelettes.)

★ ★ ★ ★ El Patio

3244 Georgia Ave. (at 33rd, a block from Williams Blvd.), Kenner. 443-1188. 5-10 p.m. Mon.-Sat.; till 11 p.m. Fri. & Sat. AE, MC, V. $$

El Patio is my favorite local Mexican cafe. Its extensive, ambitious menu is served with a high degree of polish. The two dining rooms flank an atrium with a stained-glass skylight and a fountain. Further atmosphere is provided by guitarists and singers, who are sometimes joined in rousing ensemble performances by the several members of the Rodriguez family, who own the place and work in every corner of it.

You can put together a grand feast here. Start with the ceviche — marinated fish in lime with crunchy vegetables, served cold. The nachos are rich with avocado, sour cream, cheese and beans. The black bean soup with chopped fresh onions is the best I've eaten — elegant and fresh-tasting. The avocado and tortilla soup is light, flavorful, and aromatic with herbs.

The crabmeat-stuffed squid with its creamy, spicy white sauce would be perfectly at home in a much fancier restaurant. There's a lot of other seafood here (with a long coastline, Mexico eats a lot of fish): trout, red snapper and shrimp come out in a variety of successful preparations. The dishes in which rice is central are filling and finely-balanced. These include arroz con calamares (rice with squid), arroz con pollo (chicken) and arroz con camarones (shrimp). There's also an okay paella, served for two but enough for four, with lots of chicken and seafood.

They make a blue-ribbon mole poblano — the peppery, bitter chocolate sauce — and it's great over chicken or enchiladas. Fajitas are just okay: skirt steak, charred to a pleasant smokiness, rolled up in a flour tortilla with dressings. More familiar dishes like chiles rellenos (stuffed with cheese and fried), empanadas (fried meat pies), and all the things in or on tortillas — and combinations thereof — are a cut above.

For dessert, there is the city's best flan, made with Mexican vanilla. They also have their version of bananas Foster. The wine list is decent and the service is attentive.

★ ★ ★ ★ Emeril's

800 Tchoupitoulas, Warehouse District. Reservations 528-9393. 11:30 a.m.-2:30 p.m. Mon.-Fri. 6-10 p.m. Mon.-Sat. AE, CB, DC, MC, V. $$$.

Emeril Lagasse was the executive chef at Commander's Palace during most of the Eighties, when that restaurant reached its all-time peak. He became one of the best-known chefs in the country, a fine example of the celebrated New Breed of Young, University-Trained Chefs. It was inevitable that he would open his own restaurant sooner or later, and Emeril's appeared on the scene shortly before this book went to press, in March, 1990.

It is a singular restaurant, carved from a former manufacturing plant. Heavy-duty pipes and gauges are a reminder of the past. The design would have been called punk five years ago; now it's boldly modernistic. The focus of the restaurant is a concrete "food bar." Seven stools at the counter offer a close-up view of the restaurant's entree station. Here you'll find Chef Emeril, schmoozing diners and cooking at the same time. There may be no better place in New Orleans for a single diner to eat.

Emeril has a shtick. He makes everything from scratch. I mean not just stocks, bread and pasta, but also Worcestershire sauce, goat cheese, and sausage. He has a network of farmers who raise vegetables, poultry, and even veal calves and lambs especially for him.

All of that makes good copy. Fortunately, they also know how to cook here. The wild mushroom tart is a square puff pastry filled with firm mushrooms in a sauce lightly smoky with tasso. Emeril's homemade andouille, grilled and moistened with homemade Worcestershire, is as delectable as it is substantial. Goat cheese and spinach in small phyllo pastries, crawfish ravioli with a spicy, creamy sauce, and fried calamari with a sauce of smoked tomatoes were other hits in the early going.

Roast quail Milton—a pair of birds stuffed with andouille dressing and napped with a savory brown sauce sweetened slightly with port—is the best of the first batch of entrees. Large flanks of moist fish are satisfyingly seasoned and brought to just short of perfect doneness over a hickory fire. I wanted to like the pan-roasted salmon, but the combination of its fresh-herb crust and salad underliner pushes it into green-grass territory. The rack of lamb with mustard crust and rosemary-scented jus is clearly made from first-class lamb, but it could be trimmed better. The dish also shows the penchant of the restaurant to undercook everything—and not by a little, either. Better specify medium.

Undercooking is a trend, of course, and Emeril has always kept up with those. A newer, better vogue attended to here is for very homely dishes: chicken with cornbread dressing and giblet gravy, panneed veal, and crab cakes. The mashed potatoes are some of the best you'll ever eat, and the freshly-baked cornbread actually tastes like corn.

Desserts here tend toward the very rich and chocolatey side of the spectrum. A refuge from that is the strawberry shortcake (made with real shortcake, not pound cake). The goat cheese and Creole cream cheese cake is also an original, interesting taste.

The new-restaurant mob scene was underway here during my reviews; given Emeril's fame, that condition may well continue, particularly during events in the nearby Convention Center.

ESCARGOTS. French for snails—although most of the mollusks actually come from the Far East these days. (Some California snails have appeared, but they're not very good.) Wherever they come from, 99 percent of the snails here come out in one variation or another on the classic bourguignonne recipe: butter, garlic, and green herbs. The best version is at **Brennan's**, the only restaurant that still serves its snails in the shells. **Arnaud's** and **Clancy's** serve the dish with a pastry cap atop the dish—a nice touch. At **Gambrill's**, the slugs rest in inverted mushroom caps—good flavor match. **Crozier's, Louis XVI, Galatoire's**, and **Antoine's** all cook classic garlic-butter escargots. Wherever you get this, there is no question that more than half of the joy comes from dipping bread in the sauce.

Among the more original approaches to escargots, my favorite is the proper bordelaise version at **Antoine's**, the only place in town that routinely serves snails two ways. The snails are in a complex, thick brown sauce with chunks of garlic, sherry, and a crust of cheese over the top. Another good brown-sauce version is at the **Versailles**, which serves its snails inside a small French loaf. At **Nuvolari's**, the snails are paired with crawfish in yet a third brown sauce, spicy and herbal.

ESPRESSO. Or "expresso," to use a common misspelling of the Italian word for a powerful, rapidly-brewed (hence the name) shot of coffee. Superheated water is steamed through finely-ground dark-roast coffee. The process extracts enormous amounts of flavor. That's the theory, anyway. In practice, most restaurants that serve espresso in New Orleans do a terrible job of it—they try to fill the cup which, despite its small size, should only be half to two-thirds full if the espresso is made correctly. The result should be rich and foamy; more often, it's weak and bitter. And the current craze for decaffeinated espresso is about as boneheaded an idea as I've heard—something like a car without wheels.

What's more, most people don't drink espresso correctly. You *should* put sugar into it; indeed, Italians add a great deal of sugar to espresso. The sweet flavor disappears quickly, and you are left with the chocolate-like taste of the coffee lingering on your palate for a long time. As for the little twist of lemon, throw it away. That's a practice that dates back to Mussolini, when bitter coffee substitutes were used and the lemon was added to cut the bitterness. Espresso coffee now is of such high quality that twisting the lemon is like drinking XO Cognac with Coke.

I find reasonably good, consistent espresso at **Andrea's**, the **Windsor Court Grill Room, Flagons, PJ's Coffee & Tea Co.**, and the **Bistro at the Maison de Ville**. The same places also make good cappuccino; more at **Cappuccino**.

★★Etienne De Felice's

111 Veterans Blvd. (Heritage Plaza building), Metairie. 834-7670. 11 a.m.-2:30 p.m. Mon.-Fri., 5:30-10 p.m. Wed.-Sat. AE, CB, DC, MC, V. $$$.

   A modern, airy cafe that serves lunch to the office workers in the towering Heritage Plaza, De Felice's has a bit more going for it than most such restaurants. It is the rebirth of Etienne's, a French-Creole institution during the Sixties and Seventies. The new generation has not much changed the culinary style of the old days; you can expect to find reasonably decent versions of oysters Rockefeller, shrimp remoulade, turtle soup, gumbo, trout meuniere, chicken Clemenceau, bread pudding, and the like. A few new ideas like grilled fish have worked their ways onto the menu. Both the old and the new stuff is okay, but nothing will jump off the plate and into your permanent taste memory. Beware any dish whose sauce must be described with a compound sentence. Service (other than that provided by the personable old-school maitre d') is amateurish.

ETOUFFEE. It means smothered, and it's usually applied to crawfish — to which I now refer you.

F as in file gumbo

FAMILY DINING. Parents know (until their children grow up, when they forget) that children don't always have their table manners quite down, and that juvenile likes and dislikes rarely dovetail with a menu—unless the restaurant specializes in family dining. Unfortunately, few such places are much good these days, ever since the fast-food chains staked out that market segment. (McDonald's, for example, is obviously a restaurant designed to attract children as a primary clientele.)

Few restaurants actively discourage your bringing children, even if kids would be inappropriate. Dining rooms designed to present rare cuisine in a romantic atmosphere are clearly not right for the pre-pubescent. Nor are places where cigar-smoking seems to fit in. But even places that say they welcome children would probably prefer that they be at least six and that they not come on a Friday or Saturday night. The issue is behavior. Certainly the sound of a young baby's crying is disturbing to all who hear it. But even older children, if they haven't learned the restaurant ritual, can really disrupt things.

Here are some restaurants other than fast-food franchises which, because of their menu structure, style of cooking, or policy regarding the young ones, are especially appropriate for families with children. All of them charge greatly-reduced prices for children's plates; on occasion, the kids may eat free. All of them serve food good enough to attract you even without the kiddie consideration.

Andrea's
Antoine's
Bozo's
Cafe Pontchartrain
Clancy's
Commander's Palace (brunch)
Delmonico
Dooky Chase
Gambrill's
La Cuisine
Liuzza's
Masson's
Middendorf's
Nuvolari's
Pastore's

Peppermill
Ralph & Kacoo's
Sal & Judy's

I would add to this list all the Chinese restaurants in the area, but I would advise you to insist that the MSG be left out of food for the young ones.

FAST FOOD. The problem with fast food is the fast part. In order to be able to give you your order within seconds, a fast food "operator" (as they call themselves, in the same mechanifood-speak that makes their restaurants "stores") has to have the food almost entirely prepared and sitting around waiting. Different fast food places do this different ways, but every way produces an inferior "product" when compared with the same food cooked to order. The current trend, exemplified by Wendy's, is to cook at a low temperature so that the burger can be said to be coming hot off the grill. *Warm* off the grill is more like it; the texture that results leaves me cold. I look for fast food places that allow one to defeat the system. **McDonald's,** for example, will cook a burger to order for you. Worth the wait.

When external constraints cut out all options but fast food places, I usually skip the meal. Acceptable fast food places here are **Bud's Broiler, Checkers, Danny's Fried Chicken, Dante's Pizza, Lee's, Luther's, McDonald's, New Orleans Hamburger & Seafood Company, Popeyes, Rally's,** and **Wendy's.** Unacceptable: **Arby's, Burger King, Church's, Hardee's, Kentucky Fried Chicken** (except for the original recipe chicken), **Pizza Hut, Pizza Inn.**

Tastee Donuts and their Kastleburgers—those little square burgers riddled with onions—appeal to a personal culinary perversion of mine. I like 'em, but I'm not proud of the fact.

★ ★ ★ Feelings

2600 Chartres St. 945-2222. 11 a.m.-2 p.m. Mon.-Fri.; 6-10 p.m. Mon.-Thurs., till 11 p.m. Fri. and Sat., 5-9 p.m. Sun. AE, MC, V. $$$

The building is in the hotbed of renovation on the downtown side of the French Quarter; it's pretty old, and when the weather is damp, it smells its age. There are dining rooms downstairs in the main building and upstairs in the slave quarters, with some very pleasant tables along the balcony. Before and after cocktails can be had to the accompaniment of live piano in the courtyard.

Although the original owners of Feelings have moved to Atlanta (where they are running a very good place called Taste of New Orleans), the food here continues to provide novel twists on Creole cuisine. For example, the shrimp etouffee is a spread—as are the chicken liver pate maison and the silky smoked-salmon mousse. Chicken taquitos are untouchably hot when they arrive with their cooling guacamole. There is usually a couple of soups—one a gumbo, the other something like bean—and these are almost always excellent. The house salad has a sweet, light poppyseed-and-mandarin-section dressing.

The fish with mustard sauce and fish florentine are both good entree choices. Both are fried deftly and have distinctive flavor partners. The florentine business—which implies an underlayer of creamed spinach—also works to good effect with veal and chicken. A better veal dish, though, is veal d'Aunoy, with a sauce of mushrooms, lemon butter, and hollandaise. They have always done good chicken dishes here, although the current vogue for removing the skin has lessened the chicken Clemenceau. There are a couple of varieties of tournedos, both decent if not mindblowing.

Two great pies: peanut butter, vivid and smooth, and French silk, which is sort of a chocolate mousse in a pie shell. They also put the two ideas together in a single pie, and that's good, too.

On the off-nights, Feelings has a tendency to overcook. The wine list is just okay, the garlic breads are pretty poor, and the service is friendly and informative unless the waiter is in a mood.

★★Felix's

739 Iberville, French Quarter. 522-4440. 10:30 a.m.-Midnight Mon.-Sat.; till 2 a.m. Fri. & Sat.; 10:30 a.m.-10 p.m. Sun. AE, MC, V. $$

Felix's is a great favorite of frequent visitors to New Orleans, possibly because for a long time it was the only neighborhood-style fried seafood house in the French Quarter. Recently it expanded through its back wall into what was formerly Toney's Spaghetti House; that stroke made it a much bigger, more comfortable restaurant. Neither the food nor service has changed. The essential thing to eat at Felix's is raw oysters on the half shell at the bar; you enjoy not just the taste of good, cold oysters, but also the personality of the shuckers. (See **Oysters**.)

At the table, Felix's serves up the breadth of local fish and shellfish cookery (at least the shirtsleeves kind). The baked oysters Rockefeller and Bienville are better and cheaper than in most such places; the boiled shrimp, with or without remoulade, are edible enough. The fried seafood is somewhat variable; at its best, it's light and greaseless, but not especially well seasoned. Felix's is one of the few restaurants around that still serves the once-ubiquitous whole broiled flounder, but make sure it's fresh before you order it. Stuffed crab or shrimp are very rich. They attempt to grill and blacken fish, but that's not really Felix's style.

The menu goes on to include poor boy sandwiches and a bunch of short-order platters: acceptable, not brilliant. Service has always been a bit mechanical and brusque; you get hustled around by a not-too-cordial host or hostess when you enter.

FESTIVALS. South Louisiana has more than its share of festivals, and regardless of the theme you can count on seeing a lot of food booths at them. Unfortunately, most festival food is pretty bad, even that which seems very authentic.

The best festival of the year is the New Orleans Jazz and Heritage Festival, a world-class, ten-day music extravaganza. During two weekends in late April and early May, the Jazzfest occupies the infield of the Fair Grounds Race Track with dozens of music stages and thousands of people. The food booths sell about a hundred different Creole, Cajun, and African dishes. The best of these are the Natchitoches-style spicy fried meat pies, the artichoke and spinach casserole with sweet potato pone, and the brown (not the red!) jambalaya. (The Jazzfest is a good place to see how jambalaya is authentically made — in big tubs stirred with oars.)

A couple of weeks before the Jazz Festival, in early April, the French Quarter Festival serves up some very tasty stuff in Jackson Square, to the accompaniment of lots of music. This has grown and gotten better every year.

In the dead of summer, an umbrella organization called La Fete assembles a schedule of food and wine events, most of them staged by independent entities, some of them very classy. The best have been the winemaker dinners at Flagons, in which the top California winemakers present their best stuff in a dinner planned around the wines and cooked by name local chefs, for about $100 a plate. Other events range from cooking classes for kids to the world's largest coffee break. The weekend before Bastille Day, La Fete presents Chefs on the Square, a food-booth deal with dishes from local restaurants. To be avoided at this time of year is the New Orleans Food Festival, which for the past several years has been a free-for-all of uninteresting grub. (One of the regular highlights of the Food Festival has been Takee Outee; enough said?)

Two spectacular culinary expositions support New Orleans major parks. The Zoo-To-Do is a black-tie event benefitting the Audubon Park Zoo; it features 80 or so of the city's best chefs, each cooking a dish and doling it out to the patrons, who pay upwards of $150 for the pleasure. A similar event of only slightly lesser quality is the Lark in the Park at City Park.

And then there are the Crawfish Festival, the Strawberry Festival, the Andouille Festival, the Gumbo Festival, the Creole Tomato Festival, the Jambalaya Festival... it's endless. And Mardi Gras, about which we write elsewhere.

FETTUCCINE. It's what people used to order when they wanted to eat spaghetti but felt they were in too fancy a restaurant. Now restaurants serve not spaghetti but pasta, and we don't have to worry about it anymore. See **Pasta**.

FILE. Almost impossible to find outside Louisiana, file (FEE-lay) is powdered sassafras leaves with a wonderful herbal aroma. Its only use is for dusting atop gumbo at the table, although it seems to me it could be used for other things. See **Gumbo**.

FISH. Surrounded as we are by some of the best fisheries in the world, Orleanians are accustomed to eating first-class fresh fish. But for many years the local taste devolved almost totally on just two species: trout and redfish. A disaster broke us of that bad habit. First redfish, then trout were so overfished (a result of the nationwide blackening craze) that their commercial catching became heavily restricted. But the restaurants had to have fish, so—with great trembling—they began using other Gulf fish. Surprise! Diners not only accepted the new fish but loved the variety.

Here are the species of fish most often encountered on New Orleans menus, in order of goodness (to my taste, anyway):

1. Pompano. The best-tasting of Gulf fish, pompano is medium-sized (about a foot long) and has white, fine-textured flesh and just enough oiliness to give it a distinctive delicacy. Its flavor is best when the rather flat fillets (or even the whole sides) are grilled or broiled with the skin on, as is done at **Galatoire's** and **Antoine's**. Add a little meuniere butter and you have The Best Fish Dish in New Orleans. **Andrea's** also cooks beautiful pompano, broiling it and abetting the flavors with a light, herbal pesto cream sauce. Two locally popular pompano dishes are to be avoided. Pompano en papillote is an old-style French-Creole perversion: the fish is baked with a thick sauce inside a parchment bag. The flavor of the fish is drowned with shrimp, oysters, mushrooms, and who knows what else. Waiters love it, however, because it gives them something fancy-looking to do at the table. The other odd pompano dish is pompano Pontchartrain, topped with crabmeat or even a small soft-shell crab. The two flavors, each a delicacy on their own, don't go well together.

2. Red snapper. Once and for all, this is not the same thing as redfish. Red snapper lives at considerable depths in the Gulf, must be line-caught, and is usually expensive. It's a big fish—between 10 and 20 pounds—and from it we get thick white-gray fillets with a firm texture and a great taste. It is not a fixture on local menus, usually showing up as a special. The only restaurant that seeks it out is **Andrea's**, where they make a superb buttery, herbal basilico sauce with a touch of tomato.

3. Speckled trout. This is nothing like the smaller freshwater trout sold in the rest of America. Speckled trout is a largish saltwater fish with light gray meat, big flakes, and a delicious, nutty taste. It is at its best sauteed or fried; it is much less good grilled or broiled. The ultimate and ubiquitous trout dish is trout meuniere, done especially well at **Galatoire's, Christian's, Commander's Palace,** and **Delmonico's**. The same places also scatter slivered almonds in the sauce for an equally delicious trout amandine. **Commander's Palace** developed a variation with roasted pecans; this is delicious and has spread to other restaurants.

4. Salmon. This is not a Gulf fish, but it is omnipresent on New Orleans menus these days, owing to the efforts of the Norwegians (who set the world standard for fresh salmon) and the Pacific Coast fisheries (whose product is not quite as good as the Norwegian, but much better than it once was). Salmon's pink steaks and fillets emerge from the grill, the saute pan, the broiler, or the poaching pot with a superb, distinctive flavor. It's especially good with rich sauces. I like the salmon at **Louis XVI, Christian's, Gautreau's, Andrea's,** and **Gambrill's**, although I can't say I've had much bad salmon.

5. **Flounder.** Some beautiful flounders are caught in the shallow waters of the Gulf. I'd sooner have a broiled flounder in front of me than the much more expensive Dover sole. The flesh is soft and almost creamy; as long as the skin is left on, flounder grills beautifully. Many restaurants stuff their flounder, which masks the taste of the fish. The main problem is that too much flounder is frozen. **Andrea's, Commander's Palace, Christian's, Galatoire's,** and the **Windsor Court Grill Room** have served me excellent flounder. The fish is not as often seen as it once was; even at the places above, it was served as a special.

6. "Albacore" tuna. This is not really a tuna but a cousin. The flesh is very white, unlike the dark meat of a yellowfin tuna. The texture is much lighter and flakier, and the taste more delicate than Charlie. This is another great fish for the grill, where it turns up to fine results at **Mr. B's, Commander's Palace, Flagons, Galatoire's (where they call it "oilfish"), Nuvolari's** (they call it "palu") and a few other places—but always as a special.

7. **Mahi-Mahi or dolphinfish.** The Hawaiian name is preferred by restaurants, who don't want diners to get the idea that they're eating Flipper. This is a wonderful, pearly-white fish with a sort of lumpy quality in the fillets. It has a firm texture, but explodes with flavor in the mouth. It's great for grilling, and I suspect it would even survive a preparation en papillote. Any restaurant that would seek this out can be expected to cook it well.

8. **Wahoo.** Thick, white fillets of large-flaked flesh can perform well on either the grill or the saute pan. The flavor and texture are wonderful; I find the fish lends itself particularly well to herbal or tomato sauces. I've enjoyed it as a special at **Flagons,** the **Bistro at the Maison de Ville, Windsor Court Grill Room,** and **Andrea's,** but it's showing up everywhere lately.

9. **Sheepshead.** The only problem with this delectable fish is its name. So it is called some other things: "sea bream" and "silver striper" are two I've seen on menus. Sheepshead gets its name from its mouthful of big, flat, lamb-like teeth. No chef who has ever cooked a sheepshead would let this or the fact that the fish is hard to fillet interfere with his cooking it again. The sheepshead yields beautiful, thick, firm, fillets with a satisfyingly rich, fat taste. It's so white that it has been used as a substitute for crabmeat. It sautees, broils, and grills well, and lends itself to just about any sauce treatment. We don't get this fish nearly often

enough; it is fairly regularly served at **Alex Patout's**.

10. Redfish. The red drum is a good fish, all right—but not so good that it should have been eaten almost out of existence. Redfish are big and yield large thick, gray-white fillets that poach and broil well. But what made its popularity skyrocket a few years ago (it used to be what you ate if trout were unavailable) is that it is delicious when grilled over wood. When the grilled-fish vogue hit, redfish became king. Then came blackening, which is also good—but only if the fillet is at least eight ounces. That's a bigger piece of fish than most blackening factories are willing to part with, so don't blame me if you find blackened redfish to be charred to dryness. Better you should have it poached with hollandaise at **Galatoire's**, or grilled at **Flagons, Mr. B's,** or **Copeland's**. (Despite the ban, redfish continues to come in from other areas. Much of the redfish being served in restaurants is corvina, an almost identical fish from Central America.)

11. Catfish. There is much controversy among catfish lovers as to whether wild catfish or farm-raised are better. I think this is a simple matter. Farm-raised catfish is vastly better than the nasty cats that people used to fish out of the lake and river. But it is not quite as good as this area's premium catfish, from the swamp-lake channels around Des Allemands. Either form of catfish surpasses its cheap-fish reputation. There is nothing like the taste of catfish, which has a unique sweet corniness. No matter what anybody tells you, keep in mind that the only way to eat catfish is fried—preferably coated in cornmeal. The best places to go to for fried catfish are **Barrow's Shady Inn, Bozo's,** and **Middendorf's**. **Mr. B's** and the **Bon Ton** make great finger-food catfish appetizers.

12. Yellowfin tuna. This is the red-meat tuna of sushi bars and nouvelle-Creole fish grills. Neither way does it taste or look anything like the stuff you get in cans. Tuna sells very well in restaurants, despite a penchant cooks have for grossly overcooking the fish. The fish is best cooked like a medium-rare steak—crusty on the outside, pink-red in the middle. When cooked until all the color is gone, tuna gets like sponge rubber and tastes not much better. It grills beautifully and may be the best possible fish for blackening. Look for it those ways at **Bayou Ridge Cafe, Commander's, Mr. B's, Brigtsen's,** and **K-Paul's**. Quite a few chefs like to treat tuna to an Oriental-style marinade or sauce; this has good results at **Gambrill's** and the **Grill Room**.

13. Drum. A tricky one. The black drum is a relative of the redfish, but it is tougher and not as tasty—especially if the fillets came from a large black drum. Some restaurants are featuring a small black drum called "puppy drum," and this is delicious—a lot like speckled trout, I find.

14. Grouper. My best experiences with grouper would rank it higher than this, but I've found it inconsistent. It's a big fish, and my guess is that its goodness depends on which part of the fish your piece came from. Grouper has gigantic, snow-white flakes and is very low in oil content. It's good grilled or sauteed, especially when accompanied by a cream sauce. I've done well with the fish at **Le Jardin, Arnaud's, Christian's,**

and **Galatoire's**, among other places.

15. **Amberjack.** Like grouper, amberjack has long been a staple fish in Florida, but just recently started appearing here. It too is somewhat variable, but it can be excellent. It has long, firm flakes and grills up nicely, especially when heavily seasoned. **Andrea's** does a barbecue-shrimp-style amberjack that's terrific. **Christian's** has smoked it to good effect.

16. **Salmon trout, rainbow trout, and brook trout.** All of these come from a long distance from New Orleans, usually frozen. They are much smaller than and taste completely different from our local speckled trout. They are usually served whole, either grilled or sauteed.

For recommendations on shellfish, see **Crabs, Crawfish, Oysters,** and **Shrimp.** For a great local fish recipe, see **Trout Meuniere.**

Fitzgerald's

West End Park, Lakefront. 282-9254. 11:30 a.m.-10 p.m. Tues.-Sun., till 11 p.m. Fri. and Sat. AE, MC, V. $$

From the sidewalk, Fitzgerald's is the most interesting-looking restaurant at West End Park. It's mounted on pilings above the lake waters, and for decades it has been one of the city's best-known names for seafood. For the last one or two of those decades, however, it has not been very good. As this book went to press the restaurant came under new ownership, with a promise of drastic revisions. I hope the place comes back.

★★Five Happiness

3605 S. Carrollton, Mid City. 482-3935. 11:30 a.m.-3 p.m. seven days; 5-10:30 p.m. Mon.-Sat.; till 11:30 Fri. & Sat.; Noon-10:30 p.m. Sun. AE, CB, DC, MC, V. $$

The dining room is comfortable, the menu is (for a neighborhood Chinese place) ambitious, and the regular patrons are many. But my luck here has been just average. The best meals have been on Saturday and Sunday noons, when they have a "den-shen" (a.k.a. dim sum) menu available for the asking. There are few selections, the best of them the steamed, shrimp-stuffed cabbage leaves. The rest of the menu is the standard collection of Cantonese, Szechuan, and Mandarin dishes. While I have not been greatly displeased by any of them, in every case my mind wanders to the four or five places I know of that cook the item before me better.

★ ★ ★ Flagons

3222 Magazine, Uptown. Reservations 895-6471. Bistro: 11:30 a.m.-2:30 p.m. Mon.-Sat.; 6-10 p.m. Mon.-Thurs., till 11 p.m. Fri. & Sat. Wine bar: 11:30 a.m.-1 a.m. seven nights; till 2 a.m. Fri. & Sat.; till-Midnight Sun. Food served in bar till Midnight. AE, MC, V. $$$

Flagons has a dual personality. Both sides are engaging. The original Flagons, the first wine bar in the city, is still one of the best in the country, with upwards of 40 wines by the glass. The darkish, antique premises serves an abbreviated menu of caviar, smoked salmon, cheeses, interesting sandwiches, and a few other light dishes. The crowd that hangs out here creates its own atmosphere; it's especially dense when the Magazine Street galleries are having openings.

The "Bistro" side of Flagons, added in 1986, is a full-fledged, comfortable restaurant. It is much brighter and more modern than the wine bar; in fact, it feels as if you're in a different establishment. Over the years, Flagons Bistro food has reached surprising peaks of goodness. Unfortunately, these have been punctuated with dark valleys. The succession of chefs—all of whom were encouraged to create by proprietress Eugenie Vasser—has varied widely in taste and ability. One of the more recent chefs installed a collection of robust Creole and Southern dishes that brought Flagons a long way from its early tiny-portion nouvelle preciousness.

The gratin of oysters with spinach and Pernod (nouvelle oysters Rockefeller), rigatoni pasta with four cheeses, turtle and black bean soups, and the vintner's salad are reliably delicious starters. The best of the new appetizers is the sauteed rabbit loin, paired with cabbage cooked with Champagne.

Many entrees here are daily specials. Three or four different fish species receive treatments attuned to their unique flavors daily; the grilling and sauteeing of the basic ingredient is skillfully executed. They are especially good with tuna here. I would stay away from the grilled trio of seafood; the portions are too small to take a decent grilling.

The best entree of all is roasted pork tenderloin, stuffed with andouille, glazed with a garlic-rosemary butter, served atop a pile of greens. As heavy as this might sound, it fairly leaps into the mouth and is a terrific blend of flavors and textures. Thick grilled lamb chops are rendered even more amusing by a sauce made with Dijon mustard and Stilton cheese. Rabbit is panneed, cut up, and mixed into angel hair pasta with bell peppers. Veal is turned out differently nightly; it is the most inconsistent thing on the menu. They also invent a pasta entree daily. At lunch, there are several salads composed of cooked meat or seafood morsels mixed into greens and vegetables.

The great dessert is the intense chocolate St. Emilion, a super-rich flourless cake. They also make light bread puddings with various fruit admixtures that are usually wonderful, and an excellent caramel custard.

The regular coffee is excellent, and this is one of the few places in town that consistently makes perfect espresso and cappuccino.

Wine is one of the great joys of dining at Flagons. Not only is the by-the-bottle list superb, but the enormous vairiety of wines by the glass allow one to match a wine to each course. (That can be, however, a litte expensive.) Service is a litte dull but generally efficient. They do lots of good special events here with winemakers.

FLAN. Restaurants that speak Spanish—particularly if the owners are Cuban—are the best purveyors of caramel custard, and flan is what they call it. See **Caramel Custard**.

FLORENTINE. Almost without exception, "florentine" means that there is spinach—usually creamed spinach—somewhere in the dish. It's a preparation you don't see as much as you used to. My favorite of the local florentine dishes is the trout florentine at **Antoine's**; **Andrea's** prepares a few dishes in the style (under the Italian form of the name, "Fiorentina") as specials. The veal florentine at **Vincent's** is also wonderful, completely avoiding the overrichness to which the dish is prone.

FOIE GRAS. This is the liver of a goose, duck, or other anseriform bird which has been forced to become abnormally fat. It used to be that the only way we ever saw this in the U.S. was in heavily processed form in a can from France. Now, however, foie gras—usually from ducks—is being produced in New York. It needs little preparation: just a light grilling, producing an incomparable rich, buttery flavor that I would nominate as my favorite taste. Few restaurants offer it regularly. **Henri**, as a restaurant serving Alsatian cuisine, necessarily has a lot of dishes involving foie gras, and they're the best in town at it. It is certainly the only restaurant making its own terrine de foie gras truffe in house. The stuff also turns up occasionally at **Le Jardin, Sazerac, Flagons, Windsor Court Grill Room,** and the **Versailles**.

FOOD. I know this entry is so general as to be almost ridiculous, but there are some important notes I want to make that don't fit anywhere else. The bedrock belief from which I write is that a restaurant with great food is noteworthy even if it has little in the way of service and atmosphere. On the other hand, a restaurant with poor food is unrecommendable—no matter how fine its surroundings, service, prices, or wine list.

Just like you, I know when something tastes good without having to think about it. But when I get in front of a typewriter and start analyzing why a dish was enjoyable, I come up with five qualities:

Freshness. There are some foods that are better in their canned or frozen form (San Marzano tomatoes and truffles on this side of the ocean, to name two), but they are rare exceptions. A restaurant that serves only fresh product has to do a lot of legwork to keep that standard; fresh fish is particularly troublesome. But nothing else makes as a dramatic difference in taste. I have to be reasonably satisfied in my mind that a restaurant uses fresh food exclusively before I can give it four or more stars. It is in this area that I think New Orleans restaurants have made the greatest strides in recent years.

Quality. Prime beef tastes better than choice. It's also much more expensive and harder to find. The same story holds for most other foodstuffs, from pasta to crabmeat to butter. The restaurant that buys the best will always have a head start.

Cooking skill. It would be nice if there were something like a batting average for cooks. Restaurateurs (other than those who themselves are chefs) tend to underrate the importance of the timing, nerves, and taste of a good cook. In fact, chain restaurants usually work under the belief that all they need are well researched, tightly controlled cooking procedures. They hire a minimally-skilled kitchen crew at low wages, hand them the formula, and then consider the job done. The results are predictable. Little local joints using second-rate raw materials and no recipes other than those in the cook's head usually do a much more delicious job.

Creativity. This is the most elusive quality for a restaurateur to capture, because it involves taking risks and never leaving well enough alone. The ability to create new forms of deliciousness is what marks the very best chefs and restaurants. It can be found in all corners of the restaurant business, French palaces to poor boy stands. Finding it makes the search worthwhile. The rigorous competition among restaurants these days makes them take this aspect of their kitchens more seriously. Unfortunately, some confuse novelty with creativity, and visual spectacle with taste. In both cases, the first usually precludes the second.

Consistency. This is a tough one. It is not in the nature of human beings to perform any task exactly the same way twice. But problems can be avoided if there are certain overriding standards of taste. For example, the oysters Trufant at Commander's Palace have never looked or tasted the same from sampling to sampling. But they are always good, because the basic elements are there: big oysters, fresh cream, bubbling hotness, and sufficiency of seasoning. (It must also be said that the same taste might not taste the same way twice to a critic or any other eater. Ask anybody in the wine business who has sampled the same wine two days in a row and taken notes.)

FOOD COURTS. I'll let you make up your own joke about attorneys specializing in apple tort law or whatever, and just go ahead and pronounce my own sentence. Food courts in shopping malls may represent a new appeal on behalf of fast food, but the case can be dismissed on summary judgment. The only solid achievement of the local food courts is that they introduced pizza by the slice to New Orleans. (The best pizza in town is sold by **Dante's Pizza Cafe**, a mall operation.) Some eaters like the salad bars, poor boy and muffuletta shops, and fried-or-baked-potato places which are food court staples. I find them of minimal interest. The worst food court eats emerge from the Oriental, fried seafood, and Philadelphia cheese-steak booths.

Mall dining is also uncomfortable. The frequent difficulty in finding a clean table and the universal plastic utensils and paper plates make a mockery of the joy of eating.

The first time I wrote this entry, I made a lot of specific recommendations in the larger food courts. By the time I came back through to check facts, almost all of the places I named were out of business. So I added the new places, but they had drastically changed by the next rewrite. This should tell us something. (What it tells me is to give up trying to review specific food court outlets.)

Here is a list of the major food courts in the New Orleans area, rated by our star system:

1. ★★★**Jackson Brewery**. Lots of variety, from booths to sit-down places, and an emphasis on local cuisine.
2. ★★★**Esplanade Mall, Kenner**. Good variety, including Dante's Pizza and Cafe du Monde.
3. ★★**Plaza in Lake Forest**. Dante's and a great popcorn place.
4. ★★**Belle Promenade Mall, Gretna**. A decent Philly cheese steak.
5. ★★**Oakwood Mall**. Mrs. Wheat's meat pies at Ted's; good baked potatoes and coffee.
6. ★**New Orleans Centre**. Second-rate everything, and plenty of it. The stores, however, are terrific, and Macy's has a great little lunch counter.
7. ★**Canal Place**. Lots of mediocre booths in a mall of great shops.
8. ★**Riverwalk**. Much fanfare, little decent food. Constant turnover.
9. **Place St. Charles**. Beautiful place, terrible food.

★★Fortune Garden

3804 Williams Blvd., Kenner. 443-4114. 11:30 a.m.-10 p.m. Mon.-Fri.; till 11 p.m. Fri.; Noon-11 p.m. Sat.; Noon-10 p.m. Sun. CB, DC, MC, V. $$

Fortune Garden has one of the most unusual Chinese menus in the area. In recent times the food has not shown its former consistency and polish, but it's still worthwhile. The most interesting of the first courses sets the tone: cold spiced jellyfish, whose strips look just like you'd expect them to but which feel almost crunchy in the mouth. That's really good, as are the other cold items: the pickled cabbage, the smoked fish, and the spiced beef. There is a decent hot-and-sour soup and a well-made crab-and-asparagus broth to keep things moving along well.

The best of the entrees is worth a special trip to this restaurant all by itself. It's the rice-smoked chicken, and it consists of bite-sized morsels of the bird with an elusive, delectable smoky flavor and a concentrated, dry texture. No sauce—nothing but chicken. Also good is the ta-chien chicken with its hot sauce and vegetables, the yu-shiang dishes with their orange peppery sauce, the satay beef with its unique sauce of fresh spinach, and the very hot orange-flavor beef. The whole braised fish is gigantic and delicious, if a bit troublesome to eat and somewhat overcooked. There's a long list of vegetable dishes; particularly good is the sauteed spinach with sesame seeds.

Peking duck—served with an optional soup made from the bones—sounds better than it is.

FRENCH FRIES. At least 99 percent of the French fries served in New Orleans are made from frozen product, and are therefore unacceptable to the discriminating palate. The handful of restaurants which cut, blanch, and fry their own potatoes get my special thanks; theirs are the only fries that taste like potatoes. **Ruth's Chris Steak House not only cuts fresh French fries, but does so in five different shapes, all delicious. Cafe Savanna, Casamento's, Charlie's, Crescent City, Liuzza's, Schweickhardt's, Uglesich's, and Ye Olde College Inn** are the entire remainder of the honor roll.

The last words in French fries, however, are pomme de terre soufflees—souffle potatoes, those wonderful balloonlike jobs they do at **Antoine's** and a few other places. See **Souffle Potatoes.**

FRENCH RESTAURANTS. New Orleans is not really a French restaurant town, and nobody will agree with that faster than French restaurateurs. We have always had a lot of places with French names on their doors and menus, but the cooking is typically Creole. The French chef brave enough to cook authentically French without Creole touches is rare. The best real French restaurants hereabouts are **Crozier's, Henri** and **Louis XVI** in the deluxe category, and the more moderate **La Crepe Nanou** and **L'Economie.**

FRIED SEAFOOD. Despite the increasing popularity of grilled fish, when you say "seafood restaurant" most Orleanians think of huge platters of deep-fried everything, served in a very casual setting. Such restaurants have been around since before the Civil War; then as now, the classic venue was the lakefront. (It's unfortunate that most of the seafood places on the lake are mediocre or worse.)

The seafood platter is the yardstick by which most people measure a fried seafood restaurant. The platter typically includes fried oysters, shrimp, fish (rarely specified, but usually trout or catfish), and some variant of stuffed crab, along with French fries and maybe hush puppies. A high-class seafood platter includes a fried soft shell crab. Seafood platters usually amount to less than the sum of their parts, since few restaurants cook the various seafoods separately. This is essential, since if everything is cooked together it all tastes the same, and when the soft-shell is perfect, the shrimp will be overcooked.

Two restaurants that I'm certain fry the different elements of their seafood platters seperately are **Bozo's** and **Ralph and Kacoo's**. Other good full-menu fried seafood restaurants are **Bruning's, The Bounty, Cafe Atchafalaya, Drago's, Fury's, Lakeview Seafood, Middendorf's,** and **Mike Anderson's. Casamento's,** an oyster specialist, and **Barrow's,** a catfish house, are also deft fryers of their particular seafoods.

There is one more question to consider: cornmeal versus flour as a fried-fish coating. I like both, but I like cornmeal a little better, especially on oysters and catfish; I enjoy the extra crunch they provide. On the other hand, the flour coating—particularly when an egg wash is used—is a bit more elegant and complex.

★★Fury's

724 Martin Behrman Ave. (half-block lakeside of Veterans), Metairie. 834-5646. 11 a.m.-10 p.m. seven days; till 11 p.m. Fri. & Sat. AE, CB, DC, D, MC, V. $

Fury's is an out-of-the-way Metairie seafood house run by a West End refugee. It is very popular with a growing following. Indeed, it's tough to get a table from which to watch the television in the dining room on Fridays and Saturdays. The menu is straight-ahead New Orleans fried seafood, coated with flour and fried to a very agreeable lightness. The West End-style fried seafood platter includes oysters, shrimp, soft-shell crab, a couple of fish fillets (all fried) and a stuffed crab. It's good, hot, and greaseless. They also prepare an all-broiled seafood platter, but this is less good. The French fries are nothing, but the onion rings are far above average. The dining room is small but comfortable, with a decidedly neighborhood feel.

G as in grillades and grits

★ ★ ★ ★ Galatoire's

209 Bourbon, French Quarter. No reservations. 525-2021. 11:30 a.m.-9 p.m. Tues.-Sat., Noon-9 p.m. Sun. No credit cards. $$$

Galatoire's has the best food of the old-line French Quarter restaurants. In fact, it has some of the best food in New Orleans, and it's a good choice for those who want to get the maximum feel of New Orleans from one meal. No advance planning is necessary, since they don't take reservations anyway. If you go between about 1:30 and 6:00 p.m., you should find immediate seating in the one large room. Brightly lit with naked light bulbs interspersed with motionless ceiling fans, it gains added dimension from mirrors that line the two long walls. Service is almost that of a casual restaurant.

Galatoire's hardcover eight-page menu is a lengthy catalog whose depths could only be plumbed by a compulsive. Most of the specialties are listed on page two, but others are scattered throughout the book, and some great dishes are not on the menu at all. In crawfish season, for example, they do a great etouffee, the better crawfish Yvonne (browned butter, artichokes, and mushrooms), and an interesting cold crawfish ravigote.

Galatoire's is primarily a seafood restaurant, and the best starters are the big, firm shrimp remoulade (with a zappy sauce made from scratch), oysters en brochette (fried with bacon and oysters alternating on a skewer), oysters Rockefeller (dark green lobes of spinachy sauce atop a plate of oysters), crabmeat maison (mayonnaise sauce and capers), and canape Lorenzo (a sleeper: a concoction of crabmeat and hollandaise on a piece of toast). The soups du jour are great stuff, especially Wednesday's potato and ham and Sunday's homemade vegetable (the latter has giant chunks of brisket sticking up like icebergs). The gumbo, turtle and artichoke-and-oyster soups are, oddly, not very good. The green salad with garlic is my usual choice in that course, although the salad maison (including a bunch of vegetables, some canned) and the entree-size Godchaux seafood salad fit certain moods.

If pompano are running nice, a broiled fillet of that superlative fish with the restaurant's distinctive toasty brown-butter meuniere sauce will be as good a seafood dish as you can eat. Trout meuniere is similarly good, fried to an incomparable lightness. Trout Marguery is the house specialty; a not-so-good piece of trout is poached and covered with a buttery, elusively spicy, ivory-hued sauce with shrimp and mushrooms. *Shrimp Marguery*, which is more or less an order of sauce, is better. Like every other restaurant in town, Galatoire's menu has had to admit some new fish species lately; of particular merit are the "white tuna" (sounds better than its real name, oilfish), sheepshead, and grouper.

If you like crabmeat, you're in the right place. Crabmeat Yvonne is a loose casserole with mushrooms, artichokes, and pimientos, oily but good. Crabmeat Sardou has the white morsels atop creamed spinach and an artichoke bottom, all covered with hollandaise.

Galatoire's best meat entrees are the simply broiled chops of lamb, veal and beef—perhaps napped with the restaurant's very good bearnaise. The meat is of good pedigree and gets a pleasant slight charring. Some people like the chicken Clemenceau, but it's just a broiled chicken with a bunch of peas, garlic, and potatoes dumped over it. As for the offbeat dishes on the menu, use the look on the waiter's face as your guide.

For dessert I like the crepes maison (filled with currant jelly and topped with toasted almonds and orange zest, awash in Grand Marnier). The coupe princesse is ice cream and canned fruit cocktail with the same liqueur and, believe it or not, it's more than acceptable. Although the coffee is not as rich as it once was, it still sets your knees to wobbling if you drink too much of it. The wine list is short and inexpensive and perfectly matches the food.

Equally elusive as becoming a member of the Boston Club or writing a hit novel is getting a house account at Galatoire's. After you've written several dozen checks for your meal (which they very readily accept, unlike credit cards), they might vouchsafe you a number.

★ ★ ★ ★ Gambrill's

94 Friedrichs (at Metairie Rd.), Old Metairie. Reservations 831-6917. 11 a.m.-2:30 p.m. and 5-10:00 p.m. Mon.-Thurs.; till 10:30 p.m. Fri. & Sat. AE, DC, MC, V. $$$

Many small, pleasant dining rooms were carved from a turn-of-the-century mansion in Old Metairie to create this low-key, very consistent restaurant. The owner and chef is Steve Gamble, skillful alumnus of the line at Commander's Palace. Not surprisingly, there is much of the Commander's culinary style at Gambrill's, including such elements as scrupulousness about the freshness of raw materials, a devotion to Creole flavors, and a need to innovate.

Start with the superb lump crabmeat ravigote, with its light, horseradish-tinged mayonnaise sauce. Escargots en croute, which involve not just pastry over the snails but mushrooms under them, are delectable in the standard garlic butter. The sauteed shrimp pesto has a marvelous herbalness and toothsome shrimp. Gamble makes terrific soups; his corn and crab bisque and turtle soup are flawless.

The seafood is pretty here. Trout with pecans gets a particularly good rendering. More newfangled are the steaks of such things as tuna and swordfish, abetted by sauces with hints of the Orient. Crabmeat lovers will be smitten by like the rich casserole of lump meat with mushrooms and cream. At lunchtime you find quite a few blackened fish, with good reason: Gamble's ex-partner Gerhard Brill created the blackened concept.

The most interesting non-seafood entree at Gambrill's is a plate of thin veal steaks with a fine Normandy-style sauce of apples, calvados, and cream. It's rich, but wonderful. Tournedos Rossini is an old warhorse not enough restaurants serve; this is a fine filet with foie gras in a ruddy brown demi-glace sauce. The rack of lamb is sliced, fanned out, and moistened with a fine port wine sauce. Lighter but no less flavorful is the raspberry chicken, crusty at the edges and set off with an underlayer of spinach. The same dish with duck is richer and also delicious.

The wine list is pretty good and has shockingly low prices (in fact, all the prices here are attractive). Desserts are homemade and include a bread pudding soufflee that isn't quite as good as the Commander's original, but still recommendable. Service is unpolished but decent.

★★Garce's

4200 d'Hemecourt, Mid-City. 488-4734. 10:30 a.m.-9 p.m. Mon., Wed., Thurs., till 10 p.m. Fri. and Sat.; 1-9 p.m. Sun. MC, V. $$

This well-hidden cafe started as a Cuban market. It made such good sandwiches and plate specials, however, that the dining room aspect of the place took over. Still the best food here is the Cuban sandwich and its variant, the media noche. These are quite a bit like poor boys but have a touch all their own. The fillings are ham, roast pork, cheese, lettuce, tomato, pickles, and mustard. What sets the sandwich apart is that it's grilled on both sides in a gadget that flattens the finished product out somewhat. Crusty, warm, and wonderful. They put forth spectacular black beans as a side dish, and every day brings a plate special of anything from a Cuban steak to paella (a nice try). Anglos are more than welcome to join in the lively neighborhood party that goes on here most of the time.

★★★★Gautreau's

1728 Soniat (at Danneel, four blocks lake side of St. Charles Ave.), Uptown. Reservations 899-7397. 11:45 a.m.-2:30 p.m. Mon.-Fri.; 6-10 p.m. Tues.-Sat; till 11 p.m. Fri. & Sat. MC, V. $$$

The closing of Gautreau's in early 1990 upset a lot of Uptowners, for whom the tiny restaurant represented the apex of the Nouvelle Uptown Creole Restaurant Revolution. So only a few months of darkness persisted before a consortium of former customers bought the restaurant and re-opened it. They did not change it physically. The former antique neighborhood pharmacy still has just a dozen tables; they are still always full. The tile floors, tin ceilings, and glossy, glassy walls still make for an uncomfortable ambient sound level.

Most encouraging of all, the new owners kept the basic Gautreau's menu concepts: constant change, well-below-average prices, and originality. Gautreau's new chef is as eclectic as the old guy was. If you had to name it, you might say his cuisine is Nouvelle American with a Southwest accent. This differs almost totally from the former new-Creole menu, yet the same spirit lives on. It is still unlikely, for example, that any dish on the menu will be familiar from any other restaurant.

It is impossible to predict what may be in the offing when you get to Gautreau's. But a typical menu one week started with crab cakes, sharpened with tomato salsa, mellowed with basil tartar sauce; crawfish cocktail taken in the direction of ceviche, with lime, cilantro, and cucumbers; and fusilli pasta with wild mushrooms, cherry tomatoes, and asparagus. All of that was delicious and fresh-tasting. On the other hand, a soup from that menu—shiitake mushrooms with celery root puree, leeks and pine nuts—was more contrivance than creation.

Gautreau's always put a great filet mignon on the table, dressed with offbeat, well-made sauces. That tradition continues; on the night I tried it, the sauce was tarragon butter. The side dishes here tend to the delightfully quirky; the steak, for example, came with gratin of fresh beets and potatoes, both still slightly crunchy and better than you might expect that pairing to be. The roast chicken is another perennial specialty. Although they don't say so, this is a free-range bird with a slightly wild taste. The side with this was garlic mashed potatoes—delicious.

The best of Gautreau's seafood has been a thick slab of tuna treated like a black-and-blue steak. It's charred on the outside, but red within (cool at the center). This is to my taste the best possible way to serve a good cut of tuna. You will probably also be offered some soft-shell crabs with something like the arugula and lime-ginger sauce I tried. You will find it eminently edible.

The best desserts so far are creme brulee flavored with orange and key lime pie tinged with tequila and (yes) banana whipped cream. The wine list remains abbreviated but thoughtfully chosen. Service is performed by some of the old hands and is reasonably polite and efficient.

★ ★ ★ Genghis Khan

4053 Tulane Ave. (near S. Carrollton), Mid-City. Reservations 482-4044. 5:30-11 p.m. Tues.-Sun.; till 11:30 p.m. Fri. & Sat. AE, MC, V. $$

Neither the location nor the surroundings are what you could call high-rent, but the Genghis Khan is sophisticated and popular. The menu is Korean—clearly Oriental in appearance and taste, yet very different from the more familiar Chinese and Japanese cuisines.

Lots of good appetizers and side dishes. Fried mandu is a fat fried wonton, served with an assortment of sauces. The half-dozen different tempuras—ranging from the familiar shrimp and oyster to the odder squid and pineapple—are all fried to a greaseless toastiness. Kim is seaweed dried to diaphanous squares, used to wrap the lightly-fried rice, and eaten with another complement of sauces. Kimchee is a Korean commonplace—spicy pickled cabbage—and it makes a good cold side dish, as does spinach namul, with its slightly oily, nutty flavor.

The entree to get is the whole fish—dredged in flour, fried, then disassembled at the table. Also fine is the very spicy chicken Imperial. Some big grilled shrimp come out with slices of what amounts to lobster pate. Bulgoki, the Korean national dish, is beef grilled to a char, napped with a thick, slightly sweet sauce.

Music is a highlight of dinner here. Proprietor Henry Lee plays first chair violin with the New Orleans Symphony, and he frequently performs—as do other classical musicians. Service is deft and spirited. Nothing much for dessert.

★ Ginza

3225 Williams Blvd., Kenner. 443-2749. 11:30 a.m.-2 p.m. Mon. & Wed.-Fri. 5:30-10 p.m. Wed.-Mon.; till 10:30 Fri. & Sat. AE, MC, V. $$

Ginza started out as a hybrid of French and Japanese cooking techniques, but when that didn't fly it became a conventional Japanese restaurant and sushi bar. If I were living in the neighborhood I wouldn't hesitate to dine here, but it's not worth crossing town for. The sushi is good to very good, the tempura and teriyaki are decent, but the sukiyaki is the worst I've ever eaten. Guys with legs as long as mine will find that their limbs will be jammed uncomfortably against some sort of shelf underneath the handsome, thick, light-colored wooden tables.

★★ Giorlando's

741 Bonnabel (just south of Veterans), Metairie. 835-8593. 11 a.m.-7:30 p.m. Mon.-Fri. 11 a.m.-4 p.m. Sat. No credit cards. $

The dining room is kept in the dark by drawn curtains over the windows and doors, and this gives the place the feeling of a neighborhood bar. The roast beef poor boy also give you this feeling, because it has that indefinable, classic taste: tender beef, a rich, thick gravy, warm toasted bread, and fresh dressings. All the other sandwiches are assembled with equal care. The pastrami and corned beef poor boys—both of which are harder to find than one would wish—are terrific. The rest of the self-service menu consists of the standards of neighborhood chalkboard cuisine, with a fair amount of red-sauced Italian specials daily. Prices are very low and the food is put in your hands quickly.

★ ★ ★ Great Wall

2023 Metairie Rd., Old Metairie. 833-2585. 11:30 a.m.-2:30 p.m. Mon.-Fri.; 4:30 p.m.-9:30 p.m. Mon.-Sat.; till 10 p.m. Fri. & Sat. 4:30-9 p.m. Sun. MC, V. $

Dreary-looking outside, recently redecorated but still modest within, the Great Wall has one of the best Chinese kitchens in the area. The menu emphasizes the spicier Szechuan cuisine, cooked with liberal pepper doses and an expert balancing of flavors. The hot and sour soup makes an agreeably nose-clearing starter. I also like to start with fried dumplings, with their good soy-and-garlic sauce.

The Great Wall's Peking duck is the top of the local crop. The skin is crisper and the meat less fatty than I usually find. You spread the well-made, doughy crepes with the thick, oily, aromatic brown hoisin sauce, and then roll them up with sliced scallions and duck strips. It's an elegant repast that makes a fine first course for four or more, or an entree for two.

Simpler, but no less good, is yu-shiang shredded beef; the hot flavors play intriguingly with the sweet fruitiness of the bamboo shoots. Beef with orange peel here may be the hottest Chinese dish I've ever encountered—good, too. A meal of just spicy food gets to tasting all the same, which makes one look for dishes like the king crab with straw mushrooms and broccoli, lemon chicken, and mo-shu pork. Each of those is unimpeachably tasty.

For dessert, there are good banana fritters, available with the candy coating frozen at the table. Service is minimal.

GRILLADES AND GRITS. This is a terrific Creole breakfast or brunch specialty. Prepared the old-fashioned way, the grillades would be cheap cuts of veal simmered forever in a spicy, chunky red sauce, all of which would be poured over hot grits. The dish has been greatly cleaned up for serving in restaurants—the veal shoulder, for example, generally becomes medallions of baby white. That's all right, but what restaurants generally mess up is the grits part of the dish. Grits are delicious when they're limpid, semi-liquid, and buttery. They're horrible when cold and lumpy, as they too often are. The best grillades and grits in New Orleans are at **Brennan's**. The veal is beautiful, the reddish-brown sauce is spicy and delicious, and the grits are always perfect. Also good at this dish are **Flagons, Mr. B's, Commander's Palace** (which makes the grits into fried cakes), **La Gauloise**, and **the Coffee Pot**.

Grillades and grits are so delicious and so distinctly Creole that I think you ought to have a recipe for it.

GRILLADES AND GRITS

2 lbs. veal round or shoulder, sliced about ½ inch thick
2 cloves garlic, minced
1 tsp. salt
½ Tbs. coarsely cracked black pepper
¼ tsp. cayenne
¼ cup flour
¼ cup vegetable oil
1 large onion, chopped coarsely
1 bell pepper, chopped coarsely
2 stalks celery, chopped coarsely
¼ cup dry red wine
2½ cups veal stock
2 medium ripe tomatoes, seeded and peeled, chopped coarsely
¾ cup grits
½ stick butter or margarine

1. Blend the garlic, salt, pepper, and cayenne. Sprinkle it onto the veal and pound it lightly. Cut the veal into bite-size pieces.
2. Heat a large, heavy saucepan over high heat and sear the veal quickly—no more than about 20 seconds on each side. Remove the veal and keep it warm.
3. In the same saucepan, make a medium brown roux: heat the oil briefly and sprinkle in the flour, stirring constantly to keep it from burning.
4. Add the onions, bell pepper, and celery to the roux and saute until onions turn translucent. Add the wine and, when it comes to a boil, add the veal and veal stock. Bring to a boil. Reduce heat to a simmer and cook, uncovered, until sauce has reduced to one-half original volume. The slower you cook this, the better it tastes.
5. Add tomatoes and cook until they become soft.
6. Cook grits according to package directions, adding butter when grits are near desired thickness. Serve grillades and lots of sauce atop grits, or serve the grits on the side.

Serves four to six.

GRILLED FISH. In 1976, **Cafe Sbisa** started a trend that wound up adding a new dimension to New Orleans seafood cookery. In addition to the standard fried, broiled, and boiled, it offered its fish grilled over charcoal—a method previously reserved strictly for hamburgers. Now you can get grilled fish in many restaurants of all kinds around the city. Grilled fish is also an indicator dish; if you find it on a menu, chances are you're in a Nouvelle Creole restaurant.

Cafe Sbisa still grills a large assortment of fish, though not as well as it has in the past. **Mr. B's** improved upon the idea by doing the deed over a hickory wood fire, and produced the progenitor of blackened redfish. The best grillers of fish (and, usually, other things too) include **Pelican Club, Commander's Palace, Copeland's, Flagons, Louis XVI, Windsor Court Grill Room,** and **Upperline.**

GRILL ROOM. See Windsor Court Grill Room.

GRITS. See Grillades and Grits.

GROUPER. See Fish.

GUACAMOLE. Is it a salad? a sauce? a spread? a dip? Look—I'm not going to answer every single one of your questions. I can tell you that guacamole is made from avocados, with touches of onions, garlic, milk or sour cream, tomatoes, and pepper. **Vera Cruz** makes what I think is the best local guacamole; **El Patio, Casa Garcia,** and **Castillo's** also serve decent versions. **Cu-Co's** makes guacamole tableside to order, but it's just su-so.

GUMBO. One of the essential dishes of Louisiana cooking, gumbo can be described as either a thin stew or a thick, chunky soup. And I just ran out of definition. Because more than any other dish in the cuisine, gumbo lends itself to interpretation. Every cook has his or her own distinctive gumbo. It will, however, probably fall into one of the two major phyla: seafood-and-okra, or chicken-and-file.

Seafood gumbo is by far the more common. In fact, there is hardly a Creole or Cajun restaurant that doesn't have it; it is especially unavoidable on Fridays. It's generally a seafood stock with a brown roux, okra (the African name for which is the origin of the word "gumbo"), and rice. The seafood can be just about anything: shrimp, crab claws, and oysters are most common. Sausage is often in there somewhere. A good gumbo has a wonderful aroma and a mildly spicy flavor. My favorites are those made at **Bruning's, Chez Helene, Delmonico, Drago's, Fury's, Gumbo Shop, New Orleans Hamburger and Seafood Company** (yes!), and **Ralph & Kacoo's.**

Chicken-andouille gumbo, after a long absence from menus, became trendy a few years ago. While it looks much like seafood gumbo, the taste is totally different (or should be). It's made with a chicken stock, a dark roux, onions and peppers, pieces of chicken (or duck or turkey or quail), andouille or some other smoky, spicy sausage, and sometimes a bit of seafood. It is flavored with file (pronounced fee-lay), an aromatic powdered herb (sassafras leaves). Most restaurants have the file already in the soup; others bring it to the table so you can add a pinch or two (which is all you need). Without a doubt the best chicken-andouille gumbo in the world is made at **Mr. B's,** where they call it gumbo ya-ya. It is marvelously spicy, oily, and chunky with big pieces of chicken and great andouille. A similar recipe is found at **Commander's Palace**. Also good for file gumbo are **Stephen and Martin, Bayou Ridge Cafe,** and **Gambrill's**. Bozo's makes a highly distinctive and delicious version, much lighter than most and without a roux. The quail gumbo at **La Provence** is the fanciest poultry gumbo I've encountered; there's a whole roasted quail in there, and when you cut into it the rice stuffing falls into the soup.

I nominate chicken-andouille gumbo as one of the Ten Greatest New Orleans Dishes, so here's a recipe. This is the one I grew up eating.

CHICKEN-ANDOUILLE GUMBO
1 3-lb. frying chicken
½ cup plain flour
½ cup vegetable oil
1 large onion, chopped
1 red bell pepper, chopped
2 cloves garlic, chopped
2 green onions, chopped
2 quarts chicken stock
2 quarts water
3 sprigs chopped flat-leaf parsley
1 Tbs. salt
1 tsp. black pepper
¼ tsp. Tabasco
2 bay leaves
¼ tsp. dried thyme
1 lb. andouille or smoked sausage
2-3 cups cooked rice

1. Cut up the chicken and fry the pieces in 2 Tbs. of the oil in a large kettle or Dutch oven over fairly high heat. Keep turning the chicken pieces until they begin to brown; they should not cook through. Remove the chicken and debone the pieces. Cut up the chicken meat into strips about a half-inch wide and reserve.

2. Add the flour and the rest of the oil to the pot and make as dark a roux as you can. The critical instruction about making a roux is to avoid burning it. This is accomplished by constant stirring and watching the heat.

3. Add the onion, pepper, garlic, and green onions and saute them in the roux over medium heat until the onions begin to brown.

4. Add the chicken stock, water, parsley, salt, pepper, Tabasco, bay leaves, thyme, and chicken bones and bring to a boil. Slice the andouille into one-inch-thick discs and add to the pot. Lower the heat but keep the soup at a fast simmer. Skim excess fat thrown off by the sausage.

5. After 30 minutes, add chicken meat. Reduce heat to a slow simmer and cook the gumbo for one hour, or until chicken is tender. Stir every few minutes. Serve over cooked long-grain rice with a pinch or two of

file at the table. A great side dish is baked sweet potatoes, which are for some reason spectacularly delicious in combination with the gumbo.
Serves six to eight.

★ ★ ★ Gumbo Shop

630 St. Peter, French Quarter. 525-1486. 11 a.m.-11 p.m. seven days; AE, CB, DC, MC, V. $

"The Gumbo Shop" may be the best name ever conceived for a New Orleans restaurant. It conjures up images of an old place with black cooks and blacker pots full of authentic versions of the local classics. The restaurant looks the part, too, with its alley entranceway, tiny courtyard, and ancient-looking murals.

They don't make the city's best anything here, but the goodness across the menu is consistent. They make two kinds of gumbo: a very good seafood gumbo with okra, shrimp, crab, and rice, and a chicken-andouille gumbo that tastes good but too much like the seafood concoction. (The flavors should be completely different.)

They have all the other essentials of the cuisine here, plus a few flights of fancy. Red beans and rice are available every day and are very good: firm beans, creamy sauce, a nice length of smoked sausage. Jambalaya, shrimp Creole, and crawfish etouffee are all respectable representatives of those dishes. They grill and blacken both fish and chicken to spicy tidbits (they have a penchant for overcooking these things). The most complicated dish in the house is a baked trout atop spinach, all awash in hollandaise. Rich, but better than one would expect.

H as in hush puppies

★ ★ ★ Haagen-Dazs

8108 Hampson, Uptown. 861-1005. • 3313 Severn (next to Morning Call), Metairie. 456-9500. • 621 St. Peter, French Quarter. 523-4001. All: 11 a.m.-Midnight Sun.-Thurs., 11 a.m.-1 a.m. Fri. & Sat. No credit cards. $

Haagen-Dazs was there when the public demanded a better ice cream. The stuff is expensive but expensively made; in fact, if there could be any criticism of it it's that Haagen-Dazs is *too* full of butterfat. The flavors are natural, and there are no artificial colors, either; so we get a strawberry that really tastes like strawberry, but is a pale pink-brown instead of the bright red we're used to. My own favorite flavors are black cherry, Swiss almond vanilla, cookies and cream, and boysenberry sorbet. You can also get Tofutti—a kosher dessert made with bean curd—in many flavors. And malts, shakes, sundaes, and all the rest of it, including a reasonably good, too-rich approximation of the old-fashioned nectar soda.

HAMBURGERS. Let's get right to the point. Here are the five best hamburgers in New Orleans:

1. Port of Call
2. Snug Harbor
3. Streetcar Sandwiches
4. Camellia Grill
5. Houston's

The hamburger, without question the most popular of American dishes, is nevertheless thought of as the low end of the gourmet spectrum. This is because while a great hamburger is as enjoyable as any other food I can think of, great hamburgers are outnumbered by terrible hamburgers by a ratio of, I'd guess, about a million to one.

It is the hamburger's misfortune to appear convenient to cook and serve. In fact, a great hamburger requires at least as much attention to detail as most other first-class cooking. And the corners cut by most vendors of hamburgers—particularly the fast-food places—constitute the most heinous culinary crimes perpetrated in the world today.

I don't think that any person of taste would argue with the following criteria for The Ideal Hamburger:

The Bun. The Ideal Hamburger starts with a fresh bun no larger in diameter than the meat pattie it holds. It is toasted immediately before serving and is warm all the way through. The exterior has a bit of a crustiness, in the direction of that found on French bread.

The Beef. The Ideal Hamburger Pattie is ground on at least a daily basis from a good cut of fresh beef, choice grade or better. The best cuts are chuck and round, with about ten percent fat. After grinding it is rendered into the characteristic pattie shape by hand, and it should have no perfect geometric dimensions. A meat pattie pressed by hand, with little fissures here and there, cooks up far better than a burger punched out by a die or (the worst) a machine. Its diameter should be no more than five times its thickness, so that the inside can stay juicy.

The Grilling Method. The Ideal Hamburger doesn't begin to cook until you place your order. (It is in cooking your burger before you even arrive at the restaurant that most fast-food outfits go wrong.) The cooking surface can be either a flat-top griddle or a grill open to flames (preferably coming from charcoal or wood). But it is critical that the temperature be sufficiently hot to sear the exterior of the meat quickly, thereby sealing in the juices and creating a tasty, dark-brown crust.

The Seasonings. The chef (the person who prepares the Ideal Hamburger is a chef in my book) applies some seasoning to the beef while it's on the grill — salt and pepper at the very least, but preferably some other herbs and spices, judiciously applied, to add character. My own preference is for some chopped onions pressed right into the pattie, but this is not a necessary ingredient for Idealness.

The Dressings. If this is really the Ideal Hamburger, then no dressings are necessary. It should be delicious plain — as all of the top five above are. (I consider this the acid test of a great hamburger.) But since more people eat cheeseburgers than not-so-cheeseburgers, the Ideal Hamburger has a substantial layer of freshly-grated sharp Cheddar cheese. (Grated cheese gives a much better flavor release than sliced.) Other dressings like lettuce, tomatoes, pickles, etc. would only detract from the Ideal Hamburger. The addition of mustard or relish are okay, but mayonnaise or catsup get in the way of the Ideal Hamburger's flavor.

Hamburgers of note other than those at the beginning of this entry include the works of **Bud's Broiler, Cafe Savanna, Hard Rock Cafe, Hummingbird Grill, Lee's, Mr. B's** (at lunch), **New Orleans Hamburger and Seafood Company,** and **Ye Olde College Inn.**

★ ★ ★ Hana

8116 Hampson, Riverbend. 865-1634. 11:30 a.m.-10 p.m. seven days; till 11 p.m. Fri. & Sat. AE, MC, V.

Hana is a sushi bar in the Riverbend neighborhood, and already the collegiate segment of the Camellia Grill crowd has found and adopted it. The premises are fairly large, with seating on two levels and a long sushi bar. All the sushi and sashimi I've tried here was great, and some of it was perfect. The sea urchin, for example, has a particularly fine texture, taste, and temperature. None of the choices are especially offbeat, but the chefs tell all who will listen that a bunch of the lesser-known items on the wall chart are sometimes available. On occasion, they even offer the prized, rare fatty tuna called toro. About the only departure from standard procedure here—and a minor one at that—is that they serve a small pickled salad instead of miso soup with sushi orders.

At the tables they serve the customary assortment of teriyaki, tempura, and straight-ahead grilled fish. They assemble some of these items, along with small salads and a few more exotic things, into lovely dinners. These are typically presented in enameled wooden boxes with nine to twelve pockets, each with a different delicacy. Depending on how adventuresome you seem, you will get some very unusual and even delicious items in this assortment. On the other hand, they don't seem to get into sukiyaki and the like.

★ ★ ★ ★ Hansen's Sno-Bliz

4801 Tchoupitoulas, Uptown. 891-9788. Open Easter-Halloween 3-9 p.m. Tues.-Fri.; 2-9 Sun. Closed Mon. and (!) Sat. No credit cards.$

What would summer be in New Orleans without sno-balls? I can't imagine it. There are lots of good sno-ball stands around town, but Hansen's is in a class by itself. Mary and Ernest Hansen—some of the nicest people I've ever met—opened their place in 1939 and are still going strong. Ernest built the machine they still use. Mary is the chef: she hand-picks, washes, and cuts the ice, makes all the syrups from scratch daily, and does the actual grinding between talking with her thousands of friends. It's impossible to pick out a favorite flavor: ice cream with cream, nectar, lemonade, orangeade, peach, and almond are some personal favorites. The unique pink flavor called "Sno-Bliz" is an extra-tart sno-ball that could fit as a sorbet in a gourmet dinner. Sizes range from a small for about 50 cents to giant plastic barrels full of Sno-Bliz for $300 or $400. The latter are great for parties. The signs all over the walls make interesting reading while you wait in line, as you probably will. Hansen's is very popular among Tulane students and the many adults who have been coming here every summer of their lives.

★ ★ ★ Hard Rock Cafe

440 N. Peters, French Quarter. 529-5617. 11:30 a.m.-11 p.m. seven days; till midnight Fri. & Sat. AE, CB, DC, MC, V. $$

You've probably heard the phenomenal international success story of this Corvette of hamburger joints. Two Americans living in London missed the good ole cheeseburger, so they opened up a restaurant and gave it a rock 'n' roll theme. That was a magic combination that hit big everywhere it opened—including here, in the Marketplace building of the Jackson Brewery development. The appeal is to the 15-to-25 set; the two main elements of atmosphere are the museum of rock artifacts on the walls and the loud music.

The entrees range from steaks to grilled fish to salads, but there are three real specialties. The hamburger is made from freshly-ground, hand-formed beef, grilled to order over a superheated flame that gives it a nice crustiness. It's served nice and juicy on a rather dry, chewy whole-wheat bun with grated Cheddar and good dressings. It's far from the best in town, but still a superior piece of work. Better food is the barbecued chicken—a half-bird marinated in lime juice broiled to little areas of sweet char. It's one of the best simple chickens around.

The barbecued baby back ribs, with their watermelon barbecue sauce, sound better than they are; the ribs are overcooked and too big. Starters and sides are generally disappointing. The onion rings are just okay, the salads are haphazardly thrown onto the entree plate, and the French fries are frozen. The soups range from decent (black bean) to terrible. Desserts are another matter. The apple pie gives new meaning to the hyphenation "deep-dish," the pecan pie is crusty and nutty, and the brownie a la mode is a staggering richness of chocolate.

The service kids seem genuinely happy to be part of the scene, which takes on sardine-can characteristics on weekend evenings. By the way, the line at the front door may be for T-shirts and other precious Hard Rock memorabilia, so push past it for a table. There is often immediate seating at the counter in the back, which has the added advantages of a kitchen view and a lower decibel level.

★★ Harold's Texas Barbecue

3320 Houma Blvd. (just lake side of Veterans), Metairie. 456-2832. 11 a.m.-10 p.m. Mon.-Sat.; till 11 p.m. Fri. & Sat. AE, MC, V.$

Harold is from Georgia, but his style is reasonably true to that of the Lone Star State. At least by New Orleans standards, which are not especially stringent. The barbecue here is not perfect across the board, but the good things are very good. I like the brisket, which is smoked slowly to a nice burned edge, served in substantial portion with an undeniably delicious, spicy, well-balanced sauce. The ribs are far less successful—they're too big, for one thing. The decent smoked sausage and barbecued chicken round out the menu. Side dishes—cole slaw, baked beans, and potato salad—are excellent. Corn on the cob, the best in town, always seems to have been cooked to order: crisp and buttery. The small dining room has the right cowboy look, yet it is clean and comfortable.

HEALTH FOOD. I like what New Yorker writer Calvin Trillin said on this subject on Johnny Carson one night: "Health food makes me sick." Natural-foods restaurants typically replace unhealthy ingredients with more wholesome foodstuffs, but in fairly standard American dishes. The result is often a parody that insults the palate with a shocking poverty of taste. Tofu may be better for you than eggs, but in a blind taste test the egg version of a dish would probably beat the tofu by a margin of around 98 percent. Physical health is important, but so is mental health, and if I had to eat this stuff for the rest of my life I'd die early from slit wrists.

The better natural-food restaurants develop their cuisine from the bottom up, playing to their strengths. Health food places do best with salads, sandwiches, and pasta dishes. The best such menu here is that of **Back to the Garden**, which has several locations downtown; their salads, pastas, and vegetable entrees are all decent or better. The **Whole Foods Market** makes interesting vegetarian sandwiches, but also serves real food.

There's one more thing I dislike about health food: the smugness of some of those who sell it. They affect a snobbishness about their wares that equals that of the most pretentious French restaurant. If you opine that you don't like the food, they conclude that you're just unenlightened.

HIGH TEA. The English practice of stopping everything in mid-afternoon for a snack of light sandwiches, biscuits, and tea has managed to become established in a few of the first-class downtown hotels. Absolutely without a doubt the best of them is in the **Windsor Court's Salon**. Every afternoon from about two till five, the room becomes densely populated with handsomely-attired Uptown ladies, who pile quite a bit of light conversation atop the live classical string music. The tea sandwiches—of such things as cucumber, watercress, prosciutto, and chicken salad—actually have a bit of taste. And the scones are crumbly and hot, served with a couple of different butters and lemon curd. One may choose from among a half-dozen different teas, brewed from loose tea the way it should be. The ritual ends with a plate of petits fours and chocolate-dipped fruit.

Another good tea is served in the magnificent lobby of the **Westin Canal Place**. Although the service lacks the polish of the Windsor Court's—they use tea bags, for example—it's still a very pleasant experience. Afterwards, any men who have been forced to sit through it can walk across the lobby to The Bar, where they can knock back a neat shot of single-malt Scotch, of which there are more choices than there are of teas outside.

HOLLANDAISE. Egg yolks and butter whipped into a thick flow, jazzed up with cayenne and lemon, hollandaise is capable of enriching many foods. The most unlikely of them is eggs (hollandaise atop eggs is, after all, eggs on eggs) but it's here that the sauce reaches its local zenith, particularly as applied at **Brennan's**. Everybody makes hollandaise, but I have especially vivid memories of those at **Galatoire's**, **Commander's Palace**, and **Crozier's**. In the suburbs, they love to mix crabmeat and/or crawfish into hollandaise and slather it on top of fish or veal; this is to be avoided.

★ Home Furnishings Cafe

1600 Prytania, Lee Circle Area. 566-1707. 10 a.m.-6 p.m. Mon.-Sat. AE, MC, V. $

It's a furniture store, with interesting, modern stuff. For some reason, they decided they needed a cafe and there it is, like a small cafeteria, on the second floor. It's strictly lunch, and the menu is of foods on the lighter side: salads, quiches, soups, a daily special, and a handful of desserts. One recent addition of interest is a thick, hand-made, grilled-to-order hamburger. All of this is better than it has any right to be, and the ambience is engaging.

★★ Home Plate Inn

4033 Tulane Ave., Mid-City. 488-9113. 10 a.m.-6 p.m. Mon.-Sat. No credit cards. $

The Home Plate Inn began as a place to have a sandwich or a beer after the New Orleans Pelicans' baseball games, played until 1960 in Pelican Stadium across the street. Baseball and stadium are gone now, but the good neighborhood "bar & rest." food for which the Home Plate became known remains. You place your order at the bar for a roast beef poor boy, an oyster loaf, or a beans-and-rice-type daily special, then you carry it back to one of the tables, all of which have a good view of the always-on television set. You never know what's going to be on the menu here; one day, they had some terrific hot tamales.

HOT AND SOUR SOUP. I order this automatically whenever I go to a Chinese restaurant; I've not lately seen a place that doesn't have it. Properly made, it's wonderful: a thick, glossy broth of chestnut hue, filled with matchstick-size pieces of pork and water chestnuts, straw mushrooms, curdles of egg, and slabs of tofu. It often doesn't make much of an impression with the first spoonful, but the pepper builds up on your palate as you go, till the last few slurps taste both very peppery and very good. The best hot and sour soup in town is at the **Peking**. Other tasty ones can be found at **Trey Yuen, Mr. Tai's, Golden Dragon, Dragon's Garden, Great Wall, Mandarin Cafe,** and **China Doll.** A problem I find in many versions of hot and sour soup is the presence in it of the sweet-glazed roast pork Chinese restaurants serve as an appetizer; this throws the flavor of the soup off.

HOTEL RESTAURANTS. Hotel restaurants exist in a world apart from their independent competitors. A major hotel is expected by its guests to have a restaurant or two, and so it must. Since hotel guests on average eat at least one lunch or dinner in the hotel and will never be back, hotel restaurants have little impetus to rise above the level of mere acceptability. Indeed, many of them don't even achieve that goal.

Some hotels, however, find public relations value in operating a first-class restaurant designed to appeal to locals. The first hotel restaurant to go this route was the Pontchartrain's **Caribbean Room**. It was followed a decade later by the Royal Orleans' **Rib Room** and the Fairmont's **Sazerac**. All these are at least reasonably fine places to eat, and have over the years collected such substantial local followings that the captive-audience effect is lessened.

The giddy expectations fostered by the World's Fair in 1984 brought a new crop of large luxury hotels, all with ambitious, impressive restaurants. The grim reality of the Fair and the several terrible years afterwards brought things more in line with the needs of the marketplace. The grand dining rooms of the Sheraton and the Inter-Continental—both superb—closed. Fortunately, the best of the new crop—Le Meridien's **Henri**, the Windsor Court's **Grill Room**, and the Westin Canal Place's **Le Jardin**—remain open and excellent. The Grill Room can even be said to be thriving. All are among the most lavish and comfortable restaurants ever built in New Orleans, and their menus are revolutionary and skillfully turned out.

The Grill Room set a precedent which several other hotels followed. It is the only restaurant in the hotel, and serves breakfast, lunch, and dinner. I think this is a great idea, because it brings up the level of breakfast from the dreary coffee-shop standard, while at the same time pulling down the pretensions and prices. Le Jardin, **Begue's** at the Royal Sonesta, and the **Veranda** at the Inter-Continental have all gone this way and benefitted from the change.

Here is a five-best list of hotel restaurants:
1. Windsor Court Grill Room
2. Le Jardin (Westin Canal Place)
3. Sazerac (Fairmont)
4. Louis XVI (St. Louis)
5. Rib Room (Royal Orleans)

★ ★ Houston's

4241 Veterans Blvd., Metairie. 889-2301. •1755 St. Charles Ave., Uptown. 524-1578. 11 a.m.-11 p.m. seven days. AE, CB, DC, MC, V. $$.

Houston's, an Atlanta-based regional chain of formula restaurants, has two of the busiest restaurants in New Orleans. You will probably have to wait for a table at lunch or dinner. With good reason. The food here is better than one usually finds in this kind of place. It is not, however, as good as it once was. The standard of freshness (as opposed to frozenness) for such things as fish and fries is not as strongly adhered to as it once was. But for the price they put out a very large, decently-grilled slab of tuna, orange roughy (brought in from New Zealand; why deplete the local fresh product?), or other fish.

Houston's hamburger remains first class. It easily passes my test of a well-made burger: you can eat it without dressings. The meat is ground in-house and grilled over the same hickory fire they use for the fish. The patty could be thicker and the bun smaller, but this is still one of the best burgers in town.

The menu goes on to include sandwiches, salads, prime rib, and some much-admired but grossly-overcooked barbecued ribs. For dessert there's a cinnamony apple cobbler. The wine selection is decent and service is very good—once you get a table.

★★Hummingbird Grill

804 St. Charles Ave., CBD. 561-9229. Open 24 hours, 365 days a year. MC, V. $

Good food is where you find it. Chances are you will be surprised to find it here. The Hummer is homely, smoky, not scrupulously clean, and located in what used to be the center of the wino district. However, the food is of astoundingly high quality, especially considering the prices. Item: hamburgers made from fresh ground beef. Item: big squares of wonderful cornbread, baked on the premises, served with butter. At lunchtime, there is a selection of some five or six plate specials, ranging from great red beans and rice to fried fish to roast chicken and more, each fleshed out with some vegetables and that cornbread. At off-hours, the fare is mostly sandwiches; there is a good breakfast in the morning. Safety is assured by the presence of the cops who always seem to be in here drinking coffee.

HUSH PUPPIES. The legend: As cooks carried platters of food from the kitchens in the rear of the courtyard to the main house, the dogs jumped and howled for some of the goodies. So the cook moistened and rolled up some of the cornmeal she was working with, fried the cornmeal balls, and put them on the tray to throw to the puppies to hush them. Apparently some of these fried cornmeal balls made it all the way into massa's dining parlor; massa liked 'em as much as the dogs did.

Great hush puppies are about an inch in diameter, greaseless, and have flecks of onions and peppers in the cornmeal. The only place locally that has decent-tasting hush puppies is **Mike Anderson's**. The most famous are those of **Ralph & Kacoo's**, which are nowhere near as good as the rest of their food. The best I ever ate were in **Cuevas Fish House**, one of many all-you-can-eat fried catfish houses on country roads in Mississippi, but it's a long drive. (If it's worth it to you, it's on MS 43 about 10 miles east of Picayune.)

IJ as in jambalaya

ICE CREAM. Haagen-Dazs raised the ice cream consciousness of Orleanians to a higher plane in the early Eighties. Suppliers responded with much richer, much more carefully made ice creams than ever before. But the quintessential New Orleans ice creamery remains the ancient gelateria **Angelo Brocato**. They make dozens of Italian ice creams and ices on the premises, and the quality is so good that many New Orleans restaurants serve them.

A few restaurants make their own ice cream; these products are usually superb. **LeRuth's** ice creams are 25 percent butterfat (cf. Haagen Dazs, 11 percent), and their fruit ices taste more like the fruits than the fruits themselves. **Chez Pierre's** outdoes this, with an ice cream estimated by the chef to be over 31 percent butterfat. **Commander's Palace** turns out a vanilla ice cream studded with pinpoint vanilla seeds, and an intense chocolate mousse ice cream. **Copeland's** makes its own ice creams, the best of which is a fascinating Mexican vanilla.

The best of the local ice cream stands, besides Brocato's, are **Haagen-Dazs**, **Swensen's**, and **Chelsey's** (whose product is really frozen custard).

★ ★ ★ ★ Ichiban

1414 Veterans Blvd., Metairie. 834-1326. 11:30 a.m.-2 p.m. Tues.-Fri.; 5:30-10 p.m. Tues.-Sun; till 11 p.m. Fri. & Sat. AE, MC, V. $$

Ichiban occupies the original site of Shogun (it's owned by the same people). But it's a different style of restaurant. Ichiban's menu is more ambitious than that of its sister, and its pace is less frantic. The long, bright, mirrored room has an L-shaped sushi bar near the door and a lot of bare-wood tables.

The sushi and sashimi are solidly in the superior category for freshness, eye appeal, temperature, and flavor. The fish has the lively vivid tastes one looks for, and the variety available is consistently large and interesting. The sushi chefs are frank about what they think is especially good, and unusually friendly. On more than one occasion, the chef slipped me a sample of something offbeat and delectable.

Table service here is equally good. I've detected no deficiencies in the sushi and sashimi platters served at the tables (it's not uncommon for a sushi chef to foist off his second-rate product on diners not sitting right in front of him).

They do an exceptionally good job of serving sukiyaki, shabu shabu, and yosenabe here. The first two involve thin slices of beef, the last seafood; all three are cooked in pans of boiling water by the diner at the table. The raw materials are in beautiful condition, and the waitress seems to take special delight in setting up the repast and explaining it if necessary. The menu goes on to include the usual combination boatloads; the tempura items are admirably grease-free and brought forth good and hot.

★ ★ ★ Impastato's

3400 16th Street (behind Morning Call), Metairie. Reservations 455-1545. 5 p.m.-Midnight Tues.-Sat. AE, MC, V. $$$

If you're not a regular you're already in trouble here, because there are plenty of regulars with a lot of money to spend and the man at the door definitely takes care of them first. One night, I was left to rot an hour and a half with the pianist in the bar as party after party breezed in to dine. Also, if you're a regular, you know that when Joe Impastato ambles up smiling with some freshly-made fettuccine or some such for you to try, it's not going to be free.

But that's the end of my complaint list. The food here—starting with that fettuccine—is well-made Sicilian eating, and the prices are modest. The other appetizers are good: rich stuffed mushrooms, scampi-style shrimp, oysters Norman (a fine, cheesy casserole), the garlicky crab fingers. The cannelloni are really good—the stuffing is of veal and cheese, and the sauce is of cream and tomato.

Entrees: A piece of buttery (perhaps too buttery) trout with various kinds of toppings: mushrooms, artichokes, crabmeat, etc. Veal of fine white quality, firm and flavorful, shows off best in the piccata version, but the veal Marianna with mushrooms and artichoke hearts is also wonderful. The osso buco—veal shank—is braised to tenderness and brought with a powerful, aromatic tomato sauce. Okay steak and rack of lamb.

Desserts are the usual things, and the wine list is surprisingly extensive. They move a lot of Dom Perignon and Chateau Lafite to people who smoke between sips.

INDIAN. It is only in the last decade that New Orleans has had any Indian dining at all. Even when it's good, it doesn't meet with great commercial success. There are at this writing two Indian restaurants in the area: **Tandoor**, which is reviewed under its own heading, and **Old Calcutta**, a new Uptown restaurant which has not impressed me enough to write much more about it than this mention.

★ ★ ★ Isadora

Energy Center, 1100 Poydras. 585-7787. 11:30 a.m.-2:30 p.m. Mon.-Fri.; 6-10 p.m. Thurs.-Sat. AE, DC, MC, V. $$$$

It's named for Isadora Duncan, legendary figure of the Twenties. And if you have a taste for that gilded era, you will find this a swell place. The interior design is hardly that of the standard office-building feedery (which function Isadora has at lunchtime). An enormous room is dominated by a rectangular bar with two massive, fluted columns rising some twenty feet to a pink-neon-lit recess in the ceiling. Palm sculptures stand beside low walls made of mirrors and geometric gold plaster. But the best part of the atmosphere is aural. Isadora's musical programming recognizes the indisputable fact that American popular music reached its zenith in the late Thirties, and limits itself to the writers and performers of that halcyon time.

The original chef here had a rather eccentric approach to Nouvelle-American cuisine. A certain amount of wackiness lives on, almost as if it were a tradition. Despite that, Isadora's food is reliably good. It remains, however, unpredictable, since a large part of the menu changes on a seasonal, weekly, daily, or even hourly basis.

The best food comes from the appetizer section. The greatest hit is the grilled shrimp and artichoke bottoms with a sauce of tomato and herbs—a terrific flavor. Oysters Lafayette are baked on their shells with a thick sauce of seafood and eggplant and a good shot of spice. The pasta starters are generally good—crawfish ravioli with scallops and tarragon are memorable. Essays with sweetbreads and rabbit (i.e., rabbit Wellington) also taste great.

The various grilled and sauteed fish dishes are some of the best food the restaurant prepares. Everything comes out with a distinctly Creole level of seasoning, even when all else about the dish is preciousness. Other than these generalities, I wouldn't hazard a guess as to what specific entrees the place might be serving by the time you get there.

Isadora's wine list includes quite a few interesting new releases and hard-to-find boutique labels, along with the more familiar stuff; they're priced as intelligently as they are chosen. Desserts have been wonderful almost without exception: variously flavored mousses, sometimes in duos and trios; well-constructed tartes and cakes.

Service is somewhat inconsistent, particularly at dinner.

ITALIAN. I think that the Italian cuisines are the world's greatest—and I'm not even remotely Italian. Their excellence springs from a source that will, I believe, allow them to surpass the primacy of French cooking in the coming years. In Italy, the cooking is grounded in freshness and quality of raw materials to an extent matched by few other cuisines. There is no question that Italians eat the best vegetables on earth, for example.

The style of cooking is much more elemental and salubrious, as well.

Throughout most of Italy—and certainly in the great culinary regions like Tuscany, Friuli, and Abruzzo—one rarely finds sauces involving cream or butter. What makes them explode with flavor is olive oil, fresh herbs, and the inherent excellence of the main item itself. And the national dish of Italy—pasta—is one of the most versatile and delicious foods imaginable.

New Orleans has a large population of Italian descent; most of them trace their lineage to Sicily, and in particular to the town of Cefalu. As a result, until recently virtually all the Italian restaurants in the area cooked in the somewhat heavy, red-sauce Sicilian style. What's more, since the immigration took place several generations ago, the local recipes have been heavily Creolized—to the point where I think you have to make a distinction between Italian and Creole-Italian restaurants, and refrain from comparing the two.

Here, then, are two lists of the best Italian eateries in the area:

BEST CREOLE-ITALIAN
1. Mosca's
2. Sal and Judy's
3. Pascal's Manale
4. Tony Angello's
5. Impastato's
6. Moran's Riverside
7. Peppermill
8. Toney's Spaghetti House

BEST ITALIAN-ITALIAN (more or less)
1. Andrea's
2. La Riviera
3. Vincent's
4. Pastore's
5. Maximo's
6. Sweet Basil's Bistro
7. Little Italians

In addition to these, there are dozens of restaurants with substantial amounts of Italian food (mostly Creole-Italian) on menus whose specialty is something else. Mr. B's, for example, has always had a good section of pasta dishes. I think we'll be seeing more and more of that as restaurants and diners' tastes internationalize themselves further.

See also **Pasta** and **Pizza**.

★ Jack Dempsey's

738 Poland Ave., Ninth Ward. 943-9914. 11 a.m.-1:30 p.m. Tues., 11 a.m.-8:45 p.m. Wed. & Thurs., 11 a.m.-2:30 p.m. Fri., 4-10 p.m. Sat. AE, CB, DC, MC, V. $$.

Named for a colorful former police reporter, Dempsey's recreates the old style of neighborhood restaurant that Orleanians cherish. The most authentic aspect of this is the neighborhood itself—an obscure corner of the Ninth Ward from which most of the customers departed decades ago, and which the renovators haven't reached yet. The restaurant is a pair of rooms that seem to be sagging from heavy use. The air is full of the aromas of fried seafood and the sounds of rock oldies from the juke box.

The food's main themes here are plainness and quantity. (The latter largely explains the popularity of the restaurant.) For the most part, we're looking at gigantic platters of fried and broiled seafood. These come out with a serious lack of crispness, hotness, freshness, or all three. Much is made with pasta, seafood, cheese, and garlic; these essays are interesting for about two bites, and then get gross on me.

The remainder of the menu is padded out with homely platter specials, poor boys, and the rest of the trappings of the New Orleans neighborhood restaurant. I have never had a scrap of it that rose above the just-okay level. Service is a bit rushed and sometimes borderline rude.

★ ★ ★ Jacmel Inn

903 E. Morris, Hammond. 1-542-0043. 11:30 a.m.-3 p.m. Fri. only. 5:30-10:30 seven nights. AE, MC, V. $$

A good-sized, fairly old house, surrounded by gardens and equipped with a large sun porch, has been easily the best restaurant in Hammond for at least ten years. Although there is a theme-restaurant aspect to the decor, the kitchen is completely serious about itself, and turns out its Creole and Italian food with verve. With the exception of a handful of standards, the menu changes every few weeks.

Come here hungry, and start with the oysters Jacmel—a filling casserole of the bivalves with Italian sausage, bread crumbs, and herbs. The oyster brochette adds bell pepper to the usual oysters and bacon—a tasty idea. There are a few pasta dishes; I like the rotolo verde, a pinwheel of pasta, spinach, and tomato. Soups are a bit variable and tend to the very filling side. The Godchaux salad is a fine blend of greens and crabmeat—not as opulent as the Galatoire's original, but a lot cheaper.

Jacmel has a way with roast duckling, and that's the best entree here. The skin is crisp, the interior is moist, and the sauces are terrific. The Italian shrimp are big ones, sauteed in a great sauce of olive oil, herbs, and no small amount of garlic. They occasionally put a Jamaican-style dish on the menu, like the smoky, spicy chicken fricassee.

Several species of fish are grilled, sauteed, broiled, or otherwise rendered, typically with understated herbal sauces, always to good effect. Steak is broiled accurately and sent forth with such things as tasso and cream, sauteed mushrooms, or bearnaise.

The wine list is a pleasant surprise. Paul Murphy, the owner, is an oenophile who buys small but interesting lots of wine and sells them at very attractive prices. I've found bottles here never before seen in a restaurant. For dessert, they make a spectacular peach bread pudding and a satisfyingly sour cheesecake. The waitresses are friendly and efficient.

★★ Jade East

7011 Read Blvd., New Orleans East. 246-5590. • 3600 MacArthur Blvd., Algiers. 362-0123. Both: 11:30 a.m.-10 p.m. Mon.-Sat.; till 11 p.m. Fri. & Sat.; Noon-10 p.m. Sun. AE, CB, DC, MC, V. $$

Both locations are handsome dining rooms in the corners of small shopping centers. The New Orleans East Jade East premiered Hunan food in this area. It is still one of the best practitioners of that style, using a thick, barbecue-like sauce, with an incomparable richness and balance between hot and sweet.

Finding the specialties is easier than usual, as the restaurant has thoughtfully listed them at the head of its menu. The Hunan beef is a great example of the dish, with those darling baby ears of corn. Szechuan chicken soong is a very unusual preparation, with a variety of vegetables in a spicy sauce, wrapped up into a package with lettuce. River Shiang pork is shredded and served with vegetables; very pleasant and rich. The Hunan lamb is almost nothing but meat in a very hot, thick sauce—but the lamb flavor is not especially pronounced. The milder dishes of note are the crispy duck; chicken in an interesting sauce of egg whites, mushrooms, and ham; moo-shu pork; and the smooth lemon chicken.

Elsewhere on the menu we find a good, extra-spicy hot and sour soup, a shark-fin-and-crabmeat soup wherein all the excitement is in the name, and all the usual Cantonese things.

★★ Jaeger's

1701 Elysian Fields, Mid City. 947-0111. 11 a.m.-10 p.m. Tues.-Sun. till 11 p.m. Fri. & Sat. AE, MC, V. $$

This big old restaurant on Elysian Fields is the best of a number of restaurants with the name Jaeger's (YAY-gers), a name synonymous with casual seafood dining for many Orleanians. The look is traditional: unclothed tables on a terrazzo floor, with an oyster bar lit with neon at one end. The menu (which resembles a crowded Yellow Page) vends the familiar assortment of boiled and fried seafood with the usual accompaniments. What sets Jaeger's apart from its competitors is that it serves its boiled seafood hot. This makes an immense difference in the flavor, and makes me wonder why it is that just about everybody else keeps their boiled seafood in the refrigerator. The seasoning is a little milder than I like, but the warmth more than makes up for that.

The fried seafood here is more variable, ranging from okay to very good, crisp, and light. The grilled seafood would be better if it were removed from the grill about a minute before it dries out. On a couple of occasions, I was less than positive that the species of fish I ordered was the one delivered, although all are about the same price. The oyster bar is one of the better ones in the area. The friendly waitresses have classic Seventh Ward dialects.

★ ★ ★ Jalapeno's

2320 Veterans Blvd., Metairie. 837-6696. 11 a.m.-10 p.m. Mon.-Thurs.; Noon-Midnight Fri. & Sat.; Noon-9 p.m. Sun. AE, CB, DC, MC, V. $

This pop-Mexican restaurant occupies a location where no fewer than seven previous eateries went out of business. Jalapeno's defies the jinx by maintaining packed tables at all open hours. The dining rooms are decorated with heavy Southwest-neon decor—lots of cactuses. The crowd is mostly young and slurps down margaritas by the gallon.

Despite the frivolity, the food here is decent. You can start with a delicious mess called queso fundido—sausage and melted cheese in a casserole, scooped up with flour tortillas. The Mexican pizza (a quesadilla, loaded with everything Mexican you can think of) is a little soggy, but tastes good.

The entree menu veers away from the standard platters of tacos and tamales and instead concentrates on grilled foods and fajitas (grilled beef, chicken, or fish, served with relishes and tortillas). They do a startlingly good grilled, marinated chicken. And a dish called Jalapeno's hot shrimp is terrific: the big shrimp are stuffed with jack cheese with chips of jalapeno pepper, wrapped in bacon, broiled, and moistened with a red sauce.

The desserts are terrible and the service is helter-skelter, but this is still a better restaurant than most of its ilk.

JAMBALAYA. Jambalaya is considered one of the most local of local dishes—even though it almost certainly came from Spanish paella by way of Haiti. The typical jambalaya contains chicken, hot sausage, peppers, and onions in a very oily, smoky rice matrix. But just about anything is permissible in the jambalaya kettle: duck, shrimp, and rabbit are common. Red meats are rare.

Jambalaya is associated more with festivals than with restaurants. (See

Festivals.) The best easily-accessible jambalayas are at the **Gumbo Shop, Copeland's, Olde N'Awlins Cookery,** and **Streetcar Sandwiches.** Mr. B's makes a fascinating variant: *pasta* jambalaya, with pasta in the place of rice.

JAPANESE. Japanese restaurants have finally caught on in New Orleans. There are about a dozen to choose from; all include sushi bars. The proliferation brought to town the first bad Japanese food I've encountered; fortunately, there were some good new places, too.

Four common specialties are generally available in Japanese restaurants. Sushi and sashimi revolve about cold (sometimes raw) fish, and are most often prepared before your eyes at a counter. (See **Sushi.**) Teriyaki dishes involve marinating various meats and seafoods and grilling them. Tempura is coated with a smooth, light, thick batter and deep-fried; almost any meat, vegetable, or seafood can be given the tempura treatment. And there are several dishes similar to sukiyaki; these involve cooking thin slices of meat and vegetables in a boiling broth at the tableside. (A seafood variation of this is called yosenabe.)

Japanese meals usually begin with a hot towel for your hands, followed by a light soup, drunk from the cup. Miso soup is the most common of these, made from a red bean paste; its flavor is very subtle. Courses follow in rapid succession; in the formal dinner called kaiseki, you get seemingly dozens of little tidbits, each on an elegant plate that seems to have been designed specifically for the item. Salads, usually more chunky than leafy, are is usually part of the picture; dessert rarely is. Sake, the warm, sherrylike rice wine is better before and after the meal; beer seems more appropriate during.

The best Japanese restaurants here are:
1. Ichiban
2. Shogun
3. Little Tokyo
4. Hana
5. Samurai
6. Shigure

K as in knife and fork

★★★ Kabby's

Hilton Hotel, 2 Poydras. 584-3880. 11:30 a.m.-2:30 p.m. and 6-11 p.m. seven days. Brunch buffet Sun. 10:30 a.m.-2:30 p.m. Open all afternoon Sat. AE, CB, DC, MC, V. $$

The Hilton's busiest restaurant is a spacious, bricked room with enormous windows looking out onto the Mississippi River (right outside). Kabby's menu — basically, a polished version of the New Orleans seafood house concept — grew in interest and sophistication in 1988, when the hotel hired chef Louis Evans. (Evans was for many years the chef at the Pontchartrain Hotel, and made many friends there.)

The best way to start is with soup, particularly the crab and corn chowder or the crawfish bisque. Both are spicy and lightly creamy. The entree section leads off with a big platter of boiled seafood, which includes not just the usual shrimp and crabs but also steamed oysters and clams. The fried seafood platter — a staple of local eating — is ample and crisp.

The menu extends to some more adventuresome food: shrimp Herbsaint, for example, a delectable plate of big shrimp with peppers and the anise-like taste of Herbsaint liqueur. All the grilled, sauteed, and stuffed fish I've tried has come out moist and flavorful.

Sundays, Kabby's sets up one of the most popular and best brunch buffets in the city. The emphasis is on seafood, with a veritable fleet of boats bearing iced-down oysters, shrimp, etc. The entrees include a lot of very good old-style pot food that survives the steam table experience better than most buffet fare does. The taste is distinctly Creole and more emphasis is put on flavor than on appearance.

★★ Katie's

3701 Iberville, Mid-City. 488-6582. 11 a.m.-3 p.m. Mon.-Thurs., till 10 p.m. Fri.& Sat. No credit cards. $

Katie's is relatively new, but looks and tastes just like the best of the old-style neighborhood joints we used to have all over town. The front room has a bar and a jukebox full of rock oldies; the back room has more tables and a glass-front case full of stuffed artichokes and such. The blackboard shows three or so daily specials of the red beans-meatloaf-beef stew persuasion. Almost all that I have tried have been delicious and very ample in portion. Two soups usually appear: one of these is a homemade vegetable, ruddy brown, really good. There are, of course, poor boy sandwiches, impressively oversized and made with good roast beef, ham, fried seafood, etc. The gravy on the roast beef varies in quality, and they like to slather on way too much mayo; but they are otherwise satisfying. The Katie's Special is described as a Sicilian-style hamburger, freshly made with onions and garlic in the meat; mozzarella and red gravy on top of it. A good muffuletta.

The menu, with its tiny type, includes okay fried seafood platters and forgettable fried chicken, decent stuffed artichokes and rather delicious shrimp pasta. Service is appropriately yat and attentive.

★ ★ ★ Kim Son

349 Whitney Ave. at West Bank Expressway, Gretna. 366-2489. 11:30 a.m.-2:30 p.m. Mon.-Sat., 5-10 p.m. seven days. AE, MC, V. $.

The city's best Vietnamese restaurant is a nice-looking place with very helpful personnel—the easier for you to explore this fascinating cuisine. The menu mixes both Chinese and Vietnamese dishes, but even the Chinese stuff is undiluted. Lots of dishes prepared in clay pots, for example.

Start with spring rolls or summer rolls. They're shaped like egg rolls and contain many of the same ingredients, plus fresh herbs; the difference is that they're served cold. Although the wrapper is the same as for the more familiar Chinese egg rolls, in its uncooked form it's silky and elegant. Next, have one of the very inexpensive noodle dishes (look for the word *bun*). These taste much better than they look or sound.

Any seasoned New Orleans eater will find the Vietnamese baked crabs easy to appreciate. They're crab quarters in the shell, baked with a great deal of pepper, black bean sauce, or ginger and onions. They are as irresistable as they are messy.

The menu goes on to include a great many other adventures. The meats that you grill yourself at the table are interesting, as are such dishes as "leaf-bound beef." (I never found out what the leaf was.)

★ ★ Kolb's

125 St. Charles Ave., CBD. 522-8278. 11 a.m.-2:30 p.m. and 5-10 p.m. Mon.-Sat. AE, CB, DC, MC, V. $$

Most Orleanians, when asked which is their favorite German restaurant, will answer "Kolb's." And then they'll probably tell you that they don't like German food very much. Well, no wonder. Kolb's, despite the fact that it's the only flagrantly German restaurant in town, does a much better job with its Creole dishes than with the somewhat limited selection of German offerings. That's a shame, because the premises are wonderful: dark, old, and Teutonic. A marvelous system of ceiling fans dates back to the first New Orleans world's exposition in 1884; all of the fans are turned by one motor via a complex array of leather belts.

Start your meal with the turtle soup or the shrimp remoulade—the latter a very pretty and ample array of shrimp on a bed of lettuce with a tangy mayonnaise-style remoulade sauce. If you must have a German dish, eschew the pork shank and the sauerbraten in favor of the variations on wiener schnitzel. That's glorified panneed veal, and it goes well with the six or seven different sauces Kolb's applies to it.

But the best entree in the house is barbecued shrimp. They are consistently some of the best—delicious, giant, heads-on shrimp with a thick, buttery, peppery sauce. Next best is the plate of red beans and rice, served with a giant ham shank—a great lunch. The corned beef and cabbage is also first-rate—tender and not too fatty. The menu goes on to include seafood of no particular note, and finishes with a most unusual and delicious apple strudel cheesecake.

At lunchtime, Kolb's is inexpensive, fast, and popular with the white-collar crowd. Service is a little brusque and touristy, as it usually is in places this old.

KOREAN. The only Korean restaurant in New Orleans that takes itself seriously is **Genghis Khan**, which see. A restaurant called the **Oriental Triangle** has a few Korean items, but seems to move more Chinese food.

★ ★ ★ K-Paul's Louisiana Kitchen

416 Chartres, French Quarter. No reservations; 524-7394. 11 a.m.-2:30 p.m. and 5:30-10 p.m. Mon.-Fri. AE. $$$$

K-Paul's is as much a shrine to chef-owner Paul Prudhomme as it is a restaurant, although he never intended for it to turn out that way. Chef Paul has been so celebrated by the media in recent years that he has become one of America's best-known food gurus—certainly the most famous chef from Louisiana. So, when people with an interest in food come to town, they head right over to his slightly-renovated neighborhood joint on Chartres and join their fellow travelers in the all-but-unavoidable line.

K-Paul's began in 1979 when Prudhomme—then chef at Commander's Palace—opened a little lunch place in a minimally-redecorated Quarter sandwich joint. Here he created a haven where the whims of customers would take a back seat to the pure practice of the chef's and waiter's arts, and where everybody could take off weekends. The culinary style was more or less the same as now, but at prices in the $5-$10 range. The stuff was great and such a deal that the line formed. Dinner was added, and the lines grew even longer. And then—celebrity.

Prudhomme makes much of his Cajun heritage, but his cooking incorporates ideas from many cuisines. What makes it of a piece are the levels of pepper, salt, cream, butter, and certain spices (most notably cumin), which are extreme even by Creole-Cajun standards. Prudhomme's most quoted idea concerns a harmony of hotness in red, white, and black pepper. The most interesting thing about K-Paul's is its raw materials: great, unheard-of fish, home-grown vegetables, and poultry and rabbits raised on the restaurant's own farm.

The menu changes daily, and lists about six first courses and a dozen or more entrees. The first thing that arrives is a basket of freshly-baked breads, all of which are terrific—especially the jalapeno cheese bread. Cajun popcorn is the signature appetizer, although the creation was not the dish (you have always been able to get fried crawfish tails in New Orleans restaurants) but the appealing name.

The famous entree is blackened fish, a fillet charred on the outside in a hot skillet with lots of seasonings. Good eating, particularly when the fish is tuna. Less well-known but probably the best frequently-offered dish is trout Czarina, with a rough-edged butter sauce, julienne vegetables, and a reasonable seasoning level. Panneed rabbit is pan-fried with a crumbly, herbal crust and a hillock of the spiciest fettuccine with cream and cheese you'll ever eat. In season, many dishes are prepared with crawfish; the etouffee is strictly for people who can't get enough pepper.

The dessert to get is the sweet potato and pecan pie, a delightful innovation. The coffee is good and strong. The happy waitresses insist on pasting stars to your face, the color depending on how much of your meal you've eaten.

It is a major ordeal to eat here. Unless the town is dry of tourists, the wait in line can be very long. The dining rooms retain the neighborhood-bar look; the tables are unclothed, and you are expected to share them with strangers if there aren't enough in your party to fill all the seats. Food arrives when it's ready, regardless of whether you've finished the previous course or whether your companions' dinners are ready, too. If you want the one available drink (a Cajun martini, a mason jar of vodka with hot peppers that I find undrinkable) or the one wine, you'd better order it early, because they won't bring it to you later. Forget about getting them to change spice or salt levels. I don't know why K-Paul's feels it has to put its customers through these travails, which since entree prices passed the $20 mark are hard to accept with a smile. Unless you get a charge out of being around famous people; Prudhomme is almost always on hand, ready to sell you copies of his books or some of his Magic Brand seasonings.

★ ★ ★ Kung's Dynasty

1912 St. Charles Ave., Uptown. 525-6669. 11:30 a.m.-11 p.m., seven days. No Sat. lunch. AE, MC, V. $$

The premises—a small Uptown mansion that once housed "The Explorer's Club"—are unusual for a Chinese restaurant. That and most else about Kung's breaks out of the neighborhood-cafe prison to which most local Chinese eating has been consigned. With the exception of the glass plates covering the tablecloths, the furnishings, service, and presentations are those of a grand restaurant. There's a board of daily specials, and the menu proclaims that no MSG is used.

Hot starters of note are the lettuce-leaf packages of minced squab (I've had far better, but this version is not bad), the crab Rangoon (a fried wonton stuffed with cream cheese and crabmeat) and steamed dumplings. The shrimp toast and hot and sour soup are less successful.

The main cooking style here is Hunan—spicy, but with a certain mellow fruitiness in the background. The best entree I've had is the enormous seafood delight—shrimp, scallops, crabmeat, and squid, in an intriguingly flavorful dish with a white sauce. The oysters Szechuan style are also delicious and original—nice and plump, with a robust brown sauce.

Kung's chicken has an unusual spicy, slightly sweet sauce; the chicken pieces involved have a delectable crispness. Steak kew is tender ribeye pieces in a savory brown sauce studded with good-looking, crisp vegetables. Even better is the Imperial beef, with a fine pepper level and an echo-taste of oranges. There's a great whole fish with a brown chili sauce and a crisp duck with melt-in-the-mouth skin.

If you can plan a few days ahead, they'll fix a roast suckling pig for 12 to 16 people for $275. Service is considerably friendlier and more solicitous than in most Chinese places.

L as in lost bread

★ ★ ★ La Crepe Nanou

1410 Robert St., Uptown. 899-2670. 6-10:30 p.m. seven days; till 11:30 p.m. Thurs.-Sat., till 9:30 p.m. Sun. Brunch Sun. 9:30 a.m.-2:30 p.m. MC, V. $

Nanou started out as an excellent and flagrantly French creperie, with a menu limited to crepes, omelettes, salads, and a few other things, all served in a rather bohemian atmosphere. During the past year, it became much more ambitious in its menu, adding a substantial amount of French bistro food. Meanwhile, the premises—while still refreshingly unpretentious and just crowded enough to be sociable—have become much more comfortable.

The crepes are still very well made. They're thin, flavorful in their own right, crisped slightly at the edges. Among the dozen and a half entree crepes I like the crepe florentine, with creamed spinach and bacon and the crabmeat crepe especially, but all are pretty good. They have a deft hand with omelettes; the omelette Provencale, filled with tomatoes and finely-chopped garlic, is irresistable.

On the new annex to the menu we find roasted chickens, grilled tournedos, and sauteed fish, all unimpeachable and moistened with interesting sauces. I particularly like the fine cream-and-demi-glace steak au poivre. For starters, you can get a big bowl of fresh mussels, lightly poached in their own juices, with a touch of wine, butter, and herbs: delicious. While these are not the most polished versions of such fare hereabouts, they are more than satisfactory in this inexpensive bistro milieu.

Crepes—indeed, quite a few crepes—return when you get to the dessert list. They're made with a variety of fresh fruit, ice creams, and liqueurs, and all are good except that they tend to overload them with whipped cream. Espresso and cappuccino wind up the meal nicely. There's a short wine list well matched to the food. Service has a touch of that French bistro brusqueness, but that adds to the atmosphere for me.

★ ★ ★ La Cucaracha Cafe

8513 Oak, Uptown. 861-8053. 11 a.m.-2 p.m. and 5-10 p.m. Tues.-Sat. AE, MC, V. $$

It's like a trip to Santa Fe or Taos, where one finds dozens of little cafes that look a lot like this and serve the same style of food. The restaurant has grown a little from its original Lilliputian dimensions, but it's still miniscule. A skylight makes the place bright and cheery by day. The menu is also tiny; just a half-dozen entrees, plus a daily special.

This New Mexican food has similarities with the more familiar Tex-Mex, but the tastes and ingredients are distinctive. Start with a big bowl of their soups, usually made with beans; bring your own Tabasco. There is also a cool, creamy guacamole, and that's about it for starters. Entrees are almost all wrapped in corn or flour tortillas. The goat cheese enchiladas are a fine example of the cafe's style; the tortillas are firm and tasty, and the cheese has an appealing zing. The most impressive part of this is the dark reddish-brown sauce; it has a great slightly-gritty texture and a magnificent balance between hot and bitter—perfect with the enchiladas, and not bad when it flows into the firm beans that accompany the entrees. An unusual use of this sauce is to set off the Navajo stacked enchiladas—several tortillas, interspersed with layers of cheese, topped with an egg glazed into place: excellent. Also on the plate is posole, which is something like grand-scale grits; it's big chunks of hominy, and is the universal replacement for potatoes in New Mexican restaurants.

For dessert there is a smooth flan and a berry pie—looks like a double-thick apple pie, but with unusual red berries with a tea-like aftertaste and not too much sugar. Service and amenities are minimal.

★ ★ ★ ★ La Cuisine

225 W. Harrison Ave., Lakeview. 486-5154. 11:30 a.m.-3 p.m. and 5:30-10 p.m. Tues.-Fri. 11:30 a.m.-10 p.m. Sat. Noon-8 p.m. Sun. AE, CB, DC, MC, V. $$$

I wish there were about a dozen more places in New Orleans like La Cuisine. A friend puts it this way: "The food here isn't great. But it's very, very good." Another friend: "This is the kind of place you miss when you move away from New Orleans." It's basically a glorified neighborhood cafe. The paneled dining rooms are comfortable but hardly elegant. Waitresses perform efficient, friendly, and unceremonious service.

The food is supervised by Lete Boullion, one of the city's legendary old-line restaurateurs. You could call it Suburban Creole: local standards, with a hint of Italian in the background. The best example of this is oysters Saladino, served three to a small casserole under an encrusted, oil-logged drift of herbs, bread crumbs, and garlic. This is a spectacular flavor, one I often find myself ordering in triple and quadruple portions. The other baked oysters are good too: delicious Rockefellers, and Bienvilles with smokiness from bacon or ham and a good balance of seafood and pepper. The oysters en brochette are outstanding and absurdly inexpensive. La Cuisine makes textbook stuffed mushrooms: big caps, fresh-tasting, a well-seasoned stuffing, and just enough hollandaise to mellow it out. The soups range from good to memorable.

There's a simple rule to avoid disappointment in the entree section: if there's a sauce and crabmeat on top of something else, forget it. That done, you are on safe ground. They do a great job of frying fish here, so any of the platters of trout, oysters, or shrimp make good eating. Especially interesting is the trout three ways: meuniere, amandine, and with crabmeat. They also do a nice broiled seafood platter, which those of us on a diet welcome.

A sheet attached to the menu lists specials, which are some of the best food here. For example, Joe's hot shrimp, broiled with a unique stuffing of mozzarella and jalapeno slivers and wrapped with bacon. Best dish in the house! Another specialty is the crawfish dinner, with crawfish cooked six different ways. Not all the ways are great, but enough of them are.

The menu goes on to include prime steaks, served in sizzling butter sauce; baby white veal, delicious with lemon butter or marinara sauce; chicken, broiled to tenderness; live Maine lobster broiled and brought forth with (or without) a good stuffing.

The wine list is getting better lately, but this is still not really a wine kind of place. Desserts are led by a cube of medium-light bread pudding in a weird but good sauce with the consistency of custard.

★ La Fiesta

1412 Stumpf Blvd., Gretna. 361-9142. 10 a.m.-11 p.m. Mon.-Sat.; till Midnight Fri. & Sat.; 11 a.m.-11 p.m. Sun. MC. V. $

It's a small dining room with furnishings from the ill-fated Johnny Carson theme restaurant. A jukebox plays obscure songs in Spanish. The food is limited to the Tex-Mex basics, with many different platters speaking to different levels of appetite. All of it is pretty good, none of it great. What makes this restaurant worthy of being listed is that it consistently serves the coldest beer I have ever encountered. It's a perfect match for the food.

★ ★ ★ Lafitte's Landing

Adjacent to West Bank side of Sunshine Bridge (La. 70), Donaldsonville. 1-473-1232. 11 a.m.-3 p.m. Seven days. 6-10 p.m. Tues.-Sun. MC, V. $$$

An 1812-vintage plantation building is the best possible meal stop along the standard plantation tour route up and down the River Roads — a ride

I like to take with or without visitors. In this part of the state, the culinary pickings are usually limited to standard River Road Creole. Lafitte's Landing and its talented owner-chef John Folse break out of that mold with a menu of imaginative eating.

Many of the better offerings are specials, but you will probably be able to begin with the plump fried oysters topped with a brown demi-glace sauce. The same sauce, in modified form, reappears later under a beautiful veal steak, pink and pale, topped with large lumps of fresh crabmeat and hollandaise, with patterns drawn in the sauces on the plate. Very nice. On another visit I made a meal entirely out of appetizers, a good plan; the choices are many and the flavors unique. The soups, salads, and side courses are all first class; desserts are made on the premises. The only problems I have with the place are that the antique dining rooms are a little crowded and the service a little slow. But it's probably the best restaurant between New Orleans and Baton Rouge.

★ ★ ★ La Gauloise

Meridien Hotel, 614 Canal, CBD. 525-6500. 11 a.m.-3 p.m. Mon.-Sat.; 6 p.m.-10 p.m. Mon.-Thurs., till 10:30 Fri. and Sat.; Brunch Sun. 10:30 a.m.-3 p.m. AE, CB, DC, MC, V. $$$

This is the informal, all-day restaurant of the Meridien Hotel, but it could easily pass for a much grander restaurant. It reminds me of Arnaud's, with its tile floors, big windows, and wooden chairs. The inspiration is, however, the French brasserie—a brewery-with-cafe, usually filled with conviviality. When La Gauloise opened, it had French brasserie food. Since then, it has moved back and forth so many times between Creole and French that I hesitate to guess where it is now.

One aspect of La Gauloise is consistent: its buffets. These are offered at breakfast and lunch daily, as well as Sunday brunch. There are also seafood buffets on Friday and Saturday nights. All are well above average in the quality of the raw materials used. The pates, smoked fish, and fresh cold seafoods are particularly admirable. The big roasts of red meats are of things like beef tenderloin or lamb roasts—luscious, tender, crusty stuff. At the seafood buffets, one finds lovely spreads of sushi, sashimi, curried salads, and Thai noodle dishes—a passion of chef Patrick Perie, who spent some time in the Orient. Desserts, as the usually are in first-class hotels, are glorious. At Wednesday lunch, there is an all-chocolate dessert buffet that has become something of a legend among CBD lunchers.

The Sunday brunch buffet is one of the city's best. Even steam-table dishes are edible; such things as the blanquette de poulet and the spaghetti financiere I found one day were tremendous eating by any standard. Outside the entrance to the restaurant, a man at a cart makes dessert crepes to order. Meanwhile, a magician, a jazz quartet and a clown provide diversions.

★ ★ ★ Lakeshore Restaurant

2221 Lakeshore Drive, Mandeville. 626-5115. 11:30 a.m.-3 p.m. Mon.-Fri.; 3-9 p.m. Mon.-Thurs., till 10 p.m. Fri., 5-10 p.m. Sat. MC, V. $$

This very popular Italian cafe does indeed look out over Lake Pontchartrain. In a way, it's the Mosca's of the North Shore. The rooms are minimally decorated, and the menu—written on blackboards—lists seafood, Italian food, and Italian seafood. Start with fried mozzarella, with its chunky, robust tomato sauce, or the crab fingers, awash in a garlicky lemon butter. Salad is on the house and comes out in a big bowl from which you help yourself.

The premier entree is chicken Vesuvio: a cut-up chicken half, roasted in a pan with Italian sausage, mushrooms, peppers, and no small amount of garlic and olive oil. Very, very tasty, and enough to feed two or three people. Seafood entrees range from basic fried platters to more ambitious fare, like the broiled, buttery shrimp francaise. The same lemon butter in which this appears also tastes good on veal or chicken. They also cook some tasty pasta and seafood combinations; the crawfish pasta is saucy and elemental—and, once again, enough to feed two plus a small dog. Not much in the way of dessert, but there's hardly room for it. Service is friendly but minimal.

★ ★ Lakeview Seafood

7400 Hayne Blvd., New Orleans East. 242-2819. 11 a.m.-10 p.m. Tues.-Sun.; till 11 p.m. Fri. & Sat., till 9 p.m. Sun. AE, MC, V. $$

It's a relic from the time when Hayne Blvd. was a battered two-lane road used mainly by people spending a weekend in the camps on Lake Pontchartrain—of which, oddly enough, there is no view from the restaurant's long, very casual dining room. The place is designed for family eating of boiled and fried seafood. The oyster and shrimp "boats" are the most distinctive dishes. A boat is made by hollowing out the inside of an unsliced loaf of white bread, toasting and garlic-buttering it, and filling it with the fried seafood of your choice. They make them in three sizes: for one, two or a mob. On a good day, the fried seafood here is perfectly crisp and well-seasoned; however, the performance is not perfectly consistent. Service is indifferent, and prices are low.

★ ★ ★ La Louisiane

725 Iberville, French Quarter. Reservations 523-4664. 11:30 a.m.-5 p.m. Mon.-Fri.; 5:30-11:00 p.m. seven days. AE, DC, MC, V. $$$$

Almost as old as Antoine's, La Louisiane has not enjoyed much continuity of either management or cuisine in recent years. The current edition of La Louisiane is more or less the Creole-Italian restaurant that

Elmwood Plantation used to be, complete with much of the Elmwood's staff. It's a beautiful restaurant in the old style. In the long dining rooms, Baccarat crystal chandeliers hang from high ceilings over big tables with plush chairs.

Soup is the best starting point. They are homely and wonderful; the white bean with shell macaroni is a great example of the style. Pasta is also a nice way to start; the angel hair with a light sauce of vegetables, butter, and cream is excellent. So is the malafatta, which translates "badly made"; it's a sort of dumpling of spinach pasta with a great sauce of peas, proscuitto, and cheese.

Entrees: Halves of roasted chickens, large servings of oysters Mosca, the crabmeat-topped trout Lafreniere, and the finely-broiled, fist-size filet mignon are my favorites. At night there emerges a very fine chicken grandee for two—a whole chicken roasted with Italian sausage and mushrooms. There's a good roasted duck with different sauces daily, and a few veal dishes of only moderate interest.

The dessert and wine lists are of no special note. Lunches are very popular among a certain crowd of local businessmen, and good specials at low prices are only part of the attraction. A couple of days a week, models unclad to within a hair's breadth of indecency show off lingerie. These shows are wildly popular, but leave something to be desired as far as class is concerned.

★ ★ ★ La Madeleine

547 St. Ann, Lower Pontalba, French Quarter. 568-9950. ©601 S. Carrollton Ave. (at St. Charles), Riverbend. 861-8661. 7 a.m.-9 p.m. seven days. No credit cards. $

La Madeleine is an international chain of French bakeries—the McDonald's of France, I'm told. Whether that's the case or not, there is no doubt that the pastries and particularly the breads baked by La Madeleine are in the top rank of French bakeries hereabouts. Two shops: a good-looking cafe in the Lower Pontalba on Jackson Square, and a smaller place at Riverbend. In the center of the former is a large brick oven fired by wood. This turns out a very good French bread, heavier and crustier than the standard New Orleans version. Glass cases are replete with other pastries, and these too are very well-made. The croissants are wonderful and come in several flavors—the almond croissant is especially mellow. On the other side of the place is a cafeteria line with soups, quiches, light lunch entrees, salads, and sandwiches; these are spotty at best. The coffee is not good enough to pull business from the Cafe du Monde.

★ ★ ★ La Marquise

625 Chartres, French Quarter. 524-0420. 7:00 a.m.-5:30 p.m. seven days. No credit cards. $

This is a cute little French pastry shop with a few tables inside, a few tables outside, and enough regulars working crossword puzzles to keep them all filled. The pastries are pretty good; the variety is wide, the things look attractive, and they're made with class ingredients. I like the fruit-and-custard tarte maison, the Napoleons, the caramel custard, the green cream-filled gateaus called frogs, and the croissants. They make here the best bran muffins I have ever tasted—moist, laced with carrot strips, and great with a cup of coffee for breakfast. Unfortunately, La Marquise's coffee is perfectly terrible.

LAMB. As is the case in most other red meats, the United States produces the best lamb in the world, and you should ascertain that it is from this country rather than New Zealand before you order. Rack of lamb is the most common menu manifestation of the meat. It's lamb rib steaks all in a row, with the ribs still attached. The only thing bad about a rack of lamb is that many restaurants force you to order it for two people, which requires a rare coincidence of taste with one of your dining partners. The best racks of lamb in the city are those of **Andrea's, Commander's Palace, Louis XVI,** and the **Versailles.**

Lamb chops are the same cut of meat, but served in individual portions—preferably about an inch thick. I like a lamb chop the same way I like a steak: grilled to a crusty exterior and a juicy interior. The landmark lamb chops issue forth from the kitchens of **Galatoire's, Morton's,** and **Ruth's Chris Steak House.** By the way, lamb connoisseurs like to get theirs cooked "rosy"—just the rare side of medium, with only a blush of pink remaining in the center.

★ ★ ★ ★ ★ La Provence

US 190, Lacombe (bear right at the first major intersection past the north end of the Causeway; the restaurant is six miles further, on the right, just past "Big Branch"). Reservations 1-626-7662. 5-11 p.m. Wed.-Sat.; 1-9 p.m. Sun. AE, MC, V. $$$$

La Provence is New Orleans' French country inn. It's a comfy, rustic dining room set among the lofty pines, as close to the middle of nowhere as you can get in an hour's drive from downtown. La Provence is at its most atmospheric in the winter, when the fire is burning in the fireplace and the cold breezes shuffle the trees.

The chef-owner is Chris Kerageorgiou, a delightful character who loves to cook and loves to talk. He's proud to have people visit his kitchen; it gleams with saucepans bubbling and stockpots simmering all over the place. Out back is a garden where the chef grows fresh herbs.

Start off with whatever charcuterie is being offered. The pates, sausages and such—some made from meats, others from fish—are prepared from scratch and are superb, even such homely stuff as hogshead cheese. For a hot first course, go for the calamari in a lovely pink lobster sauce or the small casseroles of oysters, which vary from day to day in composition. There is a great soup: quail gumbo, a dark-roux broth with a whole roast quail sitting the the middle. When you cut into the quail, some nicely-seasoned dirty rice falls into the broth. The flavor is as stimulating as the concept.

The two entrees for which the restaurant is best known are duck a l'orange—which is pretty good but no landmark for my palate—and the undeniably delectable rack of American lamb, which you should ask to have roasted to "rosy." The latter is marinated and prepared with aromatic *herbes de Provence.* A new lamb dish which has caught on well is a leg of lamb rolled out, stuffed, rolled back up, and baked. Just the right garlic component there.

There is much more of interest. Sweetbreads are moist and vivid with that super-veal flavor and a crawfish sauce. Medallions of veal are lovely pale pink and taste great with light tarragon butter. The fresh fish are prepared in different ways daily, usually on the simple side; watch for and get seafood with any sort of herbal red Creole sauce. And there are specials nightly.

There's a ramekin of some delicious pate maison brought to the table with bread when you sit down; be careful not to eat too much of it. At the other end of the meal are desserts of less interest than the rest of the offerings. The wine list is peculiar in selection and often outlandishly overpriced.

The problem at La Provence is and always has been one of consistency; the place has had some alarming ups and downs. Everything depends on the mood of the chef who, like many other brilliant people, can be mercurial. My favorite time to dine here is Sunday afternoon, when a relaxed pace obtains and you don't have to worry about falling asleep on the Causeway on the way home.

★ ★ ★ La Riviera

4506 Shores Drive, Metairie. 888-6238. 5-10 p.m. Mon.-Thurs., till 11 p.m. Fri. and Sat. AE, CB, DC, MC, V. $$$

Chef Goffredo Fraccaro—New Orleans' first really serious Italian chef—operated La Riviera to a very devoted following for almost 20 years. But in 1989, he sold it to Valentino Rovere, who polished up the service, the wine list, and the general demeanor of the place. Chef Goffredo is still on hand, making frequent sorties into the somewhat gaudy Metairie-anean dining room. Which is fortunate. Goffredo is an accomplished chef who can be brilliant. The best example of this is an appetizer: crabmeat ravioli, marvelous in a light cream and cheese sauce. In season, this is also made with crawfish. Neither dish is on the menu, but it's what everybody orders. Other good starters include manicotti, fettuccine, and tortellini (little ravioli stuffed with cheese). A new pasta—possetta—is filled with spinach and the slightly bitter herb borage, sauced with cream, garlic, and walnuts.

The entree list contains many good seafood entrees, the best of which is a broiled trout, convincingly herbal and peppery. It would be even better if the fish were in better shape. The Italian-style oysters, with their bread-crumb-and-herb topping, also hits the spot. And there is a lot of veal, the best of which are the picatta (lemon and butter), saltimbocca (ham stuffing and winy brown sauce), and braciolini. I have seen whiter veal in my life. There is a wonderful steak pizzaiola, the sauce for which is a chunky affair with tomatoes, peppers, and (I think) olives.

One side of the menu lists some table d'hote dinners which include La Riviera's best food at attractive prices. The service is by waiters who give a not-always-informed reading of the night's specials but who are otherwise competent. The wine list has been vastly improved since Valentino took over. On some nights, La Riviera can make you believe, as many of its regulars do, that it's the best Italian restaurant in town. But this is not an always thing.

LATE NIGHT DINING. One of the enduring mysteries is why New Orleans, celebrated as a 24-hour city, has so few decent places to eat after 11 p.m. What remains after that hour is mostly fast food and terrible touristy places on or near Bourbon Street. The probable reason for this is that Orleanians tend to consider dining out an evening's activity in itself, rather than an adjunct to another event.

The only recommendable 24-hour restaurants are **Bailey's** in the Fairmont Hotel, **La Peniche**, and the **Hummingbird Grill**. Only the former is appropriate if you're dressed up. Fancier places that stay open late include **Maestro's** and **Maximo's** (till about midnight on weekends), the **Rib Room**, (till 11:30), and **Sal & Sam'** (till 1 a.m.).

Casual late-night eateries of note are the **Camellia Grill** (1 a.m.), **Russell's Marina Grill** (1:30 a.m., 3 a.m. weekends), and **Dooky Chase** (not only open but jumping till 2 a.m. weekends).

★ ★ ★ L'Economie

325 Girod (at Commerce), Warehouse District. Reservations 524-7405. 11 a.m.-2 p.m. Mon.-Fri. 6-9 p.m. Mon.-Sat. No credit cards. (Personal checks accepted.) $$

You will probably enjoy this restaurant because of the incongruousness of its surroundings. For ages, the place was a lunchroom for workmen in this formerly industrial area; you can still see the faded "Economy Restaurant" sign painted on the wall near the corner-cutting entrance.

Inside, however, we find a Parisian bistro. Chef-owner Hubert Sandot parachuted out of the upper echelons of the hotel business in 1988 to open this highly personal, slightly eclectic cafe.

The wait staff is greatly in the thrall of the chef, and they describe each dish with a reverence that practically dares you not to like it. These are punctuated with manifestos about the use of milk instead of cream in sauces, etc. And chef's food *is* good. The style is considerably less rich than what one ordinarily associates with French cooking, and the simplicity of the fare perfectly complements the environment and the very low prices. Everything on the abbreviated menu is presented without frills on gigantic white plates.

The great first course here is a big bowl of fresh mussels, steamed in their own juices and shells, with a little wine and herbs. Delicious, and the sauce makes for a pretty good soup. They smoke salmon on the premises; that also kicks things off swimmingly. Soups have been less interesting to me; they are the very light variety that you apparently have to be European to love. Salads are enormous piles of crisp, bitter greens with a minimalist dressing.

The entree list includes a very peculiar coq au vin, served as a semi-stew; a tournedos with a sauce du jour; smoked, grilled duck breast; lovely poached salmon, and some other grilled and sauteed fish. At lunch, there is a pasta offering and a "rice du jour," the latter a very hearty plate of food in the direction of a risotto.

Desserts have not impressed me much; I think I ate the worst chocolate mousse of the last ten years here one lunch. The crowd that gathers at L'Economie attracts more of itself; there's a certain bohemian quality to the patrons, despite the jackets and ties.

★★Lee's Hamburgers

904 Veterans Blvd., Metairie. 836-6804. ●*3301 Williams Blvd., Kenner. 443-6695.* ●*2030 Woodmere, Harvey. 340-9922.* ●*103 Schlief Dr., Belle Chasse. 392-9922. All open around 11 a.m.; closing hour varies. No credit cards. $*

Lee's bills itself as the "Original New Orleans Hamburger." Indeed, its roots go back to the first half of this century, when Lee Hash had a hamburger place next to the Orpheum. The present-day Lee's stands are some sort of intricate franchise, but the basic idea remains: good-sized patties of fresh beef with chopped onions inside. They smell great and are served with good fresh dressings and grated Cheddar. At some Lee's locations, burgers are grilled to order; others have them on the grill ready. Strangely, it doesn't seem to make much difference. The French fries are just okay. The restaurants are bright and clearly suburban-looking, but not fast-foodish.

★ ★ ★ ★ Le Jardin

Westin Canal Place Hotel, 1 Canal at the River, 11th floor. Reservations 568-0155. 6:30 a.m.-2:30 p.m. and 6-10 p.m. seven days. Sunday brunch buffet 10:30 a.m.-2:30 p.m. AE, CB, DC, MC, V. $$$$$

Le Jardin took years to get off the ground, but its food has become reliably delicious and just innovative enough to be interesting. The enormous, opulent eleventh-floor space still looks like something out of a painting. Between tiger-striped wood panels, its big windows offer a view of the river, the aquarium, the docks, and Algiers Point.

The chef and most of his staff are European, but the menu is replete with local ingredients and tastes. The better part of the menu changes daily, but not in so flagrant a way that predictions are impossible. Start with the spectacular crabmeat with avocado, served hot and enriched with hollandaise. A bit more robust is the pairing of big barbecued shrimp and spicy grilled scallops. The house soup is a mushroom and crabmeat bisque—extravagantly creamy, the mushrooms giving an interesting meaty contrast to the seafoody crab lumps.

The kitchen has a way with fish, particularly grilled fish. Part of this has to do with the portion; I find grilled fish is much better when the fillet is big—eight ounces. Le Jardin's weighty flanks of interesting Gulf species appear with minimal sauces, pristine and delectable. The marinated, grilled tuna, crusty on the outside and with a blush within, is a particular specialty.

They also present some fascinating essays with pasta, wonderful pink veal chops, and a fine rendering of venison filet mignon. All of this comes from a menu which chnages frequently. A daily "fresh sheet" is fairly extensive.

Desserts come from a table of pastries made in house; they also whip up mean ice creams and surround them with good-looking and luscious fruits and sauces. The wine list is just barely decent for a restaurant like this, but there is usually a surprise to be found. Several vintage ports are offered by the glass.

Service has improved a great deal, too. About the only distraction is that of the view which, when something is happening on the river, may steal your dining companion's attention. On Sundays, here is one of the classiest—and busiest—brunch buffets in the city. Every afternoon, there's high tea; it would be better if they got rid of the messy tea bags.

★ ★ Lido Gardens

4415 Airline Hwy., Metairie. 834-8233. 11 a.m.-2 p.m. Mon.-Fri.; 5-9 p.m. Mon.-Sat.; till 10 p.m. Fri. & Sat. AE, MC, V. $$

The menu of this somewhat obscure Italian cafe differs quite a bit from what one finds in similar places. It's more Northern Italian than Sicilian, and includes dishes rarely seen in New Orleans. There is not much polish to the food, but it can be good. The best dish is veal involtini, a football of darkish veal stuffed with prosciutto and mozzarella, served with a good bit of an oily sauce redolent of rosemary. Also in the plate, soaking up the oily sauce, is a chunk of polenta, the Italian answer to cornbread; it's still rather raw after a quick grilling, and occupies the space reserved in your stomach for potatoes. The pasta selection is led off by a very good lasagne, firm and cheesy. The thick red sauce on this and other dishes is too heavy for my taste. The fettuccine with sour cream, butter, and cheese is decent. Among the starters you'll find a good artichoke casserole and a very well-made Italian salad.

The location and the exterior look of the place are unpromising, but the rough spots tend to be more charming than exasperating.

★ ★ ★ Little Greek

2051 Metairie Rd., Old Metairie. 831-9470. 11 a.m.-2 p.m. and 5-9:30 p.m. Tues.-Sat.; till 10 p.m. Fri. & Sat. Noon-8 p.m. Sun. (4-8 p.m. during football season.) AE, CB, DC, MC, V. $$

This place really is little, and it really is Greek—the only recommendable Greek food in New Orleans at the moment, and the best we've had in about ten years. The worst part of eating here is getting a table; it always seems to be crowded, which doesn't take much. The menu covers the entire range of Greek cooking, from gyros sandwiches to elaborate platters.

Start with the flaky tiritrigona—little triangles of phyllo dough stuffed with cheese. The spanakopita (spinach pie) is served as a roll instead of the usual squares, but the flavor and flakiness are right on the money. Saganaki is a slab of white cheese sauteed with butter and lemon, flamed at the table; it's more interesting to see than to eat. Taramosalata—often called Greek caviar because of the presence of carp roe—is a great dip with raw vegetables. Hummus is not really Greek, but we welcome it anyway; it's a habit-forming dip made from chickpeas, sesame, garlic, and seasonings. Yet another dip, skordalia, is a magnificent white goo made with garlic, olive oil, bread, and (I think) almond; this would be great on fried eggplant or fried seafood, if they had them.

They serve most of the standards of everyday Greek eating here. The moussaka (a close cousin to shepherd's pie and lasagne, but with a milk-and-flour bechamel sauce as the starch component) is aromatic and complex in flavor. Souvlaki is Greek shishkabob; the Little Greek allows one a choice of beef, chicken, shrimp, or swordfish as the featured skeweree. Lamb is not listed as a souvlaki meat, but it is available in many other forms. In addition to a rack of lamb for two, there's a pair of thick, luscious chops dressed with garlic and feta cheese, and slices of lamb leg in an intense, herbal natural sauce.

The menu is light on seafood; the featured fish is a trout wrapped in phyllo and baked to a crispness. Like en croute dishes in any other language, this is more presentation than taste.

For dessert you get okay baklava and pretty-good galactoboureko. The latter is an unusual custard pie, and if I could forget the spectacular version they used to make at the Royal Oak I might like this one better.

Service and surroundings are minimal but good enough for the casual, inexpensive Greek cafe this is.

★ ★ Little Italians

4634 Veterans Blvd., Metairie. 888-3008. 11 a.m.-2:30 p.m. Mon.-Fri.; 5-9 p.m. Mon.-Thurs., till 10 p.m. Fri. and Sat.; Noon-9 p.m. Sun. CB, DC, MC, V. $$

The stark exterior in an unlikely location hides a quaint dining room and good country-style Northern Italian food. The good starters are the antipasto plate, the lentil soup, and the small portions of pasta. They have one of the most interesting red sauces I've ever eaten—herbal and aromatic. From there, the menu branches out in all directions. They do some interesting things with chicken. Angela chicken, for example, has a stuffing of bread, cheese, and prosciutto and a covering of mozzarella: very good, if a little heavy. The veal is a little on the tough side, but makes a fairly decent involtini. The fish is forgettable. Salads are assembled deftly from crisp greens.

The bread pudding is surprisingly delicious, with a rather sweet sauce. The dark, rich coffee completes a superb dessert course. Service is generally good, carried out more often than not by members of the family.

★ ★ ★ Little Tokyo

1521 N. Causeway, Metairie. 831-6788. 11:30 a.m.-2 p.m. Mon.-Fri. 5:30-10 p.m. Mon.-Sat. AE, CB, DC, MC, V. $$$

Trademark: shouted greetings from behind the sushi bar to anyone entering or leaving. This is a source of great amusement to all the faithful, of which this place has many. Little Tokyo's premises are a very small room dominated by the L-shaped sushi bar. The sushi and sashimi that proceeds from it are in the front rank locally—perfect in temperature, vividness of flavor, freshness, and appearance. The highly various assortments of sushi and sashimi are especially beautiful.

The fried-and-broiled side of the menu revolves around big boats of food, the most elaborate of which is the "Love Boat." The Love Boat contains tempura shrimp and vegetables, beef and chicken teriyaki, sashimi and sushi, and stacks of shredded crisp vegetables surmounted with an orange, carrot-tasting dressing. The boat is for two people, but it's enough food for a menage a trois at least. The tempuras are a bit oily, and the teriyakis fall short of exploding with flavor, but on the whole the boat's passengers are enjoyable.

Despite the small size of its dining room, Little Tokyo performs well the tableside rituals surrounding sukiyaki, shabu-shabu (both beef dishes) and yosenabe (a seafood equivalent of sukiyaki). The sukiyake comes out particularly fine, with beautiful translucent slices of vivid red beef and stacks of crisp vegetables.

★ ★ ★ Liuzza's

3636 Bienville St. 482-9120. 10:30 a.m.-11:30 p.m. Mon.-Sat. No credit cards. $

There is no better example of the New Orleans corner cafe than Liuzza's. The neon signs on the facade, the Barq's chalkboard of the day's specials on the sidewalk, and the small windows through which orders are pushed from the kitchen or from the bar are all quintessential. And there's a unique specialty: giant frozen glass schooners full of Barq's, beer, or (for the weird) red drink.

After a period of mediocrity, Liuzza's food in the last few years has been everything one would expect from a good neighborhood joint—and then some. The sandwiches and platters are consistently terrific, and the daily specials have gotten imaginative.

One day, for example, I had stuffed cucuzza—a long Italian squash. The red beans, spaghetti, stews, fried fish, and all the other specials have been very satisfying.

They make one of the best roast beef poor boys in town at Liuzza's. The beef is far above average, and the gravy is everything roast beef poor boy gravy should be. The dressings are fresh and the sandwich is big. The other poor boys are equally impressive; the list of choices is long. The perfect accompaniment is an order of French fries, which are cut from fresh potatoes—a very rare and welcome state of affairs.

LIVER. Liver is like Roquefort cheese, caviar, licorice, okra, and oysters—you either love it or you hate it. I love it, particularly in two very different forms. One of them is foie gras, the liver of a fattened goose or duck; see **Foie Gras.** The other is provimi veal liver, the tenderest, most flavorful form of calves' liver imaginable, found on the regular menu at **Clancy's** and occasionally at **Andrea's, Le Jardin,** and the **Grill Room.** It has also surfaced at **Brigtsen's** and **Constantin's,** which both serve rabbit livers when they're available; these are as tender and flavorful as anything I can think of. They make a fine chicken liver omelette at the **Coffee Pot.**

LOBSTER. Eating lobster violates one of my basic principles of great dining: "Eat it where it lives." Lobster, even flown in from Maine, lives on its fat and its flavor fades quickly. Only restaurants that move a lot of lobster should even be considered. The two best purveyors are **Ruth's**

Chris Steak House and Morton's Steak House. The former boils the decapods, the latter broils them; both are superb. **Andrea's** prepares its live lobsters in either the standard butter sauce or the spicier fra diavolo style; they take all the meat out of the shell for you. The **Regency Room** in the Quality Inn on Tulane Avenue, **Jim Chehardy's**, and **La Cuisine** also do a creditable job with live Maine lobsters. **Tavern on the Park** broils lobster tails from the Southern Hemisphere. Many shirt-sleeves seafood restaurants and Chinese restaurants serve tropical lobsters, which can be identified immediately by their lack of big claws. While good enough and a lot cheaper than northern lobsters, neither the flavor nor the experience of either alternative lobster equal those of Maine lobster, one of the world's great delicacies.

Eating a Maine lobster is not as great a challenge as it cracks up to be. The tail is universally split open for you when it comes to the table; the hardest work before you is breaking into the claws, and some restaurants will even take care of that. If you choose not to be a wimp, you'll do it yourself by using the claw cracker right behind the hinge of the claw. Peel off enough of the claw shell so that the meat can be pulled out (a lobster pick is usually not necessary, because by the time lobster gets to New Orleans it has shrunk inside its shell). You can also go after the meat in all the other legs, which is extracted by sucking. (All of this is perfectly proper.) Inside the head cavity everything is edible except the gills. Two particular treats are the tomalley (the green liver) and the coral (the roe).

LOST BREAD. "Pain perdu," as the Old Creoles like my mother called it, got its name from its use of day-old stale French bread. Lost for most purposes to which French bread is usually put, these crusts are soaked in eggs and milk, fried or grilled, and served for breakfast. It is, you've noticed, quite like French toast, except that lost bread tends to be a good deal richer.

Lost bread is not often seen in New Orleans restaurants, mostly because not many Creole restaurants serve breakfast. The best is at the **Coffee Pot**, but they also turn it out well at the **Cafe Pontchartrain, Begue's**, and **La Gauloise**.

No lost bread I have ever tasted in a restaurant was anything like the lost bread I used to eat as a child. My mother used regular white sliced bread, soaked it in the custard until it was almost falling apart, and then deep-fried it. While this may seem to be a recipe for oil-logging some bread, that doesn't happen; the most outstanding characteristic of this stuff is its oozy richness.

As for the other nine dishes I've tapped as the Ten Best Dishes in the local cuisine for this book, here is a recipe.

4 eggs
8 slices stale white bread (preferably sliced thick) cut in half
OR 12 slices of stale French bread

2 Tbs. sugar
1 Tbs. vanilla extract
½ cup half-and-half cream
½ tsp. cinnamon
2 dashes nutmeg
1 cup peanut oil

1. In a wide bowl (a soup dish is perfect), beat the eggs while adding the sugar, vanilla, cream, cinnamon, and nutmeg, until all ingredients (especially the cinnamon) are blended in.
2. Dip the slices of bread into the egg mixture and let them get very soaked.
3. Heat the oil in a large black iron skillet to about 350 degrees. Lower two pieces of soaked bread at a time into the oil and fry about two minutes on each side. Let it cook to a darker brown than your instincts might tell you.
4. Remove the lost bread as it's cooked, and drain it on paper towels. Use another towel to blot the excess oil from the top. Meanwhile, continue cooking the rest of the bread in small batches, allowing the temperature of the oil to recover between batches.
5. Serve immediately with powdered sugar, honey, or syrup. (Warn your guests about the lava-like heat of the insides!)
Serves four.

★ ★ ★ Louisiana Pizza Kitchen

2800 Esplanade Ave., Mid-City. 488-2800. ● 95 French Market Place (near the end of the vegetable stalls), French Quarter. 522-9500. 5:30-11 p.m. seven nights. AE, MC, V. $$.

This is the most interesting member of the flock of cafes that recently opened on Esplanade. It started out as a pretty bad French cafe-bakery. The same owner came up with a much better gimmick in 1987: small, crusty French-style pizzas baked in a wood-burning stone oven. Do I even need to tell you that this is the way they do it in Italy? Or that wood-burning pizza ovens are avant-garde? Or that all of this is supposed to be somehow good?

The crust (which, to my thinking, is overwhelmingly the most important part of a pizza) is most unusual here. It is quite similar to the little snack pastries made in Alsace and Provence. It has the texture of an undercooked cracker. Small semi-blackened areas lend an interesting smoky flavor. Large areas on top remain uncovered by anything. Most of the ingredients are piled near the middle; you can redistribute the stuff yourself if you must. Some people love this oddity; others think it's bizarre and awful.

They don't use much red sauce here. A typical pizza combines Italian sausage, duck sausage, prosciutto, and mozzarella with herbs as the topping. Amazingly, the mozzarella is buffalo-milk mozzarella, imported (with great difficulty) from Italy. On the table is a bottle of olive oil with sprigs of fresh herbs inside; you are instructed to pour some of this on the pizza. Different again, but delicious.

The pizzas are about eight inches across and sell for around $5. They look insubstantial but do a good job of filling you up. The best strategy is to order several different varieties and pass them around.

The menu goes on to include a few simple pasta dishes, amply served and tasty enough. Linguini al pesto has a fine sauce of olive oil, fresh basil, pine nuts, and a very substantial amount of garlic. Pasta can also be had with a robust tomato sauce. Starters include okay fried calamari, a great plate of mozzarella di bufalo with tomatoes and a fine Greek salad. The dessert list is that of Angelo Brocato's, plus a custard.

Despite the low prices and loose atmosphere, there are tablecloths and cloth napkins on the table. Service has always been the worst part of the restaurant; its slowness is aggravated by the fact that it's not always easy to get a table in the first place.

The French Market location is bigger and has a somewhat more extensive menu, but the pizzas remain the feature and are essentially the same.

★ ★ ★ ★ Louis XVI

730 Bienville St., in the St. Louis Hotel. Reservations 581-7000. 6-10:30 p.m. seven nights. AE, CB, DC, MC, V. $$$$$

This is the restaurant which first demonstrated, in 1970, that a Continental menu could survive in New Orleans. A few years ago it moved to a smaller but more handsome space in the St. Louis Hotel. The room is colorful and made to seem spacious by walls of mirrors and big windows looking out onto a courtyard; chairs are big and comfortable. The service is by ceremonious captains who perform a good bit of tableside folderol.

Save for a few Creole fillips like oysters Rockefeller, shrimp remoulade, and blackened fish (all of which, by the way, are quite good), it's classic Escoffier all the way. It may be old hat, but it's good old hat. The best starters are the oysters, the terrine of veal and pork, the smoked salmon, and the escargots, all of which are done strictly by the book. Soups are no big deal, but the daily vegetable creams are fluffy and vivid.

Red meats—particularly roasts for two like Chateaubriand or rack of lamb in pastry—are the great specialties. Louis XVI introduced beef Wellington locally, but I never liked it much—terrible texture. A better dish— the best in the house, in fact—is filet St. Hebert, a steak marinated in the style of venison and served with a powerful, translucent brown sauce. There's also a competently-done steak au poivre.

One can eat lighter than this, however. Thick fillets of salmon and other fish are grilled until black stripes show, then sharpened with two different mustard sauces or with Louis XVI's great bearnaise or hollandaise.

A breast of chicken grilled with fragrant herbes de Provence is eminently flavorful. To be avoided is the crabmeat-topped trout Louis XVI, from which no clear flavor emerges.

The veal Louis XVI is a very simply prepared plate of tasty scallops in a light sauce of butter, lemon, and wine. Canard Grand Veneur is tender, ruddy slices of duck breast in an aromatic sauce reminiscent of the one on the filet St. Hebert.

The wine list here has a few points of interest, but the food and surroundings deserve a better selection. The prices are a touch high. Desserts are all the usual flaming ones, an ice-cream crepe with oranges and lemons and chocolate, homemade sorbets and pastries. Good coffee. The French bread served throughout the meal smells and tastes great and comes with a ramekin of very well made garlic-and-herb butter.

LUNCH. I think the best thing that could possibly happen to our culture (after, of course, the elimination of bigotry and poverty) would be for lunch to become the main meal of the day, as it is in the Spanish-speaking world. You know, a long meal followed by at least an hour's rest before re-opening the shop or office. It makes more sense to eat your major meal in the middle of the day; there's less chance that the food you eat at lunch will wind up on your hips.

Every restaurant treats lunch differently. Some places don't even serve the meal; others are lunch specialists, running more specials and doing more business around noon than they do at dinner. Antoine's and Galatoire's have the same menu and prices at both meals, but for some reason both places seem more appealing at midday than at night.

There's one class of restaurant I stay away from at lunch. Chinese places compete strictly at the price level at midday. The egg roll-entree-fried rice specials for $3.50 are of predictable quality, and the buffets that have been springing up lately are even worse.

Here is a list of the ten restaurants with the most attractive lunch offerings—considering both deliciousness and value.

1. Commander's Palace
2. Arnaud's
3. Andrea's
4. Mr. B's
5. Ruth's Chris
6. La Cuisine
7. Gambrill's
8. Delmonico
9. Galatoire's
10. Bayona

Our deft proofreader Jennifer Connell, who never hesitates to make editorial suggestions, said that this entry really needed a list of the best really cheap lunch places. Good idea, Jen—here are the restaurants with the best lunch specials under $6:

1. Uglesich's
2. Barrow's
3. Mother's
4. Dooky Chase
5. Coffee Pot
6. Mandina's
7. Liuzza's
8. Toney's Spaghetti House
9. Copeland's
10. Serio's

★Luther's

2750 Severn, Metairie. 888-6370. ● 4950 Lapalco Blvd., Marrero. 347-0624. ● 8740 West Judge Perez, Chalmette. 227-8167. All: 11 a.m.-10 p.m. seven days; till 11 p.m. Fri. & Sat. (Metairie open an hour later at night.) No credit cards. $

This Texas chain of fast-food barbecue restaurants would hardly be worth talking about if New Orleans had any serious barbecue action, but it doesn't. Luther's slow-smokes its meats reasonably well, but its sauces and side dishes are terrible. They also grill hamburgers to order, and these are surprisingly good, thick, and juicy. The onion rings are jammed into a frying basket and come out in loaf form; this makes them oilier than optimum, but not too bad. Iced tea comes in mammoth glasses. The restaurant looks and feels good, all surfaces being of weathered wood.

M as in muffuletta

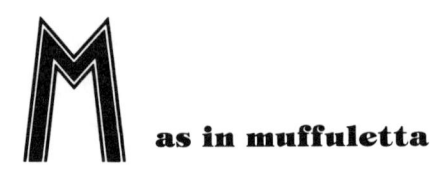

★★ Mama Igor's

4437 Magazine, Uptown. 895-5492. 5-11 p.m. seven nights. AE, MC, V. $$

A smallish, darkish, comfortably furnished Uptown corner restaurant, Mama Igor's (what a name!) specializes in complete dinners of Italian standards—pasta with red sauces, lasagne, veal, and a bit of seafood. The attraction is that the prices are low and an enormous amount of food is served in several courses. It's decent food, but not much more than that. Service is passable or less.

★ Mama Rosa's

616 N. Rampart, French Quarter. 523-5546. 10:30 a.m.-Midnight Tues.-Sun. MC, V. $

A few years ago People Magazine named Mama Rosa's Little Slice of Italy as the ninth best pizza in America. No doubt this datum came to the magazine from an overeager stringer, because while the thick-crust pizza here is above the local average, it would be of no more than routine interest in real pizza territory like New Jersey or Chicago. The sauces and cheeses are better than the crust, which tends to breadiness. Ironically, the best food at Mama Rosa's is not the pizza but the sandwiches, made on a delicious homemade bread. Italian plate specials are good enough and accompanied by the same bread (the best part). The premises are raffish but comfortable. There are times when the whole staff seems to be in a mood, and the experience becomes a mild trial.

★★ Mandarin Cafe

1011 Gravier, CBD. 566-0355. 11:15 a.m.-8 p.m. Mon.-Fri. AE, MC, V. $$

Four things that are almost always dreadful are Chinese restaurants in the CBD, Chinese lunches, Chinese buffets, and restaurants in office buildings. Although the Mandarin Cafe matches all those descriptions, it once again proves that good food is where you find it. Hot and sour soup, spring rolls, crab Rangoon, and fried dumplings are all first-class starters. The handful of entree offerings have all been pretty good; the best is the Hunan-style orange-flavor steak, with a very well-made, zippy sauce washing over tender beef slices. The crystal shrimp with its translucent ginger sauce, General Tso's spicy chicken, and the soft shell crab with garlic sauce are all as good as most other versions around town. The $6 buffet is even reasonably edible. Quick service.

★★★ Mandich's

3200 St. Claude Ave., Bywater. 947-9553. 11 a.m.-2:30 p.m. Tues.-Fri.; 5-10 p.m. Fri. and Sat. MC, V. $$

Almost unknown except to its regulars, this reliable old neighborhood restaurant, just past the tracks in the Bywater section, is a revelation to anybody who "discovers" it. Weekdays, they put out fine sandwiches and plate lunches. But the times to come here are Friday and Saturday nights—the only times the place is open for dinner. Then the menu expands to include food that seems too good for the scruffy surroundings (premises as well as neighborhood).

Shrimp remoulade, with its good homemade sauce, is a tasty appetizer; the seafood gumbo also starts a meal off well. Oysters bordelaise are great either as a starter or a main course. They're big fried bivalves with a great garlicky butter sauce. The same sauce finds its way onto my favorite entree here, the chicken bordelaise, which smells incredibly good and comes with pasta so you can get even more of the sauce into your mouth.

Trout Mandich is the best of the seafood entrees. This is pure Creole: herbal and crusty in the same way that panneed veal is, and eminently edible down to the last morsel. They also do nice broiled fish. A legend among the port and military personnel who frequent Mandich's is the lofty, beer-can-shaped filet mignon with butter sauce. This is totally delicious, especially with some of the aforementioned bordelaise sauce.

Finish the meal with the thick, tasty bread pudding. Prices are low, service and surroundings are sufficient unto the day.

★★ Mandina's

3800 Canal, Mid City. 482-9179. 11 a.m.-10:30 p.m. Mon.-Thurs., till 11 p.m. Fri. and Sat.; 3-10 p.m. Sun. No credit cards. $$

To the crowds who keep this neon-drenched old restaurant packed at all hours, Mandina's represents the happier times when we had many restaurants like this. Although I think they could find better fodder for nostalgia, Mandina's is pretty good—although not good enough to keep me there if the bar is jammed with other supplicants waiting for tables.

The menu covers the seafood-Italian-sandwich axis common to places like this; some parts of it are better than others. The sandwiches, for instance, are beyond reproach—especially the superb fried ham poor boy. Lunch specials like boiled brisket, beef stew, smothered chicken, and stuffed shrimp are the best food in the house, served in portions too big for even the very hungry.

Basic fried seafood is decent. But avoid anything with a complicated-sounding sauce; they tend to be confused in taste and unattractive in texture. The Italian dishes vary wildly from excellent to forgettable. Mandina's has an extensive sandwich menu that includes a good hot roast beef (either poor boy style or in the disappearing open-face format) and very crisp, buttery fried seafood loaves.

The bread pudding and the custard are top-notch desserts. Service is performed by waiters who don't appear to give a good damn.

MARCHAND DE VIN. A thick, heady, old-style brown sauce made (if they do it right, anyway) of a roux, red wine, beef stock, and seasonings. It reaches its apex at Antoine's, which has terrific steaks to slather it over. Most others are much less interesting; the one at Galatoire's, for example, has an oversupply of chipped marrow that makes it almost inedibly rich. Marchand de vin sauce is good with almost anything except fish.

MARDI GRAS. The Carnival season, which begins on January 6 and builds until Mardi Gras (the day before Ash Wednesday), is absolutely the worst time of the year to find a good meal in New Orleans. Especially in the last week, the restaurants are either full or impossible to get to because of parades. In the Quarter many places raise their prices and cut their menus. And the street food is unspeakable.

The best possible meal on Mardi Gras is at **Brennan's** which, despite being surrounded by crowds, manages to stay open.

★Mark Twain Pizza Landing.

2035 Metairie Rd., Metairie. 832-8032. 11 a.m.-10 p.m. Mon.-Sat., till 11 p.m. Fri. and Sat.; 3-10 p.m. Sun. No credit cards. $

What Samuel Clemens or the marks on the side of a ship have to do with pizza eludes me. More easily understood is the goodness of the pizza in this little, old-fashioned parlor. The basic item has a crust that's far from the best of my life, but the sauces and toppings are so good and so imaginative that I enjoy a pizza here anyway. The Creole pizza, with its topping of shrimp, crabmeat, andouille sausage, and zucchini, has a fine, light taste. The house combination includes first-class salami, artichokes, sausage, and basil—another winner. They can also crank out a better-than-average poor boy sandwich. Not much on looks, but nice to know.

★ ★ ★ Martin Wine Cellar Deli

3827 Baronne St., Uptown. 899-7411. • *714 Elmeer at Veterans Blvd., Metairie. 896-7300. Both: 9 a.m.-6 p.m. Mon.-Sat.; 10 a.m.-1 p.m. Sun. MC, V. $*

Finding decent deli in New Orleans is almost impossible, but the deli at Martin Wine Cellar—the city's leading wine emporium—is a good place to look. The meats, cheeses, and breads are of extremely good quality, and the sandwich combinations are clever and (most of them, anyway) tasty. My favorites are the Downtowner (a thick layer of rare roast beef, Jarlsberg cheese, and mustard on a great pumpernickel roll), the deli deluxe (hot corned beef and pastrami, Swiss cheese, and Russian dressing), and the sailor sandwich (a spicy knockwurst, corned beef, and cheese on rye). They also make things like BLTs, clubs, hamburgers, and regular poor boys.

The deli case contains a great selection of cheeses, meats, and salads; you can assemble your own thing. The lox is very good and makes a fine sandwich inside a bagel spread with cream cheese. They slice everything to go; on weekends, there are terrific specials on roast beef, pastrami, lox, etc.

Since you can pick out a bottle to go with your sandwich from the adjacent shelves, Martin's has what amounts to the best wine list in town. They'll even decant for you!

Note: Both wine stores are open an hour later than the deli hours above.

★ ★ ★ Masson's

7200 Pontchartrain Blvd. 283-2525. 11:30 a.m.-3 p.m. Tues.-Fri.; 5-10 p.m. Tues.-Sat.; Noon-8 p.m. Sun. AE, DC, MC, V. $$

Masson's was considered special-occasion dining in the Fifties and Sixties. Eating there now measures how far we have come. Masson's looks, cooks, serves, and costs less like today's grand gourmet restaurants and more like a rather fancy neighborhood place. On the other hand, after a decade or so of stasis the menu is progressing in an agreeable way, held back only by the many regulars who still demand things the old way—which, fortunately, was never too bad a way.

Masson's still starts you off with a basket of hot, peppery breadsticks. The oysters Bienville are still well above average. They still turn out a fine rack of lamb, marinated and roasted to a juicy turn, eight chops wide, for under $20, with soup and vegetables. They still have an under-$15 four-course dinner. But one night the dinner special on the dinner was a piece of delectable grilled drumfish, topped with a buster crab and moistened with a pink crawfish sauce. That was delightful, a steal at the price, and typical of the new food.

Other new dishes of note: a creamy seafood pasta, grilled tuna and salmon (quite a change for a restaurant which was stretching to put crabmeat on top of fish a few years ago), grilled chicken breast (available with a very well-made bearnaise to compromise the healthfulness of the dish), surf and surf (clever: a seafood brochette paired with a Caribbean lobster tail). The salads are now abetted by sunflower seeds and sprouts.

The dessert list includes, in addition to that awful ball of butter cream they call an almond torte, the delightful strawberry beignets—served with a sabayon sauce. Service, from the valet parking on, is far more cordial and efficient than it once was. Masson's seems to have turned the corner, and I'm optimistic about its continued improvement.

★ ★ ★ Maximo's Italian Grill

1117 Decatur, French Quarter. 586-8883. 5:30 p.m.-1 a.m. Mon.-Thurs.; 11:30 a.m.-2 a.m. Fri. & Sat.; 11:30 a.m.-1 a.m. Sun. $$

Offbeat interior architecture, especially for a French Quarter building: one long dining room done in shades of dark grey and black, culminating in an open kitchen. Surrounding the ranges is a long counter with stools, creating a sort of Camellia Grill effect. Opposite this is a row of booths, completing the diner effect in the rear half of the restaurant. A convivial, relaxing hangout.

The kitchen also takes a casual approach to the classical strictures of Northern Italian cooking, both in inspiration and execution. For example, pasta Rosa—one of the best dishes in the house—is tortelloni (bigger than tortellini, but still round and cheese-stuffed) awash in a light orange sauce with sun-dried tomatoes, shrimp, arugula, garlic, and no small amount of cayenne pepper. Another good starter is carpaccio. Ordinarily that's pounded slices of raw beef, but at Maximo's they roast it a little bit. Mussels, calamari, and a thick seafood sausage also push the appetizer button.

Lots of pasta, all available in small portions and with your choice of pasta shape. Two sauces of particular note are the spicy marinara sauce with shrimp and the gorgonzola-sharp three-cheese-and-cream affair. The pasta itself is clearly of fine quality, with a firm texture and satisfying taste.

My favorite of the entrees is the marinated half chicken, scented with rosemary and roasted to a near-crisp skin. Chicken is good across the board, for that matter; the pecan chicken has a Creole rather than Italian taste, but suffers not from the culture clash.

The standard veal dishes are here, led by a decent saltimbocca: a slice of veal wrapped around prosciutto, cheese, and a fresh sage leaf, moistened with a mushroom sauce. The veal chops look good but the treatment they get is a bit boring. Seafood is confined mostly to decent grilled specials and a chunky cioppino—the San Francisco-Italian seafood stew—with far too much pepper.

The desserts are limited and just okay. Service is a little jerky at this writing. The wine list is surprisingly good, with many selections offered by the glass.

★ ★ Mena's Palace

622 Iberville, French Quarter. 525-0217. 6:30 a.m.-6:45 p.m. Mon.-Sat. No credit cards. $

The population of this surprisingly good, very cheap neighborhood restaurant is evenly split between those wearing suits and those wearing togs suitable for manual labor. The menu is on a board and includes all the local classic plates and poor boy sandwiches, served with uncanny rapidity. The red beans are delicious, and come with the biggest (and ugliest) piece of smoked sausage I've ever had before me and a salad for about $3. The fried seafood is also decent. I have seen better beef in a roast beef poor boy, but the flavor of Mena's version is just about right. The "palace" is a bit of a joke, but the place is clean enough and not bad-looking as neighborhood restaurants go.

MENU. Most of the reviews in this book originally appeared in *The New Orleans Menu*, a newsletter-magazine about dining out I have published since 1977. Each 40-page issue reviews at least six restaurants in great depth, with reports of new openings and updates of old places. If you like the writing in this book, you'll love Menu. For a free sample, write me at MENU, P.O. Box 51831, New Orleans, LA 70151.

MENU DEGUSTATION. This is an enhancement of the table d'hote dinner concept. It is an abundance of small courses that usually includes all of the day's specials. This format has become popular in the most ambitious hotel restaurants, notably **Henri** and the **Sazerac**.

★ ★ Messina's

200 Chartres, French Quarter. 523-9225. 11:30 a.m.-9 p.m. Tues.-Sat.; till 10 p.m. Sat. AE, MC, V. $$

Two specialties: oysters and muffulettas. There's a raw bar at which one can down an agreeably cold, salty dozen on the half shell. At the tables, one discovers that the olive salad on the muffuletta is the chunkiest in memory—whole pieces of marinated cauliflower, celery, and perhaps even a whole olive. The menu goes on to include okayish fried seafood and a few other plate specials. The restaurant looks like the neighborhood cafes that used to be on corners all over town, but its Quarter location has made it a little touristy.

MEUNIERE. The name is a French reference to the wife of a miller of flour. Anything meuniere is dusted or dredged in flour and then either sauteed or fried. It is usually then moistened with browned butter, giving rise to something called a "meuniere sauce." In New Orleans, the brownness is frequently abetted with anything from Worcestershire sauce to beef stock. The best meuniere sauces—starting with one in the brown-butter style and increasing in complication and thickness—are at **Galatoire's, Christian's, Andrea's, Flagons, Arnaud's, Mr. B's,** and **Commander's Palace.** See Trout Meuniere.

MEXICAN. Mexican cuisine is spotty east of the Sabine River, and New Orleans is no exception to that rule. Our Mexican places are limited mostly to the samenesses of tortilla-based . highly-Americanized dishes—**Cuco's** being the best of that ilk. There are, however, a few places operated by Mexican families: **El Patio** (most ambitious and best Mexican menu in town, full of seafood, chicken, and broiled meat dishes), **Casa Garcia,** and **Castillo's. Vera Cruz** and **Santa Fe** have the most innovative menus. The **Bean Pot** is raffish but has tasty, unconventional Mexican food. **Taqueria Corona,** another hole in the wall, puts forth spectacular tacos grilled from big chunks of meat to order.

It's unfortunate that the public perceives Mexican restaurants as inexpensive and casual, and will not tolerate the prices the restaurants would need to charge to cook the kind of foodstuffs you'd find in a French restaurant. Yet the Mexican cuisine is so rich and interesting that it could probably produce some exciting high-end dining. This is already beginning to happen around the country, particularly in the Southwest, where Mexican and nouvelle-American tastes are forging an entirely new cuisine. We've tasted just a little of it in New Orleans—at **Cucaracha Cafe,** and on specials lists at other places—but it hasn't really hit here yet.

★ Michael's Grill

4139 Canal, Mid City. 488-2878. 11 a.m.-11 p.m. Mon.-Fri. 5 p.m.-11 p.m. Sat. 5 p.m.-10 p.m. Sun. AE, CB, DC, MC, V. $$.

This new cafe specializes in big, fresh, charcoal-grilled hamburgers that attempt to be what the Port of Call's are, but fall a bit short of that goal. The juiciness is not there, and the grilled crustiness is a bit overdone. Michael's achieves a certain notoriety for serving a $100 hamburger, topped with caviar and served with a bottle of Dom Perignon, but this is more novelty than culinary accomplishment. They do turn out a great, rib-sticking soup of black beans and andouille, some nicely-grilled and relatively inexpensive fresh fish, and mediocre but expensive prime steaks. Lunch specials are very inexpensive and decent.

★ ★ ★ Middendorf's

Manchac (Akers, La.), 38 miles northwest of New Orleans via I-10 and I-55 (Exit 15). 1-386-6666. 10:45 a.m.-9:30 p.m. Mon.-Sat.; till 9 p.m. Sun. MC, V. $$

Many Orleanians associate the eating of fried catfish with 75 miles of driving because of this restaurant, which is actually two restaurants of substantial size in the very small fishing community of Manchac. The operation is classic New Orleans-style seafood house: Formica-topped tables, bustle, noise, and large amounts of freshly-prepared seafood. Start with the raw oysters, which are consistently near the top of the range of oyster goodness. Then get into the fried seafood: oysters, shrimp, trout, soft-shell crabs, and that house specialty. The catfish can be had in either thin or thick fillets (I prefer thin, because it's crunchy; both dimensions have their adherents). You can have either a large or a small order; I always finish a large. The cornmeal coating is almost sizzling, and the fish is tasty and free of excess oil. Service is a little slow, since everything is cooked to order. But after the drive to get there, who's in a hurry to get back on the road?

★ ★ ★ Mike Anderson's

215 Bourbon St., French Quarter. 524-3884. 11:30 a.m.-10 p.m. seven days, till 11 p.m. Fri. and Sat. AE, MC, V. $$

Next door to Galatoire's, football hero Mike Anderson operates the second edition (the first is in Baton Rouge) of a seafood restaurant whose principal theme is tremendous portions. The seafood platter, for instance, comes out on a large metal fish that hardly fits on the table. Surprise! The cooking is actually quite good. The fried seafood comes out hot, crisp, and nicely seasoned, for the most part (frogs' leg have been the only real disaster for me). The menu is the familiar fried seafood with a few broiled and stuffed items, all prepared well. They also assemble multi-course dinners of shrimp, crabmeat, and crawfish; the various parts of these range from the delicious to the atrocious, but there's so much food that you can fill up easily on the best stuff.

Service is fine, but the clean-up effort could be more meticulous.

★ ★ Mimi's

10160 Jefferson Hwy., River Ridge. 737-6464. 5-10 p.m. Tues.-Sat. No credit cards. $$

The Harahan-River Ridge area has very few decent restaurants, and this is one of them. It's a cute, clean little bistro with a Leo Meiersdorff mural and a friendly feel. The menu is mostly Italian—the basics with red sauces. The best starter is the barbecued shrimp, which look a little odd and are not as spicy as I'd like but are otherwise pretty good. Skip the soups. Lasagne is served with meatballs or Italian sausage on the side and a well-made, light tomato sauce. There is also a good bit of seafood on the menu of reasonably decent quality. For dessert, there's a good bread pudding. Like most neighborhood places, Mimi's is fine if you live in the neighborhood, but probably not worth a trip across town.

★ Ming Palace

4513 Airline Hwy., Metairie. 887-3295. 11 a.m.-10 p.m. Tues.-Fri.; 4-11 p.m. Sat; Noon-10 p.m. Sun. AE, CB, DC, MC, V. $$

A pleasant enough neighborhood Chinese restaurant on the bustling corner of Airline Highway and Clearview Parkway, the Ming Palace serves very basic Cantonese food of reasonably decent quality but no great elaborateness or innovation.

★★ Miss Ruby's

539 St. Philip, French Quarter. 523-3514. Noon-10 p.m. seven days. No credit cards. $

This ramshackle little restaurant took over a corner of a French Quarter warehouse, installed some long tables which you'll probably wind up sharing with somebody else, and fired up a kitchen with some excellent cooking. The food here has a Southern, rather than Creole taste, and that sets it enough apart to make it interesting.

The menu changes daily; everything is fresh. The homemade soups are basic and wonderful—gumbo, vegetable, pea, that sort of thing. The entree to get is a half chicken—either broiled just about perfectly with a tasty complement of seasonings, or deftly fried with a fine, greaseless crust. The fried catfish, broiled trout, blackened fish, red beans and rice, and jambalaya have also been enjoyable. The desserts are mostly homemade pies: tall, homely, very sweet, and reminiscent of a simpler, happier time. Service is very friendly, the portions are large, and the prices are moderate. Miss Ruby has a dedicated following of Quarterites, who indulge in camaraderie at the communal tables.

★★★★★ Mr. B's

201 Royal, French Quarter. Reservations 523-2078. 11:30 a.m.-3 p.m. and 5-10 p.m. seven days. Sun. Brunch 11-3. AE, CB, DC, MC, V. $$$

Mr. B's opened in 1979 as a casual, pop-Creole French Quarter branch of Commander's Palace. It has since evolved into one of the most ambitious and best restaurants in the city, while retaining its comfortable, easy ambiance. There's one huge walnut-paneled room, zoned with etched-glass panels. All the tables are too small. Along one wall is a long bar; near the entrance is a grand piano; at dinner, a pianist is there, too. A back door admits directly from Westminster Parking on Iberville, whose fee the restaurant absorbs; this makes Mr. B's the most convenient restaurant in the Quarter.

In the center of the kitchen is a wood-stoked grill over which is cooked the restaurant's signature dish: hickory-grilled fish, crusty and spicy. Also ducks, chickens, steaks, brochettes of shrimp and andouille, and whatever else seems likely. All of this is inspired, exciting cooking with ingredients of superb fresh quality.

But skills extend beyond grilling here. Start with coconut and beer-battered shrimp, catfish beignets, great crusty, herbal fried eggplant sticks, or a small order of pasta. Better yet, soup — particularly the gumbo ya-ya, which is without doubt the world's greatest chicken gumbo. It's a spicy, dark-roux bowlful, chunky with chicken and discs of terrific andouille sausage. They also serve a seafood gumbo and some other old-style Creole potages, all tasty, if not quite as monumental as the ya-ya.

Mr. B's has some of the city's most interesting salads, beginning with the Solari's Market salad (sorta Greek). Chef Gerard Maras has been a leader in scouting out unusual vegetables from nearby farms, and nowhere has this proven more rewarding than in the salad department.

They perform amazing feats with all kinds of entree foodstuffs. But the dish that most turns me on is an astounding improvement on the old New Orleans classic, barbecue shrimp. Unlike most re-workings of Manale's creation, this one doesn't introduce a bunch of new flavors; it just polishes up the butter-and-pepper sauce from a rather oily affair into a creamy-looking, limpid sauce. These are far and away the best barbecue shrimp in town now.

Reduced-stock sauces show up to good effect on the meat and poultry dishes. The filet mignon with a raison and port wine sauce and the chicken with sweet garlic glaze are especially wonderful. The several daily specials bring out some great seafood: salmon, swordfish, tuna, sheepshead, and other unusual denizens of the deep, in subtly-sauced preparations. Mr. B's has always featured pasta: the carbonara and the primavera are fine examples of those dishes, and the pasta jambalaya — a dish created here and spreading around town lately — is a stroke of genius. (It tastes just like it sounds.)

The wine list is all-California (except for Dom Perignon, a favorite of Cindy Brennan's) and very well selected. The best dessert is the light, custardy bread pudding. If you really like chocolate, the Mr. B's chocolate cake is several layers of what amounts to almost solid chocolate. The coffee is great. Service is that super-efficient Brennan variety that sometimes makes you feel as if you're caught in a machine, but anything you ask will be done graciously.

★ ★ ★ Mr. Tai's

701 Metairie Road, Metairie. 831-8610. 11 a.m.-2 p.m. Mon.-Fri. 5 p.m.-10 p.m. Tues.-Sat.; till 11 p.m. Fri. & Sat. AE, MC. V. $$

Here is one of relatively few local examples of a new generation of American Chinese restaurant. It doesn't look especially Chinese—no dragons or pagodas or bright reds in the decor. The waiters at dinner wear black tie. And the menu proclaims the absence of MSG in its dishes. When Mr. Tai's opened in 1987 its menu was full of highly polished dishes with ingredients one rarely ate in a Chinese place—lamb and liver, for example. Since then, however, the menu has become more conventional and the executions less distinctive.

Start with the minced quail, mixed with vegetables and seasonings, spooned into a lettuce leaf. The cold chicken salad with its nutty sauce is also a good starter. Less good are the somewhat oily spring rolls and the uninteresting shrimp toast. The Hunan beef soup is dominated by five-spice powder, a fascinating taste that goes a little overboard here; the slices of tender beef and broccoli are needed to open your throat again.

The entrees still include a lot of offbeat food, most of it in the slightly sweet, slightly spicy Hunan style. The calf's liver is a little tough but the taste is unimpeachable; hot Szechuan chili peppers go very well with liver. Another inspired combination here is the richness of lamb with the background sweetness of a Hunan sauce. The Hunan duck, on the other hand, is sauceless and not spicy at all; presented somewhat like Peking duck, it has a pronounced smokiness from tea leaves and camphor. Its crispness arises from the deep-frying the bird gets for its final cooking step. The spicy squid is very spicy and very good. The whole fish has a gingery brown sauce studded with—of all things—pine nuts. More conventional than any of this is Mr. Tai's chicken; the sauce is a collection of vegetables bathed in a thick, well-balanced, slightly spicy sauce.

Service here is a bit cold, and prices are a touch high. For months before this writing, the background music tape had serious wows. Carelessness has clearly set in, but a meal here is still well above average neighborhood Chinese. Incidentally, despite the suggestive name there is no connection between this place and the trend-setting Uncle Tai's of Houston (formerly New York).

MIXED GRILL. As grilled foods became popular, restaurants began mixing and matching. This works very well for meats and poultry; some good ones are at **Windsor Court Grill Room, Flagons,** and **Mr. B's.** Typically, you get small pieces of grilled steak, lamb, andouille and chicken—sometimes with a sauce, sometimes not.

A trend currently gaining favor is the mixed grilling of fish. I am less sanguine about this idea. The problem is that there is an ideal size fillet for grilling — about eight ounces. This is much bigger than any restaurant will give you on a plate of three different fish. (Besides, most such platters use end cuts to begin with.) So what you get is typically dried out.

The classic English mixed grill is, sad to say, rarely seen in New Orleans. Such a platter would include mostly variety meats: liver, kidney, sausage, and the like. The last time I ran into this was at an ex-restaurant called The Quarter Deck, which slapped me with the only lawsuit of my career for my report on the dish. Although I easily beat the suit, I have been nervous about mixed grill ever since.

MONDAY DINING. See the index at the end of the book for restaurants open on Monday.

★ Monroe's

3218 Magazine, Uptown. 891-1897. 11:30 a.m.-2:00 p.m. Mon.-Fri.; 6-10 p.m. seven nights. AE, CB, DC, MC, V. $$.

Very popular with the Tulane University crowd, Monroe's is a rather tones-down fern restaurant with a salad bar, steaks, grilled seafood, and ice cream desserts, absolutely none of which rises above the level of mediocre.

MOO-SHU PORK. The fanciest commonly-found dish in Chinese restaurants, moo-shu pork (also spelled "mo-shu," "mo-shee," and "mu shu"), exemplifies the flavor and style of Mandarin cooking. The slivers of pork are stir-fried with scallions, cloud-ear mushrooms, tiger-lily petals, and egg curdles, and brought to the table with the same floury, thin crepes you get with Peking duck. Some restaurants also bring the thick, slightly sweet, aromatic hoisin sauce; this is not authentic, but it does add something to the dish.

Here's how you eat moo-shu pork. Spread the sauce on the pancakes, and spoon on about three-quarters as much of the pork conglomeration as you think appropriate in a more or less straight line, leaving about an inch of the crepe dry at one end. Then roll up the crepe and fold over the dry end to keep the contents from oozing out the bottom. (Chances are it will anyway—either that, or a crevasse will open in the side of the crepe.) Then eat. It is a virtual certainty that you'll run out of crepes before you run out of pork. So either specify that you want an extra order of crepes (communicating your intention to pay for them; for some reason, Chinese restaurateurs are more niggardly about their crepes than anything else), or just go ahead and eat the remainder with a fork or chopsticks.

The best versions of moo-shu pork are at **Dragon's Garden, East China, China Doll, Great Wall, Jade East, Kung's Dynasty,** and **Peking.**

★★★ Moran's Riverside

44 French Market (at Dumaine). Reservations 529-1583. 6-11 p.m. Mon.-Sat.; till Midnight Fri. & Sat. AE, CB, DC, MC, V. $$$$

Moran's is the major restaurant of the French Market complex, with an exceptional view of the river from its second-story aerie. The newer of its two dining rooms is a magnificent hall with a checkerboard marble floor and a look like that of a Venetian palace. The place also sports what is certainly the most luxurious ladies' room in town; the men's room is well-furnished, too.

Moran's food is slightly eccentric Creole-Italian. The specialty is fettuccine Alfredo, made at the table for two or more. It is reputed to be the best in town and it is pleasantly cheesy, rich, and firm. I have, however, had as good or better elsewhere. Another signature is the diamond-studded meatball. This is not, as you might think, a meatball with lots of garlic, but a huge, golden-hued meatball of incomparably light texture and flavor, served with a side of capellini with a wonderful spicy red sauce. (The diamond-studded business derives from the restaurant's practice of putting actual diamonds in the thing for VIPs.) These and all the other pastas are made downstairs in the restaurant's Pastaficio—which sells at retail, too.

Start with either the terrific turtle soup (I wish they'd give you more of it) or the oysters Moran (poached in a delicious tan sauce with cheese). They also have the definitive stuffed mushrooms, with crabmeat and a fine hollandaise in the upturned caps. Respectable seafood entrees occasionally rise to excellent for specials. A great regular dish is trout Candies (named for Otto Candies, not for sweets). It's an odd but delicious pairing of a piece of sauteed trout with bananas—vastly better than it sounds. Again, the portion could be a bit more generous.

More robust are the chops of beef, veal, and lamb. These are of great intrinsic merit, if not always cooked with excitement. There is nothing of note for dessert. The wine list is impressive only for old, expensive bottles. Service is by some fine old-timers with great stories to tell at the slightest encouragement.

The basic truth of Moran's moved here from the original place on Iberville: if you're not a regular, you feel as if you're missing something. And I guess you are, since the fans of the place rave accord it a level of praise that has always seemed excessive to me.

★★★ Morning Call Coffee Stand

3325 Severn Ave., Metairie. (It's actually at the far end of a small strip mall at that address, on 17th at N. Hullen.) 885-4068. Open 24 hours, seven days. No credit cards. $

The Morning Call is long gone from its original French Market home, and that's a shame, since it served consistently better coffee and beignets than the Cafe du Monde. But there has been no decline in anything but atmosphere since the Morning Call moved to its present site in a strip shopping center in the suburbs — antique marble counters, mirrors, arch and all. The coffee is still the very best in America's greatest coffee city: intense and strong enough that you'd better not even try to drink it without hot milk. The beignets have a great texture and come out nice and hot; you put the sugar on them yourself. If anything, the Morning Call is even busier in Metairie than it was in the Quarter — there's frequently a line. (While waiting, you can browse through the city's best newsstand, Lakeside News, right next door.) A second Morning Call recently opened in Covington, in a shopping mall near the intersection of US 190 and I-12.

★ ★ ★ ★ Morton's of Chicago

402 N. Peters, in the Jackson Brewery Marketplace. Reservations 523-4965. 5:30-11 p.m. seven nights; till 9:30 p.m. Sun. AE, DC, MC, V. $$$$$

Morton's, as the name implies, started in Chicago, where it is one of the two or three best and busiest places to have a steak. In its expansion around the country it has managed to keep its integrity. While the location here in the Jackson Brewery Marketplace is a bit soulless and stark (this could be remedied by fuller houses), there is little to complain about regarding the food.

To answer the inevitable question of how Morton's measures up to Ruth's Chris: It's at least as good, but it's a different style. The butter lakes have dried up here. Morton's steaks come out with just a little natural gravy. But the intrinsic merit of the beef is the equal of any: dry-aged USDA prime. Morton's cooks a steak just the way I like it: crusty dark brown on the outside, bursting with juiciness on the inside, with a pronounced aged flavor.

Morton's gives better porterhouse than anybody else in town. A true porterhouse is a T-bone with class: it has large pieces of both filet mignon and strip. Morton's serves porterhouse for one or two; the latter is a three-pound slab of meat, and comes to the table all in one piece. I like the strip next best, followed by the filet and ribeye.

They also serve prime rib, roasted to a nice exterior char and cut as thick as a steak — an impressive piece of meat.

Thick lamb and veal chops get the same kind of crusty grilling as the steaks, but somehow lack the excitement. Morton's big (three-pounders, mostly), expensive (they can kill a fifty single-handedly) Maine lobsters get a singularly meritorious cooking treatment. The lobster is shoved in the broiler and roasted until its shell becomes black in spots. The flavor of the charred shell penetrates the tender meat: fascinating. They partially debone and butterfly a whole chicken here, season it with lemon and herbs, and broil it in the same hot grill that they cook the steaks in. It comes out with a crisp skin and a juicy interior. Other light entrees include a fish of the day — they like swordfish and salmon, but buy seafood locally, too.

The service highlight is the presentation of the menu, which is show-and-tell from a cart. You see the shrimp exhibit: my goodness, what big shrimp. Also impressive are the tree trunks they call asparagus; they're much better to look at than to chew on. Things start to get silly when they show you what a potato and a tomato look like. After you run that guy off, start with some of those shrimp in a cocktail, or the very fine black bean soup. Salads are big and well-dressed. The onion bread looks andf smells great; sometimes it even tastes good.

The wine list is more thoughtfully chosen than it is in most steak houses. The collection of California Cabernets is especially good. The most interesting desserts are the hot souffles. The fluffy clouds of lemon, chocolate, or Grand Marnier are delicious vapors. Morton's also has the best steak knives I've ever used. You could butcher your own steer with one.

★ ★ ★ ★ Mosca's

4137 U.S. 90 (about four miles past the West Bank end of the Huey P. Long Bridge), Avondale. Reservations 436-9942. 5:30-9:30 p.m. Tues.-Sat. No credit cards. $$$

It's a joint way out on a godforsaken highway—but one distinguished by spectacular, unique food. Mosca's defines Creole-Italian cuisine, and its specialties are widely copied. But nobody serves them with this kind of unrepentent gall. Here is, at last, all the wonderful oily, garlicky food you always wanted but nobody else would give you.

The dining room is stark even by local standards: an old wooden building with bleached wood floors and bright light bulbs in a plain ceiling. Food is brought out in large platters which follow the battered plates, knives, and forks around the table. Wine is served in tumblers. Meanwhile outside, more insects, amphibians, and reptiles than you'd think could possibly be jammed into a unit space chirp and flutter as cars zoom by on the dark highway.

Start with crabmeat—either the marinated crab or the crab salad, both slightly oily and redolent of herbs. Then head into the main dishes. Italian oysters: a dozen or so, baked in olive oil with well-seasoned bread crumbs. Italian shrimp: big ones, roasted with lots of rosemary and oregano and whole pods of garlic. Chicken a la grandee and roasted chicken are similar, except that the former is cut up and oilier; both are fragrant and delectable. Italian sausage: made on the premises, the best I've ever eaten, roasted to a fine dry texture, redolent of anise, with a roasted potato. And spaghetti bordelaise: homemade flat pasta, cooked a little too soft, but still great with its olive oil and garlic.

Those are the essentials, but not the entire list of good food. The chicken cacciatore, all the game birds, and the filet mignon are also wonderful. The wine list is mostly Italian and well-matched to the food. For dessert, there's the kitschy but good pineapple fluff and homemade cheesecake. Service is matter-of-fact and sometimes morose.

★ ★ ★ Mother's

401 Poydras, CBD. 523-9656. 5:30 a.m.-10 p.m. Mon.-Sat.; 9 a.m.-10 p.m. Sun. No credit cards. $

For 50 years, Mother's was the definitive poor-boy-and-plate-lunch restaurant, operating in a very old style in which portion control and other insidious formulas have no place. Then the Landry brothers, who had been there since the beginning, sold it. The restaurant changed under its new owner. He opened far longer hours, fiddled with the menu a little, and upset many regulars who were unused to any change at all for decades. The current manifestation of Mother's is different, yes. But I do not detect any great decline in the joy of cramming down an enormous, heavy breakfast, lunch, or supper here.

The best sandwich is still of the wonderful ham you smell baking on the premises. The turkey is baked there too — the whole bird, brought out and carved, something you rarely see elsewhere. Roast beef is also interesting; the style of the gravy is much lighter than you usually find on a roast beef poor boy, and doesn't contain any flour. It does have a lot of "debris," the leftovers of the previous day's roasts. (The debris underwent the most drastic change of all after the management change; it's not as juicy or chunky as it used to be.) Put the roast beef and ham together, and you have the Ferdi Special, which is a bit much for me, although many like it. All the sandwiches are dressed with shredded cabbage, pickles, and both yellow and Creole mustard; this is a Mother's trademark. The bread is the best poor boy loaf in town. You can get a half-sandwich here, which is enough unless you're really hungry.

Mother's has great old-fashioned plate specials in its steam tables. Its gumbos are fantastic — rich and well-seasoned. The red beans and rice and breakfast items are also benchmarks, perhaps owing to the use of ham fat in most of the recipes. Prices are very low and the portions are huge. The dining room is usually full with the line of customers, which moves faster than you might guess. Since this is the officially-designated "Tun Tavern" for this part of the world, there's lots of Marine memorabilia. Also here are oddball characters who call to one another with the assortment of bells, whistles, and horns that seem to sound for no apparent reason every few minutes.

MUFFULETTA. A gargantuan Italian sandwich ubiquitous in New Orleans and lately spreading to other places, the muffuletta was popularized by the **Central Grocery**, which still assembles a good one. The sandwich starts with a round, seeded Italian loaf, about eight inches across and three inches thick, doughy but toasty. Its center is layered with ham (sometimes prosciutto), Genoa salami, mortadella (a somewhat fatty, rich cold cut), provolone, mozzarella, Swiss cheese, and — the most important ingredient — an oily, garlicky salad of olives, celery and other marinated vegetables. It's a unique and very enjoyable taste.

My standards for a muffuletta are that it be assembled to order from first-quality ingredients at room temperature. Many muffaletta dispensers bake them these days; I find this gives the meats a slimy texture and distorts the taste of the olive salad. Warming the bread is all right, but I'd as soon eat one at room temperature. A muffuletta is big enough for at least two people. The best muffulettas come from **R&O's**, **Come Back Inn**, and the **Napoleon House**. Less exciting but more than acceptable are the **Central Grocery's** original, as well as the products of **Progress Grocery**, **Messina's**, **Toney's Spaghetti House**, and **Streetcar Sandwiches**. **Bayou Ridge Cafe** makes an interesting muffuletta *pizza*.

MUSIC. Live music in restaurants, almost unknown in New Orleans ten years ago, has become another arena in which competition rages. The styles vary so much that a ranking would be ridiculous, so here in alphabetical order are the prime disciples of the terpsichorean muse. (Not included are lounges attached to restaurants.)

Commander's Palace. They invented the jazz brunch, and every Saturday and Sunday a trio of old-line New Orleans players strolls the dining parlors and eases out a very sedate brand of Dixieland.

Genghis Khan. The owner is a symphony violinist. He and other classical players perform regularly in the dining room.

Henri. A pianist playing French cabaret tunes and some light jazz and classical warms up the room.

Le Jardin. There is a harpist for afternoon tea and for some dinners; on other evenings, we find a great piano-violin duet.

Mr. B's. A pianist tickles the ivories with lively pop tunes at dinner. For Sunday brunch, they have a strolling jazz trio.

Sazerac. Ron Able plays the accordion and John Pacquette sings, as they have done together here for well over a decade. Very listenable.

Windsor Court Grill Room. The offerings range from a single pianist to a chamber-music trio, and the program spans classical to soft jazz. The sounds emanate from the first-floor Salon at afternoon tea and dinner, and in the upstairs lounge at dinner.

★ ★ ★ Mystery Street Cafe

3201 Esplanade Ave., Mid-City. 947-6117. 6-10 p.m. seven nights; till 11 p.m. Fri. & Sat. Brunch Sun. 11 a.m.-3 p.m. MC, V. $$$.

A little triangular building is made more spacious than it actually is by the artful use of mirrors, large windows, and a few alfresco tables. It was one of the hot new restaurants of 1988-89, and it's sometimes hard to get a place to sit. The scene is just casual enough and the food just ambitious enough to create conversations at the tables.

The cooking is described as French and Mediterranean, but there's also a touch of Nouvelle Creole. They are not much into polish here; the watercress soup, for example, has shreds of the green instead of flecks or a puree, and the beef tastes like a grade lower than prime. These conditions are, however, balanced by prices about half what you'd pay in the Quarter for comparable dishes.

Start with cold, spicy artichoke bottoms stuffed with crabmeat, escargots du jour (many interesting variations on sauces with garlic), pate-and-cheese plate, pasta with seafood, or soup (gazpacho is especially good). The small house salad that comes with entrees is well-assembled and has a great slightly sweet dressing.

The excellent grilled chicken, fish, and shellfish are subtly seasoned (as opposed to the thick layer of Cajun seasoning that's now the vogue), and never overcooked. Tuna, for example, comes out with a juicy, appetizing blush at the center. The more complicated veal and chicken dishes have unusual sauces—chutney and the like. You will find a couple of things with sauces from the hollandaise family. And a surprise: beef Wellington, a dish usually reserved for much fancier places. It's a hefty chunk of tenderloin slathered with a truffled pate and baked inside puff pastry. The rich brown sauce lacks delicacy, but at the $13 price I am more than satisfied.

The best dessert is the unique chocolate-frosted bread pudding. They also make a fine creme caramel and some decent pastries. Cafe au lait come to the table in a bowl. There's a good list of wines by the glass. Service is enthusiastic and bistro-style casual.

N as in noisette d'agneau Maison d'Or

★★ Napoleon House

500 Chartres, French Quarter. 524-9752. 11 a.m.- Midnight seven days; till 2 a.m. Fri .& Sat. and till 6 p.m. Sun. AE, MC, V. $

New Orleans' liveliest crumbling ruin, this old bar only recently added air conditioning as an astounding concession to modern times. The food consists of a variety of sandwiches of which the best is the muffuletta. It uses good bread, meats, cheeses, and olive salad, and it is warmed (although you can ask to have it at room temperature, which is how it should be served). The other sandwiches are roast beef, corned beef, ham, and that sort of thing. All certainly good enough, and the atmosphere helps. Good and very inexpensive drinks, and a somewhat intellectual crowd. Classical music comes from a stereo whose records you are allowed to change yourself.

★★ Napoli

1917 Ridgelake (at W. Napoleon, one block east of Causeway Blvd.), Metairie. 837-8463. 11 a.m.-3 p.m. Mon.-Fri, till 9 p.m. Mon. and Wed. AE, MC, V. $$

A modest lunch-only place populated mainly by regulars, Napoli has an a la carte menu that is largely non-functional. Just about everybody here eats one of the three or so daily specials, which are mostly Sicilian with good red sauces. However, one also finds tasty, homely food like stuffed chicken and fried seafood. The waitresses assume you know all about the place, so if you don't press them for complete information on what's available you won't really know what to order.

NATURAL FOODS. See Health Foods.

★ New York Pizza

5201 Magazine, Uptown. 891-2376. 11:00 a.m.- 10:00 p.m. seven days; till 11 p.m. Fri. & Sat. and till 9:30 p.m. Sun. No credit cards. $

This little closet (a counter, a drink cooler, a few tables, and the ovens are jammed in) has a reputation for making great Northeast-style pizza — enough so that several former employees have been able to spin off into their own places, making pointed reference to their former association. Much is made about the quality of the ingredients used. But I have always found the pizzas here mediocre — flaccid crust, too much topping, none of the delicacy of a really great pizza.

NOISETTE D'AGNEAU. "Nugget of lamb," literally. "Nwa-zet dahn-yoe" is a small filet mignon-shaped lamb steak from the rib rack. The best noisettes d'agneau I've had were at **Andrea's, Versailles, Windsor Court Grill Room** and the **Sazerac**. But I associate the dish with **Antoine's**, which wraps its noisettes in bacon and covers them with a peculiar brown sauce with pineapple. This is much better than it sounds. So good, in fact, that I named my big friendly Golden Retriever after the dish. (We pronounce her name "noyzet" so as not to be too franco-cute about it.)

NOUVELLE. French feminine adjective meaning "new," and lately a prefix for any style of cooking in which the names — if not necessarily the tastes — of the dishes are unfamiliar. So we have "nouvelle Creole," "nouvelle Italian," "nouvelle omelette," etc. When admitted to by the restaurant itself, this word is a reliable indicator of just one thing: small portions. Usually the portions are dolled up a bit, and usually the ingredients used are of better quality than what is found in the mainstream, and usually the flavors are more elemental and intense while having a lighter texture. Usually. There is sometimes a Japanese influence, particularly in the matter of presentation.

Here are some restaurants which can legitimately claim to be serving nouvelle whatever:

Nouvelle Creole/Cajun: Bayou Ridge, Brigtsen's, Clancy's, Commander's Palace, Emeril's, Flagons, Isadora, K-Paul's, Mr. B's, Mystery Street Cafe, and Upperline.

Nouvelle Anything Else: Bayona (Mediterranean), Bistro at Maison de Ville (French), Gautreau's and Pelican Club (American), Cucaracha Cafe (Southwestern), Windsor Court Grill Room (nouvelle everything), Kung's Dynasty and Mr. Tai's (Chinese), Nuvolari's (Italian), Santa Fe and Vera Cruz (Mexican).

★ ★ ★ ★ Nuvolari's

246 Gerard St. (the street leading from US 190 to the lake in the old part of Mandeville). 1-626-5619. 11 a.m.-2 p.m. Thurs. only; 5-10:00 p.m. Mon.-Sat.; Noon-10 p.m. Sun. AE, MC, V. $$

The premises are fun: lots of space, brass, ferns, and posters telling the story of the Italian race-car driver for whom the restaurant is named. Despite that look, Nuvolari's is one of the best of the many new restaurants which have opened on the north shore of Lake Pontchartrain in recent years.

The cooking style is refreshingly original without being too challenging; its execution is almost flawless. The best appetizer is a collection of snails and crawfish (or shrimp) in a brown demi-glace sauce, a well-conceived variation on the standard. The antipasto is a pretty plate of cold meats, cheese, and vegetables. The shrimp (or crabmeat) remoulade comes in the pit of an avocado. Soups have been marvelous. The minestrone is offbeat, fresh and peppery. The crawfish and corn chowder with potatoes and bell pepper is thick and fine.

There are as many non-Italian dishes among the entrees as Italian ones, but everything I've tried has been about equally good. The lamb t-bones with jalapeno sauce have a good new flavor; so does the duck with its sauce of both cherries and peppercorns. The tournedos are flamed not with brandy but Scotch whisky. There is fish—occasionally, unusual species of fish—grilled or fried. An especially good one is palu, a white-fleshed fish that chef Tim Eihausen marinates with Szechuan peppercorns to a stunningly delicious effect.

The Italian standards get interesting little twists. The lasagne, for example, has a layer of spinach. So does the veal Parmigiana, which also shares the thick, well-seasoned, not-too-sweet red sauce found on many other dishes. The veal picatta has darkish veal but tastes great with its sauce of lemon, wine, and capers.

The house salad with a fine Caesar dressing comes with the meal. The desserts are freshly-made and very good. The dining-room staff is a happy, skillful lot. The wine list is very well-selected, with lots of good California bottles at relatively low prices.

O as in oysters Rockefeller

★★ Olde N'Awlins Cookery

729 Conti, French Quarter. No reservations. 529-3663. 11 a.m.-11 p.m. seven days. No credit cards. $$

This was the first of the K-Paul's spinoffs, although the chef who spun here—George Rhode IV—is long gone. Since his departure, the Cookery's great recipes are haphazardly rendered. They still can be good, even very good; but I've also received my share of the opposite. The dining room, moreover, is not well run. The wait staff is noisy, overly playful, and condescending (I don't need a lengthy explanation of gumbo every time I eat here). The premises don't always meet my standards of cleanliness. Still firmly in place is the ridiculous policy of not accepting reservations or credit cards.

There's a big dining room with brick walls and a brick floor. If the weather is tolerable, you might consider dining on the patio, which is not a grand one but very New Orleans. The menu is on a blackboard, and commences with inexpensive dishes like red beans and rice or jambalaya. Much of the menu varies from day to day, but some oft-seen specialties are fried trout with pecans, with a good brown meuniere sauce and a nice shot of spice; barbecued shrimp, served unusually over rice; chicken and veal dishes, usually on the oily side, more often than not served with pasta; and the occasional steak or beef brochette. Appetizers, which you have to ask the waiter about, are rarely of interest, although the soups—particularly the gumbos and the oyster-artichoke soup—are usually pretty good.

Entrees come with an assortment of fresh vegetables, often including that most-underrated Louisiana product, yams. Desserts are a thick bread pudding and mellow lemon crepes.

★★ Olivier's

2519 Dreux Ave., Gentilly. 282-2314. 11 a.m.-11 p.m. (or later) Wed.-Mon.; open 1 p.m.-9:30 p.m. Sat. & Sun.; closed Tues. MC, V. $

In one of the most obscure locations noted in this book, Olivier's does a fine job of cooking those dishes which our neighborhood restaurants used to do well. The menu seems to get a little more ambitious every time I eat here, but my favorite dish continues to be the red beans and rice with hot sausage, despite the fact that my system has not been able to digest this kind of stuff well for years. The sausage is just oily enough to lend a wonderful flavor to the beans; its own taste is very, very hot.

But there is more to Olivier's. The gumbo is tasty, the fried seafood well-seasoned and crisp, and the other plate specials of well-above-average merit. The poor boy sandwiches are of large size and big flavor. Service is glad-to-see-you style.

ORIENTAL RESTAURANTS. See Chinese, Japanese, Korean, Thai, and Vietnamese.

OSSO BUCO. It's veal shank, the bottom part of the foreleg of the animal. The huge bone with its very flavorful, tender meat is roasted, stewed, or braised for a long time, thereby creating a heady sauce. The best versions are served by **Andrea's, Impastato's, Moran's Riverside,** and as a lunch special that sells out very quickly at **Commander's Palace.** The same cut of meat prepared more simply but better is at the **Veranda,** where chef Willy Coln has given rebirth to his famous braised veal shanks, tender and rich with gelatin.

OYSTERS. The most spectacular example of great shirtsleeves eating in New Orleans is the oyster. Oysters of very substantial size and magnificent silvery, iodine-tinged flavor are harvested by the millions in the wetlands surrounding New Orleans. For some reason, most of the fancy restaurants consider it below their station to serve raw oysters on the half shell. But few would dispute the delicacy of the local oyster.

Most casual seafood restaurants have an oyster bar just inside the door. Here you find guys in aprons brandishing stubby knives with which they pry open the stubborn (naturally—they're still alive!) bivalves. They don't even use plates; the open oysters are set on the marble counter, and you eat them while standing there. (You could get them served at the table, but that remains the advantage you have in staring at the shucker while he opens the oysters. This little bit of supervision results in much better oysters.) As the man commences the operation, fetch a cold beer—the perfect match for oysters—from the liquor bar that's always adjacent to the oyster bar.

I maintain that it is almost criminal to hide the magnificent taste of a fresh oyster with any kind of sauce. But most Orleanians whip up a concoction consisting of a shot or three of hot sauce, a squeeze of lemon juice, a teaspoon or so of horseradish, and a large blorp of catsup. It's the catsup that constitutes the atrocity here; a much better sauce can be made by substituting extra virgin olive oil for the catsup.

That done, you stab the oyster with the cocktail fork, run it through the sauce, pop it into your mouth, and savor with a minimum of chewing. It's bad form to cut even a giant oyster in half or to eat an oyster on a cracker. Raw oysters are an acquired taste, but a week or so after you lose your oyster virginity the urge to do it again will sneak up on you.

There is almost no such thing as a bad oyster bar. But some have a particularly good track record for supplying salty, cold, large, cleanly-shucked oysters. The best of them are run by people of Yugoslavian descent, who have always been the oyster moguls. **Bozo's, Uglesich's,** and **Drago's** are most noteworthy. Also superb are the oyster bars at **Acme Oyster House, Casamento's, Felix's, Middendorf's, Pascal's Manale, Ralph & Kacoo's, Cafe Sbisa,** and **Houlihan's Old Place.**

As good as raw oysters are, most of the bivalves are eaten cooked—most often deep-fried, as part of a fried seafood platter. All the places named above with good raw bars also prepare superb fried oysters. Other good places to look are **Alonso & Son, Cafe Atchafalaya, Commander's Palace** at lunch (they come with a spectacular peppery corn relish), **Compagno's, Fury's, Mike Anderson's,** and **R&O's.**

Many of the fancier places also cook mean fried oysters. But more interesting are their baked oyster dishes, like those in the next entries.

OYSTERS BIENVILLE. I defy anyone to define this dish. Every restaurant makes it differently. About the only commonalities—and you can't even count on these—are an orangish color and the inclusion of some kind of seafood in a sauce baked over the oyster on its shell. The dish was invented at **Arnaud's,** where they are just okay now. It reached a peak in the old days at **Commander's Palace,** but they're no longer on the menu. The best currently available are at **Brennan's, Delmonico, Galatoire's,** and **Masson's. Andrea's** occasionally makes a dish called oysters Andrea that qualifies as a Bienville in my mind. I would stay away from them just about anywhere else.

OYSTERS EN BROCHETTE. You could hardly find anything simpler—or better. The oysters are alternated on a skewer with pieces of bacon; the whole thing is then floured and deep-fried (or, more rarely, broiled), then served with a butter sauce. The definitive version is at **Galatoire's,** but they're almost as good at **Cafe Sbisa, Christian's,** and **La Cuisine.** Good broiled versions of the dish are served at **Andrea's** (where they use too much bacon) and the **Caribbean Room.** The **Rib Room** roasts its oyster brochettes with a rotisserie, with a great beurre blanc sauce.

OYSTERS MOSCA. Although the name is a registered trademark of chef Nick Mosca, the many similar dishes around town are frequently compared to the dish as it's done at Mosca's (where they call them "Italian oysters"). Whatever the name, the oysters are baked in a pan or casserole with a somewhat dry sauce of seasoned bread crumbs, olive oil, and garlic. They are at their peak, naturally enough, at **Mosca's. La Louisiane, La Riviera,** and **Vincent's** put out great versions of the dish. Oysters

Saladino at **La Cuisine** are a lusty variation on the theme, with more oil and crushed red pepper in the sauce.

OYSTERS "NUMBER THREE" (AND OTHERS). There are many fancy oyster dishes that are unique to the restaurants where you find them. Some of them are used as the third entry in an "oysters 2-2-2"—two each of Bienvilles, Rockefellers, and this third one. A surprising number of Oysters Number Three involve eggplant in the sauce. This, unfortunately, almost never works.

In order of my preference, here are some of the best offbeat oyster dishes around town. Most are served as appetizers.

Oysters Foch are the property of and best dish at **Antoine's**; why nobody has ever copied it is a mystery. The oysters are fried and then covered with a complex, thick brown sauce—as thoroughgoing a Creole taste as can be imagined. The whole collection rests atop a piece of pate-spread toast.

Oysters Roland at **Christian's** are a very herbal, buttery, mushroomy casserole, sharpened with parsley.

Oysters Peacock at the **Windsor Court Grill Room** constitute the best newly-created baked oyster dish of my eating career. The shells are filled with a puree of sweet peppers, hot peppers, bread crumbs, and butter.

Oysters Suzette at **Arnaud's** also contain sweet peppers, but the taste is completely different: almost like pizza.

Oysters casino at **Brennan's** are nothing like the classic clams casino; instead, they're covered with cocktail sauce and a strip of bacon and baked on the shells. They taste much better than they have any right to. An identical dish at **Antoine's** is called **oysters thermidor**. **Chez Pierre's** also prepares the dish, but adds a topping of mozzarella cheese.

Commander's Palace has gotten away from baking oysters and now poaches them with stunning success. **Oysters Commander** (with artichokes), **oysters mariniere** (with a reduction of oyster water and herbs), and **oysters Trufant** (cream reduction and caviar) are the current selections.

OYSTERS ROCKEFELLER, the first and best New Orleans baked oyster dish, were improvised from leftover relish trays one day around the turn of the century by Jules Alciatore at **Antoine's**. Antoine's still makes the definitive version, which is very different from most others in that the sauce contains no spinach. Everywhere else, the green baked-on topping covering the oyster in its shell is a variation on a pureed spinach sauce with an anise flavoring. There is nothing wrong with this style; the best of it is served at **Broussard's, Galatoire's, Louis XVI, Clancy's,** and **Delmonico**. You used to be able to find oysters Rockefeller on almost every menu in town; they are out of fashion these days, but that doesn't make them any less good.

In fact, I think that oysters Rockefeller are one of the dozen best local dishes. So, as for the 11 other such, here is a recipe. The result of many experiments, it duplicates the taste of the Antoine's version without the benefit of my knowing the actual recipe, since Antoine's will not divulge it.

½ bunch celery
1 bunch green onions, roots and bottom half-inch removed
1 bunch flat-leaf parsley, large stems removed
1 bunch fresh fennel ("anise") (if not available, use the other half-bunch celery)
2 cups watercress
3 cloves garlic
6 anchovy fillets
Water from 2 doz. oysters, plus enough more water to make two cups
1 tsp. sugar
2 Tbs. catsup
1 Tbs. salt
¼ tsp. Louisiana hot sauce
½ tsp. white pepper
1 Tbs. Worcestershire sauce
2 Tbs. Herbsaint liqueur or Pernod (omit if fennel is used)
1 stick butter
½ cup flour
¼ cup bread crumbs
Two dozen oysters

1. Cut off the roots, cores, and leaves of the celery and fennel, and discard. Cut off all but the bottom two inches of the fennel stems.
2. Put manageable batches of all the vegetables plus the anchovies into a food processor and process as fine as possible. Add the oyster water to help things along.
3. Simmer this mixture with the rest of the water in a saucepan until the excess water is gone, stirring well every now and then.
4. Add the sugar, catsup, salt, hot sauce, pepper, and Worcestershire sauce. If not using fennel, add the Herbsaint. Mix well and simmer on low heat for about five minutes.
5. Pour the mixture into a blender and puree as smooth as possible. Return the mixture to the saucepan.
6. Melt the butter in a skillet and, when it bubbles, stir in the flour' until well blended. Blend in the bread crumbs. Stir this mixture into the greens. Note how this will completely change the texture of the sauce.
7. Using a small oven-proof ramekin or casserole dish for each serving, top three to six oysters with a very generous layer of sauce. (For most attractive effect, use a pastry bag with a star tip for the sauce.) Bake 15 minutes in a preheated 450-degree oven, until the top of the sauce has begun to brown slightly. Serve immediately, with a warning

about the lava-like heat of the sauce.

Serves four. Excess sauce freezes well for later use; it is also good as a sauce for fish, particularly grilled tuna.

OYSTER-ARTICHOKE SOUP. Few food pairs are as complementary as artichokes and oysters. They seem to have been made to be eaten together, particularly in a soup. The restaurant that made this now-ubiquitous soup popular was **LeRuth's**, but since they're gone now we look to **Tony Angello's**, **Gambrill's**, and **Vincent's**. Without doubt the worst is the light, tasteless excuse at **Galatoire's**. It is so out of character with the rest of Galatoire's great cuisine that whenever I hear people complain about the place I immediately assume that they blundered into this atrocity in their first course and never got over it.

P as in panneed pork chop poor boy

★★ PJ's Coffee & Tea Co.

7624 Maple, Uptown. 866-9963. • 5432 Magazine, Uptown. 895-0273. Both: 7 a.m.-11 p.m. Mon.-Fri.; 8:00 a.m.-11 p.m. Sat. and Sun. MC, V. $

Phyllis Jordan, connoisseur and roaster of coffee, opened a small shop on Maple Street some years ago in which you could purchase coffees from many parts of the world in many different roasts, along with pots and mugs and all the other accoutrements of coffee service. Since then, the original shop moved to expanded quarters to become a pleasant little cafe, and similar new locations have opened around the area. At all of them, you can order from a menu of many coffees and teas, and match them with something from a good selection of pastries. The coffees are scrupulously cared for: they're brewed with spring water and held in thermoses instead of over warmers, to avoid the evaporation of volatiles and burning of oils. They also make good espresso, cappuccino, and decaffeinated brews.

★★★ Palmer's

135 N. Carrollton Ave., Mid-City. 482-3658. 11:30 a.m.-2:30 p.m. Mon.-Fri. 5:30-10:30 p.m. Mon.-Sat. No credit cards (checks accepted). $$.

This tiny cafe is short on creature comforts—neither the exterior nor the interior look like much. But Palmer's is very much worth a spot on your Dining Adventures list. Here chef Cecil Palmer—for many years the guy who did most of the actual cooking at Willy Coln's—cooks the food of his homeland Jamaica.

If Caribbean food seems familiar to New Orleans palates, it's because our Creole is historically an offshoot of Caribbean Creole—particularly that of Haiti. In Jamaica, an everyday dish called "rice and peas" is virtually identical to our red beans and rice.

Start off with Bahamian seafood chowder, which was the best soup in town when Palmer was making it at Willy Coln's. It still holds that title here. Pieces of various seafoods float in a light, orange broth with strips of peppers and noodles of cheese. The blend of mellow spice and fresh seafood is spectacular—gumbo ingredients made into a much lighter, much dfifferent soup.

"Jerk" cooking is a mainstay of Jamaican cooking. It's sorta like blackened barbecue, if you can imagine such a thing. Jerk pork and jerk lamb are the classics, and these turn up at Palmer's at times. But more interesting is the jerk fish, spicy and crusty, served (like everything here) in very large portions.

The chef's taste runs to fairly rich (with cream) and salty dishes. Some of it is fantastic until you're halfway through, and then your taste buds scream for mercy out of sheer fatigue. Prices are very low. Service is not especially good. The physical limitations of Palmer's keep it from being as good as it could be, given the talents of the chef.

PANCAKES. Nobody takes pancakes very seriously in New Orleans. There are two specialists, the better of which is the **Tiffin Inn**, whose variety includes the wonderful souffle-like baked German pancakes and a real potato pancake with lots of onions and bacon. **Rick's Pancake House** has shown vast improvements throughout its menu since new owners took over some months ago; the variety of pancakes is wide, and they come out hot, eggy, and tasty. (The benchmark for pancakes, by the way, is a chain called Walker Brothers in the Chicago suburbs.) See also **Crepes**.

PANNEE. This adjective (also spelled "pane," "panee," or "panne") means that the foodstuff in question—probably veal leg cutlets, but often chicken or rabbit—is washed with beaten egg, breaded and pan-fried with a small amount of oil. My sources are in disagreement on whether the name refers to the breading or the pan. The best of the many restaurants serving panneed veal are **Commander's Palace, Mr. B's, La Cuisine,** and **Gambrill's**. All those places bring the veal out with a side of fettuccine Alfredo. Panneed veal also appears warm atop a salad of romaine with Italian dressing; the best of the these are at **Andrea's,** the **Rib Room** (both of which call the dish veal Tanet), and **Ruth's Chris Steak House** (lunchtime only). Weiner schnitzel is the same idea as pannee veal, but with an outer coating of flour instead of breadcrumbs and a German name; the **Veranda** and the **Versailles** do it best, and **Kolb's** cooks it okay.

Panneed rabbit tenderloin has grown in popularity in the nouvelle Creole places; **Brigtsen's, Gautreau's, Bayou Ridge Cafe,** and **Clancy's** have provided me with the tastiest such morsels.

★★Parasol's

2533 Constance, Uptown. 895-9675. 11 a.m.-2 p.m. and 5-9 p.m. Mon. and Wed.-Fri. 11 a.m.-8 p.m. Sat. Closed Sun. and Tues. No credit cards. $

Headquarters for St. Patrick's Day activities, Parasol's is one of the few Irish strongholds left in the Irish Channel. It's a bar with a pair of shabby dining rooms in the back; these could use more careful cleaning. Parasol's on a good day puts out the best roast beef poor boy you will ever eat. However, the consistency has been slipping lately. One other change is more welcome: it no longer takes a half-hour to get a sandwich. It now comes out in ten minutes or less. The menu goes on to include poor boys made of virtually anything; the fried oyster and shrimp loaves are terrific, the ham pretty good, and the weiner poor boy something I haven't checked lately. The bread is warmed and aromatic. Drinks are handed up to you through a small window to the bar.

PARKY'S UNGULATE BARD-O-TERIA. No such restaurant exists.

★ ★ ★ Pascal's Manale

1838 Napoleon Ave., Uptown. 895-4877. 11:00 a.m.-10 p.m. Mon.-Fri.; 4-10:30 p.m. Sat. & 10 p.m. Sun. AE, DC, MC, V. $$$

It started out as Frank Manale's Restaurant in 1913. Then nephew Pascal Radosta bought it—hence the curious name, which has enough local parallels (i.e., "Ruth's Chris") to qualify as a folkway. For decades, Manale's (as it's still usually called) was one of the city's essential restaurants. But during the Eighties it declined precipitously into an expensive dump where you had to wait a long time in the bar before you were allowed to eat pale shadows of its famous dishes. I had to tell you that so you'd know that what follows is not just a foggy recollection of the golden years.

Because Manale's is heading back to its old self. In 1988, there was a change in the management: same family, but new faces. They brought prices down a bit (a shocker!), made kitchen practices a lot more rigorous, and got the staff to be friendlier. They've even begun renovating the old joint.

Manale's is thought of as an Italian restaurant, but the style could just as easily be called Creole. Barbecue shrimp—the greatest of all Creole-Italian dishes—remains the house specialty. It was found recently that the original recipe had been deviated from; it has now, we are told, come back home. In case you haven't had the pleasure, barbecue shrimp (which are badly misnamed, by the way) are enormous head-on shrimp baked in a sauce of butter and pepper. Particularly in the peak of shrimp season, this is as irresistable as it is messy.

Start the meal with the terrific oysters on the half shell or very rich oysters Rockefeller. The stuffed mushrooms, awash in a hollandaise that can almost be called fluffy, are some of the best in town (they should find some bigger plates to serve them on, though). Some delicious soups: the turtle soup is a great example of the old-fashioned lighter style. Salads are not worth the extra money.

Some great dishes that had unaccountably slipped off the menu have returned. The oyster and crabmeat pan roast, for example, is a delicious dozen oysters topped with a unique thick, bready, herbal sauce studded with lump crabmeat. (It's at its best three days after they make it, believe it or not.) Chicken bordelaise is simple and juicy; the new chicken Marsala is a satisfying lighter dish. Fish entrees tend toward the overcooked side, but are otherwise more than acceptable; the portions are very large. The best of the veal dishes is the Puccini version, a lot of small, tender slices of sauteed veal with a lemon butter and mushrooms. They grill up a thick, beautiful steak.

For dessert they make a first-class, extremely rich bread pudding. Lunch specials are very basic, mostly seafood, and inexpensive. Waitresses are very familiar and unceremonious. The wine list is better than it used to be.

Some aspects of Manale's are still in desparate need of upgrading. I know of no other restaurant in this class that serves coffee cream in little coffee-shop plastic containers. The wet paper hand towels the waitress proffers after you eat the shrimp are laughable. (The paper does absorb better than the polyester napkins they have here, but we can all think of a better solution.)

PASTA. Pasta has ceased to be the exclusive property of Italian restaurants. Almost every style of kitchen—Creole and Cajun included—now incorporates pasta into its cooking. With good reason: pasta is one of the most versatile foods there is. But there is pasta and there is pasta. The better chefs seek out pasta made with a lot of eggs and semolina flour. A very few restaurants—most notably **Andrea's, Moran's Riverside** and **Mosca's**—make their own pasta from scratch, right in their kitchens. What they and we all want is a firm pasta that stays together after cooking and holds sauce well.

Multiply the number of different pastas available by the number of possible preparations and you have a very large number of pasta dishes. Here are what I think are the premier dozen:

1. Angel hair with smoked salmon and caviar, Andrea's.
2. Crabmeat ravioli, La Riviera.
3. Ravioli with porcini mushrooms, Andrea's.
4. Angel hair with smoked mushrooms, Commander's Palace.
5. Pasta with four cheeses, Flagons.
6. Veal cannelloni, Vincent's.
7. Fettuccine carbonara, Mr. B's.
8. Angel hair marinara with diamond-studded meatball, Moran's Riverside.
9. Seafood cannelloni, Andrea's.
10. Pasta Rosa, Maximo's.
11. Malafatta, La Louisiane.
12. Stuffed macaroni, Toney's Spaghetti House.

★ ★ Pastore's

301 Tchoupitoulas, CBD. Reservations 524-1122. 11 a.m.-2:30 p.m. Mon.-Fri.; 6-10:30 p.m. Mon.-Sat.; till 11 p.m. Fri. and Sat. AE, CB, DC, MC, V. $$$

In a collection of smallish, comfortable, handsome rooms with lofty ceilings, waiters attempting ceremony serve an interesting menu of Northern Italian food. Pastore's is not perfectly consistent, but most of the time its offerings show inspiration and competent preparation.

Funghi trifolati—a giant serving of firm, fresh fried mushrooms in an herbal, buttery sauce—makes a good starting point. As do the garlic-aromatic escargots. The great ravioli in a clear beef broth are obviously home-made, thin pillows with a thimbleful of herbal meat. Great if you have a cold.

Pasta is elegantly turned out in much variety. Fettuccine Alfredo and the angel-hair pasta asciutta are prepared reasonably well tableside. The cannelloni and spaghetti carbonara are also good. They list gnocchi (pasta-like potato dumplings) and risotto (rice treated like pasta), but these are to be avoided. One wishes they'd serve small appetizer portions—something you can accomplish only by splitting a large portion with a tablemate.

The entree section promises almost everything under the sun, including a good many French and Creole dishes with Italian names. The widest choice is among veal preparations. Vitello primavera (artichoke sauce) or Piemontese (lemon butter) taste best to me. The fish is nicely seasoned and deftly broiled. Shrimp in garlic butter are big and flavorful. The beef dishes sound great but have been disappointing to me.

There's not much for dessert. Coffee is weak, espresso strong. And the wine list could use some fleshing out with more good Italian bottles. Pastore's has a cafe in the Riverwalk, but the main restaurant is nearby and vastly better.

PATE. Pate never seems to quite catch on in New Orleans, although there have been some close brushes. The public associates pate with liver, and you know what that means, prejudice-wise. News flash: pate doesn't have to contain liver. Pate applies to any ground, seasoned, formed meat. The texture can be anything from coarse like meat loaf (meat loaf more or less is a pate, by the way) to a silky, airy mousse. Very strictly speaking, a pate is wrapped in pastry; the same idea without the pastry is a terrine, after the crock it's baked in.

The king of the pates is pate de foie gras, made from fattened goose liver and truffles. (See **Foie Gras**) and very expensive. The real thing is available at **Henri** (which makes its own!) **Louis XVI** and **Antoine's**. The peasant of the pates is pate de campagne—country pate. It has a coarse texture, with nodules of peppercorns, herbs, fat, and meat. But there's nothing wrong with the flavor, as you will find by eating the superb versions at **Crozier's**, **La Provence**, **Louis XVI**, and the **Versailles**.

And there are some offbeat pates. **Feelings** has a good liver pate and a better shrimp etouffee pate, both perky companions to cocktails. **Versailles**, **La Gauloise**, and **La Provence** make delicious pates out of poultry, seafood, and vegetables.

PATIO DINING. New Orleans, particularly its French Quarter, is full of gardens and courtyards and patios that look perfect for alfresco dining. So why are there so few outdoor tables? You will discover the answer the first time you attempt to take a meal under the trees. Unless it's one of those two or three weeks in the spring or fall when the daytime temperature and humidity are in the seventies, you will find that the weather does not wear well as a dining environment. Certainly not if you are arrayed in jacket and tie.

Despite this, there are enough people who are willing literally to sweat it out that a few restaurants offer courtyard dining year-round. The **Court of Two Sisters** is by far the loveliest of these, and it is so adept at alfresco dining that it remains comfortable when everyplace else is far too warm. The **Angolo di Roma**, **Coffee Pot**, **Gumbo Shop**, and **Mystery Street Cafe** all have small dining patios. **Maggie & Smitty's Crabnett's** tables are all out on a sidewalk in West End. **Brennan's**, **Broussard's**, and **Commander's Palace** all have spectacularly beautiful courtyards open for a pre- or post-prandial cocktail; in nice weather, and if the oak tree isn't shedding, Commander's serves lunch and dinner out there too.

★ ★ ★ Pat O'Brien's

718 St. Peter, French Quarter. 525-4823. Open 24 hours, seven days. No credit cards. $

Pat O'Brien's is not a restaurant. The only food served is popcorn, and it's not very good. I think the place is worth mentioning, however, because it's almost without question the best bar in the city. It's certainly the biggest; a lovely patio dominated by a flaming fountain is surrounded by many comfortable venues for having a cocktail. Two rooms are especially noteworthy: the piano bar, where there's usually someone playing standards; and the "main bar," which offers the lowest drink prices anywhere in the Quarter. All the cocktails, including the famous Hurricane (four ounces of rum with fruit juices in a giant glass shaped like a storm lantern), are exceptionally well made from first-class ingredients. Pat O's is a great place to while away an afternoon. Unfortunately (or fortunately, depending upon your perspective), the place is extremely popular with Tulane students at night, and can be crushingly busy.

★ ★ ★ Patout's

1319 St. Charles Ave., Uptown. 524-4054. 11 a.m.-2 p.m.; 6 p.m.-10 p.m. seven days. AE, DC, MC, V. $$$

The Patout family purveys an honest but very homely style of Cajun cooking, using exclusively fresh ingredients. But the executions leave something to be desired in both taste and consistency. This seems to have leveled off somewhat since the return to town of chef Gigi Patout from the West Coast.

Alex Patout broke away from the rest of his family in 1988 and opened his own place in the Quarter (see **Alex Patout's**). But the original New Orleans restaurant is still going on in a handsome collections of rooms in the rear of a St. Charles Avenue motel. Live Cajun music plays in the dining rooms.

First courses are the best part of the meal. The stuffed mushrooms (with crabmeat), alligator sausage, and seafood pasta usually come off well. The soups here are not to be missed, particularly the chicken and sausage gumbo and the corn and crab bisque. But many of the flavors established at the beginning of the meal will repeat in the entrees—maybe not as well. Typical is the "lady fish"—not a species, but a grilled fish (whatever's available) topped with shrimp and crabmeat in a rich cream sauce. The flavors all cancel one another out for me. Indeed, one is hard pressed to find things that aren't either topped or stuffed with crabmeat, shrimp, or crawfish, or slathered with a cream sauce. They don't object to serving the food without the toppings, and through this strategem you get decent grilled fish, roasted chicken, and sauteed veal. The stuffed duck is usually quite good. Vegetables are authentic Cajun: overcooked to the mush stage.

The desserts are fairly decent; service is extremely friendly.

The Pearl

119 St. Charles Ave. 525-2901. 7:30 a.m.-10 p.m. Mon.-Sat.; 8 a.m.-9 p.m. Sun. AE, MC, V. $

This prominent restaurant in the first block of St. Charles Avenue looks like it ought to be great. The windows are filled with whole roast beef rounds, hams, whole turkeys, and the like, and there's an oyster bar in the rear. The menu features all the basic platters and sandwiches at very low prices. But in 20 years of trying, I have never had an acceptable meal at the Pearl. Its service is consistently exasperating.

PECAN PIE. Go to the **Camellia Grill**, where is found what is easily the town's best pecan pie, and get the free recipe from the cashier. See how simple it is. So why aren't there more good ones? Although I salute the fine pastry skills evidenced in the **Grill Room's** pecan torte, it's still a disappointment to a palate inured to the sweet richness of the southern-style pie at the Camellia Grill **Andrea's** occasionally makes great pecan torte; **Commander's Palace** sometimes cranks out a chocolate pecan pie. And **K-Paul's** still (I hope) makes a great sweet potato pecan pie.

★ ★ ★ ★ Peking

6600 Morrison Rd. (at I-10, in Kenilworth Mall), New Orleans East. 241-3321. 11 a.m.-10:30 p.m. Tues.-Sun.; till 11 p.m. Fri.-Sun. AE, CB, DC, MC, V. $$

Everybody has a favorite little neighborhood Chinese place, and this is mine—despite the fact that it is a long drive from where I live. It's a small, reasonably nice-looking place with about 20 tables; the owner and personnel, while not extremely conversant in English, are obliging.

The food is of purer composition than the filled-out-with-gravy-and-onions stuff served in most Chinese places. Certain dishes are the best of their kind I've ever had. The fried dumplings are firm noodles, looking like Portuguese men-of-war with their stuffing of meat and herbs, luscious with the peppery, garlicky cold sauce. The nonpariel shrimp toast are pyramids of minced shrimp piled up on a thin bread and fried, served with a gingery plum sauce. But the first thing I always get here is a cup of the definitive hot and sour soup, a fine remedy for a cold and just plain good with pork, tofu, mushrooms, and egg curdles in a thick broth.

The entree section has a few unusual items. Peking chicken is white meat made into a loaf, fried with sesame seeds, and covered with a unique white sauce: superb. The whole fish with brown sauce is fried to a crispness and brought out with a spicy concoction over all. For bean curd buffs only is the delicious Ma's bean curd, soft tofu with pork morsels and a sprinkling of red pepper. Szechuan classics like chicken with red pepper and peanuts, stir-fried pork string, and shrimp in hot garlic sauce are as well-made here as you'll find anywhere. The sauteed shrimp Chinese style is just a big plate of stir-fried shrimp with a few peas. Mo-shu pork is superbly turned out, with a lightly gelatinous consistency and a fine flavor. The Peking duck is good enough, if not the best I've ever eaten. The string beans with shrimp make a good side dish.

The Peking even makes a decent dessert: banana fritters in a lightly-sweet syrup.

PEKING DUCK. The most elaborate Chinese dish offered in these parts—and sometimes it even tastes good. See **Duck**.

★ ★ ★ ★ Pelican Club

615 Bienville (entrance is a few yards up Exchange Alley). Reservations 523-1504. 11:30 a.m.-2:30 p.m. Mon.-Fri.; 6-11 p.m. Mon.-Sat.; till Midnight Fri. & Sat. AE, MC, V. $$$

All three of the proprietors cook, but the menu is principally the work of Richard Hughes, who is from these parts but who made his mark in Manhattan with a restaurant called Memphis (among other places). He came back to town to open this handsome establishment in mid-1990.

The three dining rooms, arranged shotgun fashion, are spacious, modern, and dominated by banquette seating—a rarity in New Orleans. They have a New York look to my eyes. Service is a little on the precious side; they want you to be as impressed by the chef as they are.

The food speaks for itself. Most dishes on the menu are a step or two in the imagination away from the classics of Creole cooking. Enough Nouvelle American cooking is done at the Pelican Club for it to fit in that category. Scattered here and there on the menu are some dishes with an Oriental cast; these are the work of Chin Ling, one of the owners.

Start with the gravlax-style salmon, cured in the house. Or the collection of shellfish with avocado and melon. Or the grilled scallops, scattered atop a flower of artichoke leaves and an artichoke bottom with garlic buerre blanc. Or the beef satays, grilled on skewers with a Thai-inspired peanut sauce. Or the gigantic crab cakes with pepper corn relish.

There's a soup here that deserves its own paragraph. It's crab and corn bisque—not a new idea in itself, but with the original touches of soft-shell crab claws and a dash of bourbon whiskey. The latter is a direct flavor-blend hit, a spectacular taste.

The entrees begin with a list of grilled fish, served in most generous flanks, abetted by a selection of sauces. Then there's a Southwestern-style roasted chicken, a Chinese-style ginger duck, and a Metairie-style red snapper with crabmeat and garlic butter—all excellent eating. The best of the several pasta dishes is a pairing of shrimp and scallops with penne pasta and a pesto made with pistachios—a little strange, but fascinating.

Two dishes are presented literally by the potful. The jambalaya is wetter than the local standard, and chock-a-block with mussels, clams, gigantic shrimp with their heads still on, scallops, and big slabs of andouille. Cioppino—the Italian answer to bouillabaisse—is a bit more saucy and garlicky. Both are presented in covered saucepans in quantities easily enough to serve two, although the price in both cases is under $15. Robust and filling.

Dessert is the least inspired part of the menu, although one can't find flagrant flaws in the cheesecake, creme brulee, or chocolate mousse cake. Coffee is excellent chicory dark roast. Despite the "club" mention in the name and the filled dining rooms at dinner, the staff is welcoming.

★★Peppermill

3524 Severn Ave., Metairie. 455-2266. 7 a.m.-3 p.m. Mon.; 7 a.m.-9:30 p.m. Tues.-Sun.; till 10 p.m. Fri. & Sat. AE, CB, DC, MC, V. $$

With its forests of plants, high-back wicker chairs, mirrors, and bright colors, the Peppermill is a bit too good-looking and ambitious to be called a neighborhood restaurant, but that's essentially what it is. The cooking is familiar Creole and Italian. The best starter is artichoke Joseph, a little bubbly casserole of the vegetable with mushrooms and crabmeat. (It's no longer on the menu, but surfaces as a special.) In a similar vein are the rich stuffed mushrooms with bearnaise. They make a superb cannelloni, the veal-and-cheese stuffing inside a crepe, all awash with a fine tomato sauce. Fettuccine, tortellini (small ravioli in a cream-and-cheese sauce), crawfish bisque (with a couple of stuffed heads), and spinach salad are other fine starting points.

Veal is the best entree section. Veal Alexander, with its fried eggplant and meuniere sauce (a brown one which also contributes goodness to some of the fried seafood) is my favorite. Veal Normandy, a frequently-offered special with a sauce of sour cream and apples, is another good one. The seafood emphasis lately has moved from the fried and stuffed Suburban Creole dishes to more interesting grilled, lightly sauced fish, sometimes of interesting species. The striped-with-char grilled chicken is unimpeachable. Steaks are less interesting.

They serve a pretty good breakfast here: all the standard egg dishes, plus a fancy one or two, share the menu with Belgian waffles and the like. Prices here are very low, so one tends to forgive the less-than-best quality of the raw materials and the occasional side dish that clearly has been sitting around too long. The service staff is friendly and helpful. Wines, dessert, and coffee are passable.

This restaurant, unfortunately, has a consistency problem. Disappointments in dishes I'd previously enjoyed here have been a bit too frequent for me to feel entirely comfortable.

★★Petunia's

817 St. Louis, French Quarter. 522-6440. 8:00 a.m.-Midnight seven days. AE, CB, DC, MC, V. $$

A smallish cafe in the double parlor of a French Quarter cottage just off Bourbon Street, Petunia's serves from the early morning until late at night a menu of fried and stuffed seafood, blackened redfish, jambalaya, shrimp Creole, and other touristy fare. But the food is much better than in most similar places in the neighborhood, and there's a twist or two. Crepes, for instance: about ten different ones, big and overstuffed with interesting, if somewhat heavy, saucy ingredients. I like the crepe St. Peter, with its asparagus, ham, and hollandaise. "Maw-Maw's Cajun Breakfast" is a sort of rice omelette with shrimp and ham — very tasty.

The problems here are unattentive service, especially when the place is busy, and rather high prices on the appetizers and breakfasts. Entrees and daily specials, on the other hand, are all at or just above $10, and include soup and salad.

PHILOSOPHY OF RESTAURANT CRITICISM. In the grand scheme, writing about restaurants is a lightweight endeavor. But to one group of readers—the restaurateurs—it carries more importance than you can imagine. And for their sake, allow me to get serious for a bit and explain my motivations and thought processes.

I can sum it up briefly. My quest is for the best dining in New Orleans, and to share the discoveries with others looking for the same thing. I derive a great deal of enjoyment from both parts of that enterprise.

For reasons I fully understand, some readers in and out of the restaurant industry see this activity differently. Those who dislike the idea of restaurant criticism per se accuse me (and other critics) of looking for flaws to condemn. They say we unjustly exercise the power of the media to hurt restaurants or tell them how to run their businesses, and that it's all a sick ego game.

The first accusation is controverted by the fact that at least 90 percent of what I write is some kind of recommendation. This book, for example, contains the *best* 300 or so restaurants in New Orleans. Entertaining negative reviews are incomparably easier to write. But they don't provide any useful information—nobody looks for bad places to eat. My usual approach to substandard restaurants is to ignore them. The few exceptions to this rule are those places which have become so well known that they can't be left out.

Some restaurateurs say that 90 percent positive is not good enough—that I should *never* say *anything* bad about a restaurant. In my mind, that's unethical journalism, since it denies the whole truth. If you want to experience what that's like, tune in Radio Moscow on a short-wave radio. According to their reports, nothing wrong ever happens in the USSR. Only the most uninformed or gullible could take that kind of pap seriously.

It's interesting that the restaurateur who makes the don't-say-bad-things point to me most vociferously is a guy who frequently appears in the media, telling how he seeks out the freshest and best raw materials and even grows his own to assure quality. He says that his taking these pains makes his food better. Better than what? Why, better than the swill served by restaurateurs who use frozen, canned, and low-grade foodstuffs. The only difference between his pronouncements and mine, then, is that he doesn't name names—except, of course, his own.

Most of the controversy boils down to a question of income. Restaurateurs perceive that criticism cuts into their business. My observation is that positive commentary has a much stronger effect on restaurant volume than negative reviews do. But even if it were possible for a review to cause fiscal harm to a restaurant, what about the losses on the part of the uninformed diner? The night before I wrote this entry, I spent $60 for two in a restaurant that smelled bad, served inedible food, and had surly waiters. I'm damn mad about it—not just because I'm $60 out of pocket, but because I feel cheated out of the enjoyment I could have had if I had gone instead to, say, Galatoire's. I feel it incumbent upon me to tell the dining public about experiences like this, so they won't suffer the same fate.

Reliable information is what the people who buy my books, subscribe to my magazine, and listen to my radio show expect—not boosterism, of which they get more than enough from advertising. It is to these consumers I address my writing, not to restaurateurs. In fact, I sometimes wish that restaurateurs wouldn't read my stuff at all.

I discovered by working in a restaurant some years ago that people in the restaurant business have a completely different perspective on dining out than lay people do. It leads to their interpreting my comments as an outsider's trying to tell him how to run his business. But I'm not a restaurateur—I'm a diner. Behind-the-scenes operations are (or should be) invisible to a diner. Restaurateurs who ask my advice about operational matters get it for free; that's about what I think it's worth.

The most important aspect of all—and the one least recognized—is that I'm just one diner. What I write represents only my tastes. It would be incredibly presumptuous of me to say I speak for the tastes of others. The reviews are a guide, not a gospel.

Three kinds of people are common to all great restaurants. First are owners and managers with taste and good business sense. Second is a staff of kitchen and dining room personnel with skill. The third essential group of people for a great restaurant—and the one least congratulated by restaurateurs for its contribution—is a clientele with knowledge of and desire for good food. It's the customers that provide the reason for restaurant's existence. And a truly good customer doesn't roll over and play dead when a restaurant fails in its part of the bargain.

Some of the above may give the impression that I dislike restaurateurs. In fact, I am on very friendly terms with most of the restaurant owners I know, and I have enormous respect for them. Their job is harder than anybody realizes. The restaurant completely takes over the life of anybody who wants to do the job right. They're proud of their babies, even the ugly ones. It's a rare restaurateur who doesn't believe his is the best restaurant of its kind in the city. (I sent out a survey asking restaurateurs to rate their own places; I got back over 50 five-star ratings.)

To the restaurateurs, I offer the following credo. It comes from Ovid's "Metamorphoses"; I found it on the wall in Archie Casbarian's office, and I've always liked it:

"It is not the critic who counts—not the man who points out how the strong man stumbled, or where the doer of deeds could have done them better. The credit belongs to the man who is actually in the arena; whose face is marred by dust and sweat and blood, who strives valiantly; who errs and comes short again and again; who knows the great enthusiasms, the great devotions; who spends himself in a worthy cause; who, at best, knows in the end the triumph of high achievement and who, if he fails, at least fails while daring greatly."

Piccadilly Cafeteria

2222 Clearview Parkway, Metairie. 454-6271. • *2609 Jefferson Hwy., Jefferson. 834-2695.* •*3800 S. Carrollton Ave., Mid-City. 482-0775.* •*1701 Barataria Blvd., Marrero. 341-7525.* •*533 Lapalco Blvd., Gretna. 391-1063.* •*3200 Paris Rd., Chalmette. 271-6860.* •*8908 Veterans Blvd., Metairie. 467-4224. 11:00 a.m.-8:30 p.m. seven days. No credit cards. $.*

This large Baton Rouge-based chain of enormous, very busy restaurants proves that the cafeteria format is far from dead. It also proves that the people for whom cafeteria dining has appeal are not especially demanding about what they eat. I find the food here incredibly lacking in flavor, and replete with evidence of canned, frozen, and heavily-processed raw materials. This bland fare does have appeal to two groups in the population notorious for disliking strong flavor statements: the very young and the very old. Nor are the prices especially low; I have spent the same dollars for lunch here as I would for a comparable (in quantity, anyway) lunch at Commander's Palace or Arnaud's. Strictly for folks who look upon eating as a necessary evil.

PIZZA. The mistake most pizza places make is treating pizza crust like some kind of pasta — a base for sauce, cheese, and grease. If they would forget about the toppings for a moment and concentrate on getting out a wonderfully aromatic, perfectly browned crust with a slightly soft interior and crisp edges — in other words, if they'd approach the crust-making procedure as a way to make a great piece of bread—they'd have it made.

There is currently a trend for small gourmet pizzas, baked in stone ovens heated by wood and topped with sun-dried tomatoes and other precious ingredients. The best of these are at **Andrea's**, **Bayou Ridge Cafe**, and (in a weird style) **Louisiana Pizza Kitchen**.

The best pizzas of the more familiar, pepperoni-topped style come from **Dante's Pizza Cafes**, a chain of by-the-slice stands that looks like it ought to be terrible. Their product is consistently great, thin, crisp-crusted Northeast-style pizza, with light, flavorful toppings. Better-than-average pizzas are also to be had from **Mark Twain Pizza Landing, R&O's**, and **Toney's Spaghetti House**. Conclusions: New Orleans is not a great pizza town, and few things in the world could be worse than a delivered pizza.

★★Plantation Coffeehouse

5555 Canal Blvd., Lakeview. 482-3164. 11 a.m.-10 p.m. Mon.-Sat. No credit cards. $

A pleasant, bright parlor, the Plantation offers several different kinds of coffees and teas, along with tasty, fresh pastries. They also have coffees to take home and brew yourself.

PLANTATIONS. The great local plantation dining experience perished in a fire at Elmwood Plantation a few years ago, and there's been nothing like it nearby since. **Tchoupitoulas Plantation** is convincingly out in the country, but the building, while authentically antique, is unimpressive, and the food is just okay.

Visiting the many plantations between here and Baton Rouge is a pretty day's entertainment. Some of them even have good food. I like to take visitors on what I call Plantation Route A: Up the East Bank River Road, stopping at **Destrehan Manor, San Francisco Plantation, Tezcuco Plantation,** and **Houmas House.** Tezcuco has a decent restaurant, but instead of eating there I like to double back three and a half miles to the Sunshine Bridge, cross it, and have lunch at the excellent **Lafitte's Landing** at the West Bank foot of the bridge. Then we hie ourselves down the West Bank River Road back to town, with a stop at the arresting **Oak Alley Plantation,** which has a good little cafe.

If you give yourself the whole day, you can make side trips to two other good plantations on the West Bank: **Nottaway** in White Castle, and **Madewood** along Bayou Lafourche. Both have fine accommodations for an overnight stay, and Nottaway's restaurant has probably the best plantation eating in the state.

Here's some useful data on the upriver plantations, in the order of the tour above. Tours are generally given between 10 a.m. and 4 p.m. at all plantations; prices range from $4 to $6 for adults, $2 to $4 for children and students.

Destrehan Plantation. Built 1787; oldest standing plantation house in the state. On East Bank River Road (LA 48) near Destrehan, about eight miles past Jefferson-St. Charles parish line. 1.764-9315. Tours only, daily.

San Francisco. On East Bank River Road (LA 44) between Edgard and Garyville. 1-535-2341. Tours only, daily.

Tezcuco Plantation. Built 1855. On East Bank River Road (LA 44), about a mile past Sunshine Bridge. 1-562-3929. Bed-and-breakfast accommodations, $55-$180. Pilot House restaurant serves lunch only daily. Tours daily.

Houmas House. Built late 1700s and 1840. On East Bank River Road (LA 44), about three and a half miles past Sunshine Bridge. 1-473-7841. Tours only, daily.

Oak Alley Plantation. Built 1839. If you only have time to visit one plantation, this should be the one. On West Bank River Road (LA 18), near Vacherie, about 45 miles from Huey P. Long Bridge (US 90). 1-265-2151. Bed-and-breakfast cottages $60-$75. Restaurant open for lunch daily. Tours daily.

Madewood. Built 1846. On LA 308, facing Bayou Lafourche, between Labadieville and Napoleonville. (About 15 miles from foot of Sunshine Bridge; same distance to Vacherie via LA 304 and LA 20). 524-1988, or 1-369-7151. Bed-and-breakfast in both main house and cottages,

$85-$150. Dinner served to guests only. Tours daily.

Nottaway Plantation. Built 1859; an unusually large house on 32 acres. In White Castle, about 17 miles west of Sunshine Bridge on LA 1 via Donaldsonville. 1-545-2730. Bed-and-breakfast $90-$250. Excellent restaurant serving lunch and dinner daily. Tours daily.

POMPANO. The best-tasting of all the Gulf fish, if you ask me. Get it grilled, never en papillote. See **Fish**.

POOR BOY. The universal sandwich of New Orleans looks like the grinder, the hoagie, or the submarine from other lands, but the taste is distinctive. A poor boy is made with a foot-long piece of a long, narrow French loaf baked specifically for the purpose. The bread is sliced end to end and filled with meats, cheeses, or seafoods. When a poor boy is "dressed," the bread is slathered with mayonnaise and piled with lettuce, tomato, and pickle slices. If it is to be a really great poor boy, the finished sandwich is popped into a hot oven to toast the exterior of the bread.

The poor boy sandwich was invented during the streetcar strike of the Twenties by Bennie and Clovis Martin. The idea was to provide the poor boys with a big, filling sandwich containing only scraps of meat for a low price—originally a nickel. Martin's Poor Boy Restaurant—first in the French Market, later on St. Claude at Touro—was the all-time greatest purveyor of poor boys until it closed in 1973. (Somebody really ought to revive it.)

Here are the ten best current general practitioners of the poor-boy sandwich art:

1. R&O's
2. Streetcar Sandwiches
3. Mother's
4. Uglesich's
5. Liuzza's
6. Avenue Sandwich Shop
7. Parasol's
8. Katie's
9. Teddy's Grill
10. Ye Olde College Inn

Places which are perceived by some as having good poor boys but which I find to be average or worse are **Domilese's, Parkway Bakery, Frankie & Johnny's, Poor Boy Bakery** and the **Pearl**.

While almost any food can find its way into a poor boy, certain poor boy varieties are considered classic:

Roast beef is easily the most popular poor boy, and with good reason. There's nothing that tastes quite like a well-made roast beef poor boy—not even most other kinds of roast beef sandwiches. The beef is usually sliced about as thick as a nickel; the cut is usually round or shoulder. It is frequently overcooked or dry, but that doesn't matter as much as you'd think, since what makes the sandwich click is the gravy. The local preference is for a roast beef to be "sloppy," with enough gravy so that it oozes out. (There is a golden mean here; there shouldn't be so much gravy that the bread falls apart.) The best roast beef poor boys are at **R&O's, Parasol's, Streetcar,** and **Liuzza's. Mother's** roast beef is not a classic, but they do make a very interesting poor boy with "debris," the leftover roast beef from the day before, cooked in stock.

Ham makes a great poor boy if the ham is interesting. The leader here is **Mother's**, always fragrant with the aroma of baking hams. Ask to have roast beef gravy on your Mother's ham poor boy, but avoid the temptation to go for the ham-and-roast beef "Ferdi." A broiled ham poor boy is also wonderful, although many poorboyaterias disdain the extra work. Those that don't are **Streetcar** (which also has a fantastic barbecued ham poor boy), Avenue Sandwich Shop, and **Liuzza's.** At **Serio's** and **R&O** they don't broil, but the ham is so good that it makes a fine poor boy cold.

Seafood is the growth segment of the poor boy industry. Fried oysters, catfish, or soft-shell crabs (that last one is an interesting experience to eat in the sandwich) are the most common offerings. Although some like such poor boys dressed the standard way, I recommend getting seafood poor boys with just butter, pickles, and hot sauce. The best fried seafood poor boys come from **Uglesich's**, which fries everything to order and even shucks the oysters to order. **Streetcar's** fried seafoods are less than perfect, but they do have a superb, highly original mesquite-grilled fish poor boy. Fine seafood poor boys are also found at **Bozo's, Acme Oyster House, Felix's, Parasol's,** and **R&O**.

Italian poor boys. Absolutely the best of these is **R&O's** Italian special of meatballs, Italian sausage, mozzarella cheese and tomato gravy. **Katie's** also does a good meatball poor boy. The great New Orleans Italian sandwich, however, is the **muffuletta**, which has its own entry elsewhere in this book.

Potato poor boy. One of the cheap and filling originals; unfortunately, it's a lost art. It consists of French fries covered with roast beef gravy on mayonnaise-spread French bread. As crazy as that sounds, it's actually delicious if made with fresh-cut potatoes. All of the few places offering a potato poor boy these days use frozen French fries—and that doesn't work. **Uglesich's** has the right potatoes, but won't make the sandwich. Very frustrating.

★ Popeyes

Many locations around town; see telephone directory. Some open 24 hours; others 6 a.m.-11 p.m. or so. No credit cards. $

When most Orleanians want fried chicken they go to Popeyes, an international fast-food chain founded in New Orleans with a distinctly local flavor. Despite the local legend that some Popeyes are better than others, I find them all pretty inconsistent. Most of the time you get crisp fried chicken with that distinctive high seasoning level; sometimes, however, it's greasy or has an insane amount of cayenne. The oozy buttermilk biscuits are always terrific. But the best thing Popeyes has is its red beans. They are utterly consistent, smoky, well-seasoned, and delicious. In fact, although they're a little creamier than I like, they're among the best red beans and rice in town. Popeyes has begun serving a spicy grilled or broiled chicken, and these are welcome additions.

PORTION SIZE. There is a school of thought that a restaurant's merit can be determined by the quantity of food served for a given price. Taken to its most ridiculous extreme, this theory results in conversations such as this one, overheard one day in a restaurant noted only for large portions:
 "Boy, dis is da woist fried chicken I ever ate, I think!"
 "Yeah you right. But they sure give you a bunch of it, huh?"
 "I hear you on dat! Dat's why I come here alla da time!"
 My own view is that getting a lot of bad food is worse than getting a little bad food. On the other hand, there's nothing funny about getting too small an amount of very good food, especially if the prices are high—which, ironically, they usually are under those circumstances. The current vogue is that white space looks good on a plate, and that a crowded plate is unattractive. As usual, some restaurants have seized on the obvious opportunity this presents, and excuse their miniscule servings as avant-garde—even when their presentations are ugly.
 Some diners make the mistake of assuming that the entree (which they refer to as the "dinner") should be enough to make a complete meal. This is true in casual restaurants, but in the widening spectrum of "serious" (for want of a better term) dining establishments, the menu is designed to be eaten in several courses. It is borderline inappropriate to order only a main course in such a restaurant. More acceptable is ordering several appetizers and no main course; indeed, in some restaurants this is the best possible strategy. Meanwhile, many entrees have shrunk to the size of the appetizers of 15 years ago—but then, how did we ever pack away a half-dozen oysters Bienville as a first course?
 Two more considerations. Certain foodstuffs are so expensive that the portions have to be kept small to keep the menu price in line. Caviar and foie gras are classic examples of this, but even crabmeat qualifies at certain times of the year. Second, most of us should be eating less food anyway. (But that still doesn't excuse restaurateurs who exploit the effect.)
 All that notwithstanding, it is possible to present an ample plate of food beautifully, and slightly more food than you feel like eating is better than slightly less. Restaurants I find especially generous with good food are **Andrea's, Galatoire's, La Cuisine, Mike Anderson's, Pascal's Manale, Peking, Ralph & Kacoo's, Ruth's Chris Steak House,** and **Young's Steak House.** Places that serve large portions but also charge large prices are **Antoine's, K-Paul's** and **Brennan's.**

Restaurants whose portions seem niggardly for the money are the **Caribbean Room, Moran's Riverside, Windsor Court Grill Room, Sazerac,** and the **Versailles**—but I don't find any of them flagrant rip-offs.

★ ★ ★ Port of Call

838 Esplanade, French Quarter. 523-0120. 11 a.m.-1 a.m. seven days; till 5 a.m. Fri. and Sat. AE. $

Two restaurants in one. The formal (sort of) dining room has prime steaks. The beef is pretty decent, although not a landmark. The other half of the operation is a dark bar that has felt the ravages of time (I hope I never have to see it in bright light). The jukebox is a refugee from the Sixties, and so are many of the customers. Here we find The Best Hamburger In New Orleans: a half-pound slab of freshly-ground beef of impeccable quality, grilled to order over the coals, served with the dressings on the side and a baked potato. The buns are toasted, the cheese is grated Cheddar, and the burger itself actually has enough flavor that it could be eaten on its own as a superior chopped steak. There's also pizza and a decent seafood salad, but for me this is strictly a burger place.

The same people own **Snug Harbor,** with the same menu and quality but nicer premises and live music.

POTATOES. One of the most abused vegetables, potatoes rarely taste like potatoes after restaurants are through with them. The worst case involves fried potatoes, almost all of which are made from frozen (see **French fries**). Baked, boiled, or en casserole, potatoes are too often prepared ahead of time and lose their texture and flavor. But some restaurants do them right; here's a ten-best list.

1. Crozier's: Gratin dauphinois (a buttery, garlicky casserole).
2. Antoine's: Soufflee potatoes or brabants.
3. Ruth's Chris Steak House: Baked or French fried.
4. Commander's Palace: Creamed.
5. Crescent City Steak House: Lyonnaise (sauteed with onions).
6. Mosca's: Roasted with rosemary.
7. Cafe Sbisa: Boiled new potatoes.
8. Emeril's: Creamed.
9. Louis XVI: Gratin dauphinois (see above).
10. Galatoire's: Boiled new potatoes (the ones they serve with redfish hollandaise).

PRALINES. First of all, pronounce it right: it's PRAH-leenz. A praline is a candy made of sugar, nuts, milk, and flavorings, and tourists eat them much more often than Orleanians do. This is a pity, because good pralines are delicious. They are made by various concerns around the French Quarter, but I have always greatly preferred those at **Aunt Sally's** in the French Market (next door to Cafe du Monde, 810 Decatur; 524-5107).

Aunt Sally's makes only praline-flavored pralines; no chocolate, coconut, or other flavor perversions. They're rich, vanilla-mellow, creamy, and chock full of big pecan pieces. They make the pralines fresh before your eyes. They also package them in miniature cotton bales to take home; they make quite an impact on the friends I've given them to.

PROFITEROLES. The pastry is like that of a cream puff, but the insides are ice cream and there's chocolate sauce drizzled over the tops. Sort of an upscale ice cream sandwich. The best are at the **Caribbean Room** and **Christian's**.

PROSCIUTTO. The silky, smoky, rich ham with the arresting aroma from Parma and San Daniele in Italy is just starting to return to this country after a long absence. Restaurants which serve it (or, more probably, the good American counterpart) are **Andrea's** (which has the real thing from Parma) and **Louis XVI**. Most Sunday brunch buffets of quality (the **Blue Room**, **Le Jardin**, and **Veranda**) also put it out, usually wrapped around slices of melon. Prosciutto also shows up in the tea sandwiches they serve in the afternoons at the **Windsor Court Grill Room** and **Le Jardin**. A place where I wish we'd see more prosciutto is in muffulettas.

Q as in...

QUAIL. These little birds, once reserved strictly for gourmets, have become extraordinary popular in recent years. Item: the quail stuffed with shrimp and crabmeat at Commander's Palace (never one of their best dishes, if you ask me) is one of the hottest sellers on their menu. The Abita Quail Farm north of the lake is at least a little responsible for this trend, supplying many restaurants with fresh kill. Among the better servings of quail in town are the grilled birds at **Camelia Beach House**, the quail gumbo at **La Provence**, the roast quails with rosemary at **Mosca's**, and the pate-stuffed quails Principessa Anna at **Andrea's**.

QUALITY INN MIDTOWN. See **Regency Room**.

R as in red beans and rice

★★ Ralph & Kacoo's

519 Toulouse, French Quarter. 522-5226. 11:30 a.m.-10:30 p.m. Mon.-Sat.; till 11:00 p.m. Fri. and Sat.; till 9:30 p.m. Sun. ●601 Veterans Blvd., Metairie. 831-3177. 11:30 a.m.-10 p.m. Mon.-Sat; till 11 p.m. Fri. & Sat.; till 9 p.m. Sun. Both: AE, MC, V. $$

Ralph & Kacoo's became legendary in the late Sixties for its fried catfish and crawfish. It moved from its original location on False River to Baton Rouge, then expanded to two sites in New Orleans. It had become really great for a few years, but since the chain's sale to the company that runs Piccadilly Cafeterias, the interest level in the food has gone down.

The alleged specialties—fried catfish and the seafood platter—are to my tastes the least of its offerings. The best dish in the house is on the fancy side: shrimp Verde, broiled to a nice char at the edges, moistened with a great sauce of butter and herbs. The stuffed, bacon-wrapped shrimp are some of the best around, with a harmonious melding of flavors. Trout Ruby—stuffed and slathered with hollandaise—is a bit much, but better than most such. One more stuffed item: mushrooms, jammed with crabmeat and afloat in a great sauce of butter, wine, and garlic.

Ralph & Kacoo's has some big platters in which one seafood is prepared many different ways. The best of these, in season, is the crawfish platter: you get crawfish cocktail, fried tails, a fine spicy bisque with stuffed crawfish heads, etouffee, and fried boulettes. Similar things are done with shrimp and crab. Lighter dishes of note are the grilled or broiled redfish.

First courses include great raw oysters, brought on a tray of ice; tangy, fat shrimp remoulade; and a tasty gumbo marred somewhat by undercooked roux. The place is famous for its hush puppies, but they may be the worst ever served, completely innocent of pepper or herbs. The short dessert list features a very good bread pudding. The Ralph & Kacoo's in the French Quarter is the biggest restaurant in town, and handsomely decorated as casual restaurants go. The one in Metairie has a more conventional local seafood-house look. Both are high-volume restaurants which by rights should be more inconsistent than they are. Service is polite but geared toward speed of turning tables.

RED BEANS AND RICE. The universal Monday lunch special remains one of the great dishes of the Creole cuisine, and one of the most difficult to locate in consistently good form in New Orleans restaurants. Few restaurants have them available every day. **Eddie's** makes the best in town, by merit of serving some wonderful greasy hot sausage over them—a perfect match. **Chez Helene** serves good beans on a plate with three pieces of equally tasty fried chicken. In the Quarter, the **Coffee Pot** and the nearby **Gumbo Shop** are the best beaneries.

On Mondays, finding red beans is a lot easier. My picks would be **Liuzza's**, **Camellia Grill**, **Olde N'Awlins Cookery**, **Mother's**, **Andrea's**, and **Rocky & Carlo's**. All perform their red bean duties recommendably every Monday. (Mother's also has them on Saturdays.) Surprisingly, some of the best beans in town are the very soupy ones doled out around the clock at **Popeyes Fried Chicken's** dozens of counters; **Copeland's** serves the same fine product.

Red beans and rice are one of the ten best dishes in New Orleans. Since we have the recipes for the other nine elsewhere in this book. . .

1 lb. red kidney beans
1 oz. pickled pork, or 2 slices bacon
1 small onion, coarsely chopped
2 cloves chopped garlic
2 ribs celery, chopped
1 green onion, tops only, chopped
1 small green or red bell pepper, stem and seeds removed, chopped
¼ tsp. thyme
¼ tsp. marjoram
¼ tsp. savory
2 bay leaves
1 Tbs. salt
½ tsp. Louisiana hot sauce
½ tsp. black pepper
8 sprigs parsley, chopped

1. The night before, sort through the beans and remove misshapen beans, rocks, etc. Soak the beans overnight in a gallon of cold water. Pour off the water the next day and rinse the beans well.
2. In a Dutch oven or large saucepan, cook the pickled pork or bacon over medium heat until the fat renders. Remove the pork and, in the fat in the pot, saute the onions and garlic until translucent. Add the celery, green onion, and bell pepper and saute, stirring well, until limp.
3. Add the beans, one gallon of cold water, and herbs. Bring the pot to a boil. Stir well, lower heat to a simmer, and cover the pot. The longer the beans cook, the better they will be. Keep the heat just high enough to barely make bubbles break in the top of the covered pot. Add a little more water if necessary to keep the mixture loose.
4. When you're ready to serve, add salt, hot sauce, and pepper to taste.

Remove the bay leaves. Serve the beans over steamed rice with some smoky meat—smoked sausage, andouille, bacon, etc. Top with chopped fresh parsley. For a low-cholesterol version of the dish, don't return the pork to the pot after rendering the fat, and add extra virgin olive oil at the table. You can also serve a turkey sausage or turkey ham to great effect.

Serves six.

REDFISH. This relative of the sea bass is seen on menus all over town, but it's never served. Reason: it is currently banned from commercial fishing. That development probably did more for fish in local menus than any other event in culinary history. See **Fish**.

RED SNAPPER. Once and for all, this is *not* the same thing as redfish. See **Fish**.

REMOULADE. This sauce, usually served with shrimp but sometimes with other seafoods, occurs in two forms locally. The red or orange remoulade sauce is the more distinctly Creole; it's mostly Creole mustard, with admixtures of onions, oil, paprika, and sometimes catsup. The white remoulade, which is more classically French, is a mayonnaise with Creole mustard and herbs. Both are good and ubiquitous. See **Shrimp**.

★ ★ ★ The Regency Room

3900 Tulane Ave. 486-5541. 11 a.m.-10 p.m. Sun.-Fri.; 4-10 p.m. Sat. Sun. Brunch 10 a.m.-2 p.m. September-December. AE, CB, DC, MC, V. $$

The dining room of a Tulane Avenue motel would not be a place you'd look for great Creole food. Unless you knew better. The Regency Room—referred to as just the "Quality Inn" by its regulars—has operated one of the better kitchens in Mid-City for years, and it has enough specialties to make it worth a taste. Here is, for example, one of the few restaurants in town that consistently prepares good Maine lobsters.

Start off with the soups (which at lunch come off the salad bar) or the broiled shrimp Benjamin. At lunch, they put out good daily specials, the classic of which is boiled brisket of beef, flavorful and tender, served with the standard horseradish-catsup sauce.

The better part of the standing menu is seafood; we find the full assortment of fried, sauteed, and stuffed local fish and shellfish. I especially like the amandine treatments of fish here; the sauce is thicker and tastier than the lemon butter that usually accompanies such things.

Finish off the meal with bread pudding or caramel custard. This is not a wine kind of place. The waitresses have a lot of personality, to put it mildly. Prices and menu are such that this is a great place to bring guests from the extremes of the age spectrum.

★ ★ ★ Rib Room

Royal Orleans Hotel, 621 St. Louis, French Quarter. Reservations taken for early dinners only; 529-7045. 11:30 a.m.-3 p.m. and 6:30-11:30 p.m. seven days. Brunch Sun. 11:00 a.m.-3 p.m. AE, CB, DC, MC, V. $$$$$

The flagship dining room of the swanky Royal Orleans Hotel is informal as such places go. The room is a big cube with a generally rustic feel about it. Lanterns along the walls name destinations for some wandering bayou train? packet boat? The service is no-nonsense, with minor pretensions to elegance. Although the food has a history of goodness going back three decades, in the last few years a certain amount of boredom has crept in.

Dominating the rear wall of the Rib Room is a tall bank of rotisseries. Spits slowly turn bearing birds, meat roasts, and seafoods before open fires. There's also a grill back there for further searing. The food which proceeds from this area is all pretty good, and some of it is remarkable. The shrimp, for example, are enormous and come to the table bursting with flavor, moistened with buerre blanc, with some great rice on the side. The mixed grill of beef, lamb, sausage, and chicken at lunch also shows off the rotisserie to good effect.

The namesake prime ribs are as good as any—crusty on the outside, tender on the inside, served with sometimes-good Yorkshire popovers. The popular veal Tanet—panneed veal atop a stack of Italian-dressed romaine—is a reliable classic. And they do a decent job with the various New Orleans fish dishes. An appetizer called fettuccine forestiere is superb, with an intense tan cream sauce and several kinds of mushrooms. Nightly specials and themed festivals supply the flights of fancy.

The desserts, particularly the pastries, are grand. Of particular interest is the chocolate mousse, which is far and away the best in the city, dense and dark. The wine list is extensive and priced more reasonably than the dinner menu, which is more than a little expensive. Service ranges from competent to rare and haughty.

★ Rick's Pancake Cottage

2547 Canal, Mid-City. 822-2630. 5:30 a.m.-2 p.m. seven days, till 3:30 p.m. Sat. and Sun. AE, MC, V. $

This leaning tower of pancakes was thoroughly revamped a few years ago. They had, for instance, the good sense to pull down all those interesting but filthy lunchboxes lining the walls. Rick's is still raffish, but it's once again a pleasant place to have breakfast. The pancakes come in dozens of varieties, most of them pretty uninteresting unless you have an insatiable sweet tooth. What adult could, for example, get through these whipped-cream-and strawberry-laden pancakes?

The basic buttermilk and buckwheat pancakes are very well made, however, and contain a goodly amount of egg. There's a lazy susan of six different syrups to keep the variety going. The potato pancakes are really just regular pancakes with some potato in them, but even so they're not bad. All the breakfast meats appear to be grilled to order—the grease-free link sausages have a satisfyingly crunchy skin. Omelettes and other egg dishes are okay. Lunchtime brings a very limited menu of fried seafood and sandwiches, as well as a daily special lunch platter; the main merit of all this is cheapness. Service is fast and the prices throughout the menu are very low.

RIVERWALK. See Food Courts.

★★Rocky & Carlo's

613 W. St. Bernard Hwy., Chalmette. 279-8323. 5:30 a.m.-Midnight seven days; till 1:00 a.m. Fri. and Sat. No credit cards. $

The strange world of Rocky & Carlo's sends a shiver down my spine. The scene is immediately recognizable from childhood memories of dozens of places like this filled with hundreds of the same people. The guy in front of me in the serving line says, "Gimme dat baked macaroni—and put some brown gravy on it!" My late dad loved that odd combination. Two people in front of him are getting big oval plates loaded with lima beans over rice—my deceased parran's favorite dish. And the bread pudding in the white enamel, glass-front case is topped with a layer of meringue—something I'd never seen outside my mother's kitchen. These bits of my past intermingle with other parts of the Rocky & Carlo's experience—like the counter personnel's seeming incomprehension of your order (though they always get it right), the wrinkled faces filling the bar and watching a Cubs game on cable, and the blend of guys who look like bankers and guys who look like mobsters all packing away the food at the tables—well, it's too close for comfort.

Rocky & Carlo's is the cultural center of the mostly-white, largely blue-collar suburb of Chalmette. It's a large version of the standard neighborhood restaurant: a five-foot-high brick wall topped with plants runs the length of the room. On one side are tables for dining, on the other is the bar. At the end is a cafeteria-style serving station with a half-dozen or so daily specials in the steam table. Above it is a sign listing the other availabilities. The platters have a more or less Italian orientation; a classic dish is the hearty but meatless lasagne, served with your choice of several sides.

The best of the specials is braciolini (they spell it something like "bruculona"), a rolled steak stuffed with cheese and seasoned breading. Also good Italian sausage and veal Parmesan. Standard menu items include edible fried chicken, pork chops, and poor boy sandwiches. All of this is portioned out while you wait at the counter with your tray. You pay, then you eat. The food here is probably the best in Chalmette, but not really good enough for a trip from the city unless you want to observe the local culture of some three or four decades ago.

ROMANTIC ATMOSPHERE. This doesn't need much explaining, does it? Soft lights, elegant but understated service, beautiful (and probably French) food, relative quiet save for music. . . these are important needs for an anniversary, a birthday, or a seduction. Here are the ten most romantic restaurants in town:
 1. Sazerac
 2. La Provence
 3. Grill Room
 4. Brennan's
 5. Andrea's
 6. Le Jardin
 7. Louis XVI
 8. Commander's Palace
 9. Versailles
 10. Antoine's

There's another side to this story. Certain restaurants are not exactly romantic—they're sexy. I have always thought **Galatoire's** is sexy, because of all the flirting that bounces off the mirrors. **Flagons**—particularly the original wine bar section—can provide some delightfully anxious moments. Some nice things have happened because of the proximity of the deuces at **Christian's**. **Crescent City Steak House** and **Beef Baron** have those curtained booths, which appeal to those with a feel for high camp. There is something about the masculine feeling of **Ruth's Chris Steak House** which makes women who show up there look great. Of course, almost any place can be romantic if you're in the mood.

★ ★ ★ R&O's

210 Metairie-Hammond Hwy., Bucktown. 831-1248. 11 a.m.-10 p.m. Mon.-Sat.; till; Midnight Fri. & Sat. 5-10 p.m Sun. No credit cards. $

It's a pleasure to see that this out-of-the-way place has caught on such that it's hard to get a table anymore. The largish dining room looks like that of a pizza parlor, and in fact they do serve a decent pizza here. Also platters of good, crisp fried seafood and surprisingly delicious Italian dinners.

But the sandwich menu is the main point of interest. These are the best poor boys in the city. The bread is unusual: it's an Italian-style seeded loaf, with the same shape as but a lighter texture than regular poor boy bread. The roast beef is thinly sliced and enriched by a superb gravy. A combination of that with ham and melted Swiss is rich and tasty. The Italian Special sandwich is Italian sausage, meatballs, mozzarella, and tomato gravy on the same bread: a real stunner. They also prepare a killer muffuletta. All of the sandwiches at R&O's are too big to be finished comfortably, but that has never stopped me. This may sound trite, but R&O's was even better when it was unknown and in a shabby room next to a grocery store. I hope success doesn't spoil it.

★ Russell's Marina Grill

8555 Pontchartrain Blvd., West End. 282-9980. 7:00 a.m.-Midnight seven days; till 1 a.m. Fri. and Sat. AE, V. $

The Marina Grill is an attempt, not entirely successful, to bring an old-style diner to the Lakeview area. The need is obviously there: the place is very busy, particularly late at night. There is a lunch counter, a la Camellia Grill, but much more table and booth seating. The menu is a very standard assortment of sandwiches, omelettes, hamburgers, fried and blackened seafood platters, and daily specials of things like fried chicken. I find all of this just okay. There is one unique item: the onion mum, a whole onion sliced so that it resembles a chrysanthemum, then battered and fried. It comes to the table with a spicy, light mayonnaise sauce, and it's undeniably delicious. (So good, in fact, that the idea has spread to some other restaurants.) Waitresses are pleasant and prompt, unless the place is really busy.

★ ★ ★ ★ Ruth's Chris

711 N. Broad, Mid-City. 486-0810. • 3633 Veterans Blvd., Metairie. 888-3600. Both: 11:30 a.m.-11:30 p.m. seven days. AE, CB, DC, MC, V. $$$$

The two venues of the city's definitive, high-profile steakhouse, with their parking lots dominated by Mercedeses and Cadillacs, are macho-recharge centers for the alpha males of the community. In Metairie, you'll see a heady assortment of politicians, bankers, and businessmen, but the real Ruth's Chris Steak House is on Broad Street. There the most solid of the hard chargers, primary sports figures (sportswriters and the football players themselves), and the top political powers converge, often with their submissive females, to conduct the sacred rite of devouring what is widely believed to be The Best Steak In Town at convincingly stiff prices.

A Ruth's Chris Steak at its best is, in fact, hard to beat. The beef is prime, fresh, well-aged, and given a great broiling in a veritable inferno that quickly sears the exterior and allows the inside of the steak to retain all the juices. It comes out bubbling and deliciously aromatic in the definitive butter sauce—an overkill of cholesterol, but it tastes great. The best cut is the strip, firm and eminently beefy. The filets are large but include an ounce or two of "chain," an inferior neighboring cut. The porterhouses for two or three (really enough there for from three to five) are glorious festivals of carnivory, even though the big ones are fleshed out with filet tips. The ribeyes are okay but, as prime ribeyes usually are, rather fatty.

In the last couple of years, Ruth's has expanded its menu to include some great chops. My own favorite, served at lunch for $11, is the inch-and-a-half-thick center-cut pork chop, broiled to a char at the bone and served in bubbling butter with apples. Similarly well turned out are the tender pink veal chops and the double-thick lamb chops; both are as good as any in town.

Seafood takes a back seat here, but lately that seat has been made more luxurious. We now find thick fillets of fresh salmon, beautifully grilled. They always did serve some of the city's best Maine lobsters, taken from a tank just inside the door.

The salads are superb, with unique homemade dressings. The various shapes of fried potatoes are all wonderful, because this is one of the few places in town that uses fresh potatoes for frying. The creamed spinach and the au gratin vegetables, with their thick toppings of Cheddar, are very popular—but they leave me cold. Bread pudding is the most reliable dessert. The cheesecake they make here has a funny texture like that of soft-serve ice milk, and is way too sweet and rich.

S as in shrimp remoulade

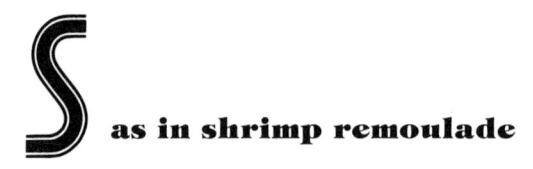

★ ★ The St. Charles

333 St. Charles Ave., CBD. 522-6600. Lunch only, 11:15 a.m.-2 p.m. Mon.-Fri. AE, CB, DC, MC, V. $$

With a former bank lobby as its dining room, the St. Charles has one of the most spacious and grandest-looking eating parlors in the city—comparable to those of the big hotels. It's a slightly-upscale lunch place, densely populated by businessmen. The menu is limited to a handful of very good if uncomplicated Creole specialties. The best dishes are oysters Jaubert (fried, atop an English muffin and a slice of Canadian bacon, with a spicy, light bearnaise), shrimp etouffee, and fried and grilled seafood.

In addition, there are a few daily specials, and these are generally edible. Some outstanding specials include trout with sauteed crawfish, double-cut stuffed pork chops, and the panneed veal with fettuccine. Crabmeat Higgins is a good, spicy, orange soup that makes a good starter or entree. A few salads and appetizers round out the menu. The prices are attractive, as are many of the career girls who lunch here. For the most part, the tables seem sexually segregated by choice of the clientele.

SALAD. A dish is a salad if you call it a salad. Although the elements of cold temperature, vegetables, and crunchiness seem essential, I can think of salads that have none of those things. But I think I see three categories of salad, whatever it is:

House or **dinner salads** are served either before or after the entree. The best of these is the Windsor Court salad at the **Windsor Court Grill Room**, with its multicolor bands of avocado, egg, Roquefort, tomato, lettuce, bacon, and red cabbage. **Arnaud's** has a pretty collection of endive and watercress. **La Cuisine** does one of Creole tomatoes, Vidalia onions, and ricotta cheese. Other salads gain distinction from their dressings: the **Rib Room** (a spicy Roquefort), Ruth's Chris Steak House (a zingy reddish French), and **Tavern on the Park** (avocado). **Crozier's** has a classic French vinaigrette with crisp romaine.

Entree salads are far more various and change more drastically with the seasons. The best of those are **Kabby's** fried chicken salad, **Mr. B's** warm grilled chicken over greens, **Galatoire's** Godchaux seafood salad, **Andrea's** seafood salad Portofino, with such things as mussels, clams, and squid; **Bayou Ridge Cafe's** salade Nicoise, made with fresh grilled tuna; and the **Coffee Pot's salad Jayne of shrimp, boiled egg, bacon, greens, and buttermilk dressing.**

Salad bars are declining in popularity; they never were commonplace in New Orleans. Few salad bars are very interesting. My experience is that restaurants with exceptional salad bars rarely have anything else worth eating. **Steak and Ale**, and **Monroe's** come to mind. So do **Wendy's** and **Shoney's**, both of which scrupulously keep up their rabbit-food buffets.

★ ★ ★ ★ Sal & Judy's

U.S. 190, Lacombe (bear right at first major intersection past north end of Causeway; restaurant is about nine miles east, on the left). Reservations 1-882-9443. 5-10 p.m. Wed. & Thurs.; 12:30-11 p.m. Fri.-Sun. MC, V. $$$

In the center of Lacombe, a tiny town on the north shore of the lake, is an old roadhouse, turned a dozen years ago into a restaurant by Sal and Judy Impastato—he the chef, she the hostess. The place is halfway decorated: the curtains are pretty, but the walls and the bar are rather shabby. This does not deter the crowds, however, with whom I agree that Sal & Judy's is one of the best kitchens in the area and an outstanding bargain. Even with a reservation or at an odd hours, there's usually a wait for a table.

The menu doesn't look promising, listing as it does the most everyday pasta, steak, and seafood warhorses. Specials are what make the lake crossing worthwhile. And they'll make anything for you if they have the raw materials.

Start off with the fettuccine—firm, a little spicy, and rich. Fried calamari are crisp and almost inhalably delectable. They do a nice plate of rather basic baked oysters with Italian seasonings. Soups are good—especially the oyster-artichoke.

The best entree is one of the specials: trout belle meuniere. It's a big fillet, dusted with flour and paprika, broiled, and covered with shrimp, artichokes, and mushrooms. The liquid portion of the sauce is a translucent lemon butter of startling goodness. This is the best seafood-atop-seafood dish I've ever had—a triumph by any standard. Variations on the theme appear, and all of those have been good, too.

The Italian sausage is some of the best you'll ever eat. It's made on the premises, aromatic with anise and herbs, and grilled with peppers and onions. It's a marvelous match for the spaghetti aglio olio. Chicken cacciatore has a wonderful, robust Sicilian tomato sauce—rough-edged, chunky, and well-seasoned.

The wine list is good enough and inexpensive. Service is by friendly, efficient waitresses.

★★ Sal and Sam's

4300 Veterans Blvd., Metairie. 885-5566. 11 a.m.-1 a.m. seven days. AE, MC, V. $$

The greatest contribution Sal and Sam's makes to our culinary resources is that it stays open very late—one of the few full-service restaurants that does. The food is not what you could call brilliant, but it's agreeable enough. The emphasis is on Italian food, although one finds a large selection of Creole seafood dishes. The appetizer tray for two, for example, includes rich, filling oysters Bienville; richer, more filling stuffed mushrooms; and okayish barbecue shrimp. This is almost enough to complete a meal, but we plunge ahead anyway through the soups—home-style, very well made, some of the best food in the place.

The best entree I've had here is the veal florentine, with its underlayer of creamed spinach—rich, but not gloppy. They boil delicious, giant cubes of tender beef brisket, and serve it with a pile of boiled vegetables. The seafood is reasonably well cooked, although the fried stuff could be crisper and lighter. The steaks are prime and more than edible. The Italian dishes are gigantic in portion; the mostaccioli, served with a couple of earthy meatballs, has a thick, robust, spicy sauce.

Bread pudding and cheesecake are the best dessert shots. The wine list is much more sophisticated than the food—distinguished, almost. Service is very friendly, owing to the fact that a large percentage of the customers are regulars.

★★★ Samurai

609 Decatur, French Quarter. 522-7356. 11:30 a.m.-2:30 p.m. and 5:30-10:30 p.m. Tues.-Sun.; till 11 p.m. Fri. & Sat. AE, CB, DC, MC, V.

Although the place has the unmistakable feel of an old Quarter building, it's bright and clean—as a sushi bar had better be. The Samurai has a large following of Quarterites, and they and the staff conspire to create an unusually happy, welcome feeling. Many regulars come here alone and wind up talking with other regulars—both at the sushi bar and at the tables.

The sushi, particularly large platters of it, is priced a touch below the prevailing local average. It is not the prettiest sushi presentation I've ever seen, but this does not impact the flavors; tuna, yellowtail, octopus, and sea urchin are all flawlessly fresh and delicious, and the rice is well-made. Most of the sushi and sashimi I've eaten at Samurai has come to the table with a nice chill, although on a couple of occasions the rice int he sushi was palpably warm.

The rather lengthy menu goes on to include all the usual tempura and teriyaki items, neither of which is worth crossing town for. But the restaurant features specials of cooked foods that can be fascinating and delicious. (These are not always listed on the menu, so press the waitress to find out what's available.) The complete dinner deals run between $12 and $18 and are very substantial. The miso soup that comes with these is satisfyingly rich.

SANDWICHES. See Poor Boy, Muffuletta, Hamburger, and Deli.

★ ★ ★ Santa Fe

801 Frenchmen, French Quarter. 944-6854. 11:00 a.m.-11:00 p.m. Tues.-Fri. 5:00 p.m.-11 p.m. Sat. AE, MC, V. $$

    The secret that all the many regulars of this Mexican place want you to know is that the chef-owner is German. He flaunts his heritage in the dessert department; the German chocolate cake is one of the best, and there are other European pastries.
    We have been through Tex-Mex, New Mexican, California Mexican, and nouvelle Southwestern cuisines. But this is the first place whose menu legitimately can be described as Creole Mexican. Although the formats are distinctly south-of-the-border—lots of tortillas, brick-red sauces flavored with cumin, and refried beans—the fillings are more likely to be seafood than anything else. Some of this is even good. The crab and corn soup, the unique Mexican gumbo, seafood fajitas, and seafood-stuffed chile relleno are as delectable as they are offbeat. The seafood burritos, enchiladas, and the jalapeno-tinged sauteed fish are also pretty good. Straight-ahead meat-and-cheese tostadas, enchiladas and the like are ordinary.
    There's a great chicken dish called the Pepian, breaded with pumpkin seeds, baked with a cheesy sauce sharpened with poblano peppers. And a few dishes that seem to have no Mexican connection at all. Aside from the pastries, the best dessert is the delicious, mellow flan—better without the whipped cream and Amaretto. Service has a certain fussbudget demeanor. The premises are colorful; tables are clothed, but covered with sheets of glass (a cheapness).

★ ★ ★ Sazerac

Fairmont Hotel, University Place, CBD. Reservations 529-4733. 11:30 a.m.-2 p.m. Sun.-Fri; 6-10 p.m. seven days. AE, CB, DC, MC, V. $$$$$

    The Sazerac is the last bastion of dining ceremony. The room—redecorated beautifully in 1988—remains palatial in a classical manner. The plush, velvet, lace, harp music, and large paintings suggest the Belle Epoque. Waiters push gueridons and trolleys around; almost nothing is served that doesn't receive a bit of tableside ministration. For special occasions, particularly of a romantic nature, there are few beter venues.
    The Sazerac's food has undergone so many jerky changes in the past

two years that I hesitate to venture any strong opinions about it. Just as this book was going to press, the place returned to the menu it junked when the dining room was spruced up. With good reason. The two California-inspired, nouvelle-cuisine concepts that were tried in the interim received mixed reviews at best from the Sazerac's established clientele, much of which drifted away. That was a shame, because some of the new food was very good.

But the old food could have its moments, as well. I feel there is a place for this kind of food, and nobody ever did it better than the Sazerac. So far, here's what I can vouch for from the New Old Menu. Start with the magnificent lobster bisque, intense with lobster flavor, chunky with tail meat, and rich with cream. The house salad is expensive but very well made, with a thick dressing fragrant with dill. (This is especially good with the addition of crabmeat.)

Poultry is the best of the entrees. They send out a magnificent roasted chicken, stuffed with an ethereally light oyster dressing, enhanced with a garlic-tinged buerre blanc. The roast duck with spinach and raspberries comes as close to melting in the mouth as a side of bird can; the skin is crispy almost to the point of crackling. Any way you get a slab of beef or lamb will be a good one; some of these are served for two with all the dining room theatre for which the Sazerac is celebrated. There is no better steak tartare in town; the dish is prepared with your oversight, served cold and delicious.

A couple of dishes from the nouvelle interregnum remain, most notably a lovely flank of grilled pompano with Creole seasoning and a corn relish. The other seafood dish of note is the trout (or whatever species is available) with a well-made light lemon butter, with crabmeat and shrimp on the side.

At dessert, consider first the fine pastry table. For unknown reasons, the Sazerac seems to be incapable of serving a decent hot souffle, although they keep trying. A very good, very expensive wine list and other high prices are still part of the picture. The Sazerac is especially interesting around Christmas, when they mount a festive table d'hote dinner attended by every avid restaurant-goer in town.

SEAFOOD. See Boiled Seafood, Fish, Fried Seafood, Grilled Seafood, or the name of the particular fish or shellfish you're interested in.

SEAFOOD PLATTER. See Fried Seafood.

★ ★ ★ Seb's

Jackson Brewery Millhouse, Fifth Floor, 600 Decatur, French Quarter. 522-1696. 11:30 a.m.-2:30 p.m. Mon.-Fri.; 5-10 p.m. seven days. 11 a.m.-4 p.m. Sun. brunch. AE, CB, DC, MC, V. $$$

From the fifth floor of the Jax Brewery, Seb's has a commanding view of the Mississippi River. Look the other way, and you peer through the kitchen's large windows. The dining room is on two levels, with a singular design punctuated by sculptures of fish in what looks like verdigris-covered copper but which is actually papier mache.

The culinary focus is on a wood-stoked grill, over whose flames Seb's offers to put stripes of black on several different species of fish. From there, the menu spreads out both into very traditional Creole cooking and into nouvelle territory. Unfortunately, the lack of a strong local clientele seems to have lessened the pressure on the kitchen to stay consistent.

Start with the magnificent shrimp and crab bisque, ruddy light brown with a bit of cream and pepper and big lumps of crab. The crabmeat ravigote, shrimp remoulade, oysters Rockefeller, and oysters Bienville are all very well made. The carpaccio—classically raw, thin beef tenderloin—is here roasted a touch around the outside and gets a great smoky flavor. The grilled Belgian endive is far tastier than it sounds: the bitter, spear-shaped green is lightly charred on one side, wrapped with cappacola ham, and brought forth with a raspberry vinaigrette. (The chef is a little nuts about raspberries, but this works.) All the salads are interestingly composed.

Other than the grilled fish, the entree which has most accurately pushed my button at Seb's is the pair of double-cut lamb chops, grilled to a magnificent exterior char, as juicy and bone-nibbling delicious as any lamb I've had in awhile. They display similar gifts with the steaks, which come dressed with exceptional versions of the classic steak sauces. There's also a fine veal chop with shrimp butter, a wonderful seafood pasta with a spicy red sauce studded with olives, and a terrible duck breast. Everything comes out with tasty fresh vegetables.

The short wine list is well chosen, with emphasis on less-expensive wines and wines by the glass. The best desserts are the raspberry-tinged chocolate mousse and the raspberry-layered ice cream meringue pie. Service gets the job done with a modicum of style.

★ ★ Serio's

133 St. Charles Ave., CBD. 523-2668. 7 a.m.-3 p.m. Mon.-Fri. No credit cards. $

The Central Business District is cursed with dozens of terrible lunch places, but this is not one of them. Serio's may turn over the greatest volume of poor boy sandwiches in the city from a menu that includes every imaginable filling and combination. Despite that, the sandwiches are generally well made, with fine fresh French bread and good fillings. I find the ham poor boy here unusually good, even though it's served cold; the ham is almost silky. The Italian sausage sandwich with red gravy will eliminate the need for supper. Daily lunch platters, which never get more ambitious than the Thursday baked chicken with macaroni and cheese (delicious!), are cheap and good. They also have acceptable fried seafood plates and sandwiches. Service, by a battery of ladies who look as if they'd been at it awhile, is fast.

SERVICE. A new class of service personnel has developed in New Orleans restaurants. It is considerably more professional than it was ten or even five years ago—probably owing to the fact that a good waiter will always have a job making better money than most other employment (or unemployment) available hereabouts. I have encountered only very few occasions of extremely poor service in recent times, and even less surly, insulting service.

The trend in the service profession is for waiters and waitresses to think of themselves as the equals of their customers. I think this is fine, assuming the essential duties of serving are performed. Beyond the "I'm Bruce and I'll be your waiter tonight" stage (thank heaven that's out of vogue), servers became more conversational and helpful. They were also bereft of the "I'm just a dumb waiter, what do you expect" excuse for bad service.

Unfortunately, equality is a short step from superiority. The suggestion that a diner might not be up to the lofty levels of comportment of which the server imagines himself an exemplar invites the leaving of a cheap tip (which, of course, will be taken by the server as proof of his theory). I notice this problem most in restaurants where the dining room staff is predominantly gay.

After incompetence and haughtiness, the service condition that bothers me most is *excessive* service. A few days before I wrote this, I was in a restaurant where, after each course arrived, four different people came by to ask "Is everything all right?" I think the question is ridiculous to start with. If something is not right, a good waiter should be able to spot my discomfort without having to ask.

Some fillips of service were nice when they occurred once in awhile, but then they got out of hand. The synchronized lifting of silver domes at the table, at the sight of which one is supposed to squeal with delight, is the current edition. (It has not completely replaced, "Would you like some fresh ground pepper?", its predecessor.)

My wife says, "I don't notice service unless it's bad." There is an essential truth in that statement. More thoughts along these lines at **Tipping**.

Here are the best service acts in New Orleans.

1. Grill Room
2. Mr. B's
3. Christian's
4. Tavern on the Park
5. Arnaud's
6. Commander's Palace
7. Andrea's
8. Sazerac

9. Louis XVI
10. Brennan's
11. Antoine's (if they know you)

SHEEPSHEAD. This is the terrible common name for a very good Gulf fish which, since redfish and trout have become scarce, has begun to appear on menus with some regularity. Its texture is somewhat like that of redfish, and it grills and poaches to good effect. See **Fish**.

★ ★ ★ Shigure

8115 Jeannette (near streetcar barn), Uptown. 866-1119. 11 a.m.-9:30 p.m. Tues.-Sat. (later Fri. & Sat.), 1-8 p.m. Sun. AE, MC, V. $$

In a minimally-remodeled house, Shigure has tables inside three small rooms, plus a couple more on the front porch. After some failed experiments in Sino-Creole cuisine, it has become a reliable, if slightly quirky Japanese restaurant and sushi bar. The sushi and sashimi are beautifully cut, eminently fresh, and satisfyingly chilled. The rice has an especially good texture and flavor. The place has become popular with the Uptown subspecies of sushihead, which exist in large numbers in that neighborhood. Their presence guarantees the essential fast movement of product.

There are some tasty non-sushi dishes here. They serve edamame, which makes an interesting appetizer: they're short green bean pods, each with two or three green beans about the size of a navy bean inside. They're boiled, salted and served hot; you pop them out of the pods and nibble them like peanuts. Their taste is subtle but interesting enough. The tempura and teriyaki stuff is okay. Service is carried out by intelligent and friendly Western waitresses.

★ ★ ★ Shogun

2325 Veterans Blvd., Metairie. 833-7477. 11:30 a.m.-2:00 p.m. and 5:30-10:00 p.m. Mon.-Fri. Noon-11 p.m. Sat. & Sun. AE, MC, V. $$

When Shogun opened the first real sushi bar in New Orleans a few years ago, it set the standard against which all comers were compared. It still does. It is the one place about which I have never received a word of complaint from the sushi freaks.

After outgrowing its original location (now Ichiban, which the same people own), Shogun moved to this space (formerly Shakey's Pizza). They installed the longest sushi bar in the city and a commodious dining room with lots of tables. The sushi bar gleams; big signs depict the various forms of sushi on hand. Shogun's selection of raw fish is superb. Even if you order a small luncheon plate of nigirizushi, they send out a thoughtful assortment, no two pieces of which are alike. Because a large percentage of the clientele is very regular, the chef doesn't hesitate to use some of the more unusual seafoods. The condition, slicing, and temperature of the fish are just about perfect.

Shogun's cooked dishes are good, too. The tempura assortment includes not only the usual shrimp and vegeables but also some chicken and fish, all light and free of excess oil. The teriyaki is also good, with a more pronounced marinated flavor than average. A few oddball items appear among the appetizers. Japanese dumplings, battered and fried into marshmallow-shaped nuggets, have the musky taste that one has to grow up with to like, but they come with a thick, slightly sweet brown sauce that makes a great dip for tempura.

Recent development: when the local Benihana went bust, Shogun bought some of the equipment and is now performing something like the phony knife-flashing act we used to have to put up with downtown. Some of the regulars are offended, but there's nothing that says you have to take advantage of the teppan-yaki service.

The menu, reprinted a few too many times from the same original, is the most unreadable in town. The staff is cold and sometimes even rude. But the experience is still dominated by the best Japanese cooking and non-cooking in the vicinity.

SHRIMP. The overwhelming majority of shrimp sold in restaurants throughout America come from our Gulf waters. They are arguably the best in the world, and unarguably a first-class food item. There are two similar species; the better of them is the brown shrimp, which are at peak in the summer months; white shrimp follow in the fall.

Shrimp receive every imaginable treatment at the hands of New Orleans cooks. They are boiled by the zillions in the shirt-sleeves seafood restaurants (see **Boiled Seafood**). Still more are boiled for a fixture of New Orleans appetizer menus—**shrimp remoulade**, the Creole improvement of shrimp cocktail. A cold sauce dominated by the flavor of brown Creole mustard is slathered over large, spicy boiled shrimp. There are two different styles: red and white. I greatly prefer the uniquely New Orleans red version, particularly the ones at **Arnaud's, Galatoire's, Commander's Palace** and **Christian's**. White remoulade sauce, closer to the classic French formula, is milder and has a mayonnaise base. The great ones are at **Broussard's, Ralph & Kacoo's**, the **Gumbo Shop, Mike Anderson's**, and **Ruth's Chris Steak House**.

You can reasonably divide the world of shrimp entrees into those made with big shrimp and those made with small shrimp. The big shrimp I'm talking about are real monsters—some six inches or more long. The best dish made from these is **barbecued shrimp**, created at **Pascal's Manale** but now prepared by many others. The dish is simple: huge whole shrimp in a tremendous amount of butter and black pepper. As far as the eating is concerned, barbecued shrimp are two dishes in one. The first is the shrimp themselves, drenched with the sauce and eaten with the fingers. The other dish is bread dunked in the sauce; some maintain this tastes even better than the shrimp. Besides Manale's, **Mr. B's** (the best in town), **Stephen and Martin** and **Kolb's** make great barbecued shrimp on a regular basis. (See **Barbecue Shrimp** for more details and a recipe).

Big shrimp also turn up on the rotisseries at the **Rib Room**; these are incredible. So are the scampi served at **Moran's Riverside**. Andrea's occasionally obtains gigantic shrimp from the Southern Hemisphere and makes a superb stuffed, sauced dish called gamberi Tommaso with them. They also make a lusty shrimp fra diavolo with a spicy, light red sauce. Bozo's broils butterflied shrimp with margarine, salt and pepper to a spectacular taste. **Mosca's** roasts big shrimp in their shells with a staggering amount of garlic and olive oil to create an unforgettable dish. Shrimp Madeleine at **Christian's** swim in an elegant, intense cream sauce heightened with a touch of mustard. In a funkier vein, Joe's hot shrimp at **La Cuisine** are bacon-wrapped, jalapeno cheese-stuffed, and fried to marvelous effect.

The classic entree made with small shrimp is **shrimp Creole**, a dish which has largely passed into the realm of cliche. The shrimp are simmered (usually to death) in a thick, tomatoey sauce with peppers, and the whole mess is served over rice. I would advise you to avoid them entirely; I have never had a really good version. (Clearly, something essential in the preparation must have been lost in the dim mists of time.) Decent shrimp Creole is made by **Brennan's**, **Christian's**, **Court of Two Sisters**, and **Galatoire's**.

Better dishes involving small shrimp are the etouffee at the **Bon Ton**, shrimp Toulouse (mushrooms, herbs, and butter) at the Court of Two Sisters, shrimp dill-icious (a creamy, rich sauce with dill) at **Copeland's**, and **shrimp Marguery** at Galatoire's. There are plenty of good shrimp-and-pasta dishes around town. And a few hundred more original creations, most of them of more than routine interest. Good shrimp rarely go wrong unless they're overcooked.

★ Sid-Mar's

1824 Orpheum, Bucktown. 831-9541. 11 a.m.-10:30 p.m. Tues.-Sun. MC, V. $

Bucktown is a wonderful pocket of the past. It's as if a small fishing village had been deposited in the center of suburbia. There's no better place in which to absorb some Bucktown culture than Sid-Mar's, with its screened porch and dining room full of tables set for the unfussy enjoyment of large quantities of boiled and fried seafood, all of which is prepared decently but not brilliantly. Very, very casual; service is sometimes terrible.

★ ★ ★ Smilie's

5725 Jefferson Highway, Elmwood Park. 733-3000. 11 a.m.-2:30 p.m. Mon.-Fri. 5-9 p.m. Tues.-Thurs.; 5-10 p.m. Fri. & Sat. AE, CB, DC, MC, V. $$

NOTE: As this book went to press, Smilie's suffered a destructive fire. The word is that the restaurant will rebuild, but the job will be enormous. Call before going.

For unknown reasons, Harahan—a nice, suburban, middle-class community—has no virtually no restaurants. So everybody in Harahan drives about a mile down the highway to eat at Smilie's. The restaurant, located at the corner of a road leading into an industrial district, has always fooled my radar into thinking that here I will find little of interest. But I have always been pleasantly surprised by what Smilie's chef-owner Rodney Salvaggio puts on the table. It's Suburban Creole, to be sure, but it's skillfully turned out.

Start with a baked oyster dish. The best of these is oysters Smilie, a variation on the oysters Mosca idea, with garlic, bread crumbs, and olive oil. Good Rockefellers and Bienvilles are served not on the shells but in auz gratin dishes. They put out a fine small plate of fettuccine Alfredo, fried eggplant sticks dusted with Parmesan, and fried calamari, too. At $4 or less each, these are priced to move.

The entree list reveals nothing unfamiliar. The best dish here is a roasted half chicken, crisp at the skin and fragrant with rosemary. It is very much like the great roast chicken they used to serve at Elmwood Plantation. Appropriately enough: a lot of people who used to eat at the Elmwood before it burned down now dine at Smilie's. They also broil a magnificent steak here. It is probably not prime beef, but the exterior crust and interior juiciness are most convincing, and the price—$17 for a gigantic filet with all the trimmings—is very attractive.

The fish here is served in magnificent flanks. The best of them is a dish that reads complicated, but tastes harmonious: trout Smilie, with a crustiness of Italian bread crumbs and a gilding with lump crabmeat. The basic trout meuniere and grilled fish are also quite delicious, and you can get a satisfyingly ample fried seafood platter. Crabmeat au gratin is very popular here, but I find the cheesiness of it gets a little out of hand.

At lunchtime, they prepare a list of classic local platters, including many stuffed things. It is difficult to spend $10 here at lunch; in the evening, most of the entrees are $10 or less, and complete meals can be had for around $16. Service can be a little rushed at times—they always seem to be short a waitress—but the people are pleasant. There's nothing fancy about the premises, but they're very comfortable for a loosened-tie evening of real food.

The handful of desserts are led by a fine, light bread pudding; the lemon ice box pie is also nice.

★ ★ ★ Snug Harbor

626 Frenchmen, Marigny. 949-0696. 6 p.m.-Midnight seven nights; till 2 a.m. Fri. & Sat. AE, MC, V. $

Same owners as the Port of Call, and the same specialty: The Best Hamburger in Town, thick, freshly-ground, charcoal-grilled, served with a baked potato. The menu is a little more various than the Port of Call's however. In addition to prime steaks, there are several seafood entrees, prepared competently if not with a great deal of polish. The basic sauteed or grilled fish with minimal saucing is the best bet. The schooner salad, a pile of chilled seafood with greens, is also welcome.

The premises are nicer than those of the Port of Call, although the same bench-style seating obtains. The walls are covered with maps and a gigantic aquarium. The lounge is one of the better places to catch live modern blues and jazz in the area.

SOFT-SHELL CRABS. These are regular blue crabs from the lake, corraled just before they're ready to molt. As soon as they slough off the old shells, they're removed from the water and shipped to restaurants for frying, sauteeing, and grilling. Soft-shells are in season from about April through August. The specialists are **Andrea's, Commander's Palace,** and **Mr. B's.** Interesting variations: **La Cuisine's** stuffed soft shells, **Antoine's** fried softies with the thick, brown Colbert sauce, and the inhalable *smoked* soft shell crabs at **Christian's** and **Clancy's. Trey Yuen, China Blossom,** and **China Doll** do nice Oriental things with the beasts. See also **Buster Crabs.**

SOUFFLES. Souffles are among the most elegant of desserts, their light frothiness vaporizing into a wraith of flavor in the mouth. If they're made right, anyway. Unfortunately, New Orleans is not a souffle town; its two best practitioners went out of business in 1989. The best hot dessert souffles—Grand Marnier, chocolate, and the like—come from an unlikely source: **Morton's Steak House.** A close second is the brilliant bread pudding souffle at **Commander's Palace.** The **Windsor Court Grill Room** sometimes has hot dessert souffles. When they do, I guarantee it will be a flavor you never heard of.

SOUFFLE POTATOES. These are the world's greatest French fries. Potatoes are sliced thin and fried twice to produce a cigar-shaped potato balloon. Many restaurants now serve them, but they are a signature dish at **Antoine's,** where a basket (woven from potatoes—don't try to eat it!) full of souffle potatoes arrives at the beginning of the meal (you have to buy them, though). It is essential that you eat them while they're hot. They vary a little, but they're best with a bit of starchy potato on the inside.

Like almost everything else at Antoine's, there's a story behind souffle potatoes. The first person to taste the treat was King Louis Phillippe of France. The king planned to take the inaugural ride of the train from Paris to St. Germain-en-Laye in the early 1800s. A chef named Collinet was in charge of the feast at the end of the tracks. When the chef saw the train approaching, he prepared some fried potatoes—a favorite of the king. But the king had chickened out of riding the contraption and was following it in a horse-drawn coach. The chef had no more potatoes to fry. When the king finally did arrive, Collinet simply dropped the original batch into the now overheated oil. To his amazement, they puffed up like little balloons. The king loved them. Antoine Alciatore, who would later travel to New Orleans to open the restaurant that bears his name, learned the trick from Collinet himself.

SOUPS. New Orleans is most definitely a soup town. You would expect, given our weather, that the local soups would be light and often cold. Quite the opposite is true. The classic Creole gumbos, bisques, and soups tend to be thick, heavy, and robust. Cold soups are little seen on menus.
Here is a list of the dozen best soups in New Orleans:
1. Gumbo ya-ya, Mr. B's.
2. Turtle soup, Commander's Palace.
3. Crab and corn bisque, Pelican Club.
4. Mushroom and crab bisque, Le Jardin.
5. Jackson potato soup, Galatoire's.
6. Bahamian seafood showder, Palmer's.
7. Chicken-andouille gumbo, Bozo's.
8. Black bean soup, El Patio.
9. Crab and corn bisque, Gambrill's.
10. Pasta fagioli soup, Andrea's.
11. Hot and sour soup, Peking.
12. Shrimp and tomato bisque, Brigtsen's.
See also **Gumbo**..

SQUID. Or calamari, to use the Italian name. The smaller ones (about six inches long when whole) are usually deep-fried after being cut up into rings plus the fried-spider-looking part with the tentacles. Fried calamari is sold in dozens of restaurants around town, and although each one has regular customers who rave about them, I can't tell you that any one place is better than another at that trick.
The most ambitious restaurant where squid is concerned is **Drago's**, which not only fries them but broils and occasionally stuffs them. At **Andrea's**, they incorporate calamari into a great many hot and cold dishes—notably the seafood salad and the cioppino. Andrea's also sometimes makes a risotto with squid and its ink—a trick also turned at **El Patio**, where a similar dish is called by its Spanish name, arroz con calamares.
The most unusual version of squid served in New Orleans is at **DiPiazza's**,, where they cut two-inch squares out of the side of giant squid.

STEAK. This may surprise you, but New Orleans is one of the great steak towns in America. It is surpassed only by New York, equalled only by Chicago. Kansas City has nowhere near the quality of the beef found here. As for Texas, the best assessment was given by Bum Phillips, former head coach of the New Orleans Saints and, before that, of the Houston Oilers: "The worst steak I've had in New Orleans is better than the best steak I ever had in Texas." One more index to back up this seemingly outrageous thesis: when new locations of the New Orleans-based **Ruth's Chris Steak House** open up in other cities, they are frequently acclaimed as serving the best steak ever cooked within those precincts.

Since the **Crescent City Steak House** started serving prime beef 55 years ago, there has been intense competition among steak restaurants at the quality level. As a result, almost all the beef in the better restaurants of New Orleans is USDA prime. There is very little prime beef raised, especially in these days when the trend is toward leanness. The USDA prime stamp means that the cattle involved are young, built low to the ground, and heavy with fat. The fat shows up as marbling, those little white flecks in the lean that give prime beef its tenderness and flavor. In my opinion, this works to best advantage in the strip. It is desireable but less important in the already-tender filet mignon. Rib-eyes, which are fatty even in lesser grades, are too fatty for me when they're prime.

The actual grading is done by an inspector from the Department of Agriculture. It would be great if it were as simple as that. But with the loosening of the USDA criteria for grading prime beef, there have arisen degrees of quality within the prime grade. These are determined by the packers, who have created a whirlwind of claims and counter-claims as to why this prime is better than that prime. The only reliable indication is—as usual—the taste and integrity of the restaurateur.

More cut-and-dried (literally) is the matter of aging. I like aged beef. The process sounds disgusting, but it is similar to that found in many other rare foods and almost identical to the "noble rot" of great Sauternes. The primal roasts are allowed to develop a mold while hanging in a cooler; in the case of Ruth's Chris' and Morton's beef, the process takes three weeks. The mold dries excess water from the beef and tightens it up, thereby concentrating the flavors. The mold is cut away before the beef is shipped.

Here are the ten best steaks served in New Orleans:
1. Ruth's Chris (filet mignon or strip)
2. Morton's of Chicago (porterhouse or strip)
3. Young's (any cut)
4. Christian's (steak au poivre or farci la Loutre)
5. Antoine's (filet or tournedos)
6. Brennan's (filet Stanley)
7. Tavern on the Park (large filet)
8. La Cuisine (filet)
9. Versailles (filet Rossini)

10. Crescent City (strip or porterhouse)

Other restaurants which buy the best prime beef and cook it deftly are the **Beef Room, Commander's Palace, Mr. B's, Windsor Court Grill Room,** and the **Steak Knife.** Choice beef cooked with a great deal of excitement puts **Charlie's Steak House** on the list. Restaurants with other specialties but with standout steak dishes include **Andrea's, Tujague's, Crozier's,** and **Arnaud's.**

★ ★ ★ Steak Knife

6263 Marshal Foch (just river side of Harrison Ave.), Lakeview. 488-8981. 5:00-11 p.m seven nights. AE, DC, MC, V. $$$

Very well hidden on a Lakeview side street is this comfortable, casual dining room, populated mostly by regulars, serving a limited repertoire of consistently good specialties. I like to start with the unique "tidbit in the oven," a pizza without the tomato sauce: cheesy, herbal. The crabmeat au gratin is mild but has a nice crusty topping. The soup menu has expanded beyond the always-tasty crab bisque to include a nice gumbo and some daily specials.

The steaks are prime; the strip and the filet are the best. They're charbroiled and only moistened with butter. More ambitious and interesting is the tournedos marchand de vin, a filet in a red-wine sauce with mushrooms. The menu has expanded beyond steak lately to include a superior roasted rack of lamb and an intense osso buco. More seafood these days, too: from the grill come interesting species, nicely encrusted. The fish with crabmeat and mushrooms is lighter and better than most such. The side dishes and desserts are okay, the wine list is minimal but sufficient, and the service is low-key and friendly. This is a decent, reliable place for a quiet supper.

★ ★ Steak Pit

609 Bourbon, French Quarter. 525-3406. 5:00-10:45 p.m. Sun.-Thurs.; till 11:45 p.m. Fri. & Sat. AE, MC, V. $

This dark room in a touristy block of Bourbon Street has any number of attempts at decor: western-style benches and tables, posters for French plays, and a backlit mural photograph of some nondescript American city in the Fifties. The steaks are not especially good, but I list this place because, consistently for at least 15 years, it's served the best hamburger steak in town. It's crusty on the outside, juicy within, and comes with a bucket of okay onion soup, a plain salad with what tastes like bottled dressing, a basket of good wheat bread, and a baked potato. The price for all that is about $4! No desserts and not much service.

STEAK TARTARE. A dish that separates the gourmets from the pretenders, steak tartare (known as "steak American" or "steak cannibale" in Europe) is mostly raw chopped beef. It's mixed with onions, egg, garlic, anchovies, cayenne, capers, and a few other condiments. The result is a raw beef salad. It is at its best when prepared tableside, so that you can demand that it be seasoned to your taste. A classic steak tartare is not ground but chopped with knives; some authorities say it should be pounded into a pulp. Some restaurants use filet mignon for tartare, but round tastes as good to me. The best practitioner (although it's no longer on the printed menu there) is the **Sazerac**. Andrea's, Commander's Palace, and the Windsor Court Grill Room also perform the deed very well. The **Camellia Grill** offers essentially the same item on a sandwich called the cannibal special.

★ ★ ★ Stephen & Martin

4141 St. Charles Ave., Uptown. 897-0781. 11 a.m.-11 p.m. (later on weekends), seven days. AE, CB, DC, MC, V. $$.

In 1977, this place started an explosion of nouvelle-Creole restaurants in the Uptown area. The old Stephen & Martin, which had served as an inexpensive neighborhood restaurant since the Forties, was renovated into a modern, attractive dining room with a semi-attached, classy lounge-hangout. Some years later, the restaurant expanded into a lovely enclosed courtyard with big windows facing the streetcar tracks. For awhile, the menus of the two dining rooms were different, but lately the best of each has been combined onto one card.

Some of the best food here comes from a hickory grill. The chicken breast with three sauces is a great light dish, nicely seasoned and satisfyingly striped with char. Also good are the various grilled fish—interesting things like swordfish, mako shark, and tuna. The ribs are very lean and tender; however, we like 'em chewy and with a bit more fat than this.

The rest of the menu is a collection of Creole and Italian dishes. Some of the latter are in the style of Manale's—most notably the barbecued shrimp. These are consistently among the best in town, made with enormous heads-on shrimp and a sauce of butter and pepper that tastes as good with bread as with shrimp. Oysters with ricotta, chicken-andouille gumbo, shrimp and garlic pasta, and steak au poivre are other hits.

The wine list is interesting; the bar has eight intelligently-chosen bottles served by the glass. Desserts include a very good bread pudding with a sort of praline-tasting sauce and a couple of other things.

★ ★ ★ Streetcar Sandwiches

1434 S. Carrollton Ave., Uptown. 866-1146. 10:30 a.m.-11 p.m. seven days; till Midnight Fri. and Sat. No credit cards. $

A couple of immigrants from Wisconsin assault logic by operating one of the best and most consistent producers of authentic New Orleans poor boys. The roast beef, for example, is good meat and better gravy, rich and thick, on toasted French bread—a first-class piece of work. The fried seafood sandwiches of shrimp, oyster, or fish are beyond reproach. The menu goes on to include all the other traditional stuffings for poor boys and more than a few innovative ones. Among the latter is the improbable but delicious mesquite-grilled fish poor boy (better without the tartar sauce it comes with) and some extra-peppery combinations. The mesquite-grilled chicken is a delicious, healthful alternative to fried. They put out a decent jambalaya. Streetcar is not comfortable for eating on premises, but it can be done. At times, the assembly of the sandwiches is slipshod, but the quality and quantity of the contents never suffers. Service is swift.

STUFFED MUSHROOMS. One of the great kitsch dishes of the local cuisine, these are upended large mushrooms filled with a crabmeat stuffing and baked, usually with a topping of hollandaise. The best such are at **Pascal's Manale, Moran's Riverside,** and **Ralph & Kacoo's.**

SUBURBAN CREOLE. When people moved from the old neighborhoods to the suburbs, they brought their demand for neighborhood Creole restaurants with them. Of course, they wanted the restaurants in the new neighborhood to reflect the new suburban lifestyle: same food, feel, and people, but a more modern, cleaner look than the dumpy old places they'd left behind. Thus was born the Suburban Creole restaurant, and over the years its cuisine has diverged far enough from what's cooking in town to have become distinctive.

Suburban Creole menus are comprised of familiar Creole dishes, some with Italian touches. Trends are followed, but about three years late; blackened foods are still hot in Suburban Creole places, for example. But the hallmark of a Suburban Creole kitchen is its penchant for mixing seafoods. It seems to be unable to send out a piece of fish without crabmeat, shrimp, crawfish, or all three on top. The same treatment is often accorded veal, steak, and even chicken. Sometimes this idea works, but more often it results in a hodgepodge of flavors.

The good side of Suburban Creole is that its restaurants are unembarrassed about serving dishes which, while good, have passed out of vogue. The old cooks one often finds in these places use funky old methods and ingredients that still produce tasty results. So, ironically, if you're looking for the food of 30 or 40 years ago, the best place to look is in the newest parts of the metroplex.

The best of the Suburban Creole restaurants are **La Cuisine, Masson's, Peppermill, Etienne De Felice's,** and **Sal & Sam's**. Less interesting but definitive of Suburban Creole is **Augie's Glass Garden**.

SUSHI. Sushi is not a food, it's a religion. Or so one would think after spending a few minutes seated next to a sushi fanatic at **Shogun** (the best sushi bar in town, and where you're most likely to run into one of these guys). If you show any signs of being a novice, they begin to proselytize, telling you not only what to eat but how to eat it in an annoyingly condescending way.

Here's my advice, humbly offered. Start with sashimi, which differs from sushi in that the pieces of beautiful raw fish are not wrapped around rice. The flavor is not at all what you'd expect of raw fish; it's something most people love the first time they taste it. The best way to begin is with tuna, yellowtail, or bluefish; then you can move on to the more exotic thrills of octopus and sea urchin. Sashimi is usually sold as an assorted plate.

Sushi, on the other hand, is sold in small orders—two to six pieces of this or that. Just point at what looks good in the glass case before you, or on the card with color photographs of the common sushi concoctions. Some sushi is just rice pressed against a slice of fish, but it can also be rather elaborate, with thin pieces of fish and vegetables surrounded by rice and then wrapped in nori, a wafer of dried seaweed. (An extremely popular beginner sushi is the California roll, with crab, avocado, and orange roe.)

For either sushi or sashimi, grab a chair at the bar, tell the waitress (who'll be on your side of the counter) that you want a beer (the perfect accompaniment to sushi), and watch the chef drop a wooden board before you with some marinated ginger and a ball of pastel-green horseradish called wasabi. The latter is incredibly pungent; mix a little of it with soy sauce for dipping. And away you go. Order a little at a time, and tell the chef when you're ready to stop. If you think there's a possibility you've eaten enough, you have; it is possible to sit there and keep ordering until your bill goes over $30, which is ridiculous. In some restaurants, you're on the honor system; in others, the chef keeps track. In either case, it always takes longer than seems necessary to get your check. It is proper to tip the chef.

The other good sushi bars besides Shogun are **Ichiban, Little Tokyo, Hana, Shigure,** and **Samurai**.

★★Sweet Basil's Bistro

3445 Prytania St. 891-2227. 11 a.m.-10 p.m. seven nights; till Midnight Fri. & Sat. AE, DC, MC, V. $$

Tables surround a large bar in a narrow building with lots of doors. The place is across the street from the Touro Medical Complex, which provides an all but captive clientele that rarely complains because it has to eat in a hurry. There are many terrible restaurants nearby, but this is not one of them. The menu is an ambitious flyer at the newer, lighter, more herbal styles of Italian cooking. While the fine edges are lacking, the results are generally good, and the prices are right.

Start off with soup (this changes daily, but is generally well made) or a small order of pasta. The oyster-artichoke casserole would be good if the seasoning balance were better and the oysters weren't cooked into rubber erasers. Salads are very well made; at lunch, there's an all-you-can-eat soup and salad deal.

The entrees cover the pasta staples: lasagne, cannelloni, spaghetti and meatballs, etc. The style tends toward Northern Italian. This can mean either light and herbal, or rich and creamy. At night, there is a seafood special which varies wildly from edible to terrific. A little veal rounds out the menu. Service is good and rapid. Prices are bargains.

SWEETBREADS. Although this word can be used to refer to the entire range of organ meats, when you see "sweetbreads" on a New Orleans menu what is being offered are the thymus glands of a young calf. These look something like cauliflower and are very light and tender. The taste is that of veal, but somehow more intense and elemental. The most common manifestation of sweetbreads is sauteed and served with a simple brown butter and capers. **Bistro at Maison De Ville, Andrea's, Arnaud's,** and **Crozier's** serve them in that style. The dish could be considered a specialty of all those restaurants. Sweetbreads are poached and served with a demi-glace sauce at **Christian's,** which was one of the first places around to offer them locally. I love sweetbreads, but have cut back on them a lot; they contain a staggeringly high percentage of fat and cholesterol.

T as in trout meuniere

TABLETOP. New Orleans restaurant tables are for the most part poorly furnished. The same cheap china you find in the everyday restaurants also appears in some of the fanciest, most expensive places, and almost everything in between. Exceptions are the extravagant hotel restaurants like **Henri, The Grill Room, the Sazerac,** and **Le Jardin.** Independent restaurants with unusually nice china and silverware are **Arnaud's, Christian's,** and the **Versailles.**

The best napkins and tablecloths are the heavy linen at **Galatoire's, Antoine's, Henri,** the **Grill Room,** and **Le Jardin.** A disturbing trend is the proliferation of polyester tablecloths and napkins, which don't absorb and so don't do their jobs; **Arnaud's** and **Pascal's Manale** are two among many restaurants that really should have better than this.

Absolutely the worst development in table-dressing has been the attempt by many restaurants to avoid the cost of laundering a tablecloth for every party it serves. Some—Chinese restaurants are numerous in this category—accomplish this by placing a sheet of glass or clear plastic atop the tablecloth. What this ignores is the fact that some people wipe their hands on the part of the cloth that drapes down; who knows how long the restaurants leave those cloths on between cleanings? A related but no more salubrious practice is that of covering the tablecloth with a piece of white butcher paper. Sometimes crayons are provided to make this seem like fun instead of a cheapness on the part of the restaurant. **Cafe Sbisa, Bayou Ridge Cafe,** and **Fitzgerald's** are the dishonor roll for the paper trick. I like to eat from a tablecloth, but if I can't have one, my next choice would be a plain Formica or wood surface. Don't try to make me think you're giving me a tablecloth when you're not.

★★ Tandoor

3000 Severn Ave., Metairie. 887-7414. 11:30 a.m.-2:30 p.m. and 5-10 p.m. Tues.-Sun. AE, DC, MC, V. $$

New Orleans has only had Indian restaurants on a consistent basis for about five years, and then only one or two at a time. The Tandoor is the best current resource, and would be recommendable even if there were dozens of other places. Formerly in Gretna, it moved in late 1989 into a small strip shopping center in Metairie. The open-to-view kitchen includes the namesake tandoor—the superheated clay oven wherein are roasted various meats on skewers. Naan, a tasty buttered flat bread, is slapped right up against the hot clay walls to bake.

A good assortment with which to begin are the vegetable pakoras—cauliflower, eggplant, and some other things, fried with a thick batter. They do a fine mulligatawny soup, chunky with chicken. Marinated tandoori chicken is wonderfully juicy and roasted to crusty corners. Kabobs of lamb sausage are also tasty; shrimp that go into the tandoor, on the other hand, don't survive the experience.

The items on the vegetarian plate range in interest from the spectacular paneer palak (a mild homemade cheese, baked and mixed with spinach) and a fine navrattan curry (a variety of finely-chopped vegetables in a zingy curry), to a completely uninteresting dal (a lentil dip). Vegetables, chicken, or lamb jalfrezi have a very spicy tomato sauce that reminds me a lot of some things I've had at K-Paul's. Service is a little slow, but the management apologizes for it with complimentary finger food.

★ ★ ★ Taqueria Corona

5932 Magazine St. 897-3974. 11:30 a.m.-2 p.m., 5-9:30 p.m. seven days. No credit cards. $

This little hole in the wall of one of those narrow blocks of Magazine Street has attracted something of a cult following, and with good reason. The menu of Mexican and El Salvadoran specialties is cooked with total abandon of concern about Anglo sensitivities, and the result is some exciting eating. The food and the place make one feel lost somewhere in Central America.

Most of the seating is at a counter. Back of the counter is a rudimentary grill. Every few minutes, flames shoot two or three feet high when the meats get going good. These are for the tacos for which the restaurant is named. They are not the tacos you're used to. The tortillas, for starters, are the soft flour kind, and the fillings are minimal. The most interesting of the meats is the beef tongue; if you don't get a tongue taco, you're missing the point of this place. Beef, chicken, and pork are also used to stuff these things; a plate of three different tacos, while extremely filling, goes down quickly. The side order of beans comes to a semi-boil on the hot plates.

The menu includes a few other oddments and a reasonably decent flan for dessert. Beer is the drink to get. The people are aggressively Hispanic, but that's what you came for.

TASSO. A spicy, salty, smoky, somewhat dry ham, tasso used to have a very limited distribution in the Cajun country until the K-Paul's-style Cajun cooking craze made it de riguer. While tasso does add an interesting twang to some dishes—notably those with rich cream sauces—beware of any concoction in which it appears to be a main ingredient. The pepper, salt, and smoke components it brings can completely take over, and the flavor wears your palate out in short order. It really should be used only as a seasoning ingredient.

★ ★ ★ Tavern On The Park

900 City Park Ave., Mid-City. 486-3333. 11:30 a.m.-10 p.m. Mon.-Sat., till 11 p.m. on Fri. and Sat. AE, CB, DC, MC, V. $$$

Across from the oakiest part of City Park, a 19th-century building was renovated with lots of windows, marble, and brass into a large, comfortable restaurant. The menu is surprisingly basic: few forays are made into anything more complicated than broiled steaks and chops, and fried and broiled seafood. The steaks are the better part of that; while the house makes no claim for their grade, they are tender, tasty, and well-trimmed, broiled to a pleasant exterior crust, and just moistened with butter. They are cut to order and can be had any size you like. All the cuts I've tried have satisfied my meat hunger completely. So does the veal chop, a nice cut of pink, tender meat.

The first courses and side dishes are exceptionally good. They make a terrific shrimp remoulade, the onion rings are some of the biggest and best in the city, and soups—especially turtle—are consistently delectable. Salads are well-composed and feature a wonderful, rich avocado dressing and crunchy, garlicky, homemade croutons. Vegetables are fresh and interesting.

The proprietor keeps urging the seafood entrees on me, but they leave me cold. A particular dud is the poached trout with Champagne sauce. Lunch specials are agreeable in both taste and price. The lunch menu also has a standing list of some very good whole-meal salads.

The wine list here is somewhat eclectic but eminently usable and attractively priced. They keep an excellent stock of vintage ports and sherries to be served by the glass. Desserts include highly-buffed pastries and an unusual bread pudding topped with rum raisin ice cream. The service staff is cheerful and helpful.

★ Tchoupitoulas Plantation

6535 River Road, Avondale (turn right from US 90 on the West Bank side of the Huey P. Long Bridge onto La. 18; restaurant is about three miles up). Reservations 436-1277. 11:30 a.m.-3 p.m. Mon.-Fri.; 5:30-9:30 p.m. seven days. AE, CB, DC, MC, V. $$

Used to be that you could experience an ancient Louisiana plantation home and have a good meal at the same time, but then Elmwood Plantation burned down, leaving us with this place, which offers more of the first joy than the second. The premises are fascinating: the main house was built in 1812, and is kept in pretty good shape. One room offers a view outside, where various fowl run about at liberty and sometimes fight with one another.

The food is not bad, but it needs the help of the surroundings. The menu has taken a slight Italian turn of late: the best starter is the barbecued shrimp, with the fried calamari a close second. Oysters Tchoupitoulas—probably the best dish in the house—have a soupy brown sauce with a good, spicy flavor. Entrees are standard Creole-Italian veal, steak, and seafood: okay trout amandine and fried catfish. Also some decent poultry. Service is on the perfunctory, rude side, with the occasional pleasant waiter full of stories.

TEN GREATEST NEW ORLEANS DISHES. A few years ago, I gave a lot of thought to this question in the course of writing a cookbook with that name. Although the cuisine and my own tastes have continued to evolve, I don't think I'd make any changes in the list. In alphabetical order, the essential dishes of Creole-Cajun restaurant cuisine are:

Barbecued Shrimp
Bread Pudding
Chicken-Andouille Gumbo
Chicken Bonne Femme
Crawfish Bisque
Grillades and Grits
Lost Bread
Oysters Rockefeller
Red Beans and Rice
Trout Meuniere

Although this is a book about eating, not cooking, I have included the recipes for these ten dishes, listed under their respective entries. They are all kitchen-tested adaptations of recipes from the restaurants that do my favorite versions.

★★Tessie's Place

116 N. Woodlawn (just north of Airline Hwy., one block east of Clearview Pkwy.), Metairie. 835-8377. 11:30 a.m.-10 p.m. seven days. MC, V. $

A classic neighborhood Bar & Rest., Tessie's looks and cooks like a survivor from the golden age of such places in the Fifties. While Tessie's has been open only a few years, it is the successor to the Club 90, a great old roadhouse that was blown down by Hurricane Betsy in 1965. Club 90's finest legacy—its roast beef poor boy, with a great gravy and thickly-sliced beef—lives on at Tessie's. It shares the menu with fairly decent fried chicken, an assortment of very ample seafood platters, a magnificent plate of buttery, garlicky spaghetti bordelaise, some tasty New Orleans-style hot tamales, and just-okay steaks. All the other poor boys are big and delicious. A card lists daily specials like red beans and

THAI. It's surpassingly appropriate that many Thai dish names include the word "yum." Decidedly Oriental in appearance, Thai food is some of the best in Asia.

Several high-profile ingredients contribute to the distinctiveness of Thai cooking. The most obvious—and most appealing to New Orleans palates—is a great deal of pepper. Indeed, some Thai dishes are among the spiciest eating on earth, and get their heat from a variety of green and red peppers. I find it a more comfortable burn than one finds in the hottest Cajun or Mexican food, although it may be as hot or hotter. Lemon grass (looks like chives, tastes like citrus), cilantro (looks like parsley, tastes pungent and sharp), and coconut milk (looks like milk, tastes like coconut) are other common flavoring elements. Nam pla—a sauce made from fermented squid—is dashed on almost everything in almost the way we use hot sauce.

Here are some specific dishes that exemplify the Thai taste. Paht Thai is practically the national dish; it's lightly fried noodles with chicken, shrimp, bean sprouts, and more than a little pepper and a faint taste of peanuts. The center sections of chicken wings are stuffed with a mixture of shrimp and pork (a common Thai stuffing) and served with a great peanut sauce. Curry comes in several colors in Thai restaurants; green is usually the hottest, yellow the mildest, and red in between.

At this writing both sources of good Thai food are Uptown. **Bangkok Cuisine** is the pioneer, having introduced Thai cooking to the area about ten years ago. The newer **Thai Pepper** is described below. The two restaurants are about equally good, although stylistically different.

★ ★ ★ Thai Pepper

8601 Oak, Uptown. 865-1340. Noon-2:30 and 5:30-10:30 p.m. seven days. AE, MC, V. $$.

This is the rebirth of the Thai House, an imaginative restaurant killed by a terrible location on Canal Street. The new Uptown neighborhood and premises are much nicer. Chef Tee Somboon Thainghtham continues to add a new dimension to the small universe of Thai dining hereabouts. Most dishes here, for example, are authentically served inside hollowed-out vegetables.

The best first course is a platter containing samples of four different nibbles. Fairly down-to-earth are the spring rolls (skinny ones, stuffed with pork, shrimp, mushrooms, and glass noodles) and the satays (slices of chicken on a skewer, rolled in a spicy batter and grilled). More exotic are the stuffed (with pork and herbs) chicken wings, brought out with a wonderful peanut sauce that tastes good on almost anything. The khanom pang looks sort of like shrimp toast, except that the topping also has pork, ginger, and garlic. The soups are also delicious, light, and palate-cleansing.

They do wonderful things with Thai glass noodles here. I love the claypot of tiger prawns (shrimp the size of small lobsters) with noodles, as well as paht Thai, a classic of the cuisine containing chicken, shrimp, bean sprouts, and the spicy peanut sauce among the soft noodles.

"Bird of the Golden Mountain" is a shrimp-and-pork-stuffed roasted Cornish hen; it is inflamed both with a creamy curry sauce and by an actual flambeeing at the table. Great eating. There are many variations of curry, all of them well-made. Thai food has been nominated by some eaters as the hottest eat on the planet. The Thai Pepper's evidence of that is a dish called Evil Jungle Prince, a chicken dish flavored with a variety of peppers and basil: potent and tasty.

Lots of good seafood. Shrimp in garlic butter, large squid with a mild curry and the vaguely fruity taste of bamboo shoots, and the spicy soft shell crab are the best shots. There is also a bit of grilling going on; those tiger prawns are pretty good that way.

Dessert: homemade ice cream surrounded by nuggets of fried banana. Coconut-milk custard. An unusual baked pear with mint and almonds. Service is understanding of the fact that not everyone is familiar with the cuisine, and otherwise accommodating.

★★Tiffin Inn

6601 Veterans Blvd., Metairie. 888-6602. Open 24 hours. AE, MC, V. $

In Chicago, a place called Walker Brothers' Pancake House is the most creative and deft purveyor of mainstream breakfasts I've ever experienced. I wish we had something like Walker's here. Since we don't, I go to the Tiffin Inn, which has many of the same ideas, if not the same sparkling executions. These are the best pancakes in the city, and they come in several dozen varieties. Some are very good: the Swedish pancakes with lingonberry butter, for example, or the potato pancakes with applesauce, onions, and bacon. The German pancakes look like giant flowers; they're baked instead of griddled, and have an unusual souffle-like texture. They also do an okay job with eggs here; three small pancakes come with egg orders.

I have two complaints. The coffee is terrible. Second, the restaurant is dreary and dark. I need a bright, cheery spot for breakfast. The fact that the prices are very low is only partial consolation.

★★Tio Pepe's

511 Toulouse, French Quarter. 529-5380. 11 a.m.-10 p.m. seven days, till 11 p.m. Fri. and Sat. AE, CB, DC, MC, V. $

A pleasant little dining room with a cordial, friendly serving staff, Tio Pepe's serves reasonably decent Tex-Mex standards with a few surprises. The appetizers, for example, include a few seafood items. The crabmeat puff and the crabmeat nachos are still great ideas. The black bean soup has a good flavor.

The various platters of tortilla-based dishes are all flawless and inoffensive; the cheese enchiladas with chili con queso make a fine mild plateful. The entree specialty is fajitas, made from superbly grilled strips of steak, thick enough to remain rare in the center while slightly charred at the outside. These are actually better eaten with a fork, since the pico de gallo and guacamole dressings are just passable, and it's hard to bite through those thick pieces of meat when they're wrapped in a flour tortilla. There's a nice flan for dessert, and a great assortment of beers. Once I even enjoyed a bock-style dark beer made by Dos XX, a rare item.

TIPPING. Unless the restaurant prominently displays "No Tipping" signs, the tip you should leave a waiter in any restaurant—*including buffets*—is 15 percent. I do not subscribe to the theory that the tip is a boon bestowed at the option of the customer to reward a worthy servant. It is part of the cost of dining out. If tipping were universally eliminated tomorrow, within a year menu prices would rise by at least 15 percent.

Some years ago, I worked for a month as a waiter to write a story about the profession. Ever since that experience, I have routinely tipped 20 percent. The only time I go under that is when the prices are extremely high for the kind of service received (by the same token, I go higher if the prices are very low), or when the waiter seems incompetent. I never go below 15 percent unless I feel I have been intentionally insulted. Even then, I leave a small tip, which hurts more than no tip at all (waiters who have been stiffed suspect the customer just forgot).

My personal tipping policy derives from a few observations I made while a waiter:

1. The work is grueling, both physically and mentally.

2. The salary received by waiters from the restaurant is only about half of minimum wage, even in the best places; tips form the bulk of a waiter's income.

3. The amount of the tip is very close to the front of a waiter's mind. A waiter can calculate within seconds what percentage you left him, and he remembers.

4. If you cheat a waiter out of a tip, he doesn't think, "Well, I'll have to try harder next time." He thinks, "What a jerk!"

If you find yourself frequently tipping less than 15 percent, that waiter is right about you. You're not playing by the rules.

★ ★ ★ Tipton County Barbecue

5538 Magazine, Uptown. 899-9626. 11 a.m.-11 p.m. seven days; till Midnight Thurs.-Sat. MC, V. $.

Barbecue is not something that Orleanians know or care much about. Despite that, every now and then we get a barbecue place as good as

Tipton County, which makes far and away the best barbecue in town. This is not the bastardized Texas style that has always dominated the barbecue scene; rather, Tipton County purveys the Memphis taste with reasonable authenticity.

Two distinctive parts of Memphis barbecue are the way the pork and the sauce are made. They serve pulled pork here—pulled off the bone in shreds, not slices. The sauce is somewhat vinegary and sloshy; it is never sent out in a puddle on the plate. You dash it on the meat at the table, more as a condiment than as a sauce.

The great specialty at Tipton Country is ribs. These are smallish spare ribs of pork—bigger and meatier than baby backs, but smaller and tastier than those gigantic hog ribs frequently seen hereabouts. They are slowly smoked in a standing position, so that the fat bastes the lean and ultimately drips off. Very little fat remains when the ribs come to the table. Meanwhile, the meat has taken on a fantastic smokiness and a perfect slight chewiness of texture. The lusty spiciness of the dry rub dusted on the ribs before smoking completes one great eat.

The beef brisket is decent, but takes a back seat to the pulled pork and ribs. Side dishes range from pretty good (onion rings and fries) to excellent (beans and cole slaw). For dessert, we find an assortment of not-especially-well-homemade pies of which the best is the rarely seen chess pie (something like a pecan pie without the pecans). They grill thick, handmade hamburgers, but these are nothing special.

★ ★ ★ Toney's Spaghetti House

3400 Hessmer Ave., Metairie. 888-0342. 11 a.m.-3 p.m. Tues.-Fri.; 5-10 p.m. Tues.-Sat., till 11 p.m. Fri. and Sat.; 11:30 a.m.-9 p.m. Sun. 308 St. Charles Ave., CBD. 568-9556. 11 a.m.-3 p.m. Mon.-Fri. AE, MC, V. $

After 53 years on Bourbon Street, Toney's Spaghetti House closed shop and went looking for a new location. It ultimately turned up at the Metairie location (formerly Nancy's Steak House), but in the meantime it opened the smaller cafe for the CBD lunch crowd. Portions are large, prices very low, service and atmosphere are minimal at both places; the Metairie location has a somewhat more extensive menu.

Toney's food is extremely basic. The red sauce, for instance, is innocent of herbs or spices, and is the thick, smooth kind that has been cooked for hours. No matter. The taste is comfortable and satisfying. The best carrier for the red sauce is Toney's classic stuffed macaroni—big pipes of pasta stuffed with a mixture of ground veal, cheese, bread crumbs, and garlic. An order of three of these with two Italian sausages makes an appealing symmetry.

All the other bedrock classics of American Italian food are done well: spaghetti and meatballs, veal Parmigiana, chicken cacciatore, chicken Marsala, and marinated Italian beef daube. So are a couple of surprises.

The eggplant Parmigiana is superb either as an appetizer or as a side dish. Seafood with pasta, for example, shows up here as a shockingly good plate of plump oysters Bordelaise with spaghetti.

Toney's still has its array of edible fried seafood, to which has been added some fairly good grilled fish. Daily specials include many standard Creole items in fine manifestations: red beans and rice, veal stew, etc. For appetizers they cook all right gumbo and an artichoke-oyster soup made to the old Nancy's recipe (delicious). They also kept Nancy's wonderful thin-cut, lightly-fried onion rings. Other starters are the Italian salad (crunchy greens), or the big, firm shrimp remoulade. The bread pudding is a very fruity one, but a good dessert.

Toney's has some consistency problems and, judging by the phone calls I get, they can be somewhat infuriating. But for inexpensive, unchallenging family food, I think it serves well.

★ ★ ★ Tony Angello's

6262 Fleur de Lis Dr. (at W. Harrison Ave.), Lakeview. Reservations 488-0888. 6-11 p.m. Mon.-Thurs. 5:30-11 p.m. Fri. & Sat. AE, MC, V. $$

It acts as if it were trying to hide its existence from the public. When it first opened, its phone number was unlisted. It still doesn't have much of a sign outside; the premises look like a large suburban house. None of this keeps Tony Angello's from being packed. Even with a reservation, chances are you'll have to wait in the bar with the fascinating antique radios awhile — unless you're a regular, in which case you'll get special treatment.

The food is rudimentary New Orleans Italian, well prepared. The classic Tony Angello's meal is a succession of courses in which nothing is identifiable as the entree. Many such meals are outlined in the menu; others are assembled by Mr. Angello if he likes you. A typical table d'hote starts with a small lobster casserole with a rich, cheesy sauce, and is followed by one of the better oyster-artichoke soups around and a salad of marinated vegetables. Then come lasagne and eggplant Tina (which is like lasagne, except that eggplant replaces pasta).

But there is other food of note. Buster crabs come in pairs, nicely fried. Good fried calamari. Spaghetti bordelaise has a pleasant garlic-and-oil sauce. Trout Rosa is topped with crabmeat and butter to good effect. Veal has an oozy herbal crust. The house dessert is lemon ice box pie, an intense square. The wine list is abbreviated but contains some interesting Italian bottles. Service, once it starts happening, is efficient.

To hear a Tony Angello's buff talk, you'd think this were the world's greatest restaurant. Take such advisories with a grain of salt.

Tortorici's

441 Royal, French Quarter. 522-4295. 11:30 a.m.-3 p.m. and 5-11 p.m. seven days. AE, MC, V. $$$

You would think that a restaurant this old, located on one of the best possible corners of the French Quarter, would be at least decent. But you would be wrong. I have not had an acceptable meal here in well over a decade—not even with one of the owners dining at the same table with me. Nor have I talked with anyone in a long time who had anything good to report. It's supposed to be Italian.

TOURIST MECCAS. Visitors to New Orleans (or any other city, for that matter) want different things from the restaurants they visit than the locals do. Natives who dine out regularly would yawn at a meal composed of shrimp remoulade, gumbo, trout meuniere, and bread pudding, even if all those things were prepared perfectly. But to a visitor from Utah, this classic Creole menu would provide an excellent, memorable taste of the city.

The other side of the same coin is uglier. The occasional or once-in-a-lifetime aspect of the tourist dining practice is an invitation to abuse. Some visitors forgive bad food as being just Creole and strange. Some restaurants actually suggest this explanation to them. For this reason, restaurants without a significant local clientele tend to experience a deterioration of taste—often accompanied by an escalation of prices.

So while I don't think it's bad for a restaurant to be touristy, I am offended deeply by places where the food is a parody of the real thing and the service is condescending. Here are the ten restaurants that offer visitors the most intense doses of the New Orleans dining experience, without taking undue advantage of the uninitiated:

1. Commander's Palace
2. Galatoire's
3. Christian's
4. Arnaud's
5. Tujague's
6. Mr. B's
7. Mother's
8. Broussard's
9. Dooky Chase
10. Gumbo Shop

TOURNEDOS. Pronounced "TOOH-neh-doe," this is both singular and plural for a cut of beef taken from the tube-shaped tenderloin. Properly, it refers to the narrow end of the roast; the middle part is the filet mignon, and the wide, somewhat misshapen end is the Chateaubriand. In most restaurants, however, this distinction is lost and the three terms are used to differentiate portion size, tournedos the smallest and Chateaubriand a large cut for two people. When a tournedos is really a tournedos, however, it is what I order, since I find it tastier than the filet mignon. A big tournedos cut comes out looking like a beer can, my favorite shape for a tenderloin steak.

★ ★ ★ ★ Trey Yuen

600 Causeway Blvd., Mandeville. 1-626-4476. 11:30 a.m.-2 p.m. Wed.-Fri.; 5-10 p.m. Mon.-Sat.; till 11 p.m. Fri. & Sat.; Noon-9:30 p.m. Sun.
• *U.S. 51 North at Columbus Dr., Hammond. 1-345-6789. 11 a.m.-2 p.m. Mon.-Fri.; 5-10 p.m. Mon.-Thurs.; 5:00-11 p.m. Fri. & Sat.; 11:30 a.m.-10:00 p.m. Sun. Both: AE, CB, DC, MC, V. $$*

Trey Yuen ("crystal garden") is a pair of staggeringly beautiful Chinese restaurants operated by the five talented Wong brothers. Each location is an Oriental palace built largely from antiques imported from China. The food is impressive, too—although it is not much more elaborate than that of the better neighborhood Chinese restaurants. (Unless you book a Chinese banquet for eight or more in a private room, which is nothing but eleganza.) And they use more distinctive local foodstuffs—alligator, for example—than any other Chinese restaurant.

The thin-skinned spring rolls and the thick hot and sour soup make good starters. Even better (but not on the menu) is the lettuce flower, a leaf of lettuce filled with a concoction made from shrimp or squab or whatever, folded over and eaten like a taco.

The great entrees involve tong-cho, a brown, spicy, intense sauce that goes well with everything from meat to seafood. Make sure you get tong-cho something, and then investigate the three or four daily specials. For example, Maine lobster is brought to the table in whole form first and then cut up in a fine ginger sauce: glorious food. The tender Szechuan style alligator is a stellar preparation using the very tender, tasty tail meat. The lemon chicken is the best I ever ate: fried pieces in a good batter, moistened with a smooth, tart lemon sauce. Other points of interest include the fresh whole fish, tea smoked duck, Szechuan spicy lamb with peppercorns, Saday beef, and wor shu op (a.k.a. Mandarin duck, a collection of duck strips with vegetables and lotus flour, fried to a melt-in-the-mouth crust, great with tong-cho).

Service is pretty straightforward, as are the desserts and the wine list.

TROUT. Almost certainly the most popular fish in New Orleans, this is a big salt-water fish quite different from the freshwater trout found elsewhere in America. See **Fish**.

TROUT MEUNIERE. This is probably the most commonly-found entree on Creole menus. Despite that, it's usually good. A fillet of local speckled trout is dusted with flour and either sauteed or fried. It's served with a sauce, which may appear in either of two distinct styles. The simpler of them is the one in French cookbooks: butter cooked until the solids brown, with lemon juice added. The definitive version of this is at **Galatoire's**, where the effect is one of toastiness. **Christian's, Clancy's,** and **Delmonico** also do their meuniere sauce that way—and well. The other style of meuniere sauce is uniquely New Orleans and generally credited to **Arnaud's** (which now does it poorly). This sauce is of butter, lemon, and enough veal stock to turn it brown. It is done exceptionally well at **Commander's Palace, Gambrill's,** and the **Peppermill.** The idea of serving a brown sauce over fish may be the most distinctive practice in all of Creole cookery.

I consider the brown-sauce style of trout meuniere to be one of the ten best dishes in the cuisine. Here is a recipe.

Sauce:
½ stick butter
4 Tbs. flour
1 Tbs. chopped onions
½ tsp. chopped garlic
1 Tbs. chopped celery
1 Tbs. chopped flat-leaf parsley
1 Tbs. chopped green bell pepper
Pinch thyme
Pinch oregano
2 cups veal stock
2 Tbs. dry red wine
2 Tbs. lemon juice
1 Tbs. Worcestershire sauce
½ tsp. salt
¼ tsp. white pepper
2 Tbs. softened butter

6 fillets speckled trout, 6-8 oz. each
1 cup flour
¼ tsp. Creole seasoning
¼ cup peanut oil

1. Make the sauce first. Start by making a roux. Melt the butter over a medium heat and sprinkle in the flour. Cook the two together, stirring constantly, until the mixture is light brown. Be careful not to burn it, and just plain be careful, as roux is hot!

2. When the roux is the right color, add the onions and garlic and stir in. Cook until the onions have become translucent, then add the celery, parsley, bell pepper, thyme and oregano. Cook while stirring until the vegetables become limp.

3. Add the veal stock, red wine, and lemon juice. Bring the blend to

a simmer, whisking to blend the roux into the sauce.

4. Strain the sauce, then add the Worcestershire and salt and pepper to taste. Remove from the heat and whisk in softened butter. Keep warm.

5. Wash the trout fillets well and shake dry. With a fork, blend the Creole seasoning into the flour in a broad bowl. Pass the trout fillets through the seasoned flour to coat, but not too heavily.

6. Heat the peanut oil in a skillet over medium-high heat and saute two trout fillets at a time for two minutes—until lightly browned on the bottom. Turn the fillets and cook about another 90 seconds. Remove and drain the fish, and keep warm until all of it is cooked.

7. Nap two Tbs. of sauce over each fillet. Serve with a lemon wedge and a sprinkling of fresh chopped parsley.

Serves six.

★ ★ ★ ★ Tujague's

823 Decatur, French Quarter. 525-8676. 11 a.m.-3 p.m. and 5-10:30 p.m. seven days; till 11 p.m. Fri. & Sat. AE, CB, DC, MC, V. $$$

Tujague's is one of the city's oldest restaurants, with a history going back through several sets of owners to Madame Begue, New Orleans' first restaurant superstar. For most of its history, Tujague's was a dining room for the workers in the French Market across the street. The serving style dates back to those times: instead of a menu, there's the dinner of the day. The current owners, who took over a badly-deteriorated kitchen in 1984 and turned it around, made one major change: there are now three choices of entree instead of no choice.

The dinner begins with a shrimp cocktail with an unusually heady red sauce, and a bowl of soup. The latter is generally too rich, but is otherwise pretty good; the spinach-and-crabmeat soup is the top of the repertoire. That's followed by Tujague's signature dish, a chunk of freshly-boiled beef brisket, tender and nicely-flavored by the vegetables in the boiling liquid, served with a red horseradish sauce.

The entrees are big platters of food. Always available are a gigantic filet mignon with garlic butter and chicken bonne femme. The latter is assertive and unforgettable: half a pan-fried chicken beneath a pile of fresh-cut fried potatoes and a colossal amount of garlic and parsley. Strictly for garlic lovers, and rather delicious. The other entrees of the day usually include a seafood and a pot dish—very New Orleans.

Dessert is usually pecan pie (which would be better if they'd warm it) and coffee in an old-fashioned glass (trademark!). Service is very friendly, and the antique bar is a neighborhood hangout.

★ ★ ★ Tula's Kitchen

3828 Hessmer Ave., Metairie. 885-5661. Noon-2 p.m. Tues.-Fri.; 6-10 p.m. Tues.-Sat. $$

A sign outside Tula's Kitchen says that it serves the finest Nicaraguan cuisine in Louisiana. This is a safe bet. Tula Lacayo, who for about 13 years was the consul for Nicaragua here, does all the cooking, most of it to order. Her daughter serves it and gives enthusiastic explanations. The dining room is small, colorful, and sparkling clean.

Nicaraguan food is obviously Central American, but much different from, say, Mexican. Nacatamales, for example, are about twenty times the size of the tamales we eat around here. They're a sort of corn meal porridge with meat, herbs, cheese, and sauce in the center. The fritanga, a collection of fried pork seasoned with achiote, fried plantains, fried cheese, and gallo pinto (a sort of warm salad of beans and rice) is a very pretty platter and seriously delicious.

The best entree is pescado Tipitapa, a whole fried fish with a spicy, chunky tomato sauce. Tasty, and an enormous serving. The arroz Tula brings shrimp, chicken, ham, sausage, and a few other things to bear in a marvelous first cousin to jambalaya. Variations on broiled beefsteak are fine, too—typically marinated in garlic, pepper, onions, wine, and oil. A filet mignon slathered with a creamy jalapeno sauce has a unique deliciousness.

For all that, the high point of your meal may be dessert—specifically, a cake called "tres leches." The "three milks" are made into a custardy cake topped with a meringue that looks like marshmallow cream, but with a distinctly lighter taste. Delicious stuff, and the perfect match for cafe con leche — the cinnamony Central American cafe au lait.

TUNA. There is delicious tuna in the Gulf of Mexico, and ever since the redfish ban it has become one of the most popular fish in restaurants—especially in those that grill fish. Tuna is probably the very best fish for blackening. Remember that tuna should still be a little pink inside when it's properly cooked. In fact, one element of its appeal is that it can be made to resemble beef. See **Fish**.

TURTLE SOUP. Creole-style turtle soup, made from the very abundant, large, and mean turtles that live in the swamps all around New Orleans, is much headier and thicker than other turtle soups you may run into in your travels. It's almost a stew and contains, besides morsels of the firm, tasty turtle meat, a good deal of lemon, onions, egg (sometimes turtle egg), and sherry. The last item is often added at the table; turtle soup must account for well over half of the sherry consumption in New Orleans. (Be careful about that. There's already sherry in the soup, and the sherry added at the table tends to throw the soup off balance.) The definitive local turtle soup is served at **Commander's Palace**, where it's extra-thick, spicy, and generally unforgettable. Also good are the turtle soups at **Brennan's, Delmonico, Bon Ton, Flagons, Gambrill's, Moran's Riverside, Pascal's Manale,** and the **Tavern on the Park.**

TWENTY-FOUR-HOUR RESTAURANTS. New Orleans is an around-the-clock party town, and there's never a time when you can't find an open bar. But eating late at night is another story. Very few restaurants are open all night, and most of them are terrible franchises or French Quarter sleazoramas. The decent 24-hour establishments are **Bailey's, Clover Grill, Hummingbird Grill, La Peniche,** and the **Quarter Scene.** Warning: all these places tend to be much busier in the wee hours than they are in the daytime—perhaps too busy for you to entertain the notion of a quick meal.

UV as in vegetable soup

★ ★ ★ Uglesich's

1238 Baronne (at Erato), Lee Circle Area. 523-8571. 9:30 a.m.-4 p.m. Mon.-Fri. No credit cards. $

The surroundings are probably the most forbidding in town. The best thing in the neighborhood is the Brown's Velvet dairy. Nor is there a lot of atmosphere *inside* Uglesich's. Come to think of it, yes, there is: so much of it that when you leave you may smell as if you've been frying seafood all day. The place is old and busy. Some of the clientele wears ties. The menu is mostly sandwiches, and the specialty is sandwiches of fried seafood. It's all fresh stuff: the oysters, even those for a sandwich, are *shucked to order* at the bar. There you can get some on the half shell while you wait. Service is not instant, but when you get your poor boy of fried shrimp, oysters, trout, or soft-shell crab, you find that it's worth the wait. The French fries are cut from fresh potatoes and taste great; for some reason, they will not make a sandwich with them. The roast beef is made with a rather spicy reddish gravy rather than the standard brown stuff: interesting. They also make a mean grilled ham and cheese poor boy.

Lately, Uglesich's has added a collection of grilled seafood entrees and such items as stuffed peppers to its menu. All of this is delicious and very inexpensive.

UNGULATE'S. See **Parky's Ungulate's Bard-O-Teria.**

UPDATE. *The New Orleans Eat Book* is unique among restaurant guides in that it updates itself. Every six months until the new edition is published, a bulletin will inform readers of interesting new restaurants, drastic changes at restaurants in this edition, and closings. Regardless of when you bought this book, I will send you the most recent (or the next) Eat Book Update free of charge—along with all prior bulletins that apply to this edition. Just write to **Eat Book Update,** P.O. Box 51831, New Orleans, LA 70151.

★ ★ ★ ★ Upperline

1413 Upperline (between St. Charles and Prytania), Uptown. Reservations 891-9822. 5:30-10 p.m. seven nights; till 10:30 p.m. Fri. & Sat.; AE, CB,DC, MC, V. $$$

    Upperline, a trendsetting cafe founded by Jo Ann Clevenger and her chef son Jason in 1982, had its ups and downs since then, but at least managed to survive—which is more than can be said for the majority of Uptown bistros that opened in the Eighties. The place took a long step forward when it hired Tom Cowman as chef in 1987. Cowman, who made his local mark at the failed Restaurant Jonathan, has a style as eclectic as that of the Clevengers, and the chemistry has been nice.

    The menu now is a well-blended amalgam of the best old Upperline specialties and Cowman's trademarks. A booklet of nightly specials adds further pizzazz. Cowman's trout mousse with dill mayonnaise is luscious as ever. So is the shrimp with both colors of remoulade sauce—the best possible solution to the long-standing argument about red vs. white remoulade. Oysters and artichoke a la Nick is something the chef picked up during his brief stay at Lenfant's; it's an inspired variation on oysters Mosca, with an herbal, well-oiled bread crumb topping that could be a little crustier. Soups, particularly cold ones like the red pepper vichyssoise, are generally good. More interesting small salads than most restaurants.

    Upperline's charcoal grill works on fish, shrimp, chicken and steak to equally good effect; I have noticed an occasional mistake on the overgrilled side, fatal for fish. Among the not-so-grilled entrees we find a very fine roasted duck, prepared with sauces which change with the seasons. Cowman's famous calves' liver a l'orange is a must for liver lovers; the sauce, only slightly sweet, is admirably suited to the meat. The chef has also installed his curries, complete with an array of little dishes of condiments; some people love this, although it never pushed my button.

    Trout Lacombe, a richness of sauteed fish with crawfish in a creamy dill sauce, is the most distinctive of the saucier fish fare. Pasta with crabmeat is tasty, and the idea of topping it with a small soft-shell crab is a great idea.

    The wine list is short but satisfactory. The desserts have improved immensely since Cowman arrived: great cakes, and the rich rum trifle are the best bets. Service is by smarter waiters than most. The premises vary pleasantly in atmosphere from the Utilitarian Deco front room to the Renovated Dwelling rear. Jo Ann Clevenger, who has the most distinctive laugh in town, presides over all—occasionally dreaming up fascinating dining themes, such as the garlic festival in summer and the Jane Austen dinner on the author's birthday in December.

VEGETABLES. New Orleans at last seems to be past the vegetable-of-the-day stage, in which one got a side dish of some grossly overcooked canned vegetable, more to fill space on the table than to provide any taste sensation. Most serious restaurants now buy good fresh vegetables; some of them actually spend some time coming up with recipes for them. A precious few buy and cook vegetables of such quality and variety that one can assemble a tasty, satisfying vegetarian plate. The best at this is the **Windsor Court Grill Room**, which always seems to have a vegetable I never heard of among its half-dozen nightly offerings. **Andrea's** maintains an antipasto table on which are ten or twelve crisp, elemental marinated vegetables; these make a great appetizer. **Mr. B's** chef Gerard Maras is a leader locally in encouraging Louisiana and Mississippi farmers to grow specialty vegetables, and he cooks a lot of them. Other good vegetable houses are **Bayona, Brigtsen's, Commander's Palace, Emeril's, Gambrill's, Le Jardin,** and the **Versailles.**

VEGETABLE SOUP. It's got to be homemade (preferably that day), the vegetables have to be fresh, and it's nice to find a big chunk of brisket in it. The best old-style vegetable soups in New Orleans restaurants come from **Galatoire's** (the soups du jour on Thursdays, Saturdays, and Sundays are all variations on the theme), **Delmonico, Camellia Grill** (cooler months only) and **Ye Olde College Inn.** Andrea's and Nuvolari's respective minestrones qualify as a vegetable soup, more or less; they're terrific.

A completely different kind of vegetable soup is the vegetable cream soup. These are usually smooth, elegant, and rich with cream. The better practitioners are **Bistro at the Maison de Ville, Commander's Palace, Louis XVI,** and the **Versailles.**

See also **Soups.**

VEGETARIAN RESTAURANTS. See **Health Food.**

★Venezia

134 N. Carrollton Ave., Mid-City. 488-7991. 5:00-Midnight Tues.-Sat.; till 1 a.m. Fri. and Sat. 5:00-11 p.m. Sun. Closed Mon. AE, MC, V. $

A large restaurant with a loyal regular clientele—much of which comes from Tulane University—Venezia knocks out a large menu of mediocre pizzas and edible to good Italian specials. The sauces in both cases tend to the rich, overcooked side to my taste. Service is quick, portions are enormous, and prices are low.

★★Vera Cruz

1141 Decatur, French Quarter. 561-8081. 5:30-10:30 p.m. Mon.-Fri; till Midnight on Fri. Noon-Midnight Sat. & Noon-9:00 p.m. Sun. • 7537 Maple, Uptown. 866-1736. 5:00-10 p.m. Mon.-Sat. Closed Sun. Both: AE, MC, V. $$

With lots of greenery, a pleasant raffishness missing from the Mexican chains, and a style of Mexican cooking not seen elsewhere around New Orleans, Vera Cruz has a very dedicated following. The generally friendly waiters are frank about the stranger food, but wax appropriately enthusiastic about such as the mesquite-roasted pork loin, loaded with garlic, sliced into pieces with some nice hard edges: delicious.

Also good here is fajitas, mesquite-grilled chicken or beef that you roll up into flour tortillas at the table with some pico de gallo (a relish of onions, garlic and herbs), guacamole, sour cream and grilled onions. The combination chicken and beef fajitas is especially good, and ample enough to split with a friend. The menu goes on to include well-made versions of the standard combination platters. An odd, popular tostada called an India is a tortilla with everything in the house on top. Appetizers and side courses are not very good. Prices are reasonable, the crowd is interesting, and the beer is cold.

The French Quarter location is a lot better than the one Uptown.

★ ★ ★ Veranda

Hotel Inter-Continental, 444 St. Charles Ave., CBD. 522-5566. 6 a.m.-3 p.m. and 5:30 p.m.-10 p.m. seven days. Sun. brunch 10:30 a.m.-3 p.m. AE, CB, DC, MC, V. $$$

A lovely, garden-like area in a large skylit atrium is the main restaurant of the luxurious Inter-Continental. The hotel had not been able to work up much of culinary interest in this space until the late-1989 arrival of chef Willy Coln. Coln had a wonderful little restaurant in Gretna that closed during the oil bust, taking with it the best German food in the area and the city's best Oktoberfest celebration.

The Oktoberfest was brought back to life in a part-time way at the Veranda, and a few of the chef's dishes have landed on the Veranda's menu. The best of these is the best braised veal shank I've ever eaten—roasted until the meat starts falling from the bone. A big pile of this tender stuff is served with lots of vegetables to absorb the copious natural juices.

As flagship dining rooms of major hotels go, the Veranda has a rather unambitious menu. For the most part, the food is a blend of standard Creole and standard hotel continental ideas. The best starter is the crab cake with mustard sauce, lightly spicy and full of lump crabmeat. The crawfish cassoulette is also nice: a small casserole of crawfish in a simple, zippy sauce, covered with a dome of puff pastry. The marinated salmon is an elegance, tinged with dill and presented with a pretty watercress puree. Crab bisque employs claw crabmeat in an otherwise gilded broth, creamy and intense.

Grilled tuna steak with a very mild tomato salsa, red snapper with crabmeat and lemon butter, and fried soft shell crab with hollandaise lead the seafood entrees, which gives you an idea of how conventional things are here, The most offbeat dish is the salmon Wellington, wrapped with crawfish in pastry. The red-meat entrees include a great steak au poivre, an all-right veal chop with mushrooms, and an interesting quail stuffed with foie gras.

Desserts come from a table of nice things, which always include the chef's trademark Black Forest cake. On Sundays, there's a stridently average buffet brunch. This is a very comfortable place to have breakfast during the week.

★ ★ ★ ★ ★ Versailles

2100 St. Charles Ave., Garden District. Reservations 524-2535. 6-10 p.m. Mon.-Sat. AE, CB, DC, MC, V. $$$$$

The Versailles evolves slowly upward, ever upward. Anything here resembling a trend does so only by coincidence. For instance, the kitchen was using fresh herbs over a decade ago, when such exotica practically had to be smuggled in by diplomatic pouch. Nor has the Versailles ever made much noise about itself. Both the restaurant and its chef-owner Gunter Preuss are low key.

Until Preuss opened the Versailles in 1972, his career had been in hotel restaurants. Logically, then, the Versailles looks and operates like a first-class hotel dining room. The main part of it has a zigzag wall of windows offering a view of the streetcar. The other rooms are classically decorated, a bit too sedate for me but liked by regulars.

The best first courses I've had have been specials or half-portions of some of the seafood entrees (they're easy about that sort of thing). A seafood boudin in mustard cream sauce with capers, assortments of pates from fish, meats, and vegetables, and the Pernod-tinged crabmeat florentine are recent hits. Superb snails come in a garlicky brown sauce ladled into a hollowed small French loaf. The only soup worth a taste is the terrific rich bouillabaisse, chock-a-block with local seafood; split this a few ways and it's a grand beginning.

Two fish dishes lead the seafood offerings. The pompano Herbsaint is a delicacy, an ideally-sauteed fillet of pompano atop a bit of spinach, napped with an anise-flavored sauce. Pompano Marcus gets an aromatic quality from the artichokes in the sauce, and the fish tastes pure and elemental. The chef also plays a good hand with fresh Norwegian salmon.

Boxed at the top of the menu as the house specialty is veal farci, a mound of crabmeat dressing hidden by slices of baby white veal. In fact, the eggy, sizzling Weiner schnitzel or the veal chop with wild mushrooms are better. An interesting new game the chef is playing is pairing small portions of entree-type foods—say, chicken and lamb—on one plate.

Filet mignon Helder (grilled onion and tomato concassee) and the tournedos Rossini (intense, translucent sauce of demi-glace and truffles, with foie gras) are polished, exciting versions of two beef warhorses. Rack of lamb, with its beautiful rosy meat edged with dark brown, is first-class. Duck is roasted to an exciting crisp skin and a tender, moist interior, served with two different sauces—one sweet, the other herbal and peppery. I like the variations on quail, even though they're on the light side.

Oversized plates hold restrained portions, but I always get enough to eat here. The prices, on the other hand, add up fast. The wine list is interesting, with many choices from France, California, and Germany. It is maddening that vintages are not marked on the list; the waiters, of course, never know.

Dessert is polite to the point of being forgettable, although I seem to remember a hazelnut-and-coffee mousse called creme noisette. The maitre d' is the capable James Kellett; the rest of the wait staff is extemely low-key.

VICHYSSOISE. It's a cold soup made from potatoes and leeks—old-fashioned, but still commonplace on local menus. The nouvelle places like to slip unusual ingredients into the pot; Tom Cowman at the **Upperline**, for example, has been known to put out watercress vichyssoise and red pepper vichyssoise. The richest version is at **Antoine's,** where there seems to be as much heavy cream as any other ingredient.

VIEW, ROOMS WITH A. For a dining room to have a view, it generally must be high up in the building. But restaurants off the first floor have rarely done well in New Orleans—either in terms of volume or, more inexplicably, cuisine. Here is a list of restaurants whose windows offer something more to see than a street, along with ratings for the food.

TOWERING VIEWS FOR MILES
★*Hyatt Top of the Dome*
★★*Marriott River View*
RIVER VIEW
★★★*Kabby's*
★★★★*Le Jardin*
★★★*Moran's Riverside*
All Riverwalk and Jax Brewery cafes
★★★*Seb's*
LAKE VIEW
★★*Bart's*
★★*Bounty*
★★★*Bruning's*
Fitzgerald's

★Visko's

516 Gretna Blvd., Gretna. 368-4899. 11 a.m.-10 p.m. Mon.-Sat.; till 11 p.m. Fri. & Sat. AE, CB, DC, MC, V. $$

Visko's is one of the big names in the seafood-restaurant biz in New Orleans. But I find the culinary performance spotty. You get off to a great start with superb raw oysters at the bar, but it's all downhill from there. Later on, at the table, try an order of oysters Meaux, with its spicy hollandaise. Gumbo is just okay. The fried seafood sometimes comes out perfect, but I've had more than my share of tepid fish with damp coatings. Service is not what you could call well-disciplined.

The "Steamroom" side of Visko's serves, as the name implies, buckets of steamed lobsters, clams, fish, and other seafoods. Both the steaming method and its classic seafoods are foreign to New Orleans; the tastes, compared to those of boiled or fried, are very bland. This would be all right if they could get the stuff to the table consistently steaming hot, but that's spotty as well. Steamed seafood that's going clammy on you (no pun intended) is uninspiring eating to me.

W as in wine list

WAITING FOR A TABLE. From the least irritating practice to the most:

1. Being told your table will be ready in a few minutes, please wait in the bar.
2. Being told there is a 30-minute wait for a table, let us have your name, we'll call you when your table is ready. Please wait in the bar.
3. Being told the above, but finding out that the wait is actually one hour.
4. Being told any of the above, but having to wait in line outside.
5. Experiencing any of the above when you have a reservation. (And show up on time, with the number of people you said would be with you.)
6. Same as Number Five, but with tables and staff available in the restaurant. In this case, it's clear that they just want to sell you a few drinks.

Busy restaurants, like airlines, overbook. The reason for this is that when a place becomes so popular that it is assumed that reservations are essential, it finds it hard to fill the places of cancellations. (This is especially vexatious for small restaurants.) Number One above is excusable. Where busy restaurants don't take reservations, Number Two might also be excusable (although for some people it has the effect of crossing the place off their list).

But Numbers Three, Four, and especially Five and Six are outrageous. A restaurateur suggested a great way of overcoming all needs for such policies: have reservations made, as they are for hotels, with a credit card number. If the party doesn't show up, a penalty is charged against the card. But if the restaurant doesn't honor the reservation within a reasonable time—15 to 30 minutes, say—the meal is on the house.

Fast way to get out of Situation Number Six: Order glasses of water at the bar.

WEST END. In the northwest corner of the city, West End was originally (pre-Civil War) a resort to which people traveled by train and where they spent weekends in hotels. The automobile made it easily accessible, and while the hotels are long gone, West End has retained a concentration of restaurants. One of them, **Bruning's**, dates back to the 1850s. It, like most of the other restaurants in West End Park, is built on stilts out over the lake waters and serves mostly seafood.

The first order of summer for many Orleanians is reblazing the trail to West End Park—reviving, along the way, the time-honored complaint that it isn't what it used to be, while hoping that maybe this year the culinary situation out there has improved. But as of this writing most of the West End dining scene is, to put it charitably, well below its potential. The menus are almost interchangeable; it's the same old fried and boiled seafood. Some of the places have the gall to serve frozen seafood. About the only major new development in recent years has been the growth of a bar scene that can hardly be called upscale.

What West End Park needs is a classy, creative Creole-French restaurant—something like a Mr. B's at sea—to get the ball rolling. Great locations are waiting; the buildings which used to house Willie G's and Port Orleans would be perfect for such a restaurant. While we're waiting, the best of the West End eateries are **Bruning's** and **The Bounty**. **Coconuts** is the best-looking (no lake view, though) and has the most ambitious menu, but it's inconsistent. I find **Fitzgerald's** and **Jaeger's** mediocre to poor.

Many other places to eat exist aside from those around West End Park proper The seafood houses are **Bart's**, a big, handsome restaurant with an extensive seafood menu and good if somewhat inconsistent food; **West End Cafe**, where the boiled is better than the fried; **Russell's Marina Grill**, a popular but spotty sandwich and short-order place; the **Windjammer** and **Masson's**, both with more ambitious menus and more formal surroundings.

See also **Bucktown**, another interesting restaurant hotbed nearby.

★★Whole Food Market

3135 Esplanade, Mid-City. 943-1626. 9 a.m.-8:00 p.m. seven days except Sun. till 7:00 p.m. MC, V. $

The Whole Food Market, as you might guess from its name, is the city's premier marketer of foodstuffs for vegetarians, heath foodists, and others. However, it also qualifies as a gourmet grocery—its produce and cheese departments are without peer, and even the meats are a cut above. With all these things and its excellent breads, the store's deli makes takeout sandwiches of distinction. Many of them are vegetarian in composition, yet even these are tasty. I like the veggie muffuletta, with several kinds of cheese, olive salad, tomatoes, and the inevitable sprouts on pita bread; and the concoction of hummus—the Lebanese chickpea paste—and cheeses. But they also deliver a superb deli-style roast beef or ham sandwich; in both cases, the meats are beautifully cooked, have intense flavor, and stretch out between slices of interesting, virtuous breads. The deli case also has quiches, pates, salads, and the like.

★★★★★ Windsor Court Grill Room

Windsor Court Hotel, 300 Gravier, CBD. Reservations 523-6000. 7:00 a.m.-10:30 a.m. 11:30 a.m.-2:30 p.m., 6-10:30 p.m. seven days. AE, CB, DC, MC, V. $$$$$

The Windsor Court Hotel, a startlingly handsome and civilized property, is the best of the several new luxury downtown hotels. It has but one restaurant, the Grill Room, serving breakfast, lunch, and dinner. Like the rest of the hotel, the Grill Room has an English theme, and is furnished expensively with comfortable tables, original art, English antiques, and expensive silver and china.

Two aspects of the Grill Room have been outstanding since the day it opened. It has had the most pleasant and able dining room staff of any restaurant in the city. And its food has been consistently innovative. Because of the second condition, the place is a singularly difficult restaurant to review. Not only does the menu change daily, the style of the cuisine doesn't sit still long enough for one to write a complete sentence about it. As likely to get an Indian or Chinese taste in a dish here as a Creole or French one. The chef, Kevin Graham, is English—which also tells us nearly nothing.

Only a handful of dishes here are served regularly, but these are solid gold. Oysters Peacock, served in shells atop a nest of pasta, are the best new baked oyster dish in town. The sauce is a puree of peppers with bread crumbs and olive oil. Spicy, but very good. Crabmeat ravigote may be the best I've ever eaten, big white lumps with a fine mayonnaise. They make great appetizer terrines, pates, sausages, meats, and fish, some of them smoked on the premises. The matchless Windsor Court salad—lettuces, bacon, avocado, Roquefort, and a few other things, layered in a glass bowl—is the best house salad I know, and the only one that I find interesting enough to have as an entree.

Grilled fish, birds, and meats are the central entree specialties. The quality of the raw materials is superb; they always have lovely salmon, prime beef the equal of that found at Ruth's Chris, and good-looking free-range fowl. All of this is blasted by a hot fire of mesquite, pecan, hickory, and other woods until stripes of char appear. The Grill Room used to have a penchant for undercooking much of its food; lately, the pendulum has swung the other way a bit too far, so let them know you won't take rubber tuna.

The Grill Room has a tradition of minimalism and has never gone in much for complicated, saucy dishes. Which is just as well, because the few essays in that direction have generally been less good than the simpler stuff. Beware of days when the entire menu seems exotic.

One area of the Grill Room's cookery that has declined is vegetables. They used to have an inspired selection—enough offbeat, fresh, and appealing vegetables to make a complete meal, if one were so inclined. They're still above average, but seem to have fallen into the realm of afterthought.

The Grill Room's wine cellar has startling breadth and depth, especially among older Bordeaux. The California selection is also fascinating—lots of wines you've heard of but never run into before. Some bargains can be found, and the sommeliers perform expert decanting and pouring.

Desserts are baked on site and are pristine. The un-traditional creme brulee is served in a pastry shell, but is eggy and flowing and crusty on the top the way it should be. The flourless chocolate cake is the ideal brownie; the lemon tart and pie-sliced bread pudding are elegant. The coffee is weak, but they prepare excellent espresso and cappuccino.

Service here is usually flawless—but sometimes they get so caught up in their own flawlessness that it crosses the line into hauteur. This happened about the time they got five diamonds from AAA—the first hotel ever to achieve that distinction.

WINE LISTS. The wine selections in New Orleans restaurants have greatly improved in recent years. In a some places an oenophile can really get a thrill. Here are the ten best wine lists in New Orleans, and what they specialize in:

1. Brennan's. Red Bordeaux, red and white Burgundies, California Cabernets and Chardonnays. A rich collection of 20-year-old-plus vintages, at strikingly attractive prices.

2. Grill Room. Extravagant collection of old red Bordeaux; well-balanced current vintage French and California.

3. Commander's Palace. Many California Cabernets and Chardonnays, red Bordeaux, and all Burgundies.

4. Flagons. Forty (at least) wines by the glass; growing collection of recent vintage wines from all regions.

5. Andrea's. Best Italian wine list in town, which takes some doing. Proprietor very knowledgeable about the confusing Italian wine world.

6. Arnaud's. A very good inventory of current-to-10-year-old vintages from all areas of France and California. The prices are a touch high.

7. Antoine's. The only list that has or needs a table of contents. Very wide, intelligently-chosen, fairly-priced selection from all regions of France, California, and Germany.

8. Tavern on the Park. A somewhat quirky selection, but in it one finds many delightful bottles. The prices are low—in some cases, extraordinarily low. Ports and Madieras by the glass.

9. Sazerac. Well-balanced and extensive but expensive stock of California and French wine, with unusually good Champagne selection.

10. Clancy's. Enormous list for such a small restaurant; eclectic but fascinating selection.

Special Mention: **Martin Wine Cellar Gourmet Deli**, where you can pick a wine from the store to go with your sandwich. They'll even decant!

★★Ye Olde College Inn

3016 S. Carrollton Ave., Uptown. 866-3683. 11 a.m.-11 p.m. seven days. MC, V. $$

A throwback to the Fifties or earlier, the College Inn is thoroughly without pretense. They seem to take pains to keep you from thinking of their food as in any way gourmet. I give them points for honesty. If you stick with the mainstays, you'll have a satisfying meal. Begin with the shrimp remoulade (recommended by the placemat) or any of the soups. Then check the list of the daily specials for anything appealing. The lamb chops and the beef stew have been good; the seafood topped with this or that tends to be heavy and gloppy, although the fried seafood isn't bad. Veal Rufin—topped with a light lemon butter sauce with mushrooms—is darkish veal, but tastes good anyway.

Sandwiches are the real stock in trade here, though. They make a terrific hamburger—hand-formed from freshly ground beef, grilled to crustiness, and sent out with fries cut by hand from fresh potatoes. The oyster loaf (recommended by the sign in the parking lot) is good enough but wouldn't make my top-ten list. The roast beef poor boy is appropriately sloppy with a good gravy. Chicken-fried steak (recommended by local legend) would inspire a revolt among Texans. Chicken-fried *chicken*, on the other hand, comes out hot, well-seasoned, and not greasy. The menu goes on to list dozens of other sandwiches, but there are no sleepers among the funny names (not even the Lone Eagle).

Salads, vegetables, dessert, and surroundings are perfunctory. Service is friendly, although you don't see the server very much. The problem with this place is that the menu is far too big, and eighty percent of it is disappointing.

★★★★Young's

850 Robert Rd., Slidell. The restaurant is unmarked; it is exactly eight-tenths of a mile from the corner of Gause Rd. (US 190) and Robert Rd., on the right. 5-10 p.m. Tues.-Sat.; till 11 Fri. & Sat. No credit cards. $$

Once you find Young's you're past the hardest part. Getting a table is the second-hardest. The place is immensely popular and doesn't take reservations; a wait for a table is inevitable except at the earliest and latest open hours. Nor do they take credit cards. Despite all that, Young's is very much worth the trouble. Its food is terrific by any standard—not just for Slidell, where it is easily the best restaurant in town.

The wait for a table, fortunately, is in a convivial lounge serving good, inexpensive drinks. The dining rooms are smallish, reasonably comfortable, and very well served. The specialty: steak, ranging in grade between choice and prime, broiled to a nice exterior crust and served very simply—no butter sauce, even. I have had steaks as good as the ones

I've had at Young's, but I've never had better. The flavor and juiciness of the beef is hard to believe; it actually pools up in the plate as you eat. Nor is there any skimping on the size: all the steaks are 14 to 16 ounces. This is especially impressive in the case of the filet mignon, which literally towers. At prices between $12 and $15, salad and baked potato included, this is an outstanding bargain.

I'd skip the short list of appetizers to save room for the steaks, which really require a big appetite. They cook a few kinds of Gulf fish on the open grill here, and this is a good alternative for those not into red meat. There are no desserts of any kind—probably so the tables will turn faster. The wine list is short but reasonably good; its prices are very low.

INDEX

CULINARY STYLE
Creole
Annadele Plantation
Antoine's
Arnaud's
Augie's Glass Garden
Bailey's
Barreca's
Berdou's
Blue Room
Brennan's
Brigtsen's
Broussard's
Camelia Beach House
Caribbean Room
Chehardy's
Chez Helene
Chez Pierre
Christian's
Clancy's
Commander's Palace
Court of Two Sisters
Delerno's
Delmonico
Dooky Chase
Doug's
Eddie's
Etienne De Felice's
Feelings
Galatoire's
Gambrill's
Gumbo Shop
La Cuisine
La Louisiane
Masson's
Olde N'Awlins Cookery
Peppermill
Quality Inn Midtown
Seb's
St. Charles
Stephen & Martin
Taylor's
Tchoupitoulas Plantation
Tujague's

Cajun
Alex Patout's Louisiana Restaurant
Begue's
Bon Ton
K-Paul's Louisiana Kitchen
Lafitte's Landing
Patout's

French
Cafe Degas
Chez Daniel
Crozier's
La Crepe Nanou
La Gauloise
La Provence
Louis XVI
Mystery Street Cafe

Continental
Rib Room
Sazerac
Veranda
Versailles

Italian
Alberto's
Andrea's
Assunta's
Ciro's
Compagno's
Dante's Pizza Cafe
DiPiazza's
Impastato's
La Riviera
Lakeshore
Lido Gardens
Little Italians
Louisiana Pizza Kitchen
Mama Igor's
Mama Rosa's
Mark Twain Pizza
Maximo's
Mimi's
Moran's
Mosca's
Napoli
New York Pizza
Nuvolari's
Pascal's Manale
Pastore's
Sal & Judy's
Sal & Sam's
Sweet Basil's Bistro
Toney's Avenue Cafe
Toney's Spaghetti House
Tony Angello's

Tortorici
Venezia

Nouvelle

Bayona
Bayou Ridge Cafe
Bistro at Maison de Ville
Bombay Club
Constantin's
Emeril's
Flagons
Gautreau's
Isadora
Le Jardin
Mr. B's
Upperline
Windsor Court Grill Room

American

Jacmel Inn
Piccadilly Cafeteria
Tavern On The Park

Seafood (Casual)

Acme Oyster House
Andy Messina's
Barrow's
Bart's
Bounty
Bozo's
Bruning's
Cafe Atchafalaya
Casamento's
Deanie's Seafood
Drago's
Felix's
Fitzgerald's
Fury's
Jack Dempsey's
Jaeger's
Kabby's
Lakeview Seafood
Messina's
Middendorf's
Mike Anderson's
Ralph & Kacoo's
Sid-Mar's
Visko's

Steak

Beef Room
Charlie's
Chart House
Crescent City
Monroe's
Morton's of Chicago
Ruth's Chris
Steak Knife
Steak Pit
Young's Steak House

Neighborhood Cuisine

Alonso and Son
Cafe Pontchartrain
Cafe Savanna
Cannon's
Coffee Pot
Copeland's
Hard Rock Cafe
Harold's Texas Barbecue
Home Furnishings Cafe
Houston's
Hummingbird Grill
Katie's
Liuzza's
Mandich's
Mandina's
Mena's Palace
Miss Ruby's
Olivier's
Petunia's
Rick's Pancake Cottage
Rocky & Carlo's
Tessie's Place
Tipton County Pit BBQ
Vita's on Broadway Cafe
Ye Olde College Inn

Sandwiches

Avenue Sandwich Shop
Bud's Broiler
Cafe Maspero
Camellia Grill
Central Grocery
Home Plate Inn
Lee's Hamburgers
Luther's
Martin Deli
Michael's Grill

Mother's
Napoleon House
Port of Call
R&O's
Russell's Marina Grill
Serio's
Snug Harbor
Streetcar Sandwiches
The Pearl
Uglesich's

Chinese
Asia Garden
China Doll
China Orchid
Chinese Kitchen
Christina's Empress of China
Dragon's Garden
East China
Five Happiness
Fortune Gardens
Great Wall
Jade East
Kung's Dynasty
Mandarin Cafe
Ming Palace
Mr. Tai's
Peking
Trey Yuen

Japanese
Ginza
Hana
Ichiban
Little Tokyo
Samurai
Shigure
Shogun

Thai
Bangkok Cuisine
Thai Pepper

Korean
Genghis Khan

Vietnamese
Kim Son

German
Kolb's

Greek/Middle Eastern
Little Greek

Indian
Taj Mahal
Tandoor

Mexican/Central American
Bean Pot
Cafe Florida
Casa Garcia
Castillo's
Cuco's
El Patio
Garces
Jalapeno's
La Cucaracha Cafe
La Fiesta
Santa Fe
Taqueria Corona
Tio Pepe's
Tula's
Vera Cruz

Jamaican
Palmer's

Natural Foods
Back to the Garden
Whole Foods Market

Dessert

Angelo Brocato
Cafe Beignet
Cafe du Monde
Chelsey's
Croissant d'Or
Haagen-Dazs
Hansen's Sno-Bliz
La Madeleine
La Marquise
Morning Call
PJ's Coffee & Tea Co.
Plantation Coffeehouse

INDEX BY LOCATION
French Quarter/CBD

Acme Oyster House
Alex Patout's Louisiana Restaurant
Altamira
Andy Messina's
Angelo Brocato
Antoine's
Arnaud's
Asia Garden
Back to the Garden
Bailey's
Bayona
Begue's
Bistro at Maison de Ville
Blue Room
Bombay Club
Bon Ton
Brennan's
Broussard's
Cafe Beignet
Cafe du Monde
Cafe Maspero
Castillo's
Central Grocery
Chart House
Coffee Pot
Court of Two Sisters
Croissant d'Or
Dante's Pizza Cafe
DiPiazza's; Emeril's
Felix's
Galatoire's
Gumbo Shop
Haagen-Dazs
Hard Rock Cafe
Hummingbird Grill
Isadora
K-Paul's Louisiana Kitchen
Kabby's
Kolb's
La Gauloise
La Louisiane
La Madeleine
La Marquise
Le Jardin
Louis XVI
Louisiana Pizza Kitchen
Mama Rosa's
Mandarin Cafe
Maximo's
Mena's Palace
Messina's
Mike Anderson's
Miss Ruby's
Moran's
Morton's of Chicago
Mother's
Mr. B's
Napoleon House
Olde N'Awlins Cookery
Pastore's
Pat O'Brien's
Petunia's
Port of Call
Ralph & Kacoo's
Rib Room
Samurai
Sazerac
Seb's
Serio's
St. Charles
Steak Pit
The Pearl
Tio Pepe's
Toney's Avenue Cafe
Tortorici
Tujague's
Uglesich's
Vera Cruz
Veranda
Windsor Court Grill Room

Uptown

Barrow's
Bean Pot
Brigtsen's
Bud's Broiler
Cafe Atchafalaya

Cafe Pontchartrain
Cafe Savanna
Camellia Grill
Caribbean Room
Casamento's
Charlie's
China Orchid
Chinese Kitchen
Ciro's
Clancy's
Commander's Palace
Compagno's
Constantin's
Copeland's
Cuco's
Delmonico
Five Happiness
Flagons
Gautreau's
Haagen-Dazs
Hana
Hansen's Sno-Bliz
Houston's
Kung's Dynasty
La Crepe Nanou
La Cucaracha Cafe
La Madeleine
Mama Igor's
Martin Deli
Monroe's
New York Pizza
Pascal's Manale
Patout's
Piccadilly Cafeteria
PJ's Coffee & Tea Co.
Shigure
Stephen & Martin
Streetcar Sandwiches
Sweet Basil's Bistro
Taqueria Corona
Thai Pepper
Tipton County Pit BBQ
Upperline
Vera Cruz
Versailles
Vita's on Broadway Cafe
Ye Olde College Inn

Mid-City

Angelo Brocato
Avenue Sandwich Shop
Bangkok Cuisine
Bud's Broiler
Cafe Degas
Christian's
Crescent City
Dooky Chase
Garces
Genghis Khan
Home Plate Inn
Katie's
Liuzza's
Louisiana Pizza Kitchen
Mandina's
Michael's Grill
Mystery Street Cafe
Palmer's
Quality Inn Midtown
Rick's Pancake Cottage
Ruth's Chris
Tavern On The Park
Venezia
Whole Foods Market

Downtown/Marigny

Alberto's
Chez Helene
Feelings
Jack Dempsey's
Jaeger's
Mandich's
Rocky & Carlo's
Santa Fe
Snug Harbor

Lakefront/Lakeview

Bart's
Bayou Ridge Cafe
Bounty
Bruning's
Bud's Broiler
Deanie's Seafood
Fitzgerald's
La Cuisine
Masson's
Plantation Coffeehouse
R&O's
Russell's Marina Grill
Sid-Mar's
Steak Knife

Gentilly/New Orleans East

Dante's Pizza Cafe
East China
Eddie's
Jade East
Lakeview Seafood
Olivier's
Peking

East Jefferson/Metairie

Alonso and Son
Andrea's
Augie's Glass Garden
Barreca's
Beef Room
Bozo's
Bud's Broiler
Cafe Florida
Casa Garcia
Chehardy's
Chez Daniel
Copeland's
Crozier's
Cuco's
Dante's Pizza Cafe
Delerno's
Drago's
Dragon's Garden
El Patio
Etienne De Felice's
Fortune Gardens
Fury's
Gambrill's
Ginza
Great Wall
Haagen-Dazs
Harold's Texas Barbecue
Houston's
Ichiban
Impastato's
Jalapeno's
La Riviera
Lee's Hamburgers
Lido Gardens
Little Greek
Little Italians
Little Tokyo
Luther's
Mark Twain Pizza
Martin Deli
Mimi's
Ming Palace
Morning Call
Mr. Tai's
Napoli
Peppermill
Piccadilly Cafeteria
Ralph & Kacoo's
Ruth's Chris
Sal & Sam's
Shogun
Taj Mahal
Tandoor
Taylor's
Tessie's Place
Tiffin Inn
Toney's Spaghetti House
Tony Angello's
Tula's Kitchen

West Bank

Berdou's
Cannon's
Chelsey's
Chez Pierre
China Doll
Christina's Empress of China
Copeland's
Cuco's
Kim Son
La Fiesta
Luther's
Mosca's
Piccadilly Cafeteria
Tchoupitoulas Plantation
Visko's

North of Lake

Annadele Plantation
Assunta's
Camelia Beach House
Copeland's
Cuco's
Doug's
Jacmel Inn
La Provence
Lakeshore
Nuvolari's
Piccadilly Cafeteria
PJ's Coffee & Tea Co.

Sal & Judy's
Trey Yuen
Young's Steak House

On The Horizon
Lafitte's Landing
Middendorf's

OPEN SUNDAY

Alex Patout's Louisiana Restaurant
Andrea's
Andy Messina's
Angelo Brocato
Annadele Plantation
Arnaud's
Augie's Glass Garden
Bailey's
Bangkok Cuisine
Bart's
Bean Pot
Beef Room
Begue's
Bistro at Maison de Ville
Bombay Club
Bounty
Brennan's
Broussard's
Bruning's
Bud's Broiler
Cafe Atchafalaya
Cafe Beignet
Cafe Degas
Cafe du Monde
Cafe Maspero
Cafe Pontchartrain
Cafe Savanna
Camellia Grill
Cannon's
Caribbean Room
Casa Garcia
Casamento's
Castillo's
Central Grocery
Chart House
Chelsey's
Chez Helene
China Doll
China Orchid
Christina's Empress of China
Ciro's
Coffee Pot
Commander's Palace
Compagno's
Copeland's
Court of Two Sisters
Crescent City
Croissant d'Or
Cuco's
Dante's Pizza Cafe
Deanie's Seafood
Delerno's
Delmonico
Dooky Chase
East China
Feelings
Felix's
Fitzgerald's
Five Happiness
Flagons
Fortune Gardens
Fury's
Galatoire's
Garces
Genghis Khan
Great Wall
Gumbo Shop
Haagen-Dazs
Hana
Hansen's Sno-Bliz
Hard Rock Cafe
Houston's
Hummingbird Grill
Ichiban
Jacmel Inn
Jade East
Jaeger's
Jalapenos
Kabby's
Kim Son
Kolb's
Kung's Dynasty
La Crepe Nanou
La Cuisine
La Fiesta
La Gauloise
La Louisiane
La Madeleine
La Marquise
La Provence
Lafitte's Landing
Lakeview Seafood
Le Jardin
Lee's Hamburgers

Little Greek
Little Italians
Louis XVI
Louisiana Pizza Kitchen
Luther's
Mama Igor's
Mama Rosa's
Mandina's
Martin Deli
Maximo's
Michael's Grill
Middendorf's
Mike Anderson's
Mimi's
Miss Ruby's
Monroe's
Morning Call
Morton's of Chicago
Mother's
Mr. B's
Mystery Street Cafe
Napoleon House
New York Pizza
Nuvolari's
Olde N'Awlins Cookery
Olivier's
Pascal's Manale
Pat O'Brien's
Patout's
Peking
Peppermill
Petunia's
Piccadilly Cafeteria
PJ's Coffee & Tea Co.
Port of Call
Quality Inn Midtown
R&O's
Ralph & Kacoo's
Rib Room
Rick's Pancake Cottage
Rocky & Carlo's
Russell's Marina Grill
Ruth's Chris
Sal & Judy's
Sal & Sam's
Samurai
Sazerac
Seb's
Shigure
Shogun
Sid-Mar's
Snug Harbor
Steak Knife
Steak Pit
Stephen & Martin
Streetcar Sandwiches
Sweet Basil's Bistro
Taj Mahal
Tandoor
Taqueria Corona
Tchoupitoulas Plantation
Tessie's Place
Thai Pepper
The Pearl
Tiffin Inn
Tio Pepe's
Tipton County Pit BBQ
Toney's Spaghetti House
Tortorici
Trey Yuen
Tujague's
Upperline
Venezia
Vera Cruz
Veranda
Vita's on Broadway Cafe
Whole Foods Market
Windsor Court Grill Room
Ye Olde College Inn

Sunday Brunch

Andrea's
Annadele Plantation
Arnaud's
Augie's Glass Garden
Begue's
Brennan's
Cafe Degas
Cafe Pontchartrain
Cafe Savanna
Commander's Palace
Copeland's
Court of Two Sisters
Flagons
Kabby's
La Crepe Nanou
La Gauloise
Le Jardin
Mr. B's
Mystery Street Cafe
Rib Room
Veranda
Windsor Court Grill Room

OPEN MONDAY

Acme Oyster House
Alberto's
Alonso and Son
Altamira
Andrea's
Antoine's
Arnaud's
Asia Garden
Assunta's
Augie's Glass Garden
Avenue Sandwich Shop
Back to the Garden
Barreca's
Bayona
Bayou Ridge Cafe
Begue's
Bon Ton
Brennan's
Cafe Degas
Cafe Florida
Cafe Pontchartrain
Cafe Savanna
Camelia Beach House
Chehardy's
Chinese Kitchen
Christian's
Clancy's
Commander's Palace
Constantin's
Copeland's
Court of Two Sisters
Crozier's
Drago's
Eddie's
El Patio
Emeril's
Etienne De Felice's
Flagons
Gambrill's
Gautreau's
Ginza
Harold's Texas Barbecue
Home Furnishings Cafe
Home Plate Inn
Isadora
K-Paul's Louisiana Kitchen
Kabby's
Katie's
La Crepe Nanou
La Gauloise
La Riviera
Lakeshore
Le Jardin
Lido Gardens
Little Tokyo
Liuzza's
Mandarin Cafe
Mark Twain Pizza
Masson's
Mena's Palace
Moran's
Mr. B's
Mystery Street Cafe
Napoli
Palmer's
Pastore's
Plantation Coffeehouse
Rib Room
Serio's
St. Charles
Tavern On The Park
Taylor's
Toney's Avenue Cafe
Tony Angello's
Uglesich's
Vera Cruz
Veranda
Versailles
Visko's
Windsor Court Grill Room

INDEX BY RATING

★★★★★

Andrea's
Commander's Palace
Crozier's
La Provence
Mr. B's
Versailles
Windsor Court Grill Room

★★★★

Antoine's
Arnaud's
Bayona
Bistro at Maison de Ville
Bozo's
Brennan's
Brigtsen's
Camelia Beach House
Christian's
Clancy's
DiPiazza's
El Patio
Emeril's
Flagons
Galatoire's
Gambrill's
Gautreau's
Hansen's Sno-Bliz
Ichiban
Jacmel Inn
La Cuisine
Lafitte's Landing
Le Jardin
Louis XVI
Morton's of Chicago
Mosca's
Nuvolari's
Peking
Ruth's Chris
Sal & Judy's
Trey Yuen
Tujague's
Upperline
Young's Steak House

★★★

Alberto's
Alex Patout's Louisiana Restaurant
Angelo Brocato
Assunta's
Bangkok Cuisine
Barreca's
Barrow's
Bayou Ridge Cafe
Beef Room
Berdou's
Bon Ton
Broussard's
Bruning's
Cafe du Monde
Cafe Florida
Cafe Maspero
Camellia Grill
Caribbean Room
Casa Garcia
Casamento's
Castillo's
Central Grocery
Charlie's
Chehardy's
Chez Daniel
Chez Pierre
China Doll
Christina's Empress of China
Coffee Pot
Constantin's
Copeland's
Court of Two Sisters
Croissant d'Or
Dante's Pizza Cafe
Delerno's
Delmonico
Dooky Chase
Doug's
Drago's
Dragon's Garden
East China
Eddie's
Feelings
Genghis Khan
Great Wall
Gumbo Shop
Haagen-Dazs
Hana
Hard Rock Cafe
Impastato's
Isadora
Jalapenos

K-Paul's Louisiana Kitchen
Kabby's
Kim Son
Kung's Dynasty
La Crepe Nanou
La Cucaracha Cafe
La Gauloise
La Louisiane
La Madeleine
La Marquise
La Riviera
Lakeshore
Little Greek
Little Tokyo
Liuzza's
Louisiana Pizza Kitchen
Mandich's
Martin Deli
Masson's
Maximo's
Middendorf's
Mike Anderson's
Moran's
Morning Call
Mother's
Mr. Tai's
Mystery Street Cafe
Palmer's
Pascal's Manale
Pat O'Brien's
Patout's
PJ's Coffee & Tea Co.
Port of Call
Quality Inn Midtown
R&O's
Rib Room
Samurai
Santa Fe
Sazerac
Seb's
Shigure
Shogun
Snug Harbor
Steak Knife
Stephen & Martin
Streetcar Sandwiches
Sweet Basil's Bistro
Taj Mahal
Taqueria Corona
Tavern On The Park
Thai Pepper
Tipton County Pit BBQ
Toney's Avenue Cafe
Toney's Spaghetti House
Tony Angello's
Tula's
Uglesich's
Veranda